Water Finance

Founded in 1807, John Wiley & Sons is the oldest independent publishing company in the United States. With offices in North America, Europe, Australia, and Asia, Wiley is globally committed to developing and marketing print and electronic products and services for our customers' professional and personal knowledge and understanding.

The Wiley Finance series contains books written specifically for finance and investment professionals as well as sophisticated individual investors and their financial advisors. Book topics range from portfolio management to e-commerce, risk management, financial engineering, valuation and financial instrument analysis, as well as much more.

For a list of available titles, please visit our Web site at www.Wiley Finance.com.

Water Finance

*Public Responsibilities
and Private Opportunities*

NEIL S. GRIGG

WILEY

John Wiley & Sons, Inc.

Published by John Wiley & Sons, Inc., Hoboken, New Jersey.
Published simultaneously in Canada.

For general information on our other products and services or for technical support, please contact our Customer Care Department within the United States at (800) 762-2974, outside the United States at (317) 572-3993 or fax (317) 572-4002.

Wiley also publishes its books in a variety of electronic formats. Some content that appears in print may not be available in electronic books. For more information about Wiley products, visit our web site at www.wiley.com.

Library of Congress Cataloging-in-Publication Data:
Grigg, Neil S.
  Water finance: public responsibilities and private opportunities/Neil S. Grigg.
    p. cm. — (Wiley finance series)
  Includes bibliographical references and index.
  ISBN 978-0-470-76755-9 (cloth); ISBN 978-111-8-09361-0 (ebk);
ISBN 978-111-8-09362-7 (ebk); ISBN 978-111-8-09366-5(ebk)
  1. Water utilities—United States—Finance. 2. Water-supply—United States—Finance. I. Title.
  HD4461.G75 2011
  338.4'336361–dc22   2011008896

Printed in the United States of America

10 9 8 7 6 5 4 3 2 1

Dedication

I would like to dedicate the book to the men and women who are laboring to solve the world's water problems with effective tools such as private initiative, appropriate regulation, and social justice for all. Some of these people have high profiles, such as staff of the Bill and Melinda Gates Foundation, and others work behind the scenes, such as those who build village-level water systems for non-governmental volunteer organizations such as the Rotary Club or Water for People. Government solutions are needed for some water problems, but in the end it will be the business approach to water management, broadly defined, that solves the problems.

Contents

List of Illustrations

List of Tables

Preface

Water is a giant global business with annual revenues of over $200 billion in the United States alone. In the decades to come the United States must replace its aging infrastructure, which has a replacement value of over $1 trillion. Utilities, industries, and governments must find innovative ways to address these needs without sacrificing basic needs, such as safety of drinking water or reliability of water for industries and energy production. This is creating many innovations, such as the transfers, exchanges, and water banks explained in Chapter 20.

While the water business is large and important and offers up many sensational stories about emergencies and disasters, in many ways it is hard to understand. To explain it as a business, my first thought was to illustrate how it works by presenting its organization and statistics, along with brief examples. After heading down this path, I faced an unexpected challenge: how to make this mass of information interesting?

Some authors and journalists make it interesting by picking out incidents to create good stories. Some even produce movies, like *Chinatown,* which is about the Los Angeles water system, or *Erin Brockovich,* which had villains who contaminated the drinking water. Giant floods, searing droughts, and climate change also make good material for movies. The sensationalism in these movies and books does not tell the full story of the water business, however.

A related problem is how to explain the business so that it does not seem like a collection of odds and ends. After all, what connection does the plumbing department at your hardware store have with the lake where you swim and water ski? That connection is obvious when you think about it, and it became the organizing concept for the book, which is: The water business is about all aspects of handling water.

My main involvement with the water business has been on the big-system side, with its dams, reservoirs, large pipes and pumps, and the like. These mainly involve utilities, government agencies, consulting firms, and the groups that derive livelihoods from running these systems. As I worked on different water problems, I came to appreciate the links between the reservoirs and the work of plumbers, and I learned that many more people were involved in the water business than I thought. I knew that its public side was large, but it was a revelation to learn how large the private side is, with its house connections, sprinkler systems, and plumbing systems for a vast array of commercial and industrial facilities.

So, the book has a lot of facts and figures, but its main purpose is to explain the whole water business as the integrated business that it is. I have to admit, however, that you may have to work hard to make the case for integration because some water linkages are crowded out by linkages to higher-profile industries, such as electric power or health care.

I hope the book will be interesting and useful to people in business who are interested in water and that it will explain the business to the one million people who work directly in the water industry or with its suppliers. These include many technical and nontechnical workers who are focused on their specific missions and do not think much about water as a business. To my fellow engineers, for example, the presentation will seem like a different way to look at what they do, as they plan, design, construct, and operate water systems.

As a final note, I have been impressed by the large numbers of business associations where attention is given to water issues. To support my university work, I follow many magazines, online newsletters, conferences, and trade shows. I have tried to collect their water issues and integrate their meanings to explain the water business. At the end of the day, it is in these meetings and publications where you learn most about the water business.

Neil S. Grigg
December 17, 2010

Acknowledgments

Many people helped me to understand the water business as we crossed paths. Maybe the starting point was as a kid as I watched a contractor dig up a house sewer and studied the primitive storm drainage system in our neighborhood. I also benefited from father-and-son time fishing in the Alabama River and its tributaries, which introduced me to the problems of water pollution and its effects on the ecology of streams. Years later, I found myself studying water subjects at the university and getting my first job as a consulting engineer, which opened up due to flood damage in Colorado.

A number of inspiring mentors and teachers helped my education in water. At West Point I was fascinated by fluid mechanics, and one of my professors was Frank Borman, who later became the commander of *Apollo 8,* the first space mission to circle the moon. Other professors inspired me with their experiences in water, including work in many developing countries. I especially appreciated the inspiration of Maurice L. Albertson, a long-time professor at Colorado State University. He showed us the practical sides of water management, and later he explained the close links of water to poverty.

After I became a college teacher, I had the good fortune to be associated with Murray B. McPherson, the director of the American Society of Civil Engineers' program on Urban Water Management. Along with his associates, Mac did pioneering work on the water business and left a legacy of inspiration to his protégés in utilities, consulting firms, and universities. Mac had been a public health service officer during World War II, and his peers in public health had made many other contributions to the water business. For example, Dan Okun, a leader at the University of North Carolina and in the drinking water industry, has also left a terrific legacy. In particular, Dan alerted me to dramatic changes in the UK water industry and later to the needs of water distribution infrastructure.

During recent decades I have benefited from association with water industry professionals in utilities and especially through work of the Water Research Foundation, which is the research arm of the water supply industry. Working with its staff and many professional men and women in the industry has given me a real appreciation for their experience, knowledge, and dedication.

In preparing the manuscript, I received valuable help from Wiley editors Bill Falloon, the executive editor of Finance and Investment, and from Meg Freeborn, my development editor. Claire Wesley helped with the production and Tiffany Charbonier added creative touches. I appreciate their continued help in developing and publishing the book.

Structure of the Water Business

CHAPTER 1

Water for People and the Environment

The water business is about the handling of water from the global environment all the way to your tap. It deals with global climate change and the health of the oceans, but it also delivers safe and palatable water to your tap. These broad responsibilities create a giant water industry across the world. But aside from scary headlines—like flood and drought—how do people learn about water as a business? Truth be told, most of the water business operates under the radar, and the goal of this book is to shine a light on it and explain it from A to Z. Let's begin with a big-picture look at the water business.

MEET THE WATER BUSINESS

Given their broad scope, water issues provide much content for the media, and you can choose what to believe about them. There are scary forecasts about climate change, drought, flooding, disease outbreaks, and legal gridlock. The people who make the forecasts benefit from a good headline, but the water stories soon recede from the public view. We are left to wonder: Will society drown in these crises or will it solve water problems?

When you think optimistically and consider our capacity to manage water systems, these forecasts don't look so scary. In fact, I believe that society will find ways to address its water problems responsibly and one at a time, mainly with local solutions. However, these won't always be pretty because water involves a lot of politics and arguments about money and value systems. If you detect an air of pessimism, it is because our success depends more on finding political will than it does on technology and money. For that reason, the subject of this book—the water business—must work within social, political, and legal systems to find its opportunities and markets. Its high level of politics is the attribute of water as a business that distinguishes it from similar businesses.

Having acknowledged that the water business can't divorce itself from politics, let's think of the opportunities in it. Water services must be provided to billions of people around the world, and this creates a gigantic business. People need drinking water, cooking and bathing water, sewage treatment, pumps, wells, and myriad other products and services. On top of all of this is a layer of government involvement that creates many jobs on its own. Both business and government are entrenched in the water business and will continue to be so.

At its core, the water business is about obtaining, processing, and selling a precious resource that has many uses. Along the way, however, these activities lead to many paths that make water a diverse and little-understood business. For example, the water business is about much more than selling water. To illustrate, I explained to friends that you don't always make money by selling water, but you can make money by saving it (promoting conservation). A friend chimed in, "Yes, you also make money by litigating over it."

Another anecdote explains a common misunderstanding about paying for water. A nun protested a water-rate increase by saying that since God provided the water, it ought to be free. The water manager replied, "Sister, we agree the water should be free, but who will pay for the pipes and pumps?" This anecdote was told by Tracy Mehan (2007), a former EPA assistant administrator for water, who explained how the pipes and pumps make up the capital of the water industry and account for much of its business activity, but there are many more pipes and pumps than you would ever imagine. In fact, just for water supply there are upward of two million miles of underground distribution pipes in the United States.

These anecdotes about pipes, pumps, conservation, and litigation illustrate just a few aspects of the water business, which faces conundrums such as that you can lose money by saving water, a lesson learned by utilities that promote conservation only to find their revenues falling and their risks increasing. A utility faces either a conflict of interest or a moral hazard. Should it neglect conservation (and the environment), or should it sell less and charge more (thus making consumers mad), or does it sell less and try to put itself out of business without government subsidies?

Although its revenues are not quite as large as giant industries such as electric power or telecommunications, the water business has megaimpacts on many sectors of the economy and society. It often flies below investors' radar because its economic statistics are dispersed, but when they are aggregated they help identify and trace how the water business affects critical issues such as energy production, housing costs, industrial development, food supplies, and environmental integrity.

IS THERE A WATER CRISIS?

People sense the importance of the water industry, but they often cannot explain it beyond saying that water is essential to life and a compelling issue around the world. Headlines about it range from drought in Africa to spectacular water-main failures caused by aging infrastructure in big cities. A story may describe a megascale project, such as China's Three Gorges Dam, or it might be about a local issue, such as the hot-button issue of where fast-growing Atlanta will get water for the future. China's massive new dam supplies hydroelectricity for a large share of the rapidly developing nation and is paired with the country's new south-to-north water-transfer scheme to win the global contest for large-scale infrastructure projects hands-down. Although not as visible on the world scene, Atlanta's water problems have been seen as a trillion-dollar issue involving the city's future.

As we will see in the next chapter, the uses of water form a spectrum according to needs that range from drinking water for life support through uses of water for recreation and discretionary activities. Naturally, the values inherent in these uses vary from one extreme, where a person dying of thirst will pay any price, to the other extreme, where people waste water without a thought. As a result, the divergent values of water applied to various uses become a core issue in decisions about managing it.

On an overall basis, it is the aggregated importance of water that is so impressive. At the microscale, every one of the world's citizens (nearly seven billion and increasing) requires a minimum amount of clean water every day for drinking, cooking, and hygiene. There is no way around this requirement, so the business of supplying water to people will always be with us. Then, businesses require water to offer their products and services and manufacturing industries use vast quantities of water. Irrigated agriculture is the largest water user in dry regions, and electric power producers require vast quantities to produce energy. When you add up all of these needs, you begin to see the big picture of water's importance.

Attention to the water business around the globe sometimes reflects balanced scientific views and sometimes it is based more on advocacy and even superstition. For example, the European Public Health Alliance (2010) publishes dramatic statistics about water on its web site. It wrote that the global demand for water has doubled in the last 50 years and that in the next 20 years the average supply of water worldwide per person is expected to drop by a third as agriculture becomes more intensive and industry and population grow. This sounds alarming. It also wrote that waste management is not keeping pace, mentioned Belgium as a European country that lags in sewage treatment, and rated and a few countries in Central and Eastern Europe and Central Asia below some African countries.

It described climate change as being responsible for 20 percent of the increase in water scarcity up to 2050 with desertification a concern even in parts of Europe. It raised an alarm about water scarcity caused by vegetables and flowers being grown for export, golf tourism, and bottled-water production. Of course, the problem of lack of access to safe water and sanitation facilities is mentioned, along with the fact that even in Europe, many people live without piped water, such as in Romania, where all of the rural population does not have access to improved drinking water sources. This account concluded by identifying the impacts on vulnerable children, who die from waterborne diseases and are exposed to threats from arsenic, fluoride, and nitrates. Also, climate change is said to raise threats of water-related vector diseases, such as malaria. They blame global mismanagement of water resources with inertia at the leadership level and ignorant populations. These result in slow reforms and global competition in the water market. They say that water has become big business with annual profits of the water industry at 40 percent of oil and higher than the pharmaceutical sector.

Do these claims ring true? They should be subjected to a truth test, as newspapers do for election campaigns. As I look at them, it seems that each allegation is connected to an important water issue but the claims seem dramatic and difficult to prove. It is like each claim is a worst-case scenario and when you add them up, it makes a scary story. Let's take the claim that the demand for water has doubled in the last 50 years. This is certainly not true in the United States. Although the population has increased, the largest uses of water, for thermoelectric cooling and irrigation, have actually dropped. Industrial water use has also dropped considerably, and even the per capita use of municipal water has decreased. Similar water use conclusions might hold up for other developed countries, but it will also be true that in emerging and industrializing nations there will be rising demands for water caused by agriculture and industrial and population growth. So, my conclusion about the claim is that it contains elements of truth but is too dramatic and simplistic.

Scary stories about water do make for compelling reading and keynote speeches. In fact, we who work in the water industry like them because they assure us that we are doing important work and will have future opportunities. An example is a recent book about the water crisis that presents similar cases as the European Public Health Alliance, but in a well-written and entertaining style. Glennon (2009) explained a range of problems in the United States, including big issues such as the future water supply for megacities like Las Vegas and Atlanta and how some scientists predict that Lake Mead could dry up by 2021. Most of the issues he explains seem like small-scale local and regional water issues that could be solved with enough political will. Examples include the drying up of farms in Colorado (where I live), how the small Tennessee town of Orme ran out of water and had to

truck it in, how Bowater (a South Carolina paper company) could not discharge wastewater due to low flows and cut jobs, how due to lack of
streamflow the Southern Nuclear Corporation was not allowed by the
Nuclear Regulatory Commission to build two new reactors in Georgia, and
several other local or regional issues.

Publications and media accounts about the water crisis do us a favor by
sounding the alarm, but they seem sometimes to go off the deep end in
describing the issues. As an engineer and manager, I may see solutions
where others just see problems, but I have to temper my optimism with the
same statement—a lot of the problems require political will and changes in
human behavior that won't come easily.

The publicity about emerging threats and their implications for the
water industry are discussed in more detail in Chapter 10.

WHAT IS THE WATER BUSINESS?

Chapter 2 presents a model of the water business, which can be explained
in different ways. You can see water through a utility view (as a narrow
utility-based business), or through a popular view (as a giant crisis), or
through an academic and policy view (as a comprehensive and complex
web of interrelated activities that focus on handling water). The approach
taken here mixes these three to view the water business as a complex arena
with many producers, suppliers, regulators, and customers and to explore
its corners and niches.

While this view is ambitious and might seem superficial to someone
looking for an in-depth treatment, it explains how the complex arena of the
water industry is an important business sector with many parts. It presents a
realistic view of the business that is devoid of sensationalism and even
explains why the exposés and media stories of a water crisis can easily
mislead us. The book discusses the readily apparent utility businesses of selling water and treating wastewater, but also probes important water-
handling services that are not so apparent and fly below the radar, such as
risk management for flood damage mitigation and dam safety.

To create a model of the multifaceted water industry a coherent framework is required. Otherwise the business is described as a collection of odds
and ends. The organizing concept for this framework is that the water business is built around a set of water handlers that have major responsibility
for the management of water. These water handlers become the producers
of the goods and services provided by water and its management. An example of a good is the supply of potable water. A service can be the prevention
of flood damage through water handling.

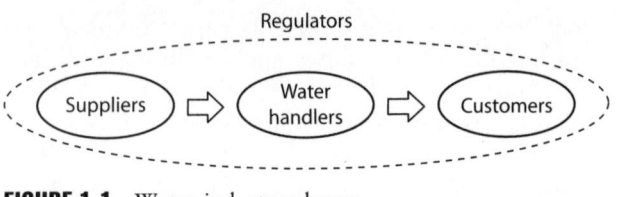

FIGURE 1.1   Water-industry players

Given the heavy regulation of water use, government regulators are also an essential part of the industry. Its other part comprises the array of suppliers of equipment and services that keep the pumps and pipes going. When you add these to its customer base, the water industry looks like other industries, with its own producers, suppliers, regulators, and customers (Figure 1.1). These players are discussed in more detail in Chapter 2.

In spite of this straightforward concept, there is no consensus about the status of the water business as a unified industry. For example, Steve Maxwell (2010), a management consultant who follows the water business closely, concluded that there is no such thing as a water industry, but instead it is a balkanized bazaar of quite different businesses focused on delivery of clean water. I think this is a valid point, and it illustrates how many of the players in the water industry also play in other industries.

It is true that that the water business is balkanized and includes many parts. In fact, water is more like an input to many industries than it is an industry itself. In that sense, it is a crosscutting industry, not one that produces distinct products and services itself. However, I believe that you can frame the business coherently by its focus on water handling as the organizing concept and that enables us to identify its suppliers, customers, and regulators to see the full picture of the business.

To its participants, the water business involves different businesses: the utility business, the point-of-use supply business, the irrigation business, the dam-building business, and several others. These players might work as utility operators, plumbers, contractors, consulting engineers, farm operators, or industrial facility managers, among other occupations. Our view of the water business depends on whether we focus on one part of it or the overall industry.

Given that the water business meets many purposes at different levels, I'd like to present a few examples of scales of business activity along the chain of water management from stream diversions to end uses. Figure 1.2 shows a map of water-industry activities that vary in scale and the split between public and private management. The examples shown range in scale from the household level to large river basins, like New York's Hudson River or even the Mississippi River. The public-private split is a variable to show whether the activity is mostly market driven or controlled by the public sector.

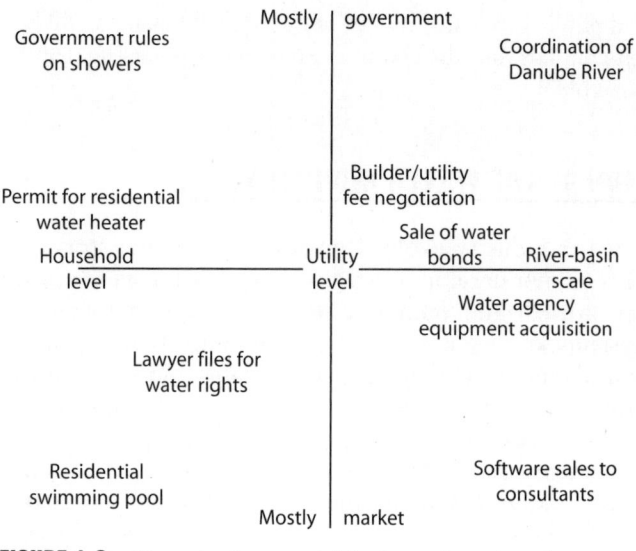

FIGURE 1.2   Water-business activities by scale and market intensity

This provides four quadrants: large scale and government driven, large scale but private, small scale and government driven, and small scale and private.

Looking at the lower left of Figure 1.2, you see a residential swimming pool, which requires pumps, pipes, and water-treatment chemicals. It involves the handling of water at a small scale and can be supplied entirely by private business, although it is subject to regulatory controls. This example and many other plumbing and household-level water-handling cases form the smaller end of the water industry. Each of these examples has larger variants, such as an Olympic-size swimming pool or even a water park, which would require much larger water-handling facilities.

Now look at the upper right quadrant. You see a builder negotiating with a utility on a water connection fee for a house, which can be as high as $30,000 for a single modest home where I live. Another example is the sale of water bonds, which might finance a new pipeline. At the highest end are the activities to coordinate a giant river basin, like the Danube River, which flows through 19 countries in Europe. While the controls on this will mainly be by government, the activity can involve river forecast software, new locks and dams, and other water-handling products or services.

These large- and small-scale examples are but a few of the many that frame the water business, which involves many types of products and services for different scales or activity and variations of involvement of the private and public sectors. A model of the overall business will be explained in the next chapter, and the chapters after that lay out the details of water-handling sectors.

EVOLUTION OF THE WATER INDUSTRY

How the water industry evolved makes a fascinating story, and today's water issues did not develop overnight. They evolved as the convergence of population growth and economic development created the pressure on natural systems that we now see. To see how the water business evolved, we can consider how technologies such as dams, pipes, pumps, valves, and treatment processes emerged over the centuries. The business still uses these technologies and continues to adapt new methods to them, including processes, instruments, and computer controls.

Early civilizations developed aqueducts and crude pipes to deliver water for household and irrigation use but they lacked a good understanding of how they worked. During the 1700s and 1800s, scientific techniques of fluid mechanics, hydraulics, and hydrology evolved to improve our understanding. Public health and environmental engineering began later in the 1800s with the emergence of the field of microbiology. The discovery of the cause of cholera outbreaks led to modern water-quality management.

As cities evolved, raw water, drainage and wastewater systems were installed and by the late 19th century, today's building plumbing systems had emerged. With the invention of the water closet or toilet, the present wastewater system was set. Treatment systems started with filtration in 1887, and disinfection by chlorination followed by 1909. By 1900, water-borne infectious diseases were on the decline, but chemical problems increased. The 1912 Public Health Act included controls on drinking-water quality, but was not very enforceable. Chemical problems led to the passage of the Safe Drinking Water Act (SDWA) in 1974, and this act frames our management approach to safe water today.

The emergence of the water-quality industry led to large- and small-scale plumbing industries, which require several crafts and trades. Plumbers and gas fitters were placed into a single category by the Census Bureau until the 1880s. The Plumbing-Heating-Cooling Contractors Association began as the National Association of Master Plumbers in 1883. The Mechanical Contractors Association of America and the United Association plumbers union began in 1889, and the American Society of Sanitary Engineering began about 1900.

Prior to 1900, state governments passed laws regulating water rights, but the federal government was not involved much in water management.

In 1902, the Federal Reclamation Act was passed. In 1917, Congress enacted the first Mississippi Flood Control Program. In the 1930s, the Tennessee Valley Authority's electric power, flood control, conservation, and economic development projects were initiated. The Flood Control Act of 1944 authorized the Pick-Sloan plan for the Missouri River Basin, including projects for irrigation, power, flood control, and recreation. After World War II, a Senate Select Committee set the stage for the Water Resources Planning Act of 1965. Today, federal involvement has shifted from project development to policy and regulation.

In the West, state governments became active in water development out of necessity. The 1950s California State Water Plan is the most prominent example and remains the largest state-level initiative in the nation. In the East, state governments were less active in water projects, but they became involved in health and environment issues. Today, state governments fill the gap between the federal government and local water providers.

Each city government or special district has its own story of water management. The stories range from small-town systems to giant organizations such as the South Florida Water Management District, which handles water management in the Everglades and other regions of South Florida, or the Los Angeles Department of Water and Power, which is one of the largest combined water and electric power utilities in the United States.

Dams are of strategic importance in water management. Many small dams have been built to store water and divert it into canals and diversion pipes. With the advent of modern earth-moving equipment, large dams could be built, and during the 20th century, thousands of dams of all sizes were built in the United States. Major dams of the 20th century include Hoover Dam on the Colorado River, Tennessee Valley Authority (TVA) dams, and Grand Coulee Dam. The government's Corps of Engineers and the Bureau of Reclamation are generally considered the nation's major dam builders, along with electric power companies and the TVA.

Dams made hydropower and inland navigation possible. Early hydropower was by waterwheels, which were used to grind wheat more than 2,000 years ago. By the early 1900s, hydropower furnished more than 40 percent of U.S. electric power. After World War I, power development focused on thermal plants, and hydropower declined as a percentage of power production to about 10 percent of U.S. production now. Hydropower is still important, however, because it can be switched on and off quickly to provide peaking power and it is one of the renewable sources of energy, like wind power. New laws such as the Public Utility Regulatory Policies Act of 1978 and the 1986 Electric Consumers Protection Act changed the regulatory climate for hydropower. Now, utilities must consider energy conservation, fish, wildlife, and recreation as well as power in their license applications.

Inland navigation brought great economic benefits to 19th-century America. Built between 1817 and 1825, the Erie Canal was so successful that the construction cost was recovered from fees in just seven years. It stimulated port development and is thought to be a main cause of New York City's ascendancy as America's largest urban area.

About 1900, the nation entered a "conservation" era during the Presidency of Teddy Roosevelt. This peaked with Earth Day in 1970 and continues today. It has added an ecological thread to public health engineering and today's environmental engineers deal with fisheries, environmental impact, and wildlife, as well as public health.

With the environmental movement, it became much more difficult to build dams, especially large dams. This increases the importance of using existing water storage well. Today, removal of dams is being considered in many places in the United States, but new dams are under consideration in some developing countries.

The history of ground water and wells goes back to the beginning of mankind when humans learned to dig boreholes to obtain water supplies. With the development of pumps, people were able to lift water more easily, and with the development of diesel and electric motors, the modern groundwater development era began. Today, groundwater is used by more than half of all public water systems in the United States.

New water systems required sophisticated management organizations, and water utilities emerged along with cities. Philadelphia initiated their water supply system in 1798 after a yellow fever epidemic. It used public and private pumping facilities driven by horses. By midcentury, other large U.S. cities such as New York and Boston followed Philadelphia's lead. Today, these giant water utilities are major players in the U.S. water industry.

Prior to 1900, many water services were private. Pressure for government involvement led to conversion to public sector management. After about 1980, the pendulum swung back. Today, there is still interest in privatization, although it is not universally favored.

Consulting engineers have much influence in water engineering and management. During the 19th century, American engineers became famous for their work and consulting engineers are a major force in the water industry today. In fact, they comprise a "shadow workforce" for public water organizations. This is explained in more detail in Chapter 18.

Water industry trade associations and professional societies began to emerge in the late 19th century. The American Water Works Association began in 1881 and the Water Environment Federation began in 1926 through an effort to create a sewage works association. A complete inventory of water industry trade associations would include many significant trade, professional, and academic groups.

These are only a few of the fascinating historical developments that lay the foundation for today's water industry. Some of this history is told in more detail in Grigg (2005). For a detailed look at the public health aspects and emergence of modern utilities, *The Sanitary City* by Melosi (2008) is recommended.

WHY IS THE WATER BUSINESS HARD TO ORGANIZE?

With these many issues driving the need for water, news stories suggest that water will be a promising business in the future. However, you have to look beyond the headlines to understand the issues, and there will be pitfalls as well as opportunities. As a business, water is complex to define and has distinct parts. It is unique because it is so political, deals with personal matters as well as societal issues, and is heavily regulated. While there is a lot of rhetoric about water problems across the globe, at the end of the day it is mostly a local matter.

The aggregate of the local issues comprises the water business. Imagine if the world's seven billion people were organized into towns of 50,000 each. They would require 140,000 local water systems to serve the needs. Of course, things are not that simple. The United States alone has more than 50,000 community water systems, but many of these serve very small populations.

The balkanized businesses making up the water industry are hard to classify, and some of them are even government owned or outright government agencies. The difficulty in classification of this gigantic public-private mixture was explained in a special report on water in the *Economist* magazine, which concluded: "No wonder a commodity with so many qualities, uses and associations has proved so difficult to organize" (Grimond, 2010).

On the private side, many entrepreneurs offer products and services, but they are mostly dependent on government decisions for their sales and market opportunities. On the government side, the World Water Assessment Programme (2007) explained that in many countries water governance is in a state of confusion with a lack of water institutions or fragmentation of authorities and decision-making structures. So, while the water business is critical for our health, survival, and quality of life, as well as to sustain the environment, its many parts and unique public-private mixtures make it "hard to organize."

In the final analysis, the reason the water business is hard to organize lies in its diversity of purposes and scales. Water services have attributes of public goods and private goods, and to manage them we must traverse back and forth between government and private sector approaches. This takes us into uncomfortable territory of embracing government and business methods simultaneously.

To serve the needs of people and the environment, water management requires many actions at scales from local homes up through river basins that cover large regions. It may be difficult at the small scale for us to connect our actions to the big picture, especially when we are balancing objectives that range from safe drinking water to using streams for recreation.

So, the water business is a mixture of activities that converge on the core issue of handling water. As it lacks identity, someone might look at the activities I include in the water business and say, "You are just adding up things that don't relate and calling it a water business!" That's an observation that you might expect, but I hold that it isn't valid because the activities do relate to one another, although it is true that sometimes the people involved in them do not recognize their relationships with others in the water business. What you can say about these activities is that while they involve water handling, most also involve other primary activities. In that sense, water is an allied industry to many others. Let me cite a few examples to illustrate this.

An employee of a company that produces, installs, or services household or business point-of-use water-treatment devices might recognize her participation in the water business but not realize how close her work is to that of a treatment plant operator working for a public water system. By the same token, a plumber would normally identify with his craft of plumbing and not primarily with the water business. Yet that same plumber deserves credit as one of the main protectors of public health by preventing waterborne disease through following codes and maintaining effective water-handling systems.

An irrigation farmer might have to learn the fine points of surface and groundwater movement, consumptive use, and water rights so that he can manage his assets productively. A landscape architect might sketch out a site drainage plan with physical and ecological features, and the plan might include the same basic analysis that a water resources engineer would perform to lay out a storm drainage plan for a subdivision. A ranger at a national park might be promoted into management and deal with permitting and access issues related to water resources, and thus deal with the same types of planning and regulatory issues as a water-resources planner.

Finally, at the residential and commercial levels, a sales team might work at a kitchen and bath exposition and explain the aesthetic and safety attributes of water-handling equipment, but think of themselves as part of the home improvement industry, rather than the water industry. All of these examples show how the water industry involves core activities of water handling, but many of the people involved in it would not identify water as their primary business.

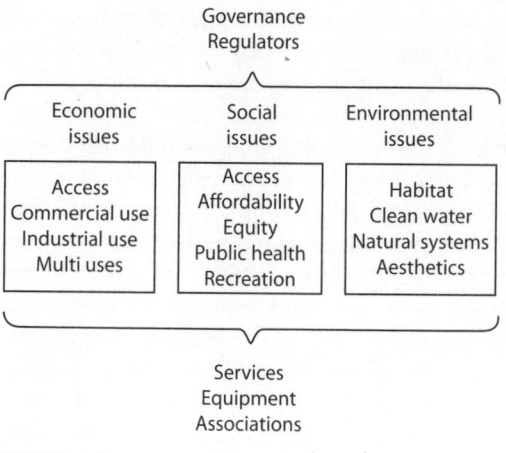

FIGURE 1.3   Water-industry interdependency

In the way of a summary of the complexity of the water business, Figure 1.3 illustrates its interdependencies among social, economic, and environmental issues and sectors and how both governance and regulators are required to deal with the many issues, while the water handlers are supported by a broad array of suppliers.

PREVIEW OF THE BOOK

The water business is organized differently from businesses that might seem similar, such as the electric power industry. The big providers of electric power are major investor-owned utilities, such as Edison International, and government utilities, such as the Tennessee Valley Authority. Also, smaller providers include cooperatives, small cities, and power districts. Electrical contractors do much of the work to hook up customers, and there is a large supplier segment that provides everything from large generators to light bulbs for appliances. Regulators consider rates, safety, and the environment.

In the water industry, the sale of water as a commodity is similar to the sale of electric power, but the water industry also provides additional services for wastewater, stormwater, and irrigation and drainage. In addition, the water industry serves instream flow and environmental water needs. It even takes care of disaster management and water drainage as water bodies pass through cities and other settlements. All of these separate facets make water different and more complex than just a commodity industry.

After the overall explanation of the water industry in Chapter 2, the book turns to the water-handling sectors: water supply, wastewater, industrial water, stormwater, irrigation and drainage, and an environmental sector named "instream flows." This section of the book also explains dams and groundwater systems, which are two important parts of the water infrastructure.

The chapters about water handling include discussions of the water-using customers. These include sectors focused on land uses such as urban development, landscaping, and floodplain management. Farming is a customer of irrigation and drainage, and it makes many demands on water and has massive impacts on the environment. Now that renewable energy is such a fast-growing sector, its water demands have increased and thickened the web of the energy-water nexus. The major source of renewable energy is hydropower, which goes hand in hand with river navigation as a control mechanism on stream flows. Large water-dependent industries, point-of-use manufacturers, and the bottled water industry are as much a part of the water industry as the utilities are.

The next part of the book contains chapters about driving forces and issues in the water industry, such as government involvement, privatization, law and regulations, financial structure, water and health, and workforce capacity. These are introduced by a chapter that looks ahead at how the emerging water industry will respond to societal trends.

The next section of the book is about product and service suppliers. The discussion is about equipment and types of services, and it is partitioned into size groups ranging from large utilities to small systems that work in individual residences. In addition to the usual products and services you think of as connected to water, this part of the book includes discussions of financial services to the water industry and the business of commodity water, which designates attempts by some entrepreneurs to develop and sell bulk water.

This final part of the book includes a chapter on the ultimate challenge of using business and philanthropy to address the critical issue of safe drinking water and sanitation for all and a concluding chapter about water investments and careers.

A Model of the Water Business

The water business is a complex web of interconnected water-handling activities with its own producers, suppliers, customers, and regulators, and it requires a rational model of valuing water so that decisions can be made about its allocation and the support of water-related services. In the past, water was largely seen as public-sector activity. Now, the picture is different. Tax revolts, environmental advocacy, and the difficulty in public-sector decision making requires that supplier-customer relationships be identified clearly to portray how water and related services should be managed according to their value. This chapter provides a conceptual map of it through a model of activities and functions from major utilities to end users at the smallest water taps.

Because the water business is not recognized as a distinct business sector by economic accounting systems, the model presents it as a cross-cutting industry that draws from recognized sectors such as utilities, government, and manufacturing. It explains that the core of the water business comprises the water handlers who meet demands for diverse water-related services, and it identifies the equipment and services that are provided by a diverse group of supplier organizations. The model rounds out the discussion by explaining the roles of the regulators who play important control roles in the health, environmental, and economic spheres. It explores the corners of the water business and explains its diverse services from the small picture to the big picture.

If the water business involved only supply, it would be similar to related commodity businesses, such as electric power and natural gas, except for the need to dispose of wastewater. However, the provision of a range of water-related services differentiates the water business from other utility businesses and water as a business is much broader than just its utility portion, although it is the dominant part. Electricity and natural gas are totally consumptive, whereas water use may be only partially consumptive and involve handling residuals as well as the commodity supplied. Electricity and natural gas focus on sale of the commodity, but they do not handle the commodity for other purposes. Another distinguishing attribute of the water business is the provision of water for agriculture, which happens mostly outside of organized utilities.

A DIVERSE AND MULTISCALE INDUSTRY

While the North American Industrial Classification System (NAICS) identifies market segments and establishes economic accounting systems for many industries, it does not recognize the water business directly. It recognizes pieces of it, such as the privately owned water utilities that are in the utility sector, but government-owned water utilities and nonutility parts of the water business are dispersed across other categories.

To address this lack of recognition, the water business can be modeled like other businesses with producers, suppliers, customers and regulators, but as a cross-cutting industry with many facets. The fact that it has a wide variety of types of producers and customers makes it somewhat like a complex and integrated industry with manufacturing to produce goods and wholesalers and retailers who add value and services to them for many types of customers.

Figure 2.1 illustrates this cross-industry feature with the water handlers and their suppliers shown across the top. The water handlers span across four NAICS categories: utilities, manufacturers, agriculture, and the federal and state governments. How these categories of establishments handle water will be explained later. The water-industry suppliers are drawn from a broad group of NAICS categories, including manufacturing, wholesale, retail, services, and construction. These are explained later in Chapters 18 and 19.

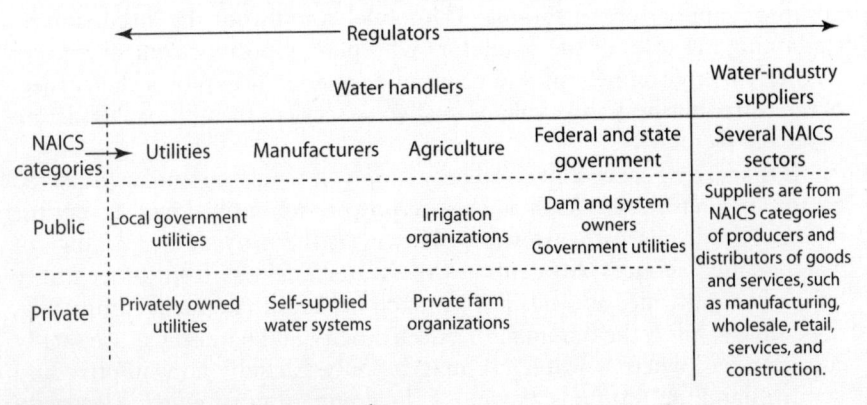

FIGURE 2.1   Model of the water industry

Regulators deal with both the water handlers and the suppliers, as shown. There are several types of regulators, and they range from the obvious ones, such as the U.S. Environmental Protection Agency (USEPA), to not-so-obvious ones, such as the U.S. Food and Drug Administration (FDA), which regulates bottled water.

Both public and private entities operate as water handlers. In particular, both utilities and agriculture involve public and private organizations. Self-supplied manufacturers are essentially 100 percent in the private sector, but government activities such as military bases share some of their attributes and although electric power utilities are included under the utilities category, in terms of their water use they are similar to self-supplied manufacturers. The state and federal government sector operates some dams and government-owned utilities. Local government water providers are shown as utilities rather than as government to emphasize their common attributes with private water companies. An example of a public sector irrigation organization would be an irrigation district in the West, while a private-sector example might be a large privately owned corporate farm.

A LONGITUDINAL VIEW OF THE INDUSTRY VIA THE HYDROLOGIC CYCLE

The common thread among the water handlers is that they are all involved with the hydrologic cycle, which is also called the water cycle. While this sounds like a concept from a science class, it is a useful tool to explain the interconnections and interdependencies among water handlers. It explains how water is used and reused as it moves from the atmosphere across land and back again and from one user to another during its journey. The hydrologic cycle is a useful concept to explain the interdependence among water users and how water is used and reused along its journey. The slogan "water flows uphill toward money" is a good way to explain the importance of infrastructure in handling it. Today, there is increasing interest in improving our accounts for water use as it moves through the cycle.

The driving force of water moving through its cycle is gravity, which is sometimes replaced by energy to explain how "water flows uphill toward money" (meaning that if enough money is provided, water can be made to flow uphill, at least in pipes and pumps and sometimes by water trading). Energy can move water, and in fact, the processing of water is a major energy user, especially of electric power.

The hydrologic cycle explains how precipitation falls in different forms, then travels as surface or underground flows to streams, lakes, and the ocean, only to be evaporated and return to the atmosphere, where it is

Watershed showing natural and human systems (Source: President's Water Policy Commission, 1950)

FIGURE 2.2 Watershed diagram to illustrate water uses
Source: U.S. Army Corps of Engineers.

available to fall again as precipitation. If water systems were free of human interference, they would be completely natural and no water industry would be involved. However, human uses insert infrastructure and its operations into the natural water cycle. Once humans interrupt this cycle, the effects become so massive that it is practically impossible to find any place on Earth that is untouched by development. In fact, the possibility of global climate change means that the entire cycle might be altered through human-induced effects such as release of greenhouse gases. Hydrologic change has been going on for a long time, and the water cycle is, in fact, a "human-altered hydrologic cycle."

Figure 2.2 shows a diagram of a watershed to illustrate how water runs downhill through communities and different land uses and to help us to understand water business issues such as demand for water for economic purposes, environmental regulation, and climate change. This diagram was actually prepared during the 1950s to illustrate a report by the President's Water Resources Policy Commission (1950). During this era, the nation was recovering from depression and war, and the commission, which was chaired by past president Herbert Hoover, was studying how to meet postwar water needs. Before we leave Figure 2.2, take another look at it to see how the water that begins uphill moves past interdependent users on its way downstream. Water in the stream at the bottom of the diagram might have flowed through networks of pipes, treatment plants, irrigation systems, and even the kidneys of people. Then, after it leaves the space shown on this diagram, it moves on downstream to other places the repeat its movement through natural, economic, and human systems.

In a science or engineering book, you would see the details of the hydrologic cycle to include precipitation, evaporation, streamflow, groundwater, and all other movements of water. Figure 2.3 illustrates how the processes occur and in it you can see how, in addition to rainfall and water supply services, the hydrologic cycle explains the processes of environmental water management in natural stream channels and aquifers. These processes include instream flows, water-quality changes, flooding, groundwater flows, and dams and reservoirs to store water. Diversions of water are required for public and industrial uses and for farm water use. Returns from these

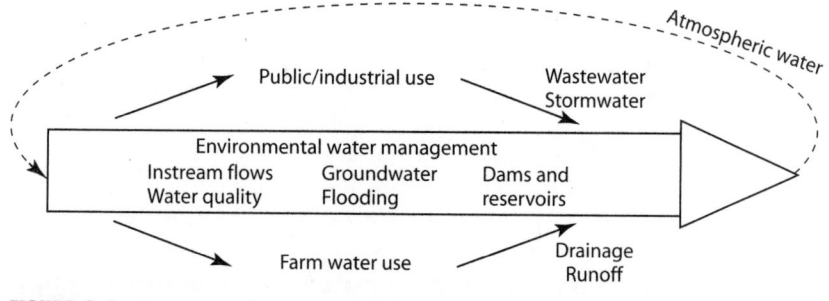

FIGURE 2.3 Water use through the hydrologic cycle

diversions show up as wastewater, stormwater, and farm drainage and run-off. Taken together, the water flows shown on the diagram cover the major water-handling activities that occur in the water business.

ACCOUNTING FOR WATER USE AND FLOW

Trends in water use belie the alarmist reports that we are running out of water. For a big picture, public supply increased with population growth, but now seems to have leveled off. Irrigation grew to about 1980, and then started to decline. Self-supplied industrial water seems to have peaked around 1980 with manufacturing, and is much less now. Thermoelectric use increased to 1980, declined, and now seems on a slow rise with increased electricity demand.

While we have a general idea of the overall uses of water across the nation, it is difficult to account for water stocks and flows accurately. This is true at the micro- and macroscales. At the microscale, an industry of engineers and lawyers is employed to account for water uses and losses so as to settle cases, especially in the semiarid West. At the macroscale, we are interested in larger-scale trends in the use of water and in tracking phenomena such as climate change effects.

A few decades ago, there was little emphasis on water accounting and many communities even lacked water meters. That is still true in some water-rich areas. Today, the emphasis on water accounting is much greater and many utilities are investing in new smart technologies for measurement, meter reading, and studies of water losses and efficiency. Even in water-rich communities, water accounting can be important to stem losses and save on infrastructure costs, regardless of whether there is plenty of raw water supply in the first place.

The major national accounts of water use and flow are maintained by the U.S. Geological Survey (USGS), a long-standing earth-science agency of the Department of the Interior. The first director of USGS was John Wesley Powell, a one-armed Civil War general who became famous for exploring the West. USGS records flows of streams and other water accounts and, starting in 1950, the agency has published a national water use report every five years; the latest one is for water use in 2005.

The basis for measuring environmental water is the national network of streamflow gages maintained by USGS, which provide data to form the basis for many water-supply decisions and allocations. To be sure that it places gages where the data are actually needed, the network is managed through a cooperative program with cost sharing from state and local governments, as well as private entities. Even with this careful approach, the budget of USGS

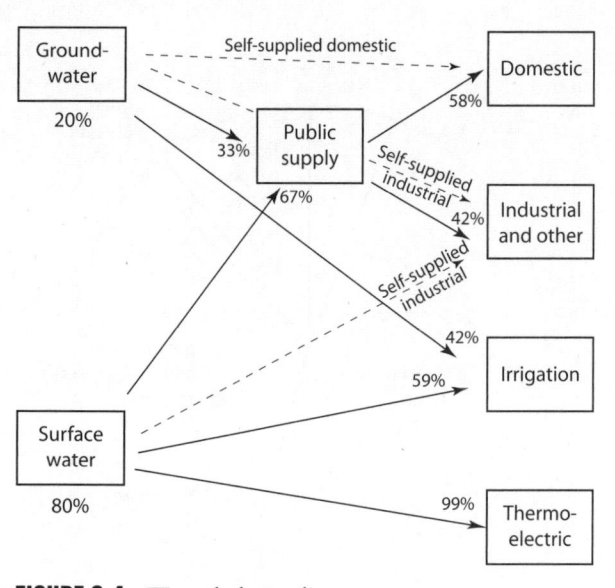

FIGURE 2.4 Water balance diagram

comes under continual fire from politicians who do not understand much about water use accounting. Their argument is that the people who use the data should pay for it, but this ignores the many public purposes that water management serves. Of course, budget watchdogs are needed to prevent the unneeded growth of programs such as streamflow gaging.

The data needed to explain the uses of water are collected by the water use program of USGS, which explains how water supplies from surface water, groundwater, and saline water are processed through infrastructure systems of the public and private sectors.

Figure 2.4 shows a water balance of the distribution of sources and uses of water based on the 2005 USGS data. The USGS report contains statistical detail that is difficult to show visually and is omitted from the diagram. The data shown are for water withdrawals, and a great deal of the water withdrawn is returned to the streams and made available to divert again. The amount not returned is named consumptive use and is not reported by USGS, although it was in the past. Consumptive use is difficult to estimate accurately, a problem that fuels the demand for water engineering and legal services to argue about water rights and entitlements.

The figure shows that 80 percent of the nation's water withdrawals are from surface water and 20 percent from groundwater wells. While this gives us an idea of water quantities, it masks the fact that it takes millions of wells to pump that 20 percent of the water supply, whereas one stream diversion can account for large quantities of surface water.

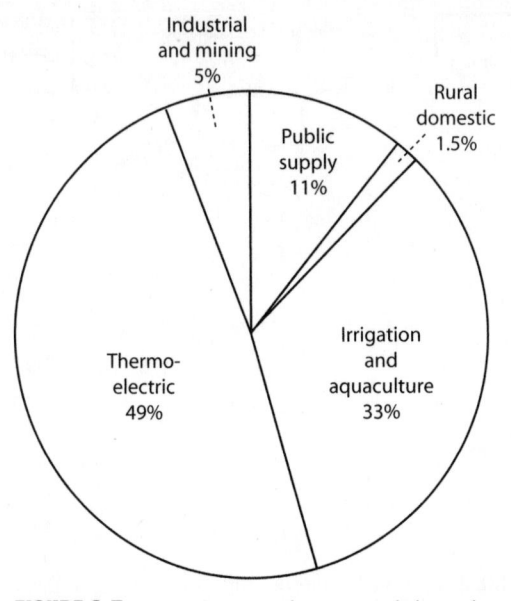

FIGURE 2.5   Distribution of water withdrawals

Water uses are displayed for domestic, industrial, irrigation, and thermo-electric uses. In addition, USGS reports aquaculture, livestock, and mining as separate categories, but these are comparatively small.

Public supply is the business unit that processes water for domestic and other users, and it is displayed as an intermediary between initial withdrawals and end users. Sixty-seven percent of public supplies are from surface water and 33 percent from groundwater.

Figure 2.5 illustrates the data on water use in pie chart form to illustrate the distribution of water supply as reported by USGS for 2005 (Kenny et al., 2009). On a percentage basis, thermoelectric cooling water is the largest withdrawal at 49 percent of the total, but it is mostly diverted from streams and then returned with an added heat load after the water cools electric power plants. Some of this cooling water is from saline sources, such as bays, estuaries, and even seawater.

Irrigation and aquaculture are next largest at 33 percent of the total. Irrigation alone, which is largest in the western states, is 31 percent of the total. Aquaculture, or fish farming, occurs in the East as well as the West. If the overall statistics did not include thermoelectric water use, irrigation would be a much larger fraction of the total and it dominates consumptive use on a national and regional basis, whereas consumptive use of thermo-electric water use is much smaller on a percentage basis.

Public supply is 11 percent of the total, and 58 percent of it goes to domestic uses and 42 percent goes to an aggregated category of all other commercial and industrial uses that are connected to public systems, as well as system losses.

Self-supplied industrial and mining uses were 5 percent of the total. To assess their total demands, this must be added to their uses from public systems. The last time that industrial uses from public systems were reported separately was 1995, when 11.8 percent of public supply went to industrial and mining uses. This comprised 17 percent of all industrial and mining uses, and the rest was self-supplied from ground and surface water supplies.

The unit of water use is million gallons per day (mgd), which is commonly used to express large rates of flow, such as the total daily use of a community. Other units in common use are cubic feet per second (cfs), acre-feet (AF) per year, and millions of cubic meters (MCM) per year.

The national totals of public and industrial water uses for 2005 were as shown in Table 2.1.

Of the total withdrawals for residential, commercial, and industrial uses in 2005 of 66,200 mgd, 25,600 mgd or 39 percent was for domestic public water supply or piped water for residential use. For the population served of 258 million reported by USGS, that represents 100 gallons per day per capita (gpcd). The unit gpcd is commonly used to measure the consumption of water in urban areas.

The unit of gallons per day per capita is commonly used to express use of water by each person, which ranges from a low of a few gallons to highs of more than 200 gpcd in affluent or high-water-using areas. Reports by utilities of per capita water use are higher, usually in the range of 150 gpcd, but their reports include commercial and other uses, as well as residential. This is one of the difficult issues of water-use accounting: Different uses are aggregated into total indicators such as average gallons per capita per day for a city.

The report for "all other and losses" was 18,600 mgd, and when you add this to the domestic use, the per capita use rises to 147 gpcd, which is

TABLE 2.1 National Totals of Water Use

Category of Water Use	National Total
Public water supply (domestic)	25,600 mgd
Public water supply (all other and losses)	18,600 mgd
Self-supplied (industrial)	18,200 mgd
Self-supplied (rural domestic)	3,800 mgd
Total	66,200 mgd

Source: U.S. Geological Survey (2009)

TABLE 2.2   Use of Water by Category from 1996 AWWA Survey

Water-Use Category	Use, MGD
Residential	6,208
Commercial/industrial	3,725
Municipal	301
Agricultural	128
Wholesale	3,790
Other	713
Total uses	14,865

Source: American Water Works Association (1996)

closer to the averages reported by utilities. The other part of the population receives water from self-supplied domestic systems (normally water wells), and the reported national total for them was 3,800 mgd.

The other large category of water use was self-supplied industrial water, at 18,200 mgd, which will be explained further in Chapter 7.

We can gain more perspective on commercial and industrial water uses from previous reports and from the utility survey taken by the American Water Works Association (AWWA, 1996). The AWWA water systems survey gives us an approximate picture, but the data were not reported consistently and the 898 reporting utilities represented a population served of 136 million, or only about half of the 1996 population. Another issue is that the reporting utilities tend to be the larger and better organized ones, so we lack a comprehensive picture of the operations of the many smaller utilities.

The utilities reported total water produced of 20,232 mgd, indicating that 27 percent of the water was not accounted for. This high value may indicate inconsistent reporting as well as low water efficiency and high losses.

To estimate the ratio of commercial and industrial to all other uses we can remove the wholesale category and compute the remaining percentages as: residential (56 percent); commercial/industrial (34 percent); municipal government (3 percent); agricultural (1 percent); and other (6 percent). The data do not indicate the split between commercial and industrial uses, but to estimate the commercial and industrial uses separately, we can consult past USGS data.

The last time that industrial uses from public water systems were reported separately by the USGS water-use study was in 1995. In that year, 11.8 percent of public water supply or 4,743 mgd was for industrial and mining. Also, 87.9 percent of water went to domestic and commercial uses.

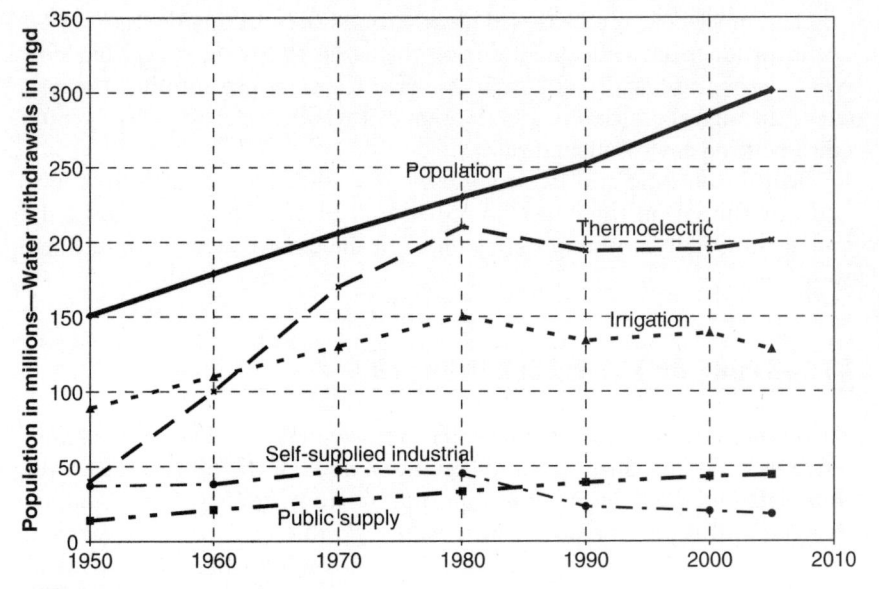

FIGURE 2.6   Trends in water use

From these data we can infer that residential use from public supply systems is about 55 percent, commercial use is 20 percent to 25 percent, industrial use is 10 percent to 15 percent, and all other miscellaneous uses are about 15 percent. These totals do not take into account system losses, which can be on the order of 15 percent even for well-managed systems.

Trends in water use reveal ongoing changes in the economy and the water industry. Figure 2.6 shows changes in water use as the U.S. population doubled between 1950 and 2005. Public supply increased by a factor of three and now seems to have leveled off. Part of the increase was due to population gain and part due to increased living standards. This seems to reflect the increased awareness of the limits to water use and interest in green or sustainable water uses.

Irrigation grew steadily to about 1980, then started to decline. Part of the decline is due to increased efficiency, part due to the end of new government water projects, and part due to conversion of agricultural water to urban use.

Self-supplied industrial water seems to have peaked around 1980 and has been cut by more than 50 percent from that peak. Part of that might be due to increased efficiency, but the greater part might be due to the loss of basic industries from the U.S. manufacturing base.

Thermoelectric use increased greatly to 1980, reflecting the rise in electricity production. It declined during the early 1980s recession, but now seems on the rise again, although slower. Electricity use continued to rise, event through the recession, so the reduced water use must reflect greater efficiency and environmental rules.

Rural domestic and livestock uses of water are at a fairly low level and not shown on the chart (about 6 mgd total). They seem to be flat and are normally not major consumers in the overall scheme of national water use.

STRUCTURE OF THE WATER INDUSTRY

The public-private nature of the water industry makes it difficult to characterize its economic structure and the interactions of the players. However, to understand the industry, it is important to study its characterization, the demand and supply of water, how water is valued for resource management, and how the industry responds to incentives and regulatory signals.

The water industry is controlled by its players, which are shown in Figure 2.7 as a map of producers, customers, suppliers, and regulators. Take a moment to familiarize yourself with this diagram, which is a starting place to distinguish roles and relationships in the water industry.

At the first ring of the diagram, you see the producers, or water handlers, which comprise the eight services of water management that are explained in subsequent chapters. These are linked to the coordinators and regulators, who are shown at the center of the diagram as enforcing the rules and establishing relationships that hold the water industry together. Regulators are explained in Chapter 14, and they include government entities such as USEPA and state departments of water resources, for example. We do not have a separate chapter about coordinators, but they involve formal and informal mechanisms, such as compact commissions, councils of government and river basin planning groups.

The second ring out shows the major customers of water handling, which include residential users, major industrial and energy water users, businesses and government users, farming, land development, landscaping and erosion control, the environment, fish and wildlife, recreation, hydropower, and navigation. In some cases—such as industrial users—the customer might be a water handler as well as a customer. This awkward arrangement is explained by the fact that an industry such as a paper mill might have one group responsible for manufacturing processes and another responsible for providing water and wastewater services. So for practical purposes, the arrangement involves an embedded water utility.

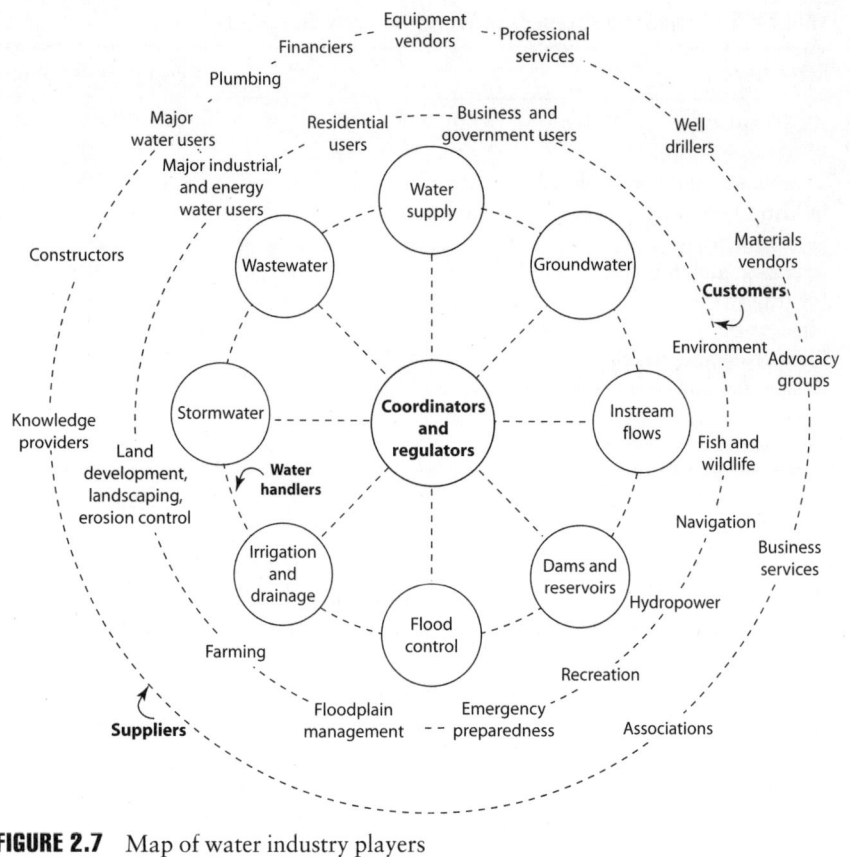

FIGURE 2.7   Map of water industry players

While the water handlers are themselves a supplier industry (that supplies water), it requires its own suppliers (of equipment and services) to function, and these are a major force in driving the water business. They are shown in the fourth ring of Figure 2.6, and their products and services can be placed into the same three classes as water systems: small, medium, and large.

The bottled-water category of the water business proved difficult to place on the diagram. It, along with the point-of-use (POU) supply industry is explained in Chapter 21. The POU business seems to fit well with the plumbing and kitchen and bath businesses as a combination of products and services aimed at the end users. Bottled water is more like a competitor to the public water-supply systems, but only for that portion of their water supplies that is for drinking. As a result, the way to conceptualize bottled water on the diagram seems to be as a competitor for a small part of the

TABLE 2.3 Estimated Revenues of Water-Industry Subsectors

Subsectors	Revenue in $ billions
Water utilities	40
Wastewater utilities	40
Stormwater and flood control	20
Industrial self-supply water and wastewater	40
Government	20
Irrigation and drainage	20
Hydropower	20
Navigation	NA
Recreation and fisheries	NA
Residential and commercial plumbing and irrigation	20
Bottled water and POU services	20
Total water-industry revenues	240

overall water supply business, and I have omitted it from the diagram to cut down on clutter, but I would like to emphasize that bottled water is an important part of the water industry and may have a larger role in the future as the water industry grapples with increasing complexity and aging facilities.

My estimates are that the annual revenues of the consolidated water industry are in the range of $240 billion. These estimates are shown in Table 2.3, which is taken from Chapter 12 and is an aggregation of estimates of revenues for the individual water sectors. As Chapter 12 explains, these are only order-of-magnitude estimates and are not based on any rigorous system of classification and accounting. Some of the categories, such as water utilities, at least have survey information and government statistics to back them up. Other categories, such as industrial water and wastewater, are based on rough extrapolations of other data, such as volumes of water use. The only redeeming attribute of such a compilation is that it shows the approximate total expenditures of an industry that is unified by the common task of handling water and this provides a basis of comparison with other, more recognized industries, such as electric power.

The value of the fixed assets of the water industry may also be of interest, and I estimate it as on the order of $1.1 trillion (Table 2.4). This helps us gain a perspective of the comparative size of the industry's assets and to interpret the reports of media and interest groups about giant unmet infrastructure needs. There might, for example, be a headline about $300 billion in unmet water and wastewater infrastructure needs over the course of the next 20 years. The asset values show that this report would represent nearly 40 percent of the replacement costs of the entire inventory in those sectors.

TABLE 2.4   Estimated Fixed Assets of the Water Industry

	Fixed Assets, $ billions
Water-supply sector	400
Wastewater and water quality	400
Stormwater and flood control	100
Dams, reservoirs, and levees	100
Irrigation and drainage	100
Total fixed assets*	1,100

*The table includes mostly public systems, but some of the facilities such as hydropower dams and infrastructure of private water companies will belong to private-sector entities.

Compiling tables such as these captures some of the ongoing activity of the water industry, but sudden events such as Hurricane Katrina can dramatically demonstrate the stakes involved. Katrina caused $100 billion-plus of damages and spurred massive rebuilding. It also stimulated plans for giant new investments, such as Houston's plans to consider a $2 billion to $4 billion protective dike to protect itself and the energy infrastructure along the Gulf coast (Casselman, 2009). As a result of disasters, the water industry can involve spikes in activity as well as regular, ongoing expenditures.

LARGE- AND SMALL-SCALE OPERATIONS

Products and services for the water industry are organized generally according to the scale or size of water-handling operations. For example, a water utility serving a population of 100,000 requires water-handling equipment that is much different in size than what a residence or small business needs. Suppliers of products and services align themselves somewhat along this scale of operations. One supplier may provide large water-handling products to water utilities while another one may produce small valves for residential sprinkler systems, for example.

Figure 2.8 has been prepared to explain this difference of scale and to provide a model of market segmentation by showing water-handling by categories. It is a complex diagram but it illustrates the different markets available to water-industry suppliers.

The diagram drills down to the level of detail of an individual household and considers that a residence is a water handler as well as a customer. The rationale for this is to identify the premise plumbing system as part of water infrastructure and the homeowner as having responsibility for its

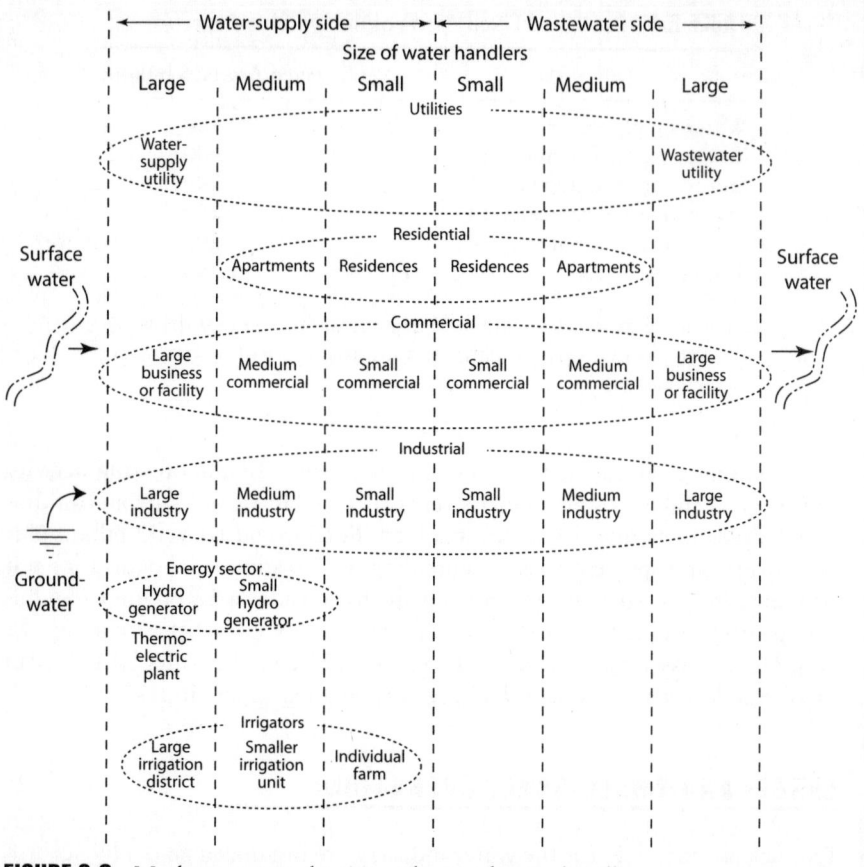

FIGURE 2.8 Market segments by size and type of water handler

operations and maintenance, just as a utility has responsibility for its infra-structure. As the water passes from the utility water main into the service line, responsibility for infrastructure (and to a great extent water quality) passes from the utility to the homeowner.

This may seem like a fine point, but the fact is that major issues of obliga-tion and liability depend on the distinction between utility and homeowner responsibilities. Utilities normally consider that they have responsibility for service lines from the connection to the main to the property line, and then the homeowner has responsibility. Most homeowners do not think much about that, until some problem occurs and they must pay a large repair bill. The only water-quality measurement that utilities are required to make inside of homes is lead at the tap. If a homeowner has a cross connection and the water gets contaminated, that is normally not a utility responsibility,

TABLE 2.5   Examples of Water-Handler Categories and Infrastructure

Water-Handler	Description	Infrastructure
Utilities	Municipal water utility serving 100,000 population or similar operation	Full range of water-handling and processing equipment
Large businesses or service organizations	University campus, large shopping center, recreation park	Water-handling and processing equipment, normally for distribution
Large industries	Paper manufacturing complex, refinery, chemical processing plant	Water-handling and processing equipment, maybe self-supplied
Hydropower generators	Electric power utility with dam, penstocks, and turbines	Dam, penstocks, turbines, other raw-water-handling systems
Thermoelectric power plants	Electric power utility with diversion, canals, pipes and water processing system	Large-scale raw-water-handling systems
Large irrigation providers	Large irrigation district that distributes water to farm operations	Full range of water-handling equipment for agriculture

although utilities will take actions to educate homeowners and look for problems like this when they have the opportunity.

On the left of the diagram, you see the two main sources of groundwater and surface water. At the large scale of operations, we have the utilities and another group of water handlers that require similar large-scale equipment. These include large commercial businesses or similar operations, large industries, hydropower generators, thermoelectric power plants, and large irrigation providers. Table 2.5 shows examples for each of these categories.

As you can see, these large water handlers require similar equipment and services, such as high-capacity pumps, large-diameter pipes, large valves, special materials to handle corrosive fluids or serve in difficult-to-reach locations, and fire protection systems.

At the medium scale and at each category of water user you find organizations that use pipes and processing systems that are larger than the household scale but smaller than those of utility scale. Medium-scale apartments, businesses, and industries might form a market cluster that requires similar products and services. Small hydro generators and irrigation organizations have different needs and form distinct market segments.

TABLE 2.6 Fort Collins Plant Investment Fees for Different Meter Sizes

Meter Size, Inches	Plant Investment Fee, $
1	21,700
2	69,700
3	157,200

Data source: City of Fort Collins (2010)

For an example of the commercial market, a big-box store might require a water tap large enough to serve multiple areas of the store and the sprinkler system, which will require large pipes and hardware. To illustrate this, in the case of Fort Collins, the 2010 plant investment fees for commercial meters are as shown. The rapid increase with diameter of service shows the city's belief that its capital costs go up markedly with size of service (Table 2.6).

At the smaller scale, you have the household plumbing system, small businesses and industries, and the individual farm irrigation units. These end users can be self-served or tapped into utilities, but most residences and small businesses are in cities and are served by utilities.

The wastewater side of the diagram applies to residential, commercial, and industrial end users and to the wastewater utilities that process the sewage from these building types. Electric power producers discharge raw water back to streams, sometimes adding tremendous quantities of heat, and irrigations discharge nonpoint sources of water.

To summarize the market segments shown on the diagram, they are:

- Water and wastewater utilities
- Residential market (segmented by size)
- Commercial market (segmented by size and type of business/facility)
- Industrial market (segmented by size and type of industry)
- Hydroelectric market (segmented into hydro and small hydro)
- Electric power cooling water market
- Irrigation market (segmented by size)

The market segments are classified into small, medium, and large groups. Small systems are at the household level and involve kitchen and bath supplies, plus outdoor sprinkler systems at the smallest level. Medium systems serve commercial centers, office buildings, and small utilities up to, say, 5,000 taps or so. Large systems would serve big cities, water districts, and large infrastructure plants such as hydroelectric generators.

As we will see later, while the same equipment types are used in each size group, the sizes of components differ greatly. For example, at the household level, half-inch copper pipe is used. At the largest size, steel pipes might reach 120 inches or larger. These can be produced by the same companies, but the suppliers to the water industry are very diverse.

On the production side, the water business sells water as a commodity (such as public supply and irrigation) and provides water-related services, such as treatment and disposal of wastewater. These water-related services involve water handling, but they do not always supply water. They may instead protect people and/or the environment from water or contamination.

WATER-INDUSTRY INFRASTRUCTURE

The asset value of the infrastructure required to provide water-industry services ranges slightly above $1 trillion, according to my estimates shown in Table 2.2. Most of this value is in the supply sources, buried assets, and treatment systems of water-supply and wastewater systems. Substantial amounts are also in dams and river control structures, including those owned by electric power utilities as well as the federal government. Constructing and maintaining these physical assets comprises one of the major business activities of the water industry.

This is a partial list of infrastructure types, which is not complete but assembles a representative set of categories that cut across the major purposes of large-scale water management.

Municipal and industrial water supply	Dams, wells, pipe systems, meters, treatment plants, pumps, tanks, valves, supervisory control and data acquisition systems
Urban and industrial wastewater	Sewer pipes, pretreatment, treatment plants, pumps, sludge facilities, hazardous liquid systems, outfalls
Irrigation and drainage	Dams, wells, diversions, canals, distribution systems, sprinkler systems, drip and subsurface irrigation, drains
Instream flow and water-control structures	Dams and reservoirs, spillways, tunnels, pumping systems, river structures, pumps, levees, bridges, constructed wetlands, penstocks, surge tanks, powerhouses, pumped storage locks, ports
Stormwater management	Collectors, culverts, headwalls, pipes, ponds, tanks, outfalls

The infrastructure components can also be classified by the functions they fulfill, which range across conveyance, storage, treatment, energy conversion, and flow control. For example, water-supply systems use pipes, canals, and tunnels for conveyance, and wastewater systems use the same but with different configurations. Water-supply systems use dams, reservoirs, tanks, and aquifers for storage, but wastewater involves much less storage infrastructure. Both water and wastewater require treatment plants, but they use different processes. Pumps are used by most water-management systems, but they require different types. Controls such as valves, meters, and hydrants are found in different forms in the different water-management systems. Hydropower and navigation require larger-scale infrastructure systems, to include large penstocks, turbines, surge tanks, and locks to go along with dams.

Water management infrastructure for in-building use takes on one additional function—providing access for personal service at sinks, toilets, faucets, tubs, and showers. Otherwise, the infrastructure comprises smaller versions of the main systems used for water management. The components that provide access to water services are faucets, toilets, sinks, tubs, and showers. Storage is by water tanks, hot-water tanks, and cisterns. Conveyance is by service lines, building pipes, building sewers, drains, and gutters. Treatment is smaller scale, to include point-of-use treatment and water-heating systems. Control and measurement are by smaller meters and valves, of which there are hundreds of millions.

WATER HANDLERS—THE PRODUCERS OF THE WATER INDUSTRY

The water-handling sectors are the producers of the water industry because they manage the water, either directly, as in water supply, or indirectly as in ensuring environmental water for natural species. They are classified in eight sectors, which are introduced in this section and explained in more detail in later chapters.

The larger-scale water-handling sectors provide a range of services that goes well beyond the supply of piped water to customers. In addition to municipal water, they provide water to the environment and for irrigation, manage water in streams and aquifers for various uses, and collect and treat wastewater. They even protect people and property against damage from too much water. Figure 2.9 illustrates these large-scale systems for water supply and wastewater, as well as raw-water handlers and the industrial self-supply users, who are named point-of-use water handlers on this diagram.

The lead water-handling service is the service that brings drinking water into your home. This water-supply sector is sometimes called municipal and

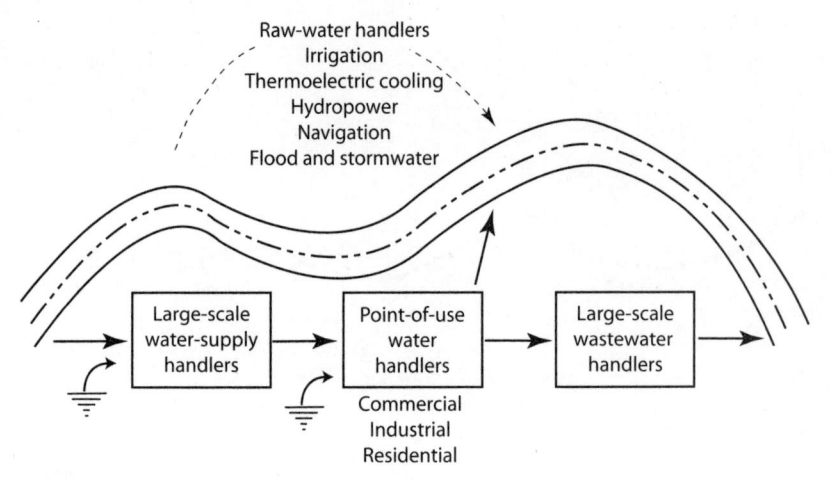

FIGURE 2.9   Large-scale water handlers

industrial or M&I water. Wastewater is also a familiar service because it takes the used water away from your home or business. Stormwater is also familiar because it is the service that collects your roof drainage and carries it away down the street. Once you get past these three services, you get into larger-scale activities that are not always household words.

The larger-scale water-handling activities for irrigation and drainage, dams and reservoirs, groundwater, instream flows, and flood control are usually much larger and more remote from view than the household services. However, as water-handling services, they require the same kinds of equipment, supplies, construction, and professional services as the water-supply, wastewater, and stormwater sectors. These products and services are needed at scales that range from the smallest household devices to the gigantic scales seen in large dams.

The focus here is on large-scale water handlers, rather than the functions undertaken by smaller systems, down to the level of the individual home. However, to get a full picture of the infrastructure and responsibilities of water handlers, you must eventually drill down to this level. Figure 2.10 shows how the water distribution system leads to the premises plumbing systems in buildings, which are accompanied by sewers and site drainage systems.

The water-supply sector serves residential, commercial, and industrial properties, mostly within urban areas. In addition to organized utilities, it includes the industries and other entities that operate their own separate water services for customers and their industrial process water systems. The utility part of the water-supply utility sector is a $40 billion industry with 250,000 employees who work directly for public water supply producers.

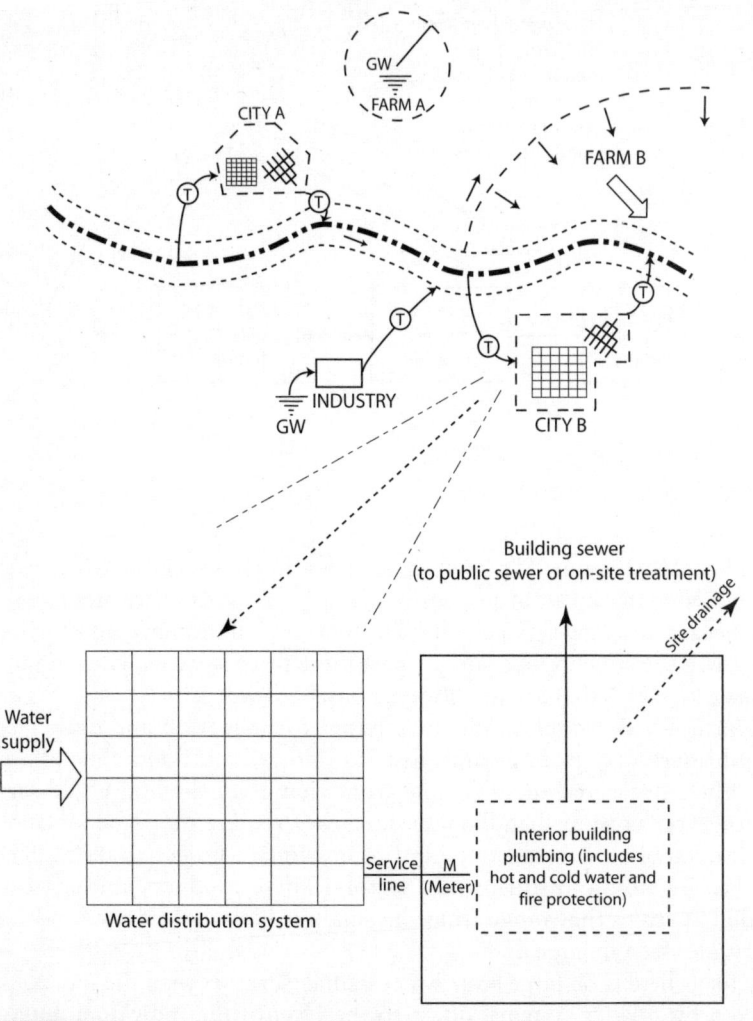

FIGURE 2.10   From large- to small-scale water handlers

If you map the chain of responsibility for water-supply infrastructure all the way to the tap, then the sector involves practically everyone with some level of responsibility, and many more employees work to provide private sector water-supply products and services (Grigg and Zenzen, 2009).

Wastewater and water quality are lumped together in a unified sector, which includes a range of services from access to sanitation through disposal of wastewater and protection of environmental water quality.

At the utility level, it is also a $40 billion industry and has 225,000 employees involved in public wastewater services. The sector also includes industrial and other users, and it is similar in structure to water supply but has a separate regulatory structure, a separate trade association, and different types of equipment and facilities.

Water supply and wastewater seem similar but have important differences. One sector diverts water from the environment, and the other disposes of wastewater to it. One provides safe water for consumption and the other processes contaminated water for disposal. One involves pressurized clean water systems and the other uses mostly gravity systems to drain contaminated water away. The two services also have different regulatory structures and professional associations.

The stormwater sector provides management and water-quality control of runoff, mostly in urban areas. It is a $20 billion industry with 50,000 employees and is managed mostly by local governments. However, on-site stormwater is managed by facility owners. Stormwater management is subject to increasing regulation for water quality and is one of the main water services affected by low-impact development (LID) and related green technologies. Stormwater management is of great interest to the landscape industry as well as to engineers.

Flood control and floodplain management are sometimes included with stormwater in a single sector, but they have distinct properties. Flood control is the mission of a diverse collection of government agencies. As Chapter 6 explains, it involves control of streams and rivers to prevent flooding, and floodplain management involves land-use regulation to remove vulnerable parties from harm's way as in floodplain management.

This diverse sector owns and operates dams and water control structures for water that remains in streams for uses such as hydropower, navigation, fish and wildlife, and recreation. It is separated out as a distinct sector because of its strategic nature in controlling large quantities of water on behalf of multiple water-handling organizations. As explained in Chapter 3, the size of this sector has not been estimated, but the United States has 85,000 dams that are large enough to be regulated.

The instream flow sector is closely connected to the dam management sector because dams and reservoirs provide the basic tools to manage instream flows. The instream-flow water handlers might be thought of as a "virtual" water-management sector because they normally lack the infrastructure and means to manage water themselves, but they may determine its use for water-based recreation, sport and commercial fishing, hydropower production, floodwater passage, and other environmental or scenic purposes. While it is not a well-organized business sector, it provides a mechanism to help us see the combined actions of groups who determine flows in rivers and streams.

The irrigation and drainage sector provides water for farming and land-scaping and it disposes of drainage water, which can be required even when irrigation is not practiced. Irrigation takes massive quantities of water from streams and water wells. It is mostly practiced in the arid West, but it is increasingly used in humid areas and for the landscape industry. The size of this sector has been estimated in terms of water used but not in financial terms. It is discussed in more detail in Chapter 8.

The groundwater sector is identified separately because it involves well drillers, hydrogeologists, and other distinct categories of business. The size and employment of the water handlers in this sector have not been estimated, but the support sector is large due to widespread use of individual wells.

CUSTOMERS OF THE WATER BUSINESS

The customers of the water business are shown at the second ring of Figure 2.7. By characterizing water users as customers, we can see how water is distributed in the supply-demand balance. The customers receive three categories of goods and services: water supply as a commodity, collection and cleaning of wastewater, and protection from water damage.

Customer demands for water services can be explained largely by their uses of land. Figure 2.11 shows six categories of land uses with demands for and impacts on water (NLUD Partnership, 2010). These land uses mirror construction categories, and residential is the largest, which coincides with domestic water use being the largest category.

The three top land use groups have similar requirements for residential, commercial, and industrial water uses, but they also have important differences that stem from the types of commercial and industrial operations. They represent the supply of water to residential dwellings; to hotels, retail shops, offices, restaurants and bars; to special institutions such as hospitals, schools, and sports facilities; and to a range of manufacturing, distribution, and military bases. When you combine these, you have a composite picture of water use in urban areas.

The category of transportation and other public uses is different in that it includes a range of infrastructure and utility locations, such as roads, tracks, terminals and interchanges, car parks, energy facilities, water utilities, and public facilities such as landfills and cemeteries. The last two categories represent open lands that are worked and those that remain in natural condition. They include agriculture, forestry, mining, and all kinds of natural environmental settings and unused land. These categories of land use do not, for the most part, use water from public systems in the same way as urban land uses do.

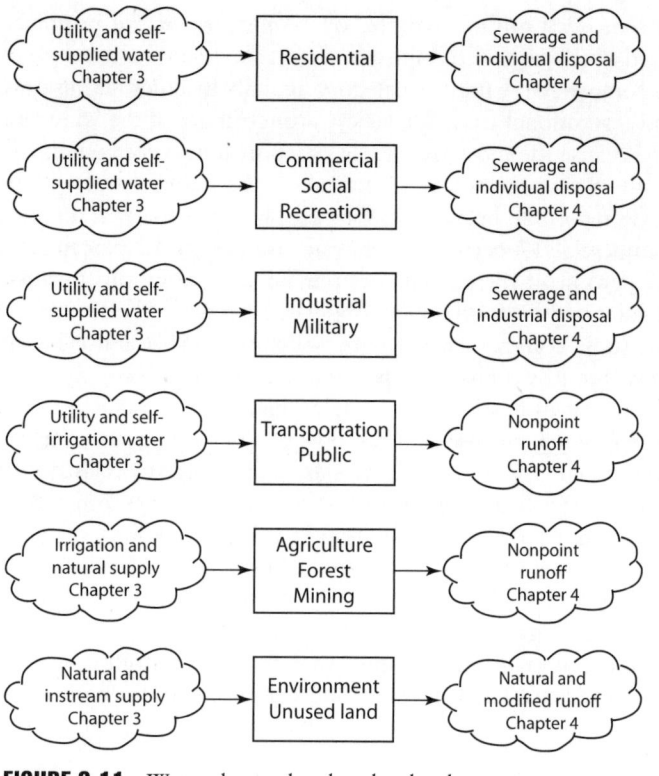

FIGURE 2.11   Water demands related to land uses

Of all water uses, the one that affects us most directly is piped water in residential homes. Some customers are connected to utilities and receive water as a piped commodity. Other customers provide their own water services, and act both as producers and consumers of water services.

The USGS data showed that 58 percent of the public supply, or 25,600 mgd, goes to domestic uses (based on 2005 data). To visualize this quantity on a nationwide basis, imagine that a small town with an average use of 100 gpcd has a water system to deliver 1 mgd, which would serve around 10,000 people. That would mean the national total is equivalent to 25,000 small towns, with each withdrawing 1 mgd. This is a fairly accurate depiction, as the number of municipalities in the United States is on that order of magnitude, according to the U.S. Bureau of Census. The remaining part of the population would be served by rural domestic systems.

Rural domestic self-supply systems comprise a large market for well drillers and POU water-conditioning systems. The 2005 USGS report showed that 42.9 million people, or 14 percent of the population, used 3,830 mgd of self-supplied domestic water.

The commercial water use category actually includes all business, government and institutional uses. We lack a firm estimate of the water used in this category because the most recent USGS report lumps commercial, industrial, and all other uses together at 42 percent of the public supply. However, the 1995 USGS report did break the public supply out as follows: domestic 56 percent, commercial 17 percent, industrial and energy 12 percent, and system losses 15 percent. If the percentages remain valid now, this means that total commercial water use from public supply in 2005 would be around 7,500 mgd.

Also, some commercial use is by self-supply. This is not broken out by USGS now, but it was about 85 percent of domestic self-supply in 1995, so in 2005 the equivalent would be about 3,250 mgd. When added to the public supply going to commercial uses, the national total would be some 10,750 mgd.

Commercial land and water uses are a challenge to classify by type, but one way to do it is by the categories of construction spending tracked by the Census Bureau. Analysis of these shows the following major categories:

- Lodging
- Office buildings
- Commercial (a broad category that includes automotive, food/beverage, multiretail such as shopping centers, other commercial such as drugstores)
- Warehouses
- Health care (hospitals and medical buildings, and special care)
- Educational (including preschool, primary/secondary, higher education, and other educational, such as gallery/museum)
- Religious
- Amusement and recreation (such as theme/amusement park, sports, performance/meeting center, social center, and movie theater/studio).

As you can see, this very diverse group of water users will range from a small store with only a sink and bathroom to a major water amusement park.

Within the commercial category we also place government uses to meet public needs, such as firefighting. Institutional uses are included within the list above, such as religious, health care, and educational institutions.

Industrial water users are also a major category, which also includes the water-energy nexus. Like commercial uses, industrial water uses are diverse and hard to classify. The USGS (2010a) explanation of them is:

The industries that produce metals, wood and paper products, chemicals, gasoline and oils, and those invaluable grabber utensils your dad uses to pull out the car keys you dropped into the garbage disposal are major users of water. Probably every manufactured product uses water during some part of the production process. Industrial water use includes water used for such purposes as fabricating, processing, washing, diluting, cooling, or transporting a product; incorporating water into a product; or for sanitation needs within the manufacturing facility. Some industries that use large amounts of water produce such commodities as food, paper, chemicals, refined petroleum, or primary metals.

This latter group is what we call water-dependent industries.

Much of the water use in urban areas is nonresidential and used to irrigate lawns and rights-of-way. These uses might be masked by the "residential" or "public categories," but they can be substantial. We cannot speculate accurately on the total of these because they cut across the categories. If we could, the total would be the aggregate of outdoor water use for residential, commercial, industrial, and public uses. Urban farming is increasing in popularity, and a good bit of it will use water from public supply systems as well.

Farming is a water customer, especially where irrigation is practiced. Drainage from farming is handled by pipes, canals, and water management organizations, even in nonirrigated areas. In many of these, farmers will consider using supplementary irrigation if it raises their profitability.

As explained in Chapter 9, supplying water to the natural environment is an indirect service that results from all other activities, including regulation to ensure that not too much water is taken away from natural systems. Water use for the environment sustains natural habitat, fish and wildlife, and plant systems. Water for fish includes sport fishing, which is included in the recreation category, and commercial fishing. Aquaculture or fish farming is included in the farming category. Water utilities and users must devote some of their resources and efforts toward supplying environmental water, even if they are forced to by regulatory controls. In some ways, this is like a tax on your activities that provides a return to the common welfare.

Water is used for several forms of recreation, such as boating, sport fishing, swimming, and sightseeing. The value to recreational users is high, although it would be difficult to finance water projects for recreational uses alone.

Hydropower and navigation are coordinated uses of instream waters. Any form of boating can be considered as navigation, but commercial navigation requires navigable rivers and lakes and the Intracoastal Waterway system.

Floodplain management is paired with flood control as a customer for water-related services as a comprehensive approach to preventing damages. Flood control involves dams, reservoirs, and levees but nonstructural actions such as zoning of floodplains, flood insurance, flood warnings, and flood proofing also mitigate the damage of floods. These require flood prediction models, consulting studies, engineering reports, and similar water-related services as other flood control measures.

Emergency managers participate in flood response and so are customers in the sense that they must prepare for and respond to floods as they do to other emergencies. That means they might use dam break models and other water-related services.

COORDINATORS, REGULATORS, AND SUPPLIERS

Coordination and regulation are important features of water governance, which comprises the institutional arrangements of the water industry (Grigg, 2011). Regulators control water quantity and use, water quality in the environment, public water systems safety, land use in floodplains (floodplain management), and emergency preparedness for droughts and other water emergencies. As we will see in Chapter 14, these regulators control a number of business aspects that range from public health protection to water requirements for endangered species.

The diverse groups of suppliers shown on Figure 2.6 are described briefly here and in more detail in later chapters. Some of them are equipment manufacturers that provide parts and assembled products. Others provide professional services and are in ways like a shadow workforce for

TABLE 2.7 Water-Industry Suppliers

Category	Description	Chapter
Equipment and materials	Capital equipment such as pipes, pumps, and instruments; materials and supplies for water treatment; energy sources	19
Professional and business services	Advisory and design services across a range of categories; outsourced operations support; system maintenance	18
Constructors and well drilling	System construction and maintenance; well construction services	17
Financiers	Financial assistance for water handlers	12
POU systems and bottled water	POU assemblies for end users and bottled water	21
Associations, advocacy, knowledge providers	Capacity development and decision assistance	15

water-industry services. Still others are secondary water handlers, such as the bottled-water industry. As a preview to these later chapters, Table 2.7 shows a list of the main categories of water-industry suppliers.

RISK IN THE WATER INDUSTRY

The water industry manages a large amount of risk across several categories, and it will be explained briefly here. Risk is discussed in the chapters about the sectors, and it might be appropriate to add it to the chapters on finance and health as well. In any case, it is such a large and crosscutting issue that it deserves an overall discussion as well.

One reason for the risks of the industry is that it deals with large issues, such as the flow of rivers, the health of people, and potential damage to the environment. These can involve large floods and disasters, causing millions and maybe billions of dollars of liability to people, businesses, and the insurance industry. When disease outbreaks occur, such as the current (2010) cholera outbreak in Haiti, thousands of lives can be threatened. Water-related environmental disasters, such as oil-spill contamination, can lead to long-term and high levels of damages. Business risk, such as preventing pipes from breaking, is an everyday concern of utilities. Perhaps the ultimate risk is that a large dam above a developed area will fail. The consequences of such a gigantic failure are difficult to imagine.

Risk differs somewhat across the water sectors. For example, dams and river improvements can involve dam or levee failures, erosion and sedimentation failures, and navigation incidents. Water-supply utilities are concerned about drinking-water contamination, infrastructure failures, and regulatory risks. Wastewater and water-quality agencies face similar risks, especially those involving water pollution. Stormwater and flood control agencies face disasters and property damage, as well as infrastructure failures. In the private sector, industrial water and wastewater facility managers face similar infrastructure risks as public utilities, as well as risks of water pollution and regulatory sanctions. Irrigation and drainage agencies must worry about their infrastructure failures, crop contamination, and salinization of soils. In the instream sector, various environmental risks must be faced, including loss of habitat.

WATER-INDUSTRY SUMMARY

While the water industry does cut across other industries, it can be explained through its driving forces, purposes and agencies, and its suppliers.

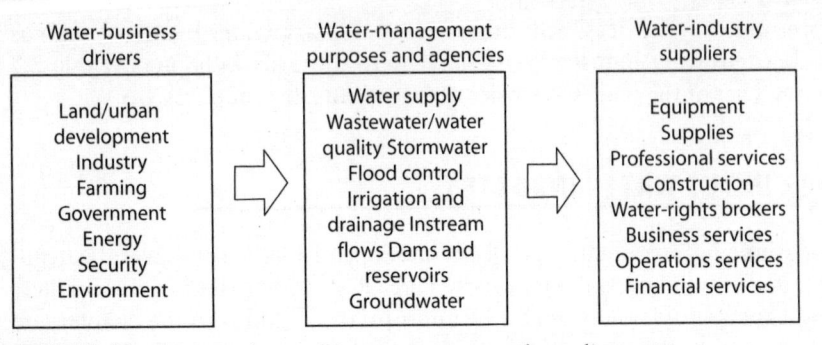

FIGURE 2.12   Water-industry drivers, purposes, and suppliers

Figure 2.12 illustrates these in some detail to display its diversity and scope. From the diagram you can see how (through the drivers) the water industry is linked to many areas of society, the economy, and the environment. You can see the broad scope of its purposes and players, and you can also see its dependence on an array of suppliers of products and services.

CHAPTER 3

Dams and Reservoirs for Multiple Purposes

In this first chapter of a series about water-industry sectors, dams and reservoirs are introduced because they provide high-level controls on natural water systems for all water uses, including water supply, hydropower, navigation, fish and wildlife, and recreation. They also influence stream water quality and have a central role in flood control.

Dams are important to the water industry because they control rivers, generate electric energy, and create major recreational venues. Their distinct services often benefit multiple parties, but their large impacts on natural systems draw fire from environmental activist groups. Although dams are developed for multiple water-management purposes and offer many benefits, they are inevitably controversial and can be the centerpieces of long-standing water disputes. In addition to political heat, these can generate expensive lawsuits and government decision processes that extend over many years. They also create serious security risks, because failure of a dam can have disastrous consequences.

For the most part the infrastructure of dams and reservoirs was developed by the utilities, local agencies, and industries that process and deliver water-related services in vertically integrated systems, but in many cases, dams were developed or assisted by federal agencies, mainly the U.S. Army Corps of Engineers (USACE), the U.S. Bureau of Reclamation (Burec) and the Natural Resources Conservation Service (NRCS). Also, the state of California has a unique and large-scale state-owned system of dams and reservoirs.

While not many dams are currently being constructed in the United States, we have an inventory of 85,000 dams that are large enough to be regulated for risk of failure. Other nations have new dams on the drawing boards, particularly in countries with rapidly expanding economies. For example, in China, the massive Three Gorges Dam was completed between 2005 and 2010, and it has the world's largest hydroelectric plant with a planned eventual capacity of 22.5 gigawatts (GW). If each person required 1 kilowatt (KW) of capacity, which is about what is needed in many developed countries, this single structure would provide the hydroelectric energy required for 22.5 million people. In developing regions of China, the electric power would serve many more, of course.

The companion feature to a dam is the lake or reservoir that it impounds. A reservoir is a lake where water is stored naturally or artificially and a pond is a small reservoir. In the United States, there are countless thousands of small lakes, compared to relatively few giant reservoirs. These small impoundments even extend down to the level of urban stormwater detention ponds, which function the same way as flood control reservoirs, but hold less water and respond faster to inflows.

The chapter explains dams and other river structures, how they are used and the issues they present to business and other interest groups. No matter how you look at it, dams are major infrastructure facilities and forces to be reckoned with. They provide many benefits but generate much controversy, are expensive and risky, and will attract a great deal of attention in the future. Levees are similar to dams and pose some of the same risks. They will also be discussed briefly in the chapter.

EVOLUTION OF DAMS AND RIVER INFRASTRUCTURE

From the earliest civilization, rivers and streams have met human needs such as water for drinking, cooking, irrigation, fishing, washing, and navigation. People recognized the energy potential of flowing water early on, and the Greeks were using water wheels for hydropower to grind flour 2,000 years ago.

Early river development focused on economic goals, and navigation went hand-in-hand with hydropower development as a productive use of waterways and attraction for capital investment. The construction of the Erie Canal was the principal driver of increased 1800s commerce between the East Coast and the Great Lakes. It opened in 1825, after a frenetic period of canal development in Britain when people started to appreciate the many economic benefits that could be provided by inland waterborne transportation. The Erie Canal is credited with much of the success of New York City as our major eastern port and city, and some people believe that it explains why New York edged out Philadelphia as a major port and became the largest city in the United States (Bernstein, 2005).

Hydropower was based on stored water to turn water wheels for many centuries, and with the advent of electric power in the 1880s it was being developed to light cities in the United States. Then, the dam-building era began in earnest as engineers and business leaders saw the great possibilities of hydropower. By 1920, hydropower was providing 25 percent of the electric energy of a rapidly developing United States, and in the 1930s the creation of the Tennessee Valley Authority's system of dams was a centerpiece of FDR's New Deal. It harnessed a mighty river for economic and social development in an underdeveloped region. Along with development of dams came new lakes, land developments, and a water-based recreational industry that did not exist before.

Many dams were built in the United States between the 1930s and the 1960s, but few major dams or river structures have been built since the 1960s. This means that the youngest of America's major dams and navigation systems are passing the 50-year mark, and the same can be said for most developed countries, as well as many developing countries. This means that the legacy of aging dams will require vigilance and investments for renewal in the decades ahead.

Today, the United States has about 85,000 dams that are large enough to warrant regulation, about 80,000 megawatts of installed hydroelectric capacity, and systems of river management that extend even to small streams across the nation (U.S. Department of Energy, 2010). The major issues are operation, maintenance, and renewal of these vital facilities. In the developing world, major dam sites remain attractive targets for new facilities.

TYPES AND PURPOSES OF DAMS AND RESERVOIRS

The basic functions of dams, to control stream flows and impound water, create many situations, as stream flows occur from the smallest headwaters to giant bays and estuaries that empty into the ocean. In the United States, this involves big river and lake systems such as the Mississippi River and Great Lakes down to small headwater streams in hill or mountain areas.

Dams can be large or small, as measured by their height, width, and quantity of water impounded. The oldest design is the earthfill dam, which has an impervious core and upstream and downstream faces with pervious rock material. A rockfill dam is similar to an earthfill design, but it uses rock as a structural element and has an impervious membrane to seal water flows. A concrete gravity dam is normally a massive structure with a pervious foundation, a cutoff wall, a downstream and upstream apron, and anchor walls to aid in prevention of sliding. Slim, graceful arch dams are built of concrete but are much thinner than the concrete gravity dams. All dams have auxiliary features for required functions, such as outlet works for water flow and spillways to protect them. A dam normally has a service spillway for ongoing releases and an emergency spillway to release large storm flows. The size and capacity of these spillways can be contentious issues in dam risk analyses and lead to the need for large reinvestments for dam upgrades.

Most reservoirs serve multiple purposes, and in terms of numbers, the purposes of dams in the United States are (in order) recreation, farming, flood control, irrigation, water supply, mine waste retention, and hydropower (Association of Dam Safety Officials, 2010). The largest dams are usually those built with government funding and are for multiple purposes as outlined in the authorizing legislation.

The value added by a water-supply reservoir is to increase reliability of a surface water source of supply, which may even go dry during droughts. By capturing excess water during wet periods, the reservoir can equalize flows and release water for use when needed. As you can imagine, the saying "you will know the worth of water when the well goes dry" illustrates how valuable having a reliable source of water during dry weather can be.

By storing water behind a power dam, water can be released to generate energy on demand. The value of such peaking power is greater than the average value of power that might be generated by a coal- or gas-fired steam plant or even a nuclear plant. Many dams are owned by power utilities, which benefit from real estate sales as well as hydropower generation. Hydropower producers control many miles of the nation's streams through a network of dams and lakes to generate electricity. In the United States, hydropower systems range from small plants generating only a megawatt or so to large systems that control major rivers. For example, the Tennessee Valley Authority's (2010) hydro system has 3,305 MW of capacity, which is about 10 percent of the utility's total capacity.

In some other nations, hydropower can be substantial percentages of overall energy. Guri Dam in Venezuela, the Iguaçu project in Latin America, and China's Three Gorges project are examples. In Latin American countries such as Brazil, Colombia, and Venezuela, the percentage of total electric energy generated by hydropower can be over 50 percent and range as high as 75 percent.

Flood-control reservoirs work by capturing the high rates of flow during storm events and releasing the water slowly to avoid damage downstream. The Army Corps of Engineers has been responsible for many of these, such as the Cherry Creek Dam upstream of Denver, which protects the city from devastating flash floods.

A reservoir for irrigation is similar to one for municipal and industrial water supply in that it captures water during wet periods for release when needed. In contrast to municipal water supply, which meets human needs and can be practically priceless, the value of irrigation water supply is more variable. Irrigated farming usually depends on rainfall and supplementary supplies, and water may be required if the crop is to survive at all or it may be used to add to the yield of crops from doses of water to finish crops off at the end of a season. Also, the value of irrigation water depends sharply on the types of crop, which vary from lower-value rough crops, such as hay, to higher-value crops such as flowers and vegetables.

Recreation is normally provided as a side benefit of other purposes of reservoirs, but it has tremendous value to people enjoying the water and to the local areas and businesses that benefit from it. Economists debate how to compute the benefits from recreation so as to assess its feasibility in justifying a water project, but normally the willingness-to-pay is insufficient to finance water projects only by recreation interests.

Navigation is facilitated by backing up water to increase the depths of river channels. In the United States, the main inland waterway system includes a number of dams, mainly constructed by the Corps of Engineers (see Chapter 9).

Environmental flow control is normally a regulated side benefit of reservoirs that is controlled by the regulators or authorizations of a project. For example, a utility might be required to release certain levels of flow to sustain a downstream fishery. Normally, environmental entities or natural resources agencies do not pay for these purposes, so the water releases must be forced, so to speak, by regulatory controls.

Dams and reservoirs are also used for waste retention for mines and other industrial facilities. These pose special hazards, as was dramatically illustrated by a high-profile 2010 failure of a sludge-holding dam in Hungary.

INVENTORY OF DAMS

While there are 85,000 regulated dams in the United States—an average of almost 30 for each county—many more small ponds are used for rural purposes, aquaculture, and recreation. No count of these is available as there are so many and they are not regulated by any central authority.

The place where dams are counted in the United States is in the National Inventory of Dams, maintained by the Army Corps of Engineers with data on more than 85,000 dams (American Society of Civil Engineers, 2010). To qualify for listing, a dam must be more than 25 feet high, hold more than 50 acre-feet of water, or be considered a significant hazard if it fails. The purpose of this database is to serve the dam safety regulatory program.

Ownership of U.S. dams is about 65 percent private and 2 percent by public utilities. The rest of the dams are in public or unknown ownership. Of the publicly owned dams, only 4 percent are by the federal government.

TABLE 3.1 Distribution of Ownership of U.S. Dams

Ownership	%	Number
Private	65	55,250
Local	20	17,000
State	5	4,250
Federal	4	3,400
Unknown	4	3,400
Public utility	2	1,700
		85,000

Data source: Association of State Dam Safety Officials.

State governments own 5 percent, but local governments own 20 percent (Association of State Dam Safety Officials, 2009). Table 3.1 shows the breakdown of ownership.

We have not analyzed the data on ownership by size, but many of the federal and public utility dams would be large, and many of the dams owned by local governments and private owners are apt to be smaller. Nationally, the Corps of Engineers and Bureau of Reclamation own many of the nation's major dams. The Tennessee Valley Authority (TVA) also operates a network of large dams.

The U.S. Natural Resources Conservation Service (2010) has assisted local governments with construction of more than 11,000 dams in 47 states since 1948, but it does not own and operate them in the same way as the USACE and Burec.

The Federal Energy Regulatory Commission (FERC) regulates more than 1,700 nonfederal dams in the United States, and these can include local and state governments as well as investor-owned utilities.

Each state's dam inventory is different. For example, in Colorado the dam owner with the greatest reservoir volume is the Bureau of Reclamation (3,577,305 acre-feet), followed by the Denver Water Board (667,864 acre-feet). The Corps of Engineers is third (427,080 acre-feet), followed by many other reservoir owners, including major irrigation districts and cities, which control less than 150,000 acre-feet of storage each (Grigg, 2003).

EXAMPLES OF HIGH-PROFILE DAMS

In the class I teach on water resources management, we discuss many cases related to dams and a few of them can serve to highlight important issues. One case is about the Aswan High Dam in Egypt, which impounds Lake Nasser and is clearly the most important infrastructure feature in Egypt and on the Nile River. It has a long story, but the short version is that after Nasser came to power in the 1950s, there was a need to upgrade the older dams on the Nile. The United States was interested in helping, but after the Suez War of 1956 Egypt found more promise in cooperation with the Soviets than with the United States, and the dam was built with Soviet assistance. It was completed in 1970 and, after the United States reestablished relations with Egypt, I visited Egypt in 1975 when the reservoir was about to become full for the first time. I discussed the many issues of the dam with Egyptian and U.N. officials and was amazed at the dramatic transformation in the national economy due to the dam and its benefits. The nation was also discussing its side effects, which included loss of Mediterranean fishery, loss of annual silting along the Nile Valley, and increase in schistosomiasis, a waterborne disease based on a parasitic snail.

This discussion of environmental effects of the large dam were fascinating to me in 1975, and I wondered about the long-term future of that major structure. Today, 35 years later, no one seems to be very concerned about these effects, and the focus seems to have shifted to long-term management issues. This makes me think that today's dialog about the environmental and social effects of China's Three Gorges Dam will also pass away, but I cannot be sure, of course.

Three Gorges Dam impounds the Yangtze River to create the world's largest hydroelectric facility, protect the downstream from flooding, and enhance navigation along the river. It produced many environmental and social effects and is still being implemented. Whatever its effects turn out to be, it is by far the largest and highest-profile dam project in the world.

Another famous dam of the Aswan Dam era is Guri Dam in Venezuela. One of its chief planners was Victor Koelzer of the Harza Engineering Company. He had worked for the Bureau of Reclamation and developed the class about water-resources management that I took over from him. When he taught the class, he explained how Guri was planned and financed with international assistance, and today the dam has one of the world's largest hydro capacities and provides the lion's share of Venezuela's electric power.

While it was never built, plans for the Two Forks Dam project in Colorado led to a dramatic showdown that was won by environmentalists. The major advocate was the Denver Water Department, which led a consortium of water utilities to plan a new structure on the South Platte River above Denver. After spending more than $40 million on environmental studies, the consortium gained approval for a permit from the Corps of Engineers, but it was vetoed by Bill Reilly, the new administrator of the USEPA under President George Herbert Walker Bush.

Lake Lanier above Atlanta on the Chattahoochee River is impounded by Buford Dam, a Corps of Engineers reservoir that has provided much of

Atlanta's water supply. However, this water supply is at risk because a court ruling cut off part of Atlanta's access to the federal reservoir (Evans, 2010). Atlanta thought it had more entitlement to water from Lake Lanier on the Chattahoochee River than it now has. Atlanta had the opportunity to share the costs of the reservoir when it was built, but then-mayor William Hartsfield refused to pay anything as he thought Atlanta had plenty of water. This was a mistake. A federal district judge ruled that unless Congress reclassifies the lake for water supply, Atlanta will lose its access by 2012. The judge found that the Corps was illegally selling nearly 25 percent of the lake's capacity to Atlanta. The judge wrote that the ruling was "draconian," but his goal was apparently to set the record straight. It seems to be a legal precedent.

This can be an issue for many other lakes. The Corps of Engineers sells water from 135 federal reservoirs around the country and gave Congress a list of 40 projects in 14 states that sell water but were not authorized for water supply. Georgia is trying to get other states to support re-classification, but it is having a hard time as many cities think they have enough water. Two locales with the same issue as Atlanta are eastern Wisconsin, where 500,000 people in several communities use Lake Winnebago for water supply, and southern Kentucky, where tens of thousands of people use Laurel River Lake, which was built for hydropower and recreation.

During 2010, Pakistan suffered record floods that created tremendous misery, which some people claimed was avoidable if the planned Kalabagh Dam had been completed. It would be part of a system of dams on the Indus River and adjacent rivers. The Indus River drains northeastern Pakistan and provides much-needed water to large areas and many farms. It is joined to other Pakistan rivers through a series of "link canals" that were planned during colonial days and are now central features of the water management plan. They are under management of the Pakistan Water and Power Development Authority (WAPDA) (2010), which was created in 1958 to coordinate and direct the development of the water and power sectors of Pakistan. Since 2007, the organization has been divided into WAPDA and the Pakistan Electric Power Company (PEPCO).

THE IRON TRIANGLE OF DAMS AND RIVER IMPROVEMENTS

Interest groups for dams and river improvements have evolved to be government agencies, congressional committees, and an industry of hydropower, navigation, and water development interests. Added to this is the support industry that focuses on dam maintenance and safety.

Some of these interest groups reach back to the dam-building era, and they are no longer as visible as they once were. As an example, the National Water Resources Association (2010) was established in 1932 as the National Reclamation Association to focus on irrigation and reclamation in the arid and semiarid West and to lobby for federal financing for water reclamation projects at a time when funding was low. It established a Washington, D.C., office in 1948 and created links with the western membership of Congress. By the late 1960s it broadened its focus to include water quality, farm issues, environmental protection, national water policy, and water rights. In 1969 it changed its name to the National Water Resources Association, and today it is a federation of state associations and caucuses representing a broad spectrum of water-supply interests.

State associations and caucuses also support Corps of Engineer projects. In North Carolina, for example, I was involved with the state water congress, which had a platform to support the water-resources development plan for navigation, hurricane protection, flood control, and other water-management purposes. It was associated with the National Water Resources Congress and its predecessor, the National Rivers and Harbors Congress.

Today, the interest groups are more focused because the general goal of water resources development has fragmented into niches of water resources management. For example, the National Hydropower Association (2010a) is an advocacy group for nonfederal hydroelectric generation and has members from utilities, power producers, equipment manufacturers, and consultants and attorneys.

Several organizations focus on dam technologies and management. The International Commission on Large Dams, based in Paris, and its U.S. committee, the United States Society on Dams (2010), focus on topics such as dam maintenance and security. The Association of State Dam Safety Officials (2010) was formed in 1984 for members who focus on dam safety, including government officials, engineering consultants, contractors, manufacturers and suppliers, researchers, teachers, dam owners, and operators and students.

The dam-advocacy organizations can be viewed as an iron triangle (Figure 3.1), that is, a diagram with corners for the industry, politicians, and government officials involved with dams. As explained above, these interest groups are not as powerful as they were in the heyday of federal spending on dams, but they are still in operation.

ECONOMICS OF DAMS

Dams are controversial for a number of reasons, including their high costs, risks, and sometimes-disputed benefits. Costs can be measured by cost of

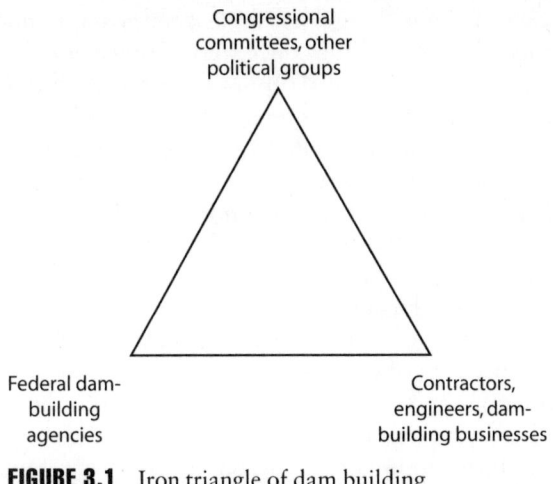

FIGURE 3.1 Iron triangle of dam building

storage and cost of yield. Storage refers to the total volume of water impounded behind the dam and is divided into zones. In many dams, the lowest zone is dead storage, which is available to be filled with sediment. The next zone is for usable or working storage, which can be used to release water for various purposes, such as water supply during a dry period. Finally there is a margin of reserve storage for flood control. These zones are shown conceptually in Figure 3.2.

Let's say a dam impounds 200,000 acre-feet of water and costs a total of $500 million to construct. This is based on current planning for a new reservoir in northern Colorado and can only be considered a ballpark estimate. Based on this, the cost per acre-foot of storage is $2,500, which is a significant unit cost in itself, but it still compares favorably on a per-unit basis to the cost of storing water in urban water distribution system tanks. Now, the cost of working storage will be more. If, for example, the working storage is 50 percent of total storage, then its cost will be $5,000 per acre-foot. You would expect an economy of scale in reservoir storage, with per-unit costs declining with size of the reservoir.

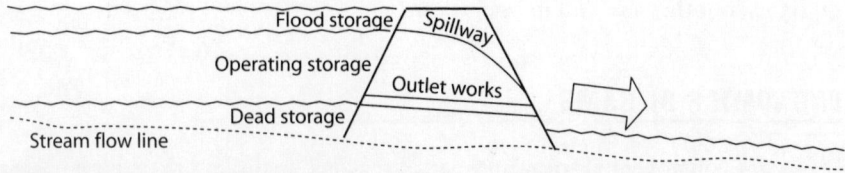

FIGURE 3.2 Zones of reservoir storage behind a dam

In most dams, the cost of the reservoir's yield is a more significant number, particularly for water-supply reservoirs in dry regions. The yield of a reservoir is the added secure water supply that is made available by storing water during wet periods for release when the natural flows are lower. Say the hypothetical reservoir above has a yield of one-third of its volume. Then, the cost per acre-foot of the yield is $7,500. If the interest rate is 3 percent, this means that the cost of each acre-foot that is delivered will be $225. This is only the annualized capital cost, and to it must be added the operations and maintenance cost.

Cost of the dams determines their initial asset value, and if each of the 85,000 dams in the United States had a current asset value of $10 million, the total would be $850 billion. The value is probably higher, although no one really knows what it is. For example, what would be the asset values for national treasures such as Hoover Dam on the Colorado River near Las Vegas, which depends on Lake Mead for much of its water supply and is one of the control structures that secure water for southern California. Most of the 85,000 dams are much smaller, of course, and there is no feasible way to estimate their average asset value.

As the inventory of dams ages, the deferred maintenance and renewal costs build up. According to federal data, the average age of dams is over 51 years and the number of deficient dams has risen to more than 4,000, including 1,819 high-hazard-potential dams (American Society of Civil Engineers, 2010). The causes that lead to the deficiency rating are aging, deterioration, lack of maintenance, and reclassification due to increased data. In terms of ongoing construction work, the important figure today is the cost of repairs and renewal.

According to the ASDSO (2009), the national cost of needed nonfederal dam repairs is $50 billion, which includes $16 billion for high-hazard-potential dams. Needs for high-hazard dams are split roughly evenly between publicly owned and privately owned dams. To respond to this increasing problem, ASCE recommends more effective state dam safety programs, emergency action plans for high-hazard dams, a national funding program and state programs for nonfederal dams, dam failure studies as part of the National Flood Insurance Program, and public education.

INTERNATIONAL FINANCING

The World Bank is a focal point for global activity. It reports that it has assisted only 3 percent of the dams in developing countries and is now financing about four dam projects a year, which is about half as many as in the 1970s and 1980s. It has approved 39 dam projects since 1986: 33

mainly for hydropower, 3 mainly for irrigation, and 3 mainly for water supply or navigation. The total lending for these projects was $7.4 billion, or about 3 percent of total World Bank lending in 10 years.

The bank assessed the economic outcomes of 50 completed large dams that it had supported. The dams have created installed power capacity of 39,000 MW and annually replace 51 million tons of fuel in electricity production. They control floods, provide urban and industrial water supply, and have added irrigation for 1.8 million hectares and improved it for another 1.8 million hectares.

For example, the irrigation benefits of Pakistan's Tarbela and Mangla dams are $260 million annually. The irrigation water made it possible to grow two crops a year on 400,000 hectares of existing irrigated land and another 400,000 hectares of rainfed land. Farmers increased their incomes, are spending them on consumer goods and on education for boys and girls and stimulating local industries for fertilizer production and agricultural processing.

RISKS AND DAM SAFETY

Risks of dam ownership and operation are formidable, and dam failures can be devastating. Early in the 20th century, many dams failed due to poor engineering and maintenance, and regulatory programs were initiated, starting in California in the 1920s. Federal agencies also established safety standards. It was only after several dam failures in the 1970s that new initiatives emerged to control the risks from dam failures. In spite of these damage-control measures, failures continue to occur. For example, in 1982 a high mountain irrigation dam failed in Colorado, causing havoc in a recreational community and the loss of several lives. Even as this is being written, an industrial waste dam failed in Hungary and devastated a community with toxic wastes. Levees are like dams, and their failures in New Orleans during Hurricane Katrina caused the biggest urban disaster in modern U.S. history. Nebraska had several low-risk dam failures in 2009, but no one was killed and the failures were not on the national media radar screen.

The Federal Emergency Management Agency (FEMA) administers the National Dam Safety Program, which was established in 1996 and includes an Interagency Committee on Dam Safety. The National Dam Safety and Security Act was passed in 2002. This legislation was enacted to assist states in improving their dam safety programs, to support increased technical training for state dam safety engineers and technicians, to pump money into dam safety research, and to maintain the National Inventory of Dams. Today, almost all states have dam safety programs and states have regulatory responsibility for 95 percent of the 78,000 dams within the National Inventory of Dams. Programs include safety evaluations of existing dams, review of plans for construction and major repairs, and review of emergency action plans.

The hazard potential classifications include "high hazard potential" (anticipated loss of life in the case of failure), "significant hazard potential" (anticipated damage to buildings and important infrastructure), and "low hazard potential" (anticipated loss of the dam or damage to the floodplain, but no expected loss of life). According to the ASDSO (2010), when you summarize the issues with dams, the main risks are risk of failure, the increasing hazard, lack of financing for maintenance, upgrade and repair, lack of adequate authority and resources for state dam safety programs, lack of emergency preparedness in case of failure, and lack of public awareness.

Dams are part of the critical infrastructure. In spite of their dispersed ownership, responsibility for dams has become a national security issue. The issue of security was important even before September 11, 2001, and the advent of terrorist threats to the United States, and a series of laws, up through the National Dam Safety and Security Act of 2002 (HR4727), has addressed dam safety.

While dam safety is a clear and present danger, the possible failure of levees has a lower profile. At least that was the case until the New Orleans levees failed and flooded out the city during Hurricane Katrina. Levee risks are well known, even to the fable of the Dutch boy sticking his finger in the dike to prevent the failure of the North Sea levees. This risk was not imaginary, as in 1953 failure of North Sea dikes led to nearly 2,000 deaths in Holland. As a result of the 1927 Mississippi River flood, authorities breached levees above New Orleans and caused great social unrest as well as many deaths.

Of the nation's many miles of levees, the condition is largely unknown. This can lead to unexpected hardship, as in the case of Granite City, Illinois. To protect itself from Mississippi River flooding, the city has a 60-year-old levee that is 52 feet high and wide enough for a two-lane service road on top. The problem is that the 174-square-mile area around the city, across the river from St. Louis, is seeing its flood maps redrawn and is being designated as a special flood hazard zone, so its residents will have to buy flood insurance to get federally backed mortgages. The three-county area that is affected has already passed a special 0.25-cent sales tax and is preparing to begin a $180 million improvement project, which will take three years. However, the redesignation is already taking place. Some residents complain that the motivation of FEMA in the redesignation is to raise money to backfill the National Flood Insurance Program, which is $18.5 billion in debt as a result of Hurricane Katrina. FEMA officials say it is about safety and risk and has nothing to do with the fund (Barrett, 2010a).

ASCE (2010) reported that while there is no definite record of all levees, most of the 100,000 miles of levees in the United States are locally owned with unknown reliability. Many were built to protect cropland, but development has occurred behind them. The estimate is that the cost to rehabilitate them is more than $100 billion. The Water Resources Development Act (WRDA) of 2007 mandated establishment of an inventory of federal levees and the nonfederal levees where information is provided voluntarily by state and local agencies. The inventory is to be shared between the Corps, the FEMA, the Department of Homeland Security (DHS), and the states. Initial results from the inventory show that about 9 percent of federally inspected levees are likely to fail during flooding. WRDA 2007 created the National Committee on Levee Safety, which recommended comprehensive national leadership, new and sustained state levee safety programs, and the alignment of existing federal programs. To address lack of resilience in the levee system, DHS included levees within the critical infrastructure protection program.

DAM CONTROVERSIES

Construction of dams is inevitably controversial because, although dams have many positive effects, they also have substantial environmental and social impacts. The dams described earlier included some with environmental opposition, social hardships, increase in waterborne disease and other negative effects that lead to antidam movements.

Water quality in reservoirs is an important issue as well, and the reservoirs impounded by dams have their own dynamics of water quality, temperature, and ecological activity.

The World Bank (2010) has been a lightning rod for controversy due to its support for infrastructure in developing countries. In recognition of the side effects of dams, the bank has issued guidelines on dam safety, on involuntary resettlement, on safeguards for indigenous people, on natural habitat, and about environmental aspects of dams and reservoirs. In the bank's study leading up to the guidelines, resettlement was shown to be a problem, and the 50 dams studied displaced 830,000 people. In particular, problems with treatment of indigenous people have been frequent where people living in remote areas are vulnerable to development.

The 50 dams were assessed as having a mixed record on environmental consequences. In tropical areas, waterborne diseases might increase with new reservoirs. Fishery impacts can be controlled by new fisheries in the reservoirs. A few projects enhanced natural habitats by creating protected areas for wildlife. Some projects (for example, Bayano in Panama and Kariba between Zambia and Zimbabwe) resulted in major irreversible degradation of pristine natural habitats. Watershed degradation and sedimentation of reservoirs may result from dam building, resettlement, and deforestation.

The bank believes that the majority of dams yield benefits that outweigh costs, including the costs of mitigation. Of the 50 dams studied, it assessed that 45 yield acceptable benefit/cost ratios. Mitigation and resettlement could have been financed without jeopardizing the dams' economic returns and the bank believes that resettlement policies are better now than in the past. Therefore, by current standards the bank determined that 13 of the 50 dams are acceptable, 24 are potentially acceptable, and 13 are unacceptable. This review was sponsored by the bank's Independent Evaluation Group. Lessons identified by the bank include the need to consider social and environmental issues at early stages; that if a project is economically feasible, then resettlement and environmental impacts are likely to be affordable; that institutional capacity and commitment are crucial; and that it should include environmental and resettlement assessments for dams that it might assist, as well as dam safety evaluations.

The Asian Development Bank (2006) also summarized the arguments for and against dams. They explained how one side sees the necessity of dams for water, electricity, irrigation, and flood protection to serve growing populations. The other side sees the negative sides of dams: disrupting the environment (sediment changes, obstructing fish migrating and spawning, and water-quality degradation) and displacement of people and communities. Dam projects are also criticized for their costs, outcomes, and inequities.

In some cases, controversies over dams reach the level where removal of old dams is considered. This is just beginning in the United States, where removal of a number of dams is being considered and a few smaller dams have been removed. Major environmental problems of dam removal include sedimentation, release of stored contaminants, and changed hydraulic conditions along streams.

REGULATION OF DAMS

In addition to safety, dam construction and operation are regulated for their impacts on streams. Much of this regulation comes via water laws (see Chapter 14), but regulation of nonfederal hydropower facilities is a specific program with strong control over dams. Nonfederal hydropower dams are licensed by the Federal Energy Regulatory Commission (FERC), which has oversight over privately owned and public power authority dams. The federal government also generates power through water projects, mainly by the Corps of Engineers and the Bureau of Reclamation. Then it markets and distributes power through the regional power administrations, operated by the Department of the Interior. These programs are not regulated by FERC.

Investor-owned power companies, which provide electricity within monopoly service areas, are regulated by state public service commissions. These commissions have oversight of infrastructure expenditures and are interested in hydropower dams, but they normally leave the licensing of projects to FERC and dam safety inspections to other agencies.

Much of the burden of dam safety regulation is on the states, but their capacity to operate regulatory programs is mixed. Texas has seven engineers to regulate more than 7,400 dams. Alabama has more than 2,000 dams but no dam safety program (ASCE, 2010).

FUTURE ISSUES

As we consider the future for dams, it seems clear that they will remain essential for economic and social purposes. How else can we guarantee the security of water supplies, generate renewable hydroelectric energy, navigate streams, and protect life and property in many floodplains? As a social benefit, dams also create lakes used widely for recreation and they increase the value of real estate around them.

Given the construction period of most U.S. dams from about 1900 to 1970, the oldest ones are more than a century old and even the newest ones are now more than 40 years old. Although you can imagine a problem-free dam as lasting for centuries, many dams will require extensive renewal programs. In the best case, most dams will last indefinitely, but a worst-case scenario would show massive renewal needs that would appear in a short interval. Our local dams that impound Horsetooth Reservoir, for example, recently required investments of over $100 million to raise the dam heights and fill in sinkholes. The federal government paid 85 percent of the cost, with water users paying 7.5 percent and power customers paying 7.5 percent, even though those particular dams do not generate any hydropower (Northern Colorado Water Conservancy District, 2010).

In general, the kinds of dam renewal required in the future will range from simple maintenance tasks, such as dressing up the erosion protection on the faces of dams to extensive reconstruction. Reservoir sedimentation is an ongoing maintenance issue, which is difficult to carry out in many places due to the cost and the environmental impacts of removing sediment. Once a reservoir fills with sediment, it creates a dilemma for which there are no apparent or easy solutions.

While few new dams will be constructed in the United States, other nations need more of them to meet the needs of rapidly growing populations and economic development. For example, China recently pushed ahead with the Three Gorges Project and, after the disastrous 2010 flooding, Pakistan might revisit its old plans for more dams on the Indus River system. The World Bank is tracking a number of proposals for new dams in developing countries, especially in Africa and Asia, and China is studying proposals for new dams on the Upper Mekong River.

Given the interest in new dams and the side effects of old ones, the World Commission on Dams (2001) was convened to look into the effects of dams and how they should be built in the future. It identified five core values for future dam plans (equity, efficiency, participation, sustainability, and accountability). It advocated an approach to identify stakeholders in negotiating choices and agreements; seven strategic priorities (public acceptance; assessing options; existing dams; sustaining rivers and livelihoods; recognizing entitlements and sharing benefits; ensuring compliance; and sharing rivers for peace, development and security); and criteria for assessing compliance, along with guidelines for review and approval of projects at five stages of decision-making.

Although dam removal has not been a high-profile issue so far, it might heat up as cost and environmental pressures mount. In 2009, a multiparty agreement was reached to dismantle four hydroelectric dams blamed for depleting salmon in the Klamath River basin in southern Oregon and northern California. The plan is to accomplish this by 2020, but it remains to be seen who will pay and how it will occur. If it does happen, it will be the largest dam-removal project so far, with an estimated cost of $450 million (Barnard, 2009).

CHAPTER 4

The Water-Supply Utility Business

Chapter 2 presented a map of the parts of the water business, and Chapter 3 explained the dams and reservoirs that control rivers and provide storage for multiple water uses. Of these uses, drinking-water supply is unquestionably the most visible and most important to people, and it is provided by an industry of water utilities and support organizations that focus on gaining sources of supply, treating the water, and keeping it safe and reliable through the process of delivery to customers.

This chapter explains the structure and business issues of the water supply industry. Its main focus is on potable municipal supplies, but information about self-supplied water for domestic, commercial, and industrial uses is included to set the stage for later discussions of these end-user topics. Bottled water is actually a competitor to municipal drinking water from the tap, but it is a distinct business and is discussed in Chapter 21.

THE CENTERPIECE OF THE WATER BUSINESS

For the water business, the first image that comes to mind is the supply of drinking water that is delivered to your tap by your local utility. These water supply utilities are the centerpiece of the water industry because clean and safe drinking water takes first priority among all the uses of water. The potable water supply that they provide is also used for many additional domestic and outdoor residential uses, and it provides water for commercial, industrial, and public uses as well.

Water-supply utilities are often bundled with wastewater for management because the two services have many common attributes. In these cases, the two can be combined and described as water and wastewater. However, they also have a number of distinctions that justify separate explanations and chapters.

The irrigation business also involves supply of water, but it is very different from the water-supply business and is explained in a separate chapter. Therefore, water-supply utilities serve a relatively fixed set of customers who are located to tap conveniently into a central supply system. The facilities of water-supply utilities comprise one of the infrastructure networks that bind urban areas together.

Although the water-supply business is dominated by government-owned utilities, many private water companies also operate in it. In fact, much of the water-supply business was initiated by private water companies, even in the largest cities, such as New York City's water supply system. Private water companies are even listed on stock exchanges, such as American Water, which is listed on the New York Stock Exchange. These are discussed in more detail in Chapter 16.

In spite of the staid and solid look of this water business sector, many changes are afoot. Raw water supplies are harder to get, new challenges to public health are evident and the industry relies on a vast and expensive legacy infrastructure that is aging and creating a buildup of deferred maintenance.

Community and Noncommunity Water Systems

While the focus of water supply is on supplying safe, reliable, and affordable tap water, the business offers choices to consumers. People can draw their drinking water straight from the tap, purchase bottled water, or hire a vendor to install a point-of-use treatment device. If they live in the right place and can get permission, they may even drill a well and provide their own drinking water. Industries can also get their water from utilities or from their own supply systems. People also expect to get safe water if they visit a highway gas station just as they would from a public building in town. Thus, safe water is expected to be available everywhere that people live, do business or travel.

The infrastructure required for water supply operations comprises source of supply, treatment, and distribution of treated water. The facilities required are shown on Figure 4.1, which illustrates a chain of processes that involves environmental water, a raw-water chain, treatment, and a finished-water chain that includes distribution to end users. The chain and hub terminology is useful to show processes (chains) that involve some sort of pipeline or operation that involves transportation and hub-type activities, where the operations take place in a confined area. This concept was published by Mintzberg and Van der Heyden (1999) to illustrate work distribution in companies, but it applies to water utilities as well.

You can compare the infrastructure of the water-supply industry with the electric power industry as shown on Figure 4.2, which illustrates the division between the larger systems and the smaller systems. The main

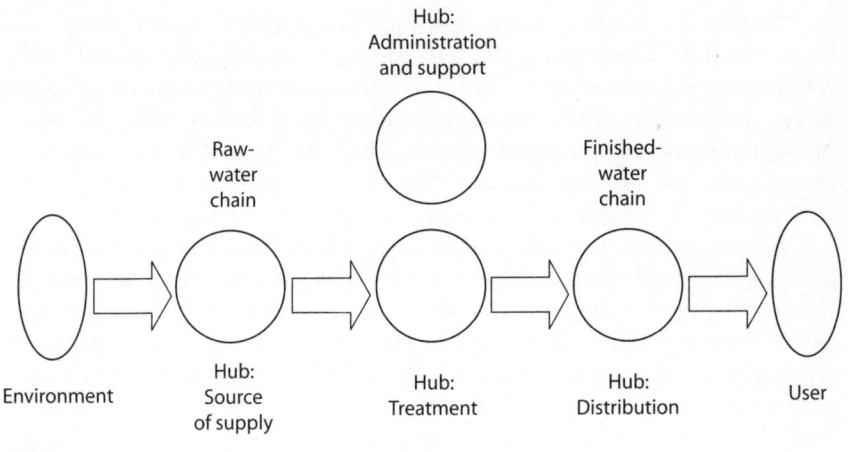

FIGURE 4.1   Water-supply system components

difference between the two industries is the water services go well beyond pure commodity status, as was explained in Chapter 2.

The regulated utility systems that provide water to customers at these many places are classified as community water systems (CWS) and noncommunity water systems (NCWS), two designations that stem from the Safe Drinking Water Act (SDWA) and its implementing agency, the U.S. Environmental Protection Agency (USEPA). These systems receive special scrutiny from USEPA because they are regulated under the SDWA as "public water systems," which may be publicly or privately owned. Their definition is that they serve at least 25 people or 15 service connections for at least 60 days per year. The rationale here is that if you are serving this many people, you are subject to public regulation. If you are serving only your own family or fewer than 25 people, you are to be self-regulated.

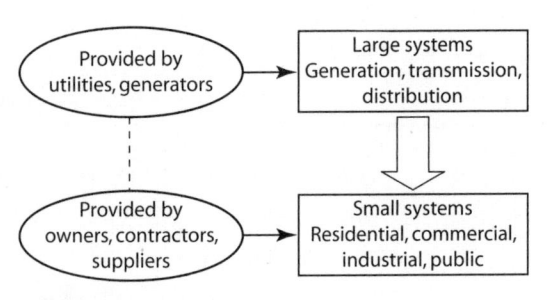

FIGURE 4.2   Comparison of water supply and electric power

Community water systems serve the same population year-round, and noncommunity water systems serve other transient and nontransient public water systems. Community water systems mostly provide water for people at home, shopping, and in businesses and industries located in cities and towns. Noncommunity water systems provide water for people in places not connected to regular utilities, in stand-alone schools and factories (nontransient facilities) and in gas stations and campgrounds (transient facilities).

USEPA (2009) has maintained statistics on these systems from the 1970s in the Safe Drinking Water Information System. Most community water systems are water-supply utilities, but a few systems can be managed as auxiliary services by a business or other organization or by contractors serving military bases or similar facilities. The systems range in size from very small to very large, and their main business is to treat and deliver potable water through buried distribution systems.

Statistics on community water systems do not change rapidly, and data for the third quarter of 2009 showed 51,651 community water systems serving 294,339,881 people, distributed as shown in Table 4.1 (USEPA, 2009).

Notice that the 410 very large systems serve 46 percent of the population, but the 28,804 very small systems serve only 2 percent. This illustrates the preponderance of small water systems, which creates the dilemma known as the "small water-system problem." This problem is caused by the complexity and cost of providing safe drinking water while the small systems may lack money and workforce capacity to do the job. The flip side of this problem is that it can create business opportunities of outsourcing work for consultants and others to serve these small utilities if they have the funds to pay.

The count of noncommunity water systems in 2009 showed 18,325 nontransient systems (like factories, office buildings, schools, and hospitals with their own water systems) and 83,484 transient systems (like campgrounds, stores, rest stops, or gas stations with their own supplies). These counts do not include industrial water supplies used for process water only,

TABLE 4.1 Statistics of Community Water Systems

	Very Small	Small	Medium	Large	Very Large	Total
	500 or less	501 to 3,300	3,301 to 10,000	10,001 to 100,000	More than 100,000	
Number of systems	28,804	13,820	4,871	3,746	410	51,651
Percentage of population	2	7	10	36	46	100

Data source: U.S. Environmental Protection Agency (2010a)

which would be classified under self-supplied industrial water. The water systems in most of these facilities require products and services that are similar to those in smaller businesses and residential facilities.

When you add up all of the community and noncommunity water systems, the count reaches 153,460 management units that must be regulated (51,651 CWS, 18,325 nontransient NCWS, and 83,484 transient CWS). Taken together, these comprise the universe of organizations that provide public water-supply services.

PLAYERS AND WORKFORCE OF THE WATER-SUPPLY AND WASTEWATER BUSINESSES

While the water-supply and wastewater businesses are different in many ways, their employment structures are very similar and will be compared in this section. Additional employment and player information for wastewater is presented in the next chapter.

Given the structure of the businesses, it follows that the main players are the key officials in utilities, regulatory agencies, and support organizations. There is enough similarity in the businesses so that most workers can easily migrate between water and wastewater jobs, although they must learn about some important differences, such as the technologies and details of the regulatory controls.

In the one million jobs of all types in the water industry, around 500,000 jobs are in water and wastewater utilities. The rest of the jobs are in public water organizations such as stormwater, hydropower, government water agencies, soil and water districts, and special districts (about 100,000 jobs) and all water-related jobs in professional service firms, suppliers, knowledge sector providers, associations, advocacy groups, construction contractors, and financiers and insurers (Grigg and Zenzen, 2009, Grigg, 2005).

The water supply and wastewater utilities in the United States offer many jobs for directors, managers, and technical leaders. In addition to management jobs, the technical jobs in water and wastewater utilities are treatment plant operators, technicians for distribution and collection systems, laboratory analysts, information technology support staff, engineers, scientists, and technical managers.

Our estimates of these job totals are based mainly on interpretation of data from the Occupational Employment System of the U.S. Bureau of Labor Statistics (BLS, 2007). The statistics require interpretation because BLS does not have a category that aggregates water industry jobs. We are also able to draw on AWWA's (1996) Water://Stats database, which is the drinking water industry's best source of data on utility operations. AWWA surveyed jobs for divisions within utilities, to include source of supply, pumping, transmission lines; water treatment, laboratory; distribution pumping, main maintenance; customer accounts, meter reading, billing, collections, customer service; administration and general; and other accounts.

Extrapolating AWWA data to the U.S. population indicates that water supply utilities employ 215,000 workers, but USEPA's Community Water System Survey indicates that the total is closer to 300,000 employees. Combining these data, we estimate 250,000 as a round number for water-supply utilities.

We lack a comparable estimate to AWWA's for wastewater, but we were able to study data from USEPA and the National Association of Clean Water Agencies to estimate that local wastewater departments employ slightly fewer workers than water supply utilities, and we set that estimate at 225,000 nationally.

Based on these statistics, we estimate that for water supply 15 percent of employees are treatment operators, 40 percent are engaged in distribution, another 20 percent in customer service and metering, and 25 percent in administration of various kinds, including engineering and technical jobs. If we assume the same distribution for wastewater systems, we can present this table to summarize the numbers of jobs by type (Table 4.2).

The consultants who serve the water supply and wastewater industries are like a shadow workforce, as explained in Chapter 18. They have a great deal of influence in policy, operations, and regulatory responses. Water and wastewater utilities require a substantial amount of consulting work to assess issues, design facilities and upgrades, and deal with regulatory issues.

Supplier representatives also have a great deal of influence in the water supply industry. They represent each category of product and service (see Chapter 19), and thus they tend to watch carefully over policy, standards, research outcomes, and public pronouncements.

While regulators are relatively few in numbers, they have disproportionately greater influence over setting rules, issuing permits, and enforcement. Regulators for water supply and wastewater may or may not be in the same organizations. Two separate branches of USEPA handle these

TABLE 4.2 Number of Water and Wastewater Jobs

Occupation	% of Jobs	Water Supply	Wastewater
Treatment operators	15%	37,500	33,750
Distribution/collection	40%	100,000	90,000
Customer service and metering	20%	50,000	45,000
Administration and other	25%	62,500	56,250
Total		250,000	225,000

services; in state governments, regulators for water supply might be in a health department, whereas those in wastewater might be in a water resources or state environmental agency.

The history of water-supply and wastewater regulation is interesting in the sense that the water-supply regulators came up from public health channels, whereas the wastewater regulators came on the scene later. As a result, most states will have water-supply regulatory capabilities down to the level of county health departments, but wastewater might be regulated only by state or regional offices of the state EPA. I witnessed this while serving in the wastewater regulatory agency in North Carolina, which was completely separated from the water-supply regulatory agency, which was part of the state health department. Subsequently, the two organizations were merged. While I lack a national study of these organizations, it seems logical that for the purposes of organizational efficiency the two would be merged almost everywhere by now.

Academics are active in the water-supply and wastewater industries, and their influence can be seen in research outcomes such as the quality of drinking water and in policy studies, such as a recent study by the National Research Council (2006) on the status of drinking-water distribution systems.

Activities by the players tend to converge in their professional and trade associations, which include for the water-supply and wastewater industries the following key groups:

- American Water Works Association (AWWA)
- Water Environment Federation (WEF)
- National Association of Water Companies (NAWC)
- Association of State Drinking Water Officials (ASDWO)
- Association of Metropolitan Water Agencies (AMWA)
- Association of State and Interstate Water Pollution Control Administrators (ASIWPCA)
- National Association of Clean Water Agencies (NACWA)

In addition, several professional associations focus on the science and technology of the water-supply and wastewater industries. Two that are especially active in them are the American Society of Civil Engineers (ASCE) and the American Academy of Environmental Engineering (AAEE).

The work of these associations in meeting member needs and influencing policy is important to the water industry. I've been active in several of the associations and on the national boards of two of them, and their activities fit a pattern of focusing on member needs and influencing local, state, and national policy. The two associations where I served on boards had

Washington, D.C., offices and arranged regular visits to Congress to discuss water policy issues. ASCE, where I have served on national policy committees, has gained a lot of publicity by publishing the "Infrastructure Report Card" to highlight deferred investment problems.

EXAMPLES OF WATER-SUPPLY UTILITIES

As shown by USEPA statistics, water-supply utilities range from the smallest to the largest, on the basis of population served. To illustrate some of the largest ones, this list is a top-10 roster on the basis of number of customers served, although some of the providers are wholesalers only and degrees of service differ. Therefore, with a different classification scheme, other utilities might have been included and different rank ordering might result. For example, MWD is only a water wholesaler. LADWP sells power as well as water services, and MWRA offers regional wastewater as well as water services (Table 4.3).

All of these large water supply utilities are government owned. The largest utility, the Metropolitan Water District of Southern California, serves 16 million people, but only with wholesale water. The next three, the New York City Dept of Environmental Protection, Chicago Department of Water Management, and Los Angeles Department of Water & Power, also serve giant cities. The scale of the business operations of these utilities is massive, as you can imagine.

For the most part, private water utilities are not as large as these, but some of them, such as American Water, operate large systems over wide areas and there are tens of thousands of smaller private water utilities. The proportion of U.S. water services provided by private water companies has

TABLE 4.3 Top Water Supply Utilities by Population Served

Rank	Utility Name	Acronym
1	Metropolitan Water District of Southern California	MWD
2	New York City Department of Environmental Protection	DEP
3	Chicago Department of Water Management	DWM
4	Los Angeles Department of Water & Power	LADWP
5	San Diego County Water Authority	SDCWA
6	Massachusetts Water Resources Authority	MWRA
7	San Francisco Public Utilities Commission	SFPUC
8	Houston Public Works and Engineering Department	PW&E
9	Miami-Dade Water & Sewer Department	WSD
10	Dallas Water Utilities	DWU

remained close to 15 percent for over 50 years (measured by customers served or volume of water handled). The investor-owned water-supply utilities accounted for about 14 percent of water revenues and about 11 percent of water system assets in 1995. The private U.S. water companies are represented by the National Association of Water Companies (2010), which was founded in 1895 and has about 340 members.

By and large, most water-supply utilities are smaller ones. The previous table showed, for example, that the 28,904 very small utilities serving 500 or fewer people serve only 2 percent of the population.

INTERNATIONAL PRIVATE WATER COMPANIES

The international water companies have made marked shifts in their strategies during the last 20 years, and their experiences tell us something about the global nature of the water business. Information about British and French water companies is presented in this section, as they have been most active on the international scene.

British Water Companies

The United Kingdom's transformation of the water industry received attention in the 1970s and 1980s because it regionalized water services and then privatized them. These transformations mirrored other moves in the UK during a series of flip-flops between nationalization and privatization brought about by postwar experiments with Labor governments, followed by a return to the Conservatives.

The regionalization of water utilities was a move toward greater efficiency in a sector that was dominated by public utilities. I learned about it during the 1970s from Okun (1977), who visited the United Kingdom and studied its water industry in detail. Okun had been a careful student of how water utilities were organized and run, and he was impressed by the added efficiency that resulted from the regionalization. He was a passionate advocate for the reforms brought about by the regionalization. I visited the United Kingdom in 1978 and was hosted by the Water Research Centre, which explained how it did research to serve the newly regionalized water authorities. This impressed me at the time, but I had no idea that such dramatic changes toward privatization lay ahead. At the time, all of this was a state-run system, although some private water companies continued to operate.

The water services were regionalized in the 1973–1975 period throughout the United Kingdom, which includes England, Scotland, Wales, and Northern Ireland. The 10 regional water authorities provided comprehensive water services on a river-basin basis. Later, the regulatory system was over-hauled to create the structure in place today.

After World War II, the Atlee-led Labor government started the nation-alization efforts that led to many changes, including the development of the British National Health Service. During the 1950s Churchill government, some nationalizations were reversed, especially the iron and steel industry, and during the 1980s Thatcher era, the stage was set for privatization of a number of public services, with state-owned enterprises being put on the block. By 1983 the Thatcher Government had sold all or part of British Aerospace, Cable and Wireless, Amersham International, Britoil, and Asso-ciated British Ports. British Telecom was privatized in 1984 and the electric-ity industry was privatized beginning in 1989, with the British Water Industry and British Airports Authority also privatized in the 1980s. British Gas became a private company in 1996, and British Rail was privatized in stages during the 1990s (Grigg, 2010).

I visited the United Kingdom in 1987 and was treated to an explanation of how the Severn Trent Water Authority was preparing for privatization. The emphasis in our briefing was on valuing assets, which was of enormous impor-tance because if they were undervalued, the stock would sell too cheap at the initial public offering, but if the opposite occurred, investors would be cheated.

Each of the newly formed water companies went its own way, and there have been a number of acquisitions and divestures since privatization. Buyers of British utilities have included conglomerates such as Suez of France and Enron of the United States, banks, and private equity firms. The industry is heavily regulated for business practices by the UK Office of Water (Ofwat). So, the freedom of action of the companies is limited. Still, the companies make attractive targets for acquisition because they offer steady if un-spectacular profits. Growth can occur only through acquisitions, international operations, and expanded activities in markets such as equipment or services.

Today's map of UK water utilities, shown on Figure 4.3, shows the 10 largest, which mostly offer both water and wastewater, and a number of smaller water-only utilities. In addition, water services in Scotland are pro-vided by Scottish Water and in Northern Ireland by Northern Ireland Water.

Brief descriptions of the operations of the largest companies are pro-vided next.

Anglian Water   Anglian Water (2010) serves the largest geographical region of the 10 companies, a drier part of England in the Southeast. It is now the principal subsidiary of Anglian Water Group Limited (AWG), which be-came the parent company following the acquisition of AWG Plc by Osprey Acquisitions Limited in 2006. Osprey is a consortium of pension funds and infrastructure investors and fund managers. Anglian Water Plc was listed on

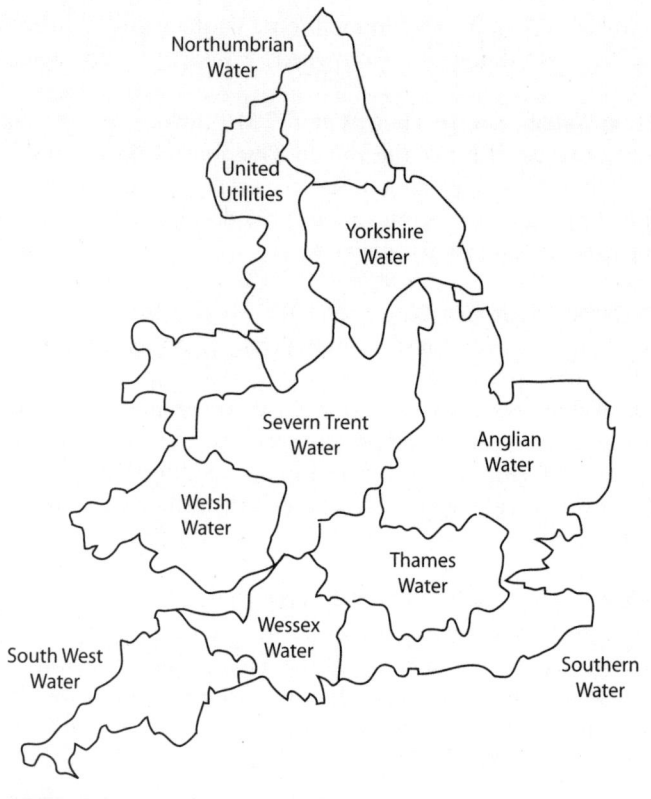

FIGURE 4.3 Service areas of British water companies

the London Stock Exchange in 1989 but it was delisted in 2006 following its acquisition

Dŵr Cymru (Welsh Water) The ownership of Welsh Water (2010) is by Glas Cymru, which is a not-for-profit company. This is similar to some U.S. water companies, such as Louisville Water, where the water utility has been spun off into a private company but it has no shareholder (other than public entities) and profits are reinvested in the company.

Northumbrian Water The Northumbrian Water Group plc (2010) has companies in three areas: UK water-supply and wastewater services, water and wastewater contracts, and technical and consulting services. The water utility is Northumbrian Water Limited, which operates in the northeast of England as Northumbrian Water and in the southeast as Essex & Suffolk Water, with a total service population of 4.4 million. Northumbrian Water Limited also has a tourist business of accommodations, conferencing, recreation, and fishing facilities. Northumbrian was owned by Suez, but it divested its shares.

Severn Trent Water   Severn Trent Water (2010), which serves eight million customers across the heart of the United Kingdom, is now part of an international corporate group named Severn Trent Plc, which also includes Severn Trent Services. It operates with three divisions: Water Purification, Operating Services, and Analytical Services.

Southern Water   Southern Water (2010) is owned by Greensands Investments Limited, which is a consortium of pension and infrastructure funds.

South West Water   South West Water is part of Pennon Group plc (2010), which also provides waste management services. Southwest Water provides drinking water and wastewater services in the southwestern part of England around Cornwall and Devon. It also takes responsibility for swimming and coastal waters.

Thames Water   Thames Water (2010) is the United Kingdom's largest water and wastewater services company in terms of customers, with 8.7 million water customers across London and the Thames River region, as well as 13 million wastewater customers. It was acquired from RWE in 2006 by Kemble Water Holdings Limited, which is composed of Macquarie-managed funds and other institutional investors.

United Utilities   United Utilities (2010) is the largest water and wastewater company in the United Kingdom in terms of financial results. It was created by merging Northwest Water plc and Norweb plc and includes electricity distribution as well as its largest businesses, which are water and wastewater.

Wessex Water   Wessex Water (2010) provides water and sewage treatment services in the southwest of England. It was acquired by YTL Power International of Kuala Lumpur in 2002. The Enron Corporation bought Wessex Water in 1998 and formed the Azurix Company with an IPO for part of Wessex's shares. This was a disaster for Enron as the opening stock price fell from $22 to $2 within two years. Enron then sold Azurix North America and Azurix Industrial Operations to American Water. Wessex had been profitable, but regulators required it to cut its rates by 12 percent, and its aging infrastructure required an upgrade.

Yorkshire Water   Yorkshire Water (2010) provides water and sewerage services to 4.7 million people in the Yorkshire region. It is owned by the Kelda

Group (2010), of which Kelda Water Services manages the nonregulated contract operations. The Kelda Group was listed on the London Stock Exchange, but was delisted after acquisition by Saltaire Water, an infrastructure fund.

French Water Companies

The French model of water management involves municipalities, large corporations, and the central administration. The country has been divided into six river basin regions to coordinate overall water management. There are six river basin committees and six river basin financial agencies (Grigg, 1996). For water supply, France has a long tradition of systems operated by private companies. The three main water companies were SAUR (Société d'Aménagement Urbain et Rural), Société Lyonnaise des Eaux, and Compagnie Generale des Eaux. Each of these has now undergone transitions, which are explained next.

SAUR is now the SAUR Group. In 1984, the Bouygues Group acquired a majority stake in it, and a 1994 agreement between Bouygues and Électricité de France (EDF) created Saur International, which is expanding with electric power and water subsidiaries in Africa. EDF divested its shares in 2001 and in 2005, Bouygues divested all but 10 percent interest to PAI Partners. Suez Lyonnaise des Eaux was formed in 1997 by a merger of Compagnie Financière de Suez and Lyonnaise des Eaux-Dumez and now operates in 130 countries. Lyonnaise des Eaux itself was formed in 1880 and expanded its operations up to 1990, when it merged with the Dumez construction group to form Lyonnaise des Eaux-Dumez. The Compagnie Financière de Suez traces its beginnings to the construction of the Suez Canal. The origins of Compagnie Générale des Eaux date to 1853, when it was created by an imperial decree to irrigate the countryside and supply water to towns and cities. Its first contract was to supply water to Lyon and then it received a 50-year concession to supply water to Paris. It is now called Veolia Water, which is part of Veolia Environnement. The company's divisions of water, environmental services, energy, and transportation were merged into the single name of Veolia in 2005, which operates in more than 100 countries (Grigg, 2010).

INTERNATIONAL WATER OPERATIONS: THE RISKS OF COCHABAMBA

Private water companies and investors can run into rough sledding when seeking to privatize a public water system, as shown by the Cochabamba (Bolivia) "Water War," which took place around 2000. This incident illustrates a fundamental issue of the water business: Is water as commodity or human right?

The water system of Cochabamba (the third-largest city in Bolivia) was managed by a state agency named SEMAPA. The World Bank pressured Bolivia to auction SEMAPA for privatization, but only one bid was received. It came from a consortium named Aguas del Tunari, which comprised International Water Limited (England), an Italian utility firm Edison, Bechtel Enterprise Holdings (US), a Spanish engineering and construction firm Abengoa, along with two Bolivian companies.

The plan was to double the coverage area and introduce electrical production to more of the region. The Bolivian government signed a 40-year concession and guaranteed a minimum 15 percent annual return on its investment. It is a long story, but after Aguas del Tunari imposed a large rate increase, the city entered a period of emergency. More issues than water came into play and it is a complex story not told in full here, but the lesson for water privatization was clear. It is not always easy.

Perhaps the final chapter in the Cochabamba Water War has yet to be told. After the protests and a long period of postadjustment, the system was eventually returned to SEMAPA, but service has remained poor (Chávez, 2006). It illustrates a critical issue in the water business: Is it a commodity business, or must water be treated as a human right and provided no matter what the cost? When asked this question, most (but not all) of my students agree with the human-right argument, but this leads to the next question: What if the state company providing the water is inefficient and even corrupt? What happens if the inefficiency and corruption are so bad that the state-run company cannot provide minimum levels of acceptable water service? It is a dilemma for which there is no fixed answer, but it is very important to understand to see the correct picture of water supply.

RURAL DOMESTIC SELF-SUPPLY

As explained in Chapter 2, rural domestic self-supply systems also comprise a significant segment of the residential water supply sector. Of course, this is even much more the case in developing countries where much of the supply is self-supply anyway. Even in the United States, the 2005 USGS report showed that 42.9 million people or 14 percent of the population relied on these mostly water-well systems.

The percentage of self-supply is a little uncertain and there is an apparent inconsistency between the USGS and USEPA statistics on the percentage of people who are served by community water systems. USEPA's (2010a) report was that 294,339,881 (96 percent of the population) people used community water systems, but the USGS report shows that 14 percent are self-supplied. The reason for the different reports may be explained by double-counting in the USEPA statistics of water use from systems which serve wholesale as well as retail customers. A utility reporting to USEPA may provide wholesale water to another utility and count its customers among its own. Then, the utility drawing the wholesale water may report those customers again. USEPA is still working out its statistical reporting systems to resolve "consecutive system" issues such as this.

USGS collects its figures directly from state and local governments and from private industries. It then estimates total water use from per-capita values. It is difficult to estimate the number of wells in the United States, but using USGS's report of a national average of 89 gallons per capita per day, and assuming an average occupancy per residence of three persons, the indication is that the United States has 14 million residential water wells, or 4,667 for each of our approximately 3,000 counties. The number is probably higher because water-well users would be expected to use less on a per capita basis. According to USGS, most of the rural domestic use is in Michigan, California, Pennsylvania, North Carolina, and Texas.

Many commercial and industrial water systems are also self-supplied. They would be reported as Non-Community Water Systems if they serve more than 25 persons in factories, offices, stores, rest stops, or gas stations, for example. Self-supplied systems comprise a large market for point-of-use treatment systems, which are described in Chapter 21.

WATER RECLAMATION

One business trend to watch in the water supply group is the rising use of reclaimed water, which is water that has been treated in wastewater treatment plants to remove contaminants. The United States and communities in other water-short countries, such as Australia, are increasing the use of reclaimed water mainly to offset shortages. The estimate is that use of reused wastewater in the United States is growing by about 15 percent per year (USEPA and U.S. Agency for International Development, 2004).

This increased interest in reclaimed water opens a new market for water supply systems. In effect, when a dual distribution system provides reclaimed water to customers through a network of mains separate from the potable distribution system, the reclaimed system becomes a third water utility to go along with wastewater and potable water.

Reclaimed water is used mainly for nonpotable applications such as landscape and agricultural irrigation, toilet flushing, industrial process water, power plant cooling, wetlands, and groundwater recharge.

This interest in reclaimed water grew slowly over the decades. When municipal water supply systems were introduced in the 19th century, all of the distributed water was raw water because water treatment had not been introduced yet. After the advent of water treatment, the drinking water in distribution systems was considered as treated water and it became possible to reclaim the water by advanced sewage treatment and reuse.

One early application of water reclamation occurred in 1926, when a dual water system was developed for Grand Canyon Village in Arizona. Later, applications for industrial and power plant cooling were brought on line. Today, thousands of reclaimed-water systems are in operation for diverse nonpotable purposes. Internationally, use of reclaimed water is also on the rise. For example, in Japan, areawide water recycling is used in the Shinjuku district of Tokyo for toilet flushing in high-rise buildings.

Many interesting cases for use of reclaimed water are in evidence. For example, St. Petersburg, Florida, has had an extensive system in operation since 1977. Pomona, California, began using it in 1973 to serve California Polytechnic University and new commercial, industrial, and landscape applications.

In Burbank, California, reclaimed water storage tanks are the only source of water serving an isolated fire system, which is kept separate from the potable fire service. Altamonte Springs, Florida, enacted a requirement in 1984 for developers to install reclaimed water lines so that all properties within a development are provided service. The Irvine Ranch Water District in California has one of the largest comprehensive systems, and many other coastal cities have followed its lead.

Use of reclaimed water is not without its critics. For one thing, it does not always pay for itself. The economics of source substitution with reclaimed water depend on the location and the costs of new sources and the costs of wastewater treatment and disposal. Reclaimed water transmission and distribution lines are expensive and disruptive in established areas so the most attractive applications are in new areas.

Generally, reclaimed water is more mineralized than potable water, enhancing the potential for corrosion on the interior of the pipe. Because reclaimed water lines are often the last ones installed, there is an increased opportunity for stray current electrolysis or coating damage.

The future seems certain to see much more use of reclaimed water. After all, with new raw water supplies hard to get, why not reuse what you already have? Many scenarios can be imagined. For example, a city can simply start near its wastewater treatment plant and begin to deliver reclaimed water to nearby industries and businesses. Then, as it makes economic sense, it can expand its coverage to respond to opportunities. Another scenario is for reclaimed water systems to be used initially for agricultural needs, to be shifted later to new urban development. This is like the city-farm programs of the West.

ACCOUNTING FOR URBAN WATER USES

Accounting for urban water use is drawing much more attention than in the past, when most water was sold on a flat-rate basis and little attention was given to metering. All of that has changed, at least in many places, especially in water-short areas of developed countries. That was even the case in my city in Colorado up to the 1990s. Finally, the push toward water efficiency overcame the inertia and opposition. In places where little water metering is practiced, such as the United Kingdom and parts of Canada, talk about metering seems on the increase as interest in water efficiency continues to grow.

While a few forward-looking utilities studied water use in the past, it is today's difficulties in obtaining supplies and paying for infrastructure that are driving the increased attention to water metering, rate structures, and water efficiency. These moves require systems in place to account for water use.

Accounting for water use requires water meters to measure water deliveries. Arguments against meters, such as high initial cost, ongoing cost to read and maintain them, and questionable benefits, seem to have evaporated (at least in many places) as water efficiency advocates cite conservation, reduction in peak-day demands, better rate structures, and tracking of system losses as proof of benefits. Advancing technologies are making water meters more high tech, and they may become part of the smart grid being developed for electric power systems. The emerging term for these systems is advanced metering infrastructure (AMI).

The place to start with water accounting is with a water audit. While these are popular now, their use actually goes back more 100 years. The first time I became aware of them was in the 1970s when interest in water conservation started to increase. I noticed a 1982 paper in the *Journal of the American Water Works Association* that explained how to do a systematic audit (Siedler, 1982). The paper explained how to check master meters for accuracy, test industrial meters, check for unauthorized use of water, and locate underground leaks through surveys. The audit would produce a balance sheet to show total accounted-for water, including known leaks, and total unaccounted-for water, including unmetered uses and unmeasured leaks. Today, it seems amazing that these basic steps would be considered as such advances even as recently as the 1980s.

At its highest level, urban water auditing classifies water uses in categories that include residential, commercial, industrial, public, and non-revenue-producing water. These lead to more detailed reports, such as those shown on Figure 4.4, which explains how the supply is either metered or unmetered and how some water is lost. The water that reaches customers is distributed according to customer classes, which include a range of uses. This water is either consumed or sent to wastewater systems as sewage.

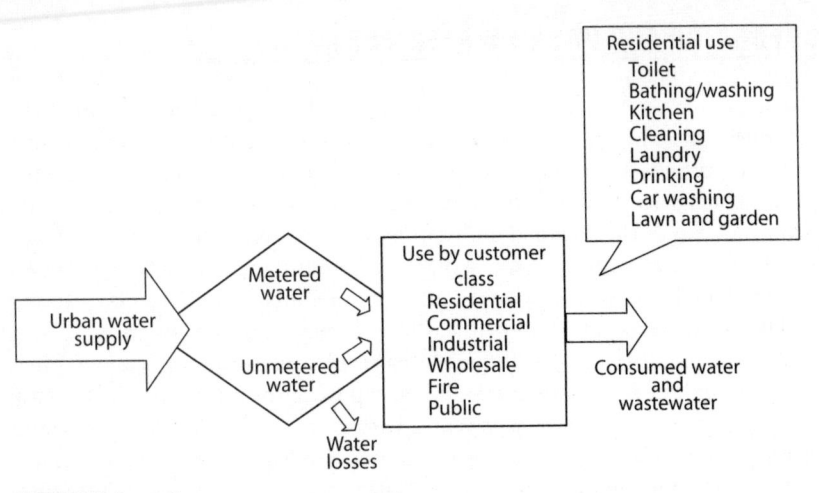

FIGURE 4.4   Urban water-use accounting

Each use by a customer class can be broken into components, such as those shown for residential use.

The water-auditing procedure used from about the 1970s would identify unaccounted-for water, but this metric proved inadequate. As the concept of water auditing advanced, industry groups such as AWWA (2010) sought to develop standards and measurement techniques for unaccounted-for water. Now, a dimensionless procedure is recommended that should apply in any country. It breaks water use into authorized consumption and water losses. Authorized consumption is billed or unbilled, metered or unmetered. This procedure leads to estimates of revenue water and nonrevenue water. Water losses are either apparent (meter inaccuracies, data errors, unauthorized consumption) or real (leakage or overflows).

Measuring water use after the fact helps us understand and charge for water use, but sometimes it is desirable to forecast future water uses. A simple approach would be a regression model that predicted total demand on the basis of population, season, day of week, temperature, and selected other variables. A model like this would normally be close enough to predict annual or monthly demand to plan for water supplies and treatment.

A detailed model named IWR-MAIN was developed for water-use forecasting. The name comes from the original supporting agency (IWR or Institute of Water Resources) and the model purpose (Municipal and Industrial Needs) (Baumann et al., 1998). The model is now available only through the CDM engineering company.

IWR-MAIN disaggregates urban water use and enables the user to forecast changes in total use when variables change. Total urban water use is

TABLE 4.4   Water-Use Coefficients for Industry Groups

Major Industry Group	Water-Use Coefficient (gall/employee/day)
Construction	20.7
Manufacturing	132.5
Transportation, communications, utilities	49.3
Wholesale trade	42.8
Retail trade	93.1
Finance, insurance, real estate	70.8
Services	137.5
Public administration	105.7

Data source: Baumann et al., 1998

summed from residential, nonresidential, and unaccounted uses. These can be estimated from regression equations that rely on multipliers, which are based on data collected for water use in selected urban areas.

The residential sector is simulated according to census categories of housing, such as single-family and multifamily data. The simulation equation takes into account determinants of water use such as income level, household size, and other demographic variables.

As shown in Table 4.4, nonresidential water use for the eight industrial codes shown was evaluated through data available to the model developers (Baumann et al., 1998).

Obviously, these aggregated categories can be at best approximate and subject to change, especially in the manufacturing group. Some other values, such as public uses, must be supplied by the user of the program. For example, these could be for irrigation of turf in medians or golf courses and for makeup water for public swimming pools. Unaccounted water can include categories such as leakage, meter errors, hydrant flushing, main breaks, firefighting, unbilled water, illegal connections, street cleaning, and construction.

RIGHT TO DIVERT SURFACE WATER OR PUMP GROUNDWATER

In the past, a utility's search for local raw-water supplies might have involved drilling wells in aquifers or tapping a river or lake. Now, even if the utility can find acceptable sources it may face a firestorm of opposition to its plans. The water history book is filled with stories of epic struggles involving expensive studies, political battles and lawsuits over water supplies. Out where I live in Colorado, this is certainly the case and the difficulty continues to increase in the context of the appropriation doctrine of water law (see Chapter 14), but it is tough to get new supplies everywhere.

Take the experience of Virginia Beach, Virginia, for example. Prior to World War II, Virginia Beach was a small town with a 1940 population of 22,584, but the war and its aftermath fueled rapid growth for five decades or more. The population has now leveled off around 440,000 and the city is part of a metro area of around two million. Virginia Beach's water supply was inadequate for this growth, and it started looking hard for new supplies in the 1970s. At the time, I was working for the North Carolina state government and was able to follow its quest for water from a nearby vantage point. It was a compelling study of water supply politics, which I described in two books on water resources management (Grigg, 1985, 1996).

On the face of it, Virginia Beach should have been able to find water supplies easily because there seems to be plenty of water in southeastern Virginia and nearby, and it could also cooperate with its neighbor cities to form a metro system. However, water problems in coastal areas are common because much of the water is saline and they often lack large supplies of freshwater. It is a long story as to why none of the obvious solutions worked for Virginia Beach, but the bottom line is that getting permission and building a new pipeline took something like 20 years. Now, Virginia Beach has a reliable supply of around 60 mgd from Lake Gaston.

Why did it take so long and cost so much? As I explained in the more detailed case study in Grigg (1996), it required a tremendous effort by Virginia Beach to overcome opposition to its water supply plans. The effort involved expensive studies, federal permit applications, political actions, media campaigns, and lawsuits. All of these are part of the cost of gaining access to the water. Virginia Beach now has around $150 million invested in the project, which works out to $2,300 per acre-foot of average yield under best-case scenarios. A local project in my area now has a price tag of about double that. These costs translate directly into significant added costs to water supply customers.

A higher-profile issue today is water supply for Atlanta, which faced a storm of legal problems and drought in recent years. So far, Atlanta has not built any major new water-supply infrastructure as Virginia Beach did, but its approach has been to seek permission to divert more water from the Chattahoochee River or to gain legal permission to increase its interbasin transfers of water from basins that are tributary to Alabama. All of these proposals have encountered very choppy water and there have been many, many meetings, including those between governors and some involving a federally appointed mediator. The inability to bring resolution to a number of related issues illustrates the complexity of large regional water supply issues such as Atlanta's.

REGULATION OF WATER-SUPPLY UTILITIES

In addition to regulation for water allocation, water-supply regulation includes health and safety (such as to maintain safe drinking water), rates and charges (such as rates of a private water company), and service access and quality (such as adequate water pressure). The major regulatory law for health and safety is the Safe Drinking Water Act (SDWA), which indirectly controls service quality parameters such as water pressure.

The rules of the Safe Drinking Water Act have evolved for many years, and have led to one of the world's safest national water-supply systems. The law is explained in more detail in Chapter 13.

In the United States, only private water companies are normally subject to rate regulation through formal mechanisms. Regulation of service delivery and business performance is through public utility commissions for privately owned utilities, but it is through self-regulation through the political process for publicly owned utilities. In the United Kingdom, the situation is markedly different, as Ofwat exercises strong control over economic operations of the water companies.

Industries and other entities with self-supplied water services and not connected to community water systems are also regulated by USEPA if they supply water to more than 25 people. They must test their water and report in some of the same ways as community water systems.

ISSUES OF THE WATER-SUPPLY BUSINESS

The water-supply business is changing significantly, even if the change seems slow compared to faster-moving industries. The change in the United States is from a centralized, government-dominated, and supply-side industry to a more distributed and flexible industry with more demand management and new opportunities for the private sector.

One way to identify issues is by concerns of water-utility managers, which include energy, workforce, political involvement, population and demographic trends, regulatory changes, and total water management (Means et al., 2005, 2006). These issues wax and wane, depending on the state of society and the economy, and as you might expect, business issues rose on everyone's radar after 2008 due to the turmoil in the financial markets. The following issues are listed regularly by water managers as areas of concern, but the list is not meant to be exhaustive.

Business Factors and Revenues

Although water supply managers report other issues, their inability to raise rates and pay for needed improvements is probably their major concern. In fact, the business factors on their minds focus on ability to finance renewal and improvements, falling revenues, and delinquent customers (Mann and Runge, 2009). Of course, these issues rise and fall with the shifting economics of the nation, but they are endemic in the water industry, which seems averse to full-cost pricing.

In addition to basic attitudes that water should be cheap, there is a built-in conflict in water pricing caused by conflict between goals to charge for water according to use but also impose water efficiency and lower use. In a supply-driven paradigm, water utilities would provide all the water that might be used under a cost-of-service pricing approach. However, this approach does not encourage water conservation. Under a demand-driven paradigm, there will be more emphasis on conservation. So, the utility is in the unenviable position of charging more for less. This is just one of the many revenue issues facing water utilities.

Another issue is that decision makers are reluctant to approve rate increases even when they are shown to be justified. The decision makers will often opt for going easy on ratepayers or holding up a renewal project because they know that the negatives from the rate increase will be harder on them than the negatives of putting off a problem for someone else to solve later. Because this keeps on going, the "can just gets kicked down the road," as some managers lament. As this is written, the Denver Water Department has just proposed a 31 percent rate increase over four years and its staff was raked over the coals by the city council. What can the managers do? They need the money to maintain a good system, so they must take the flak given out by public and political opposition leaders.

Source Water

Worries about access to new water supplies and even maintaining existing supplies under the threat of climate change is on the minds of water managers. To see this dilemma, consider two scenarios. In the first one, you are the water supply director for a rapidly growing city in the Sun Belt and have only enough water supply for the next few years. Everyone knows that it takes a long time to develop new water, so what do you do? In the second scenario, maybe you are in a similar situation but you depend heavily on a single source, which is vulnerable to climate change, such as a mountain reservoir. If severe drought hits, what do you do?

Water-supply managers are risk averse and do not, under any circumstances, want to be the ones responsible for running out of water. This can mean loss of reputation or of a job, even at the minimum. So, water managers will work hard to overcome these barriers and find new supplies. They have options, of course, and these include reclaimed water (discussed earlier), desalting, new projects, and cooperation with neighboring water suppliers. At the end of the day, however, the message may be that very little new water is available, and a number of utilities are making their plans accordingly.

Aging Infrastructure

The aging infrastructure problem of water systems is embedded in the overall aging problem of all U.S. infrastructure. In a nutshell, the problem is caused by underinvestment in renewal. Take buried water pipes, for example. Let's say that they have a lifetime of 100 years (and many of them do last that long!). Nationally, we have an inventory of these pipes with various ages, and to avoid failure, they must be replaced before they reach age 100.

Let's suppose we manage a system of these pipes, which will serve a population of 100,000. This would require around 350 miles of pipe, based on national averages. That pipe, of various sizes, might have a replacement value in the range of $300 million, again a very approximate number. Obviously, this pipe was not all built at once and the inventory has different ages. On the average, if you replaced 1 percent of it per year, you could keep up, barring expansions and upgrades. However, your replacement rate is only 0.5 percent per year (and many utilities do not reach that level).

We can plot a graph of how the deferred investment will build up by graphing investments and current value of the system, which is a condition-based number that takes into account both original cost and deterioration. The curve will look somewhat like Figure 4.5, which illustrates how the curve grows. This is a simplified portrayal of a complex situation, but it is based on the realistic notion that pipe installation dates and deterioration rates are highly variable. This depiction has actually gained some notoriety among fixed-asset managers in the water industry and is known as the "Nessie Curve" (2010), after the Loch Ness monster.

Water Efficiency

All indications are that emphasis on water efficiency will continue to rise in the years ahead. The term *water efficiency* means more than the older term *water conservation*. While it might sound redundant, water efficiency means using water efficiently or to use only as much as is needed for any

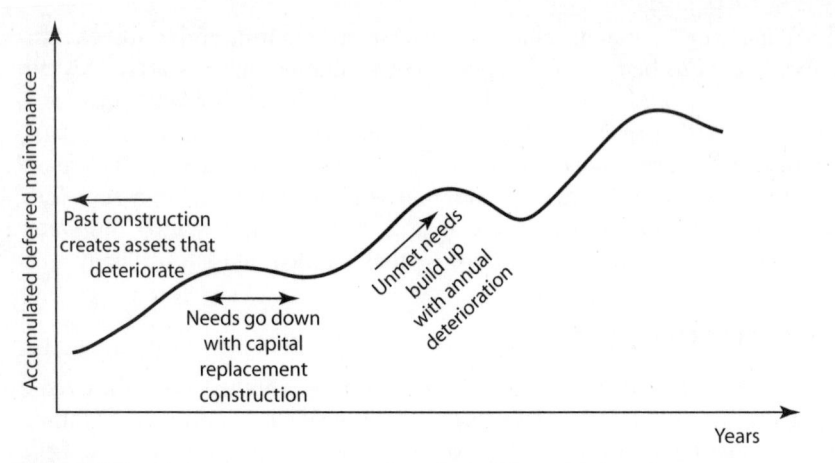

FIGURE 4.5 The Nessie Curve to explain the buildup of deferred maintenance

particular application. Given that there are so many uses of water, the identification of "as much as needed" can become complex.

Outdoor uses of water are a particular challenge because they create more consumptive use and require large quantities of water.

In any case, with supplies getting tight, demands increasing, and competition for water getting tougher, it makes sense that water efficiency should be the answer for many supply problems. This can mean water conservation, with its attendant problems of revenue shortfall or rate increases. It might mean use of reclaimed water, which brings in questions of health and safety. It might also mean introducing new financing systems to create incentives to use water more wisely. Large numbers of people are interested in or involved in these issues. *Water Efficiency* magazine was started by Forester Publications to respond to this interest, and in 2010 the second Water Smart Innovations Conference (2010) attracted more than 1,000 participants.

Workforce

The water-industry workforce "crisis" is explained in Chapter 15. This problem is similar to other industries with aging workforces and less-than-optimal employment conditions. As the demands on the industries ramp up—such as to protect public health, manage aging infrastructure systems, and respond to complex technological changes—they have difficulty in responding if they are underfinanced and subject to rigid public-sector conditions. This problem afflicts several water sectors but is particularly acute with water-supply utilities, and, of course, the financial crisis only delays the problems by creating more applicants for jobs. It does not address the underlying issue of loss of valuable institutional knowledge.

Risk Management

After the Safe Drinking Water Act was passed in 1974, USEPA went into a phase of setting maximum contaminant levels for a large number of micro-organisms, disinfectants, disinfection byproducts, inorganic chemicals, organic chemicals, and radionuclides. The number of regulated contaminants continues to increase, not decrease. When you add in the heightened public interest in emerging problems such as endocrine disruptors that might be caused by pharmaceutical wastes in water, the challenges and risks to water-system operators continue to build up. No wonder water-utility managers list regulatory challenges as one of their main areas of concern. Responding to this area will require improvements in risk management, which is an emerging management area in the water industry.

Another concern of water-system managers is security from sabotage or other threats, whether from humans or natural events. When water systems are subjected to attacks of any kind, they become vulnerable to shutdown, contamination, and loss of capacity, which threatens entire cities. Yet to protect the systems against any and all threats will add to the upward pressures on costs, and in the future water managers must learn better techniques to assess the risks and take mitigating actions.

Water-supply utilities face many additional issues. They have a watchful eye on public consumption of bottled water, not so much because of competition from sales as because of image. Public suppliers are committed to maintaining high-quality service and not to be thought of as the second choice by their customers. The utilities also wonder if new organizational forms—such as people going "off-grid" for their water systems—will affect them. Use of reclaimed water is another emerging issue that makes operation of utilities more complex. Of course, public water supply takes place in the public spotlight, so utility managers are very sensitive about their overall images and reluctant to have problems such as water-quality violations occur. They worry about the next big problem to hit their systems, whether it is a disease outbreak or natural calamity. Given many issues such as these, it seems certain that management in the water industry will become more complex and that costs of water, in response to the issues, will rise for the foreseeable future.

CHAPTER 5

The Wastewater and Water-Quality Business

While the business of wastewater and water quality seems like a mirror image of the water-supply business, it has important attributes that are different from water supply. In some ways, wastewater and water-quality management are different businesses, but they are treated together in this chapter. They are a composite of the business of handling wastewaters from diverse sources, treating them to restore their condition, and monitoring and managing the quality of water in the environment. These activities comprise the number one business of managing the water quality of the aquatic environment.

One of the differences between the water supply and wastewater sectors is that one focuses on health and human needs (water supply) and the other is more focused on environmental water quality (wastewater). This does not take away from the obvious links between wastewater and safe drinking water, but there is an important disconnect in our incentives to manage and pay for these services.

This disconnect became an important policy issue in the 1970s when the Clean Water Act (CWA) became law. It occurs because of the reality that your wastewater affects the health of downstream water users more than it does your own health, and this blurs your view of how your wastewater expenditures benefit you directly. The opposite is true of your drinking water, where you see a direct benefit to cleaning it up before drinking it. Thus, while we have common stakes in making water cleaner, it is more difficult to gain public support for wastewater treatment than it is for safe drinking water.

This chapter focuses on community wastewater systems and utilities as the centerpieces of the wastewater and water-quality business. These serve residential, commercial, industrial, and other customers who connect to urban networks. They are operated mostly by publicly owned utilities, which are in many cases integrated with water-supply utilities.

EVOLUTION OF THE BUSINESS

From the time of the first human settlements, disposing of wastewater has been necessary to maintain sanitary living conditions, but it was handled crudely until modern wastewater-handling systems emerged. Much of the disease and filth that afflicted cities in the past occurred from poor management of wastewater, which sadly continues in many places. As populations and economies grow, polluted streams in many places show the neglect of environmental water-quality management.

Until modern times, few if any people would have seen in these tremendous loads of wastewater the business opportunities that are apparent today. Of course, engineers, contractors, and plumbers were aware of the work required to design and build pipelines, but when filtration and chlorination were introduced for drinking water treatment, it ushered in a new era of complexity for both water and wastewater. In fact, you can trace the evolution of modern consulting firms to the business generated by this new system for water treatment and other features of the rapidly improving drinking-water system.

However, on the wastewater side, things moved more slowly. People were not willing to invest in sewage-treatment infrastructure to the same extent as water supply. For example, I can recall the wastewater system of my hometown of Montgomery, Alabama, as it was in 1950, and while it had sewers connected to most older built-up areas, the discharge from the whole town went untreated directly to a creek, which was a disaster zone.

Things began to move in the 1950s, however, and more wastewater treatment systems were built. The wastewater and water-quality business expanded slowly until the Clean Water Act was passed in 1972, launching what amounted to a revolution in both infrastructure construction and environmental management. The nation saw a big spike in construction of wastewater treatment plants and new attention to regulation of environmental water quality. Today, wastewater management is as large as the water supply business and in many ways more complex. The differences between the two focus on their functions and customers, their infrastructures, how they are regulated, and their business operations.

WASTEWATER SERVICES AND SYSTEMS

While wastewater customers are generally the same as those for water supply, commercial enterprises such as the customers listed in Chapter 2 can have unique needs for wastewater service. The categories of these that might have special needs include large office complexes, food and beverage outlets, hospitals and medical facilities, schools, and sports or performance venues. Industrial wastewater systems also comprise a large and complex category, including those attached to centralized systems and those with stand-alone systems.

In rural areas and in industries not served in urban areas, on-site systems and package plants are the norm. Millions of rural residential systems use individual treatment units such as septic tanks and comprise a large but dispersed market. They are served by the smaller-scale products and services sectors of the water industry, which are explained in Chapters 18 and 19.

If wastewater systems serving the public are not connected to networks, they mirror the transient and nontransient noncommunity water systems that are regulated in the water supply sector. However, no central statistics are kept on these systems. They might serve factories, schools, campgrounds, stores, rest stops, gas stations, and other freestanding facilities and in most cases, they will probably use on-site systems such as septic tanks or package units. If they are large, they may require a discharge permit under the Clean Water Act.

Manufacturing and process industries may be connected to networks and be subject to pretreatment regulations, or they may have their own discharge permits. Their operations are explained in Chapter 7.

The last part of this business sector to be discussed is the regulatory system of monitoring, modeling, and enforcement that are required for environmental water-quality control. These are important in the water business as they levy requirements on dischargers that can lead to large expenditures for infrastructure and services.

PUBLIC WASTEWATER SYSTEMS

The infrastructure required for wastewater and water quality management is extensive, expensive, and hard to maintain and operate properly. The nation learned about this during the Construction Grants Program implemented after the Clean Water Act of 1972. I had oversight responsibility at one time for one of the state government grant programs, and this provided me with insight into the infrastructure challenges.

The basic infrastructure required is shown in Figure 5.1, which illustrates the collection sewers, lift station, treatment plant, interceptor and outfall sewers, and sludge processing facilities. These facilities require investment and reinvestment, as well as careful and professional operations management.

The services provided by community wastewater systems are to collect, treat, and dispose of used waters. To provide these services, wastewater systems in cities include collector sewers, transmission lines or outfalls, wastewater treatment plants, and sludge processing and disposal facilities. As you

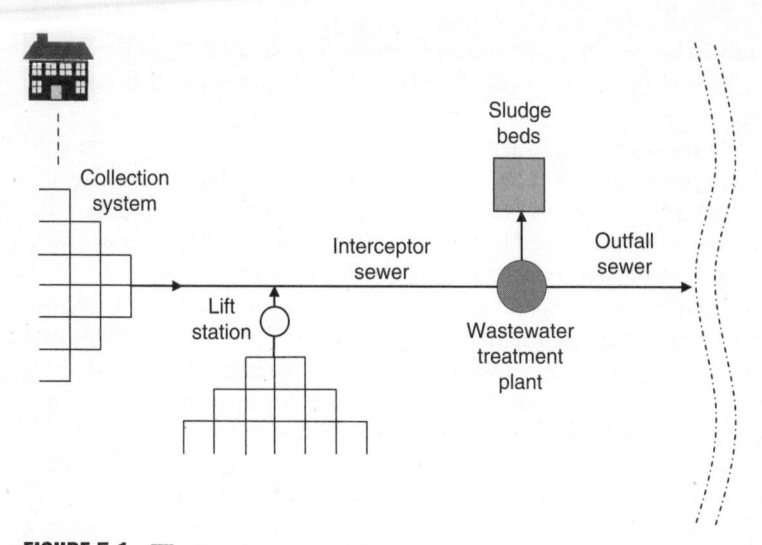

FIGURE 5.1 Wastewater system components

can imagine, these infrastructure systems are complex, expensive, and difficult to manage and maintain.

In cities most wastewater service is provided by government-owned utilities, although private operation of publicly owned treatment facilities is frequently practiced on a contract basis. Usually, a wastewater utility is a division of a city government or a special district organized under state laws. Given the large number of small systems, many other types of ownership occur in rural areas, including small businesses, associations, and auxiliary enterprises connected to other organizations.

Wastewater systems are more difficult to count than water systems, mainly because fewer of them operate with utility status than is the case with water-supply systems. Often, they are embedded in departments of city government, and sometimes treatment and collection are even contained in different management units. For this reason, no count of wastewater utilities is available to compare with the USEPA inventory of drinking-water systems, which was explained in Chapter 4. However, USEPA (2010b) maintains a count of publicly owned treatment works (POTWs) and a count of sewer collection systems, and these give us a basis from which to estimate the number of management units.

The count of POTWs has hovered around 16,000 facilities for over 10 years, which indicates that the trend is not to build new facilities but to expand older ones. Statistics on these are maintained in conjunction with USEPA's biennial needs surveys, which inform Congress about the need to

TABLE 5.1 Number of Wastewater Treatment Facilities by Flow Range

Flow Range, mgd	Number of Facilities
0.000 to 0.100	5,703
0.101 to 1.000	5,863
1.001 to 10.000	2,690
10.001 to 100.000	480
100.001 and greater	38
Total	14,774

Data source: U.S. Environmental Protection Agency (2010b)

appropriate funds to assist in maintaining the infrastructure systems. In its most recent survey, USEPA (2010) estimated that if the funds were provided, in the next 20 years a total of 15,618 facilities would serve a population of 284.2 million people, or 79 percent of the U.S. population. This implies that by 2028 the population will be about 360 million and that 75 million will remain unconnected to sewer networks.

Similar to the case with water supply, most wastewater systems are small. While no report of number of systems by population served is available, USEPA (2010b) does report number of treatment facilities by flow range (Table 5.1). This report enables us to see the size distribution of treatment works but, as some utilities have more than one treatment plant, it cannot be compared directly to number of utilities.

The service of wastewater collection in sewer systems may be unbundled from treatment operations and operated by separate management units. USEPA reported that in 2008, there were 19,739 collection pipe systems in operation. This number seems to be static or even declining, because in 1996, the report was 20,670 systems in operation. The explanation for the decline might be found in the data collection methods.

The total of 16,000 to 18,000 treatment facilities and 20,000 collection systems is of the same order of magnitude as the number of municipalities and special districts providing wastewater service as reported by the Census Bureau. The number of municipal and town governments in the United States is about 35,000 and, given that many of these are very small, the number of wastewater collection systems represents those organized local governments that are large enough to have sewer collection systems. The remaining communities are probably too small to have systems or to be connected to larger systems. As the number of collection systems is static, new land developments must be connecting to existing systems.

If stormwater systems are connected to sewer systems, it creates the special category known as combined sewers. In 2008, there were 767 of these combined sewer systems that reported investment needs to USEPA. Most of these are in nine states (Indiana, Ohio, Pennsylvania, Illinois, New York, West Virginia, Michigan, Maine, and New Jersey) (USEPA, 2010b).

PLAYERS IN THE WASTEWATER BUSINESS

The players in wastewater are generally in the same categories as in water supply as well as in the utilities, regulatory agencies, and support organizations. Chapter 4 showed that the number of employees in wastewater is nearly the same as those in water-supply utilities. Backgrounds of utility officials are similar to those in water supply and managers and technical workers can migrate from one field to another, but the certifications of operators are different.

Investor ownership of wastewater utilities is less common than water-supply utilities for several reasons, including requirements stemming from federal subsidies of construction of wastewater treatment plants. Nevertheless, once you get past these subsidies, ownership and operation of wastewater systems can be attractive as a utility enterprise. Operation of wastewater treatment plants, rather than ownership, is the most common private initiative, and the extent of this business is explained in Chapter 16.

The consultants who serve wastewater are usually from the same firms, but treatment specialists and pipe systems specialists will normally be distinct for water supply and wastewater specialists. Some supplier representatives serve both water and wastewater, and others only serve one of the two fields. Regulators may or may not be the same. State government regulators for wastewater might be in the water resources agency or state EPA, whereas water supply might be regulated through a health department. Academics tend to be the same in water and wastewater, although research fields are sharply focused.

To summarize the information about wastewater players that was presented in Chapter 4, we estimated a total of 225,000 wastewater jobs nationally, distributed among treatment operators, collection systems, customer service, and administration. Professional and trade association for wastewater are focused on the Water Environment Federation, Association of State and Interstate Water Pollution Control Administrators, and National Association of Clean Water Agencies.

TOP WASTEWATER SERVICE PROVIDERS

As in the case of water-supply systems, the largest wastewater services providers are in the major cities or urbanized areas. Also, they are all

TABLE 5.2   Largest Wastewater Service Providers

Rank	Utility Name	Acronym
1	New York Department of Environmental Protection	DEP
2	Los Angeles County Sanitary District	LACSD
3	Metropolitan Water Reclamation District of Greater Chicago	MWRD
4	City of Los Angeles	LABS
5	Metropolitan Council Environmental Services	MCES
6	Orange County Sanitation District	OCSD
7	San Francisco Public Utilities Commission	SFPUC
8	Massachusetts Water Resources Authority	MWRA
9	Houston Public Works and Engineering Department	PW&E
10	Miami-Dade Water & Sewer Department	WSD

government owned, and no private companies rise to the top of the list. Some of these providers offer only treatment or collection service, while others offer integrated services and some also provide water-supply services. This list of the largest providers was assembled from population data and analyses of the utilities' web pages (Table 5.2).

REGULATION OF MUNICIPAL AND INDUSTRIAL DISCHARGERS

The Clean Water Act (CWA) is the regulatory vehicle to impose discharge rules on cities and industries. It is a good example of a regulatory program that stimulates a lot of business. Some would probably have said in the beginning that it hurt their businesses, but in the end it shifted business from one sector to another. In other words, environmental regulations are not necessarily an overall burden on the economy but they create winners and losers.

Say the year is 1972 and you have a business that generates a heavy stream of industrial wastewater, which you treat and discharge to a stream. The CWA program imposes new rules on you and you must spend investment capital to comply so that your operations costs go up as well. This will seem like a new cost of doing business and make you less competitive.

Your investments in infrastructure go to engineering, construction, and equipment companies. Your operating expenses translate into jobs for your own employees, purchases of equipment and materials from vendors, and perhaps use of more energy for wastewater treatment. Perhaps you are able to offset this increased cost of doing business with cost reductions and productivity increases elsewhere so that you can remain competitive. Another option is that you have to change your business in other ways, perhaps by changing your products and markets. All of these expenditures reverberate in other parts of the economy. Another facet of the increased regulation is the creation of jobs to provide the environmental products and services. All of this change is too complex to analyze in a generalized way, but it illustrates the general effect of wastewater regulations.

ISSUES IN THE WASTEWATER SECTOR

Given the heavy public-sector character of the wastewater and water-quality industry, it is natural that high-profile issues will be those with public policy implications. For example, if we examine the statements of American Society of Civil Engineers (ASCE) in its Infrastructure Report Card, we find that the emphasis on the investment needed is to deal with aging infrastructure. You will find that same emphasis in USEPA's statements related to the gap between needed and planned investment levels, and these areas of emphasis imply that our national policy is that if existing and planned systems are fully funded, there will be no significant residual problems with wastewater management and environmental water quality.

This implication seems to be mostly true, but it assumes that we are doing enough to protect environmental water quality through control of point sources, while we still have quite a few streams where water quality is unacceptable. Therefore, it seems to me that we still have many issues to solve in our mixture of solutions to environmental water quality problems.

The main issue seems to be "out of sight, out of mind." To people loving the outdoors, visible water quality is a big issue, but it is local in nature. The concept of water quality somewhere else attracts our attention, but it may not compete with larger political issues as public concerns. For example, the dead zone in the Gulf of Mexico that is created by Mississippi River discharges is a major environmental issue. But how many people know about it and are willing to accept water quality changes in the Corn Belt to deal with it?

My conclusion when identifying business issues of the wastewater and water quality sector is that major gains in environmental water quality will be tough to obtain in the United States, but we should look for innovations in maintaining current levels of service and making incremental gains where possible. Of course, in the many places around the world where wastewater treatment is not practiced and environmental water quality programs are missing, major gains are possible.

Now, let's turn to some specific issues of wastewater and water quality.

Holding the Line on Point Sources and Cleaning Up Nonpoint Sources

Financially speaking, the largest business category in the wastewater sector will be dealing with wastewater collection, treatment, and disposal. The giant systems required for this are aging and will require massive sums for their renewal. This category is the focus for the USEPA needs studies, which show sums on the order of $200 billion to $300 billion per year just to keep up in this area. These funds are needed in the following categories:

While point sources will require large investments, so will our responses to the nonpoint source problem. However, systems are spread out more and expenditures will be dispersed among more types of systems and work. The work to be done varies by economic sector, including urban stormwater, agriculture, septic tank fields, construction, and others. Additional detail on stormwater is provided in Chapter 6.

Risk would not seem to be as large an issue for wastewater as it is for water supply, but infrastructure failures, regulatory violations, pollution, disease outbreaks, and sabotage are still large risks. If you add in the overall risk to society from poor environmental water quality, then the risk calculation looks more impressive.

Financing Water-Quality Infrastructure

Financing water-quality infrastructure, mainly wastewater treatment plants and the integrity of sewer networks, will be a major issue for the United States in the future and is explained here in more detail than the other issues. The overall need for capital financing for the water industry is explained in Chapter 12, including the Clean Watersheds Needs Survey (CWNS), which outlines the official USEPA assessment of clean-water financing needs. This survey is published every four years in response to Sections 205(a) and 516 of the Clean Water Act. The reports for 2000, 2004, and 2008 are available on the web site (USEPA 2010b), and planning is underway for the 2012 survey.

When the CWNS numbers started appearing during the 1970s, they served to inform the nation of the true extent of wastewater financing needs. It took a while to develop cost-estimating standards, but now the approach is that utilities must submit their needs through state agencies, and the cost estimates must be documented with detailed studies such that they represent real needs rather than guesses. This adds credibility to the process, but there is still a good bit of uncertainty in the final estimates due to the approximate nature of the studies and the large amount of information to be processed. The categories of information used in the survey are capital improvement plans (37 percent); facility plans (15 percent); state-approved areawide and region basin plans (8 percent); final engineer's estimates (5 percent); and intended use plans under the Clean Water State Revolving Fund (5 percent).

The categories of facilities that must be financed and included in the CWNS are publicly owned wastewater collection and treatment facilities, stormwater and combined sewer overflows control facilities, nonpoint source pollution control projects, and decentralized wastewater management. To estimate the costs, the survey includes estimated needs to address water-quality or water-quality-related public health problems; the location and con-tact information for facilities and projects; the facility populations served; flow, effluent, and unit process information; and information about NPS best management practices. The survey contains information about approxi-mately 33,000 facilities and projects, including about 50 percent wastewater treatment plants permitted under the National Pollutant Discharge Elimina-tion System; 25 percent wastewater collection systems; 20 percent nonpoint source projects; and 5 percent stormwater projects (Plastino, 2008).

A comparison of the 2000, 2004, and 2008 surveys shows that report-ing formats have been evolving. In the 2000 survey, wastewater treatment and collection and conveyance were estimated at $63.7 billion and $60.2 billion, or 31.6 percent and 29.9 percent of a total of $201.3 billion. Other categories were stormwater management programs ($6.1 billion, 3 percent), nonpoint source control ($15.4 billion, 7.6 percent), and com-bined sewer overflow correction ($56.3 billion, 28.0 percent).

In the 2004 survey, the total was $202.5 billion and percentages changed slightly, with combined sewer overflow correction rising to 22.7 percent and nonpoint source control rising to 15.9 percent. A new category of recycled water distribution appeared at 1.8 percent. The 2008 total was $298.1 bil-lion, and the terminology changed a little, reporting $192.2 billion for waste-water treatment plants, pipe repairs, and buying and installing new pipes (to combine the categories of wastewater treatment, collection and conveyance); $63.6 billion for combined sewer overflow correction; and $42.3 billion for stormwater management.

Why stormwater management increased so much may be explained by USEPA's statement about the 17 percent increase from the 2004 report as being due to improved reporting, aging infrastructure, population growth, and more protective water-quality standards. The total needs actually appear to be larger, as USEPA reports that "in addition to the $298.1 billion in wastewater and stormwater needs, other documented needs for nonpoint source pollution prevention ($22.8 billion) and decentralized/onsite waste-water systems ($23.9 billion) are included in an appendix to the report." Apparently, these were separated out because they are not specified by sec-tion 516(B)1(b) of the Clean Water Act. This totals documented needs of

$344.8 billion. Apparently, $334.5 billion of this is eligible for Clean Water State Revolving Fund support and another $81.5 billion may be eligible for support from USEPA's Nonpoint Source Grants Program.

The totals are creeping up, and this is as you would expect, given the aging water quality infrastructure. Attention to these reports rises and falls. Currently, the nation has many other financial issues, and the tendency seems to be to take large obligations like this as one more of many national funding challenges. Once during the Reagan administration, I recall, the report was suppressed as the political climate seemed to be not to chronicle government spending obligations.

Although widespread private ownership of wastewater plants seems unlikely, there are many opportunities for outsourced operating contracts and concessions, and these are discussed in Chapter 18.

Access to Sanitation and Wastewater Service

Access to sanitation and wastewater service is not a major problem in the United States, but it remains a very serious issue in developing countries, where much work is necessary to educate people about sanitation and provide the appropriate low-cost technologies to create sanitary communities. The market implication is for sales of point-of-use devices to improve access across the board in villages and communities around the world. Given the nature of these devices, most can be provided by local firms and little opportunity for export businesses would seem to be indicated, except in the case of the low-cost producers who serve markets in wealthier countries. This issue is discussed in more detail in Chapter 22.

New Threats to Health

Adequate sanitation provides one of the essential barriers that protect us from waterborne diseases such as cholera, typhoid, and dysentery. These diseases have been known for centuries, but they remain a scourge in some parts of the world. As this is written in 2010, for example, a major outbreak of waterborne cholera is occurring in Haiti. In fact, water management is a critical determinant of risk for a number of infectious diseases, such as dengue hemorrhagic fever, which is transmitted by mosquitoes that thrive around poor drainage and water management. Work required to respond to threats of disease will focus on governmental and nongovernmental agency programs, rather than on new technologies or products and services.

CHAPTER 6

Stormwater and Flood Control

This chapter broadens the perspective beyond the water and wastewater businesses to include stormwater and flood control services and organizations. As participants in two related but different business sectors (stormwater and flood control), these agencies handle water to provide protective services to shield people and property from water damage, and sometimes they also regulate the vulnerability of people and property by controlling land use and imposing requirements such as flood proofing. The stormwater service has an added function of managing the quality of runoff from rainfall.

So, when you combine stormwater and flood control services they form an important part of the water industry, but one that is quite different from water supply and wastewater. Not only are they different from the other water-handling services, but they also are different from each other in some ways.

As Figure 6.1 shows, stormwater and flood control services operate at the interface between water management, emergency management, pollution control, and land-use management. This attribute of operating at the interface of other services makes them hybrid services and blurs their identities as distinct services, making them hard to explain, measure, justify, and finance.

This chapter explains the stormwater and flood control sectors as involving several types of essential services, which can be difficult to measure and finance. Some of their benefits serve public purposes and some serve private purposes. Local governing boards are often surprised at how many controversies stormwater and flood control services generate when decisions about policies or investments are needed.

SYSTEMS AND SERVICES

Stormwater and flood control systems are found both in urbanized and rural areas, but they are mainly needed to protect built property and places where people live. Figure 6.2 illustrates their layouts and the basic purposes

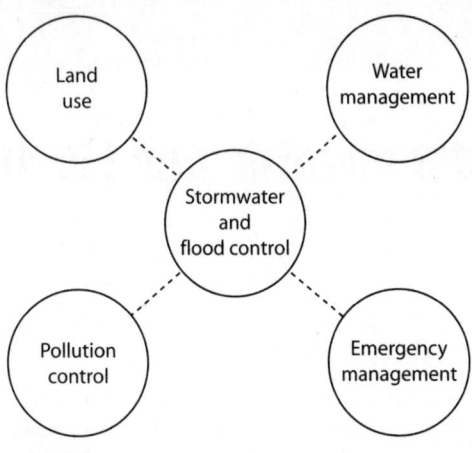

FIGURE 6.1   Flood and stormwater interfaces

that they serve. The stormwater collection systems focus on convenience drainage in neighborhoods and developed areas. The term *convenience drainage* means that the systems might not be needed for protection of property so much as they provide a way for people to walk on dry land, to

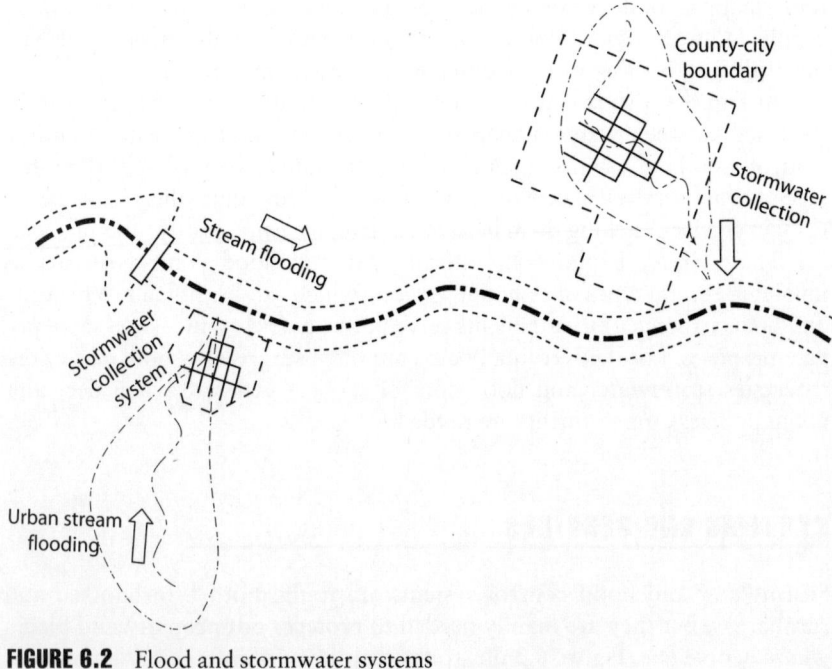

FIGURE 6.2   Flood and stormwater systems

drive their cars during storms, and generally to live conveniently even when it rains. The term connotes that it is not possible to justify the systems on the basis of strict economic analysis, but then it is sometimes difficult to quantify the value of convenience.

Urban stream flooding can occur in major drainage ways through the same areas. These major drainage ways are needed to convey larger floods than is the case with minor or convenience drainage systems. Along these major drainage ways and urban streams, the floodplain management function focuses on land-use regulation to reduce vulnerability and flood damage.

Superimposed on the work of the stormwater and flood systems are the requirements for environmental water quality. Stormwater systems are considered quasi-wastewater systems because urban runoff can be so polluted. Flood systems also carry polluted runoff, and due to the magnitudes of their flows they also have additional environmental benefits to floodplains, wetlands, and stream corridors.

While flood disasters generate more headlines, stormwater is a larger business sector in terms of employment and purchase of products and services, so it will be discussed first.

Stormwater Programs

The basic service provided by a stormwater program is drainage of sites and streets. At one extreme, this is convenience drainage because it is not avoiding damage so much as it is providing for convenient living but at the other extreme, it involves protecting people and property by providing for major drainage along streets and urban waterways. Engineers struggle to classify these extremes and call them "minor drainage" or "initial drainage" and "major drainage." None of these terms has been adopted as a standard, and stormwater managers still struggle to explain the benefits of their systems.

At the level of small sites, stormwater systems comprise the drainage systems from roofs, driveways, small commercial centers, and other small areas. The more development and impervious area you create, the more the runoff problem worsens. As the sizes of the sites increase, the stormwater problem takes on larger scales. On small sites, drainage facilities start with small sizes, and the industry that provides them tends to involve landscaping more than it does engineering and large-scale construction.

When stormwater arrives at streets and is minor, the convenience benefits of drainage are experiences, and they can be provided by gutters, overland flows, and underground pipes that discharge to streams and ditches.

When stormwater flows increase above the inconvenient or nuisance levels, they begin to cause actual damage and can be called urban flooding rather than stormwater. Again, it is difficult to explain exactly when this occurs, but the problem is addressed by the major stormwater system, which comprises streets, ditches, major pipes and outfalls, and urban stream networks. The major system should be capable of discharging large flows to prevent damage except during rare events.

While there are no standards about the differences between minor and major systems, there is today general agreement on the general approach to classify them, although variation among local codes and standards persists. The search for standardization started in the 1960s, and a leading effort was the preparation of the *Urban Storm Drainage Criteria Manual,* which is available in a current version (Urban Drainage and Flood Control District, 2010). These codes are important because they have economic implications and there is often uncertainty in how much investment is required to provide safe facilities.

Almost all towns and cities have stormwater programs, located in different departments and divisions. The organizational location of these programs ranges widely. Location with street management and public works programs is common, but stormwater is increasingly located with water and wastewater services as an integrated utility. Stormwater services are similar to wastewater services and fees for them can be assessed in many cases. They can also be associated with local floodplain management programs.

While stormwater programs reside mostly in departments of municipal governments, other local agencies and state governments also have substantial programs. In fact, stormwater services are widely distributed and more difficult to put into a classification system than water-supply services are. Organizations with stormwater services range across local (city and county) government departments of public works, utilities, street management and environmental services, state transportation departments, and special drainage and flood control districts.

After World War II, developers during the housing boom paid little attention to stormwater, and drainage was an afterthought in the development of subdivisions. A site would be drained with little thought about the ultimate disposition of the water, and many streets lacked stormwater systems. However, stormwater services have changed radically over the next 60 years.

I became involved as a consulting engineer with stormwater planning and design in the mid-1960s, and our municipal clients wanted retrofits of their 1950s and earlier systems that had proved inadequate. Typically, they wanted to create standards where none existed and provide buried storm sewer systems to get nuisance drainage off of streets. The engineers were interested in preventing damage, but city planners and neighborhood improvement interests began to object to pipes and rigid concrete channels that seemed at odds with natural development; bolstered by environmental thinking, they began to insist on more natural designs, which were sometimes called "blue-green" systems. These were the predecessors of today's green movement.

Today, there is much more realization that stormwater is a key component of green development, and might be called "low-impact development," or LID. At the site level, an ideal stormwater design will result in efficient handling of stormwater and minimization of the impact of water releases. The idea fits into the concept of sustainable development and would involve methods such as local detention storage of stormwater, use of pervious pavements and on-site water storage, minimization of stormwater runoff, and treatment of stormwater to remove contaminants.

Once stormwater leaves a site, it enters the public stormwater system with its minor and major parts. Now, the concept of green development can take on a larger scale and be translated into neighborhood and regional parks and demonstrate the alignment of stormwater systems with open space. Major systems can open up in waterways that traverse urban areas, creating opportunities for bike paths and recreational venues.

Beginning with the 1972 Clean Water Act (CWA) and its emphasis on nonpoint sources of water pollution, the quality of stormwater came onto the national radar screen. The early years of the stormwater quality effort featured data collection and attempts by USEPA regulators to design a coherent program.

The history of stormwater regulation in the United States involves a number of court cases. At first, USEPA resisted implementing a stormwater regulatory program, but a successful lawsuit led to an order to initiate a program. After the CWA was passed, USEPA issued exemptions from the National Pollutant Discharge Elimination System (NPDES) permit program for most stormwater sources. The Natural Resources Defense Council (2010) sued USEPA to require permits for all point sources, including storm sewers, and a federal district court ruled that the exemptions were contrary to the Clean Water Act. The decision was upheld by a federal court of appeals in 1977. This led to a set of USEPA rules and eventually, after direction from Congress in the 1987 Clean Water Act Amendments, phased rules were issued for cities and industrial sites. These were implemented for cities of different sizes and, given the complexity of the program, they are still being phased in and implemented.

The phased-in regulatory program for stormwater is now part of the NPDES permit program that applies to point-source dischargers. The stormwater component of the NPDES systems regulates discharges from municipal separate storm sewer systems (MS4s), construction activities, and industrial activities. The operators of large, medium, and regulated small MS4s may be required to obtain permits. Construction sites larger than one acre must comply with EPA's general permit for construction. Industrial activities may also require NPDES industrial stormwater permits.

The problem addressed by the stormwater quality program is polluted runoff from streets, parking lots, and buildings, which contains debris, chemicals, sediment, or other pollutants. The main control method is use of best management practices, which can involve a range of structures and programs. For example, filters or settling basins can be used to trap pollutants and a street sweeping program can be implemented.

Flood Control Services

In my graduate class about water-resources management, we track the daily news about water, and the number of stories about flood disasters is overwhelming. In 2010, the major story was an epic flood in Pakistan that killed 1,500 and affected millions of other people. The disease and hardship go well beyond the media accounts because so many individual untold stories are involved. These flood problems continue, and flooding remains the most costly natural disaster in most countries, even in the United States. The Pakistan flood was due to big-river problems, but flood threats occur in other forms that include major urban floods, coastal and wind-induced flooding, flash floods, and dam-break floods. All of these can involve tremendous loss of life and damage. In some countries, devastation and loss of life can be extensive and threaten the economies and societies of whole nations.

The flood management community has learned a lot about adapting to floods. The United States suffered many devastating floods as it became an advanced nation, so it initially developed responses in the form of flood control programs that were based mostly on engineered structures. Its earliest programs began with local efforts based on levee districts, conservancy districts, and individual landowner efforts. However, after experiencing devastating floods, such as the Johnstown (Pennsylvania) flood of 1889 and the Galveston flood of 1900, the nation began to develop larger-scale flood policy and flood control works with federally supported reservoirs as the favored solution. This was an era of faith in constructed works, and by the 1960s the government and its Corps of Engineers had completed many dams, levees, floodwalls, and flood channels.

Then, the nation began to see that such structural measures did not always solve the problems, and emphasis changed to nonstructural measures, with the national Flood Insurance Act of 1968 becoming the centerpiece of flood policy. Congress passed the act to establish the National Flood Insurance Program (NFIP) and enable property owners to buy flood insurance if their community participates in the program and passes floodplain management regulations. Insurance was to replace disaster response and recovery, with the high costs of repairing flood-damaged buildings and their contents. The concept of the NFIP has moved continuously toward more nonstructural and environmental solutions and away from pure protection of property and economic objectives.

The antecedents of the Flood Insurance Act were the flood disasters during the 1920s and 1930s that led to the Flood Control Act of 1936, which introduced benefit-cost analysis to federal projects. The 1927 Mississippi River flood was particularly devastating and led to great social disruptions. A federal flood insurance program was proposed but not passed during the 1950s because it became clear that private insurance could not provide coverage because of catastrophic flooding and the resulting inability to develop actuarial rates to reflect the risk. After Hurricane Betsy in 1956, Congress passed the 1965 Southeast Hurricane Disaster Relief Act, which authorized a feasibility study of a national flood insurance program. After several other studies, a document named "A Unified National Program for Managing Flood Losses" (House Document 465) was prepared with five major goals: improve basic knowledge about flood hazards, coordinate and plan new developments in the floodplain, provide technical services, move toward a practical national program of flood insurance, and adjust federal flood control policy to sound criteria and changing needs. This provided the basis for the National Flood Insurance Act of 1968.

A problem occurred in that providing subsidized flood insurance was not enough of an incentive to adopt flood insurance programs. In 1972, Tropical Storm Agnes caused so much river flooding that Congress passed the Flood Disaster Protection Act of 1973 to prohibit financial assistance in floodplains in communities that did not participate in the NFIP. This led to a Mandatory Flood Insurance Purchase Requirement, which resulted in many more communities joining the NFIP.

Today, nearly 20,000 communities participate in the NFIP, including nearly all with significant flood hazards. In addition to flood insurance and floodplain management regulations, the NFIP identifies and maps floodplains to provide data for floodplain management programs and to rate properties for flood insurance with flood insurance rate maps (FIRMs). The FIRMs reduce the extent of federal subsidy in the program.

To access subsidized insurance for existing buildings, communities must protect structures through floodplain management ordinances. After a FIRM is available, the 1968 act requires full actuarial rates on all buildings constructed or improved substantially. Construction techniques have extended the useful life of pre-FIRM buildings, but their numbers are decreasing due to flooding, redevelopment, natural attrition, acquisition, and flood control projects.

The National Flood Insurance Fund finances the NFIP, and premiums are deposited in it to cover losses and operating costs. The NFIP has authority to borrow up to $1.5 billion from the Treasury Department, to be repaid with interest. Initially and until 1986 program expenses and flood hazard mapping were supported by congressional appropriations. Now, expenses are paid from premiums and a fee on policies. The program continues to operate with three basic components: identifying and mapping flood-prone communities, floodplain management regulations, and flood insurance.

Meanwhile, the nation came to understand more that improved nonstructural approaches were needed. After the Great Mississippi River Floods of 1993, a national review committee wrote:

> By controlling runoff, managing ecosystems for all their benefits, planning the use of the land and identifying those areas at risk, many hazards can be avoided. Where the risk cannot be avoided, damage minimization approaches, such as elevation and relocation of buildings or construction of reservoirs or flood protection structures, are used only when they can be integrated into a systems approach to flood damage reduction in the basin. (Interagency Floodplain Management Review Committee, 1994)

Today, while the strategy of building dams to control floods and reclaim land is outdated, some flood control structures are still being built. These include smaller dams and reservoirs, local detention ponds, dikes, levees, and floodwalls. Also, bridges must be designed to withstand floods, and culverts and conveyance structures are built where required. In addition to flood insurance and floodplain regulations, nonstructural flood programs include disaster preparedness and assistance, floodproofing, flood forecasting and warning systems and information and education.

Flood insurance is not without its critics. The U.S. system encourages people to live in flood-prone areas and may undermine the private, unsubsidized flood insurance market. Practices in other countries vary from no compensation to victims, to compensation only in hardship cases, to compensation only by degree of hardship.

So, flood control services operate at two levels. At the local level, they focus on controlling land use in the floodplains. At regional and riverine levels, they are more large-scale and focus on hard-to-measure benefits that affect many people. Thus, national-level flood management is mainly through federal agencies. The most active of these are listed in Table 6.1.

Many state governments also have offices to coordinate federal flood programs but are not as involved as federal agencies. The floodplain management offices in state government are normally in natural- or water-resources departments, but in some cases these programs are located in state emergency offices.

TABLE 6.1 Major Federal Agencies with Flood Responsibilities

FEMA	Lead agency for coordinating flood policy. Issues reports on flooding and software on flood loss estimation (HAZUS)
Corps of Engineers	Major agency with flood control responsibility
NOAA	Operates gages and advisory programs on flood magnitudes
USGS	Operates stream gaging network and issues bulletins about flooding
FHWA	Controls planning and design of highways and bridges that are involved in flooding incidents
NRCS	Controls network on small watershed programs, including reservoirs with flood control purposes; operates snow gages
TVA	Operates a regional network of flood control reservoirs
FERC	Relicenses and regulates power dams that are involved in flood control
BUREC	Operates a number of dams that are involved in flood control

Local governments are active in regulating floodways and responding to flood hazard within their jurisdictions. At the intrastate regional and county level, flooding and stormwater require regional management because the problems do not obey jurisdictional lines. County government may be the best place to locate programs, and in some cases, special districts are organized for that purpose. The following list shows a few examples of multijurisdictional programs, including county government. All counties shown and most other organizations are members of the National Association of Flood and Stormwater Management Agencies (NAFSMA).

- Albuquerque Metropolitan Arroyo Flood Control Authority (NM)
- Clark County Regional Flood Control District (NV)
- Connecticut River Valley Flood Control Commission (CT)
- Contra Costa County Flood Control and Water Conservation District (CA)
- Urban Drainage and Flood Control District (CO)
- Flood Control District of Maricopa County (AZ)
- Fresno Metropolitan Flood Control District (CA)
- Kern County Water Agency (CA)
- King County (WA)
- Miami Conservancy District (Ohio)
- Napa County Flood Control & Water Conservation District (CA)
- Orange County Flood Control District (CA)
- Pima County Flood Control District (AZ)
- Santa Clara Valley Water District (CA)

UTILITIES

The difficulty of measuring stormwater and flood control benefits always meant the facilities were difficult to finance and, as cities developed their stormwater and floodplain management programs, they faced many dilemmas about how to organize and finance them. Stormwater programs were usually organized under a public works department or lumped in with streets management.

Cities began to realize that the property tax was too limited as a financing mechanism for stormwater, and the concept of the stormwater utility was born (Cyre, 1982). The idea of the stormwater utility is that the service provided and its beneficiaries can be identified and measured and that user charges can be levied accordingly. The legal standing of the fees and charges is based on specific benefits, which are mainly found in the drainage of private property. I participated in a 1970s Colorado research project in which a specific bill was passed in the legislature to define these benefits, at least in a limited way.

Fort Collins was one of the first communities to embrace the stormwater utility concept, and now many other U.S. communities have developed utilities, although the concept is far from universal. Fort Collins's program had its basis in a 1976 ordinance and was initiated in 1980. From the beginning, financing was via a monthly stormwater fee and a connection or impact fee. The monthly fee, which was phased in, was initially about $2 per month per house, split among operation and maintenance (O&M) and capital. The connection fee for new residential developments ranged from about $1,200 to $2,000 per acre or from $200 to $500 per house depending on lot size (Engemoen and Krempel, 1985).

Today, Fort Collins manages stormwater within a combined utility department that also includes electric power, water supply, and wastewater. In another city, stormwater management in Raleigh, North Carolina, is 1 of 11 divisions in the Public Works Department. Both cities include similar program elements: stormwater services, water quality, infrastructure management and O&M, development review, and floodplain management. Both programs are entirely funded by stormwater fees.

Financing under the stormwater utility concept has some problems. It is difficult to separate general and specific benefits of stormwater facilities because drainage systems are interconnected, making it hard to identify exactly who pays and who benefits for each project. The way around this dilemma is to mix the issues together into drainage basins, which is the case in Fort Collins. However, the city has moved away from differential fees among the basins and now has uniform fees. As long as fees are uniform across a city, there seems to be little controversy over their use instead of a general tax.

The initial Fort Collins stormwater fees were relatively modest and did not attract much attention, but that has changed now. However, in Fort Collins some local leaders are concerned about whether charges levied in one part of town are properly used in another part for stormwater projects. However, as long as the monthly charge is small enough, people do not seem to object. Once the charge increases, then the objections begin. Monthly charges and connection fees are based on lot size and land use. Currently, the connection fee for a new home in Fort Collins is about $1,100 and a typical monthly bill is about $15.

Given the higher fees and additional controversies, Fort Collins organized an assessment of its stormwater program in 2008, and I was a member of the review panel. Our experiences could help other communities with similar policy questions. We interviewed the staff and all city council members, then reported our general findings to the council at a work session. Stormwater fees, both the level and their distribution, were an issue. The council wanted a review of standards and to know whether the storm drains were overengineered and the levels of protection were too high. While there was no disagreement about a policy of uniform charges across the city, the council was concerned about benefits and costs to citizens and businesses, especially where convenience and aesthetics are the goals. How impact fees are assessed was an issue, especially where a development is charged a fee even if it mitigates its impact through land modifications. The council also wanted to see if the city was making more land developable or creating more open space through its flood programs, and it wanted an explanation of whether the floodplains are overregulated.

PROFESSIONAL AND TRADE ASSOCIATIONS

Because they are hybrid services, there is no single professional or trade association for flood and stormwater programs. However, the services have been receiving more attention from broad-based associations and the technical media. Civil engineers and landscape architects give particular attention to stormwater, and their professional associations and publication outlets provide technical information and guidelines. In particular, the American Society of Civil Engineers has published extensive materials about stormwater and flooding for many years. The American Public Works Association also devotes attention to stormwater agency practices.

The National Association of Flood & Stormwater Management Agencies was organized in 1978 with a Washington office to represent stormwater and flood agencies. For the most part its membership comprises local agencies, such as city governments and flood control districts.

Another flood-related association is the Association of State Floodplain Managers, which tracks floodplain management policy and represents flood hazard specialists of local, state, and federal governments, as well as their support groups.

Given its link to land development, stormwater involves a wide range of design and public works professionals. In ways it is more interdisciplinary than water supply and wastewater and there is an ongoing demand for professional development literature and training. Given the rise of interest in stormwater quality, the Forester Company launched a magazine titled *Stormwater* and runs an annual meeting called StormCon.

BUSINESS ISSUES OF THE SECTOR

The cost and financing of stormwater and flood control programs are major concerns in many areas. While they are not implicated as much in the aging infrastructure issue as water and wastewater systems are, they still cost billions of dollars annually to manage and are major expenditures for local governments, which are strapped for funding across the board.

The nation's flood insurance program will continue to be controversial because it involves large sums of money and risk allocation. Subsidies from the federal budget are increasingly controversial due to the nation's debt level. It is difficult to map floodplains and issues such as whether you recognize levees will continue to make mapping a complex task. Regulating land use in floodplains is a continuing point of controversy and, as this is being written, Colorado is thinking of restricting critical facilities from 500-year floodplain, which would be a tighter policy than in the past.

The interdependence of stormwater and flood corridors with natural systems opens attractive possibilities for combining stormwater and green development. We see this in use of river corridors to preserve natural systems and for recreation, such as bike trails along streams. However, it also creates possibilities for conflicts between environmental and economic objectives. Stormwater quality will also continue to be a major environmental issue, and cleaning up nonpoint-source runoff will be very expensive and difficult.

At the global scale, disastrous flooding remains a critical issue around the world. As I explained earlier, flooding is the costliest natural disaster of all. In a typical year, many deaths and losses occurred from flooding around the world. Both riverine and coastal flooding cause death and destruction, and more world-shaking events such as Katrina and the Great Tsunami can be expected in the future.

Given that structural solutions have failed to protect us from events such as these, the emphasis on local solutions has evolved out of necessity. Local solutions can address many issues, but the regional interconnection of stormwater systems requires cooperation that can be difficult politically in some cases. Local solutions to stormwater and flood problems can seem expensive and be hard to understand by citizens and public officials alike. The problems are out of sight, out of mind until emergencies occur, and then everyone wonders why someone did not prevent the problems.

CHAPTER 7

Industrial Water and the Water-Energy Nexus

While water-supply and wastewater utilities handle most public water services, large sectors of self-supplied industries and electric power producers act independently of them and also handle significant quantities of water and wastewater. In some cases, their systems are as large and complex as those of small and medium water utilities. These water-handling industries and electric power producers have diverse needs for water and wastewater services and comprise an important market. In this chapter, we combine what is known as industrial water with thermoelectric cooling water and with other energy-related water uses and impacts, such as refinery water, process water for resource development, and even stormwater residuals from oil and gas sites. This lumps all efforts by industries of diverse types and energy producers together into a sector that, for convenience, we are calling industrial and energy water.

The category of industrial water use is a hybrid anyway, and the classification of water use as "industrial" is not rigid. The businesses that provide equipment and services to such water users do not agree about the classification (Michaud, 2009). There are many types of industrial and energy water uses and impacts, but it is worth the effort to analyze them as a group because the scale of their water-handling and impacts on water make this sector a major player in the water business. When you add energy water use to industrial water and wastewater, the impact of the sector is on the same order of magnitude as the better-known municipal water and wastewater sectors. They are similar in that they must employ skilled workforces that perform the same general functions as water and wastewater utilities.

Industrial water users are diverse and create markets for many types of water-handling equipment. Due to this diversity, there is no central source of statistics about the industrial water market. While data on water used through public systems is fairly good, data on industrial water use is dispersed and harder to find. In the first place, if an industry is connected to a public system, it is one of the user categories, and you must drill into the utility's database to determine percentages of water use by industries.

In the second place, much of industrial water use is self-supplied, and while we have data on totals it is difficult to know how much is used by particular types of industries.

This chapter explains the range of industrial and energy water uses and services and how industries and energy producers develop, process, use, and discharge water. Other chapters explain the products and services they use.

CONFIGURATION OF INDUSTRIAL AND ENERGY WATER SYSTEMS

Industries in any country must take necessary actions to secure their water services, whether public water and wastewater systems are available or not. In many cases, they are connected to public water-supply systems but have their own wastewater systems and discharge permits. In other cases, they may be connected to public systems for both water and wastewater. These variations are shown on Figure 7.1, which illustrates an industry that is entirely self-supplied with water and wastewater, another one that gets public water supply

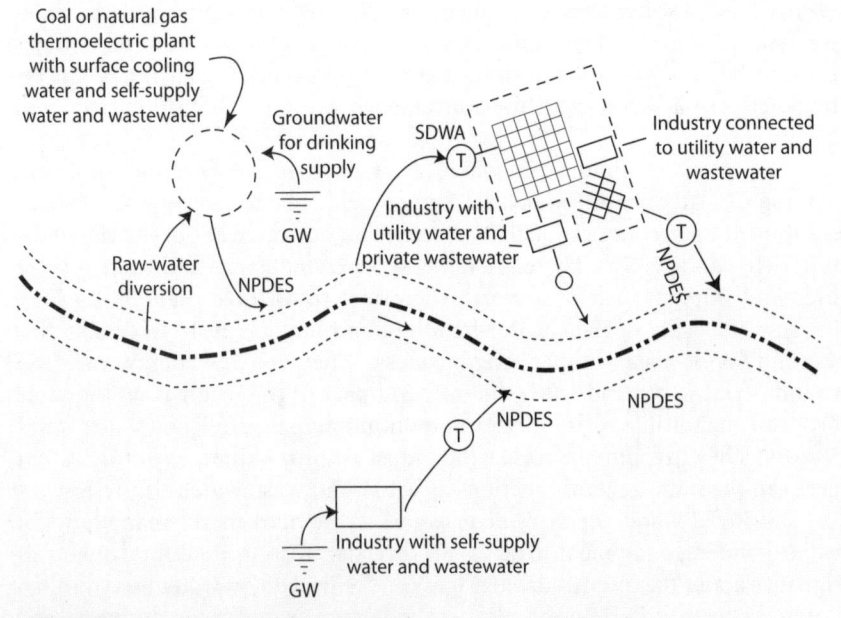

FIGURE 7.1   Examples of industrial and energy water systems

but has its own wastewater system and discharge permit, and another one that is connected to city services for both water and wastewater. Also shown is an electric generating plant with surface water for cooling and its own self-supply water and wastewater systems for the workforce and other uses.

If industries are not connected to public systems, then their only choice is to be self-supplied. In developing countries in particular, where adequate public water supply infrastructure may be lacking, industries often must develop their water services or none will be available. This can create a difficult problem of regional water management in developing countries, where uncontrolled industries exploit water resources in an uncoordinated manner, causing spinoff problems such as groundwater declines, land subsidence, flooding, pollution, and related issues.

Sometimes industries might provide water supply or wastewater services to an adjacent community as an extra service or ancillary system. This might arise, for example, in a "company town," which was built in the first place to support an industry, construction project or mining operation. A number of the Community Water Systems in the United States are of this type. USEPA's (2010a) Community Water Systems Study (CWSS) shows that of the 52,000 CWS, 51 percent are privately owned as for-profit businesses and not-for-profit entities. About 20 percent of all systems are ancillary systems, where the primary business is not water supply but water is an integral part of the principal business and the systems often do not bill customers separately for water.

OVERALL USE OF WATER BY INDUSTRIES

Worldwide, about 22 percent of all water use is industrial water for energy, process water, and for products, which can be called embedded water or virtual water (World Business Council for Sustainable Development, 2005). Many of the industries around the world rely on water piped from utility systems, but a large fraction of them are self-supplied. In any case, once water supply is obtained from the public system, their processing systems may not differ that much from self-supplied systems.

Estimates of U.S. industrial water use by USGS, presented in Chapter 2, show that thermoelectric cooling-water withdrawals dwarf those for other categories of industry. However, manufacturing and process industries process and manage water more intensively and require relatively more infrastructure than the large-volume cooling systems. The estimates are derived from individual facility reports for state or federal permit programs that require reporting of industrial withdrawals or return flows and from employee water-use coefficients by industry group.

To estimate the total industrial water use in the United States, the self-supplied water must be added to industrial water provided through public water systems. We lack a recent estimate of this total, and the data are hard to collect because each utility is different, but we have a good sense of the overall totals. Of the 44,500 mgd of public supply reported by USGS in 2005, about 12 percent goes to industrial uses. Another 17,000 mgd is provided through self-supply, so the national total of industrial water supply is about 22,000 mgd. This data is consistent with utility surveys through AWWA (see Chapter 2), so we can have some confidence in this as an order-of-magnitude estimate. For comparison purposes, this is about half of the total water withdrawn for all public systems.

INDUSTRIAL CLASSIFICATION AND WATER USE

Classifying water for industrial uses is more difficult than for residential or even commercial uses. The difficulty is caused by the diversity of industrial types and the fact that water is used for processing, cooling, and other purposes, as well as for human uses that mirror those in a home or business. As USGS (2010a) explained, industrial water uses are for fabricating, processing, washing, diluting, cooling, or transporting a product; incorporating water into a product; or for sanitation needs within the manufacturing facility.

The two-digit codes of the North American Industrial Classification System show that the main industrial water use is for manufacturing and that commercial uses include diverse categories such as retail trade, health care, and arts and entertainment. Expanding manufacturing codes to three or four digits produces a list of categories to identify manufacturing water uses by industry type. This generates a long list that includes manufacturing of food, beverage and tobacco products, textiles, wood products, paper, and chemicals.

USGS explained this further:

> The industries that produce metals, wood and paper products, chemicals, gasoline and oils, and those invaluable grabber utensils your dad uses to pull out the car keys you dropped into the garbage disposal are major users of water. Probably every manufactured product uses water during some part of the production process. Industrial water use includes water used for such purposes as fabricating, processing, washing, diluting, cooling, or transporting a product; incorporating water into a product; or for sanitation needs within the manufacturing facility. Some industries that use large amounts of water produce such commodities as food, paper, chemicals, refined petroleum, or primary metals.

Historically, the manufacturing centers in the United States used the most water for industrial purposes. This includes the Great Lakes and Ohio regions including, for example, the steel industry area around Gary, Indiana. The USGS water-use reports include survey information on water use by states. USGS (2009) wrote:

> As you might expect, states such as Indiana, Texas, and West Virginia used a lot of water in 2000 for industrial purposes. Louisiana was first, using about 2,680 million gallons of water per day, mainly in the chemical and paper industries. Louisiana, Indiana, and Texas accounted for almost 38 percent of total industrial withdrawals. The largest fresh ground-water withdrawals were in Georgia, Louisiana, and Texas, which together accounted for 23 percent of the total fresh ground-water withdrawals. Texas accounted for 71 percent of the saline surface-water withdrawals for industry.

A report series by the U.S. Energy Information Agency (USEIA, 2010) provides information on energy-related water use, under the assumption that high energy-using industries might also use more water. Table 7.1 is a list of industries to show how chemicals, paper, primary metals, food, and nonmetallic mineral products are the highest energy users.

To prepare this section, I searched for up-to-date summaries of industrial water use and forecasting, but it proved difficult to find summarized

TABLE 7.1 Energy Use by Industries

Industry	Energy Use, Trillion BTUs
Chemicals	5,149
Paper	2,354
Primary metals	1,736
Food	1,186
Nonmetallic mineral products	1,114
Transportation equipment	477
Wood products	451
Fabricated metal products	396
Plastics and rubber products	337
Machinery	204
Textile mills	178
Computer and electronic products	142
Electrical equipment, appliances, and components	103

Data source: USEIA, 2010

information. During a 1970s research program about urban water use, a report on industrial water tapped into data of the Department of Commerce (Tucker, Millan, and Burt, 1972). If this data is still collected it is not available in an organized way. To prepare their text on forecasting water use, Baumann et al. (1998) searched for statistics on water use by industry. They found scattered data, such as California industrial water use, but it dates back to 1979 and, with increased water efficiency, it seems likely that the data are not current. My conclusion is that no centralized database of industrial water use is available and that the industries and their water uses are so variable that a study could only characterize the statistics but could not reach industry-wide conclusions.

The future of industrial water use depends on the future of manufacturing itself and on economic variables such as the cost of water and the availability of alternatives, such as recycling. It is apparent that overall industrial water use in the United States has declined since the 1980s, consistent with the decline in the manufacturing base. In spite of outsourcing and offshoring a lot of manufacturing, the United States is still the world's largest manufacturer. However, the manufacturing economy has been changing for a long time and old industrial water-use statistics are outdated. The USBLS (2010a) forecasts that overall manufacturing employment will decline due to productivity gains, automation, and international competition. Sectors to decline include household appliance manufacturing, machinery manufacturing, apparel manufacturing, and computer and electronic product manufacturing. Sectors to increase include pharmaceutical and medicine manufacturing.

Some U.S. regions are beginning to tout their abundant water supplies as an attractor for manufacturing. See, for example, the discussion of the Milwaukee water cluster in Chapter 23.

INDUSTRIAL WATER TREATMENT

Much of the expenditure for industrial water is on water treatment, which requires more varied and complex processes than municipal water treatment. For municipal water the goal is to produce a similar quality of safe water for human uses, but with industrial water you require many different qualities for different applications and you have to handle a wide range of wastewaters.

Section 204(b)(1) of the 1972 Clean Water Act required industrial cost recovery (ICR) to ensure that manufacturers and other businesses paid their full share of treatment costs. However, this proved difficult to implement. The CWA Amendments of 1977 required an assessment of the ICR program, and it concluded that it was not achieving its purposes. The reasons for the conclusions were that changes in the tax code offset any subsidies to industry provided by the Construction Grants Program, ICR had an insignificant effect on industrial decision making or water conservation, and ICR was hard to manage, especially for small communities. It concluded that the user-charge system worked better than the ICR requirements (USEPA, 1978).

The concept of the ICR program was to expire after 30 years from the date of a construction grant, so most requirements have expired anyway. Today, industrial user charges in communities vary widely according to local ordinances.

To utilities, the concept of industrial water management is to require industrial pretreatment and to levy charges for industrial water discharges into sewers according to strength of wastewater. In my community, Fort Collins, for example, we have very light industry. The city requires monthly water rates for commercial uses based on meter size, and a small industry without significant process water would fall into this category. The levy of wastewater rates is similar. The city has an industrial pretreatment program that ensures that industrial users meet applicable pretreatment standards and do not damage the treatment plants. This will prevent the introduction of toxic and incompatible pollutants into the treatment system and biosolids system. Fort Collins also has special guidance for pharmaceutical waste disposal. The city negotiates with industries one at a time if they have significant industrial wastewaters, but most are like commercial users and do not require special treatment.

To treat water for their own uses, to implement their pretreatment programs or to treat their wastewaters for disposal through their own NPDES permits, industries must choose among a broad array of processes.

If they require special water qualities for their manufactured products, such as semiconductors, beverages, or pharmaceuticals, industries must assess their source waters and quality requirements and take actions to purify the water, often going well beyond the treatment levels of public water supplies. At the same time, they may treat water for domestic uses within their facilities.

For cooling water and boilers, industries must deal with scaling and corrosion. Warm water is often conducive to bacterial growth, and industries must take care to avoid problems such as Legionnaires Disease.

Sometimes effluent from one process might be reused in other processes, with obvious lower total water consumption, lower charges for effluents and lower energy costs due to the recovery of heat.

Information on industrial water treatment is available from diverse sources. For example, GE Power and Water (2010) offers an online handbook with guidance on water chemistry and basis processes, such as aeration, clarification, filtration, precipitation softening, ion exchange, membrane systems, and boiler water systems. It also addresses special topics, such as boiler corrosion control and other issues and cooling water system issues, such as deposit and scale control and microbiological control.

Industries are subject to the same general rules as municipalities for diverting water from streams, pumping groundwater and discharging effluents to receiving water (see Chapters 5 and 6). This exposes them to a range of regulatory controls that can add substantially to the cost of doing business. When water services are critical to business success, as in the brewing industry, the industries will have specialized staff to deal with them. Here in Colorado, for example, we have large brewers and microbrewers, and they are normally represented among water users and environmental interests in local and state water business meetings.

WATER-ENERGY NEXUS

The uses of water for thermoelectric cooling and to generate hydropower are well established parts of the water management puzzle, but many other connections between water and energy have been added to create the water-energy nexus, as it has come to be called. This is an appropriate term because water and energy are closely related in so many ways. Energy production is a prime issue for the future, and it will place stresses on water systems in different ways. Energy issues continue to move to center stage, such as higher oil prices, reduced oil and gas reserves, geopolitics, and the 2010 Gulf of Mexico oil crisis. The U.S. Department of Energy (USDOE) studied the water-energy nexus and noted:

> *The continued security and economic health of the United States depends on a sustainable supply of both energy and water. These two critical resources are inextricably and reciprocally linked; the production of energy requires large volumes of water while the treatment and distribution of water is equally dependent upon readily available, low-cost energy. The nation's ability to continue providing both clean, affordable energy and water is being seriously challenged by a number of emerging issues. (Sandia National Laboratories, 2010)*

After a round of studying the issues, the water-energy nexus report was submitted by USDOE (2006) to Congress in January 2007. The study group focused on how the United States developed its water and energy resources in the form of coal, oil, natural gas, and uranium. The water is needed for resource extraction, refining and processing, and transportation, as well as for hydroelectric generation and cooling and emissions scrubbing in thermoelectric generation. Many power plants, especially newer ones, withdraw less water but consume more than in the past by evaporative cooling. Much of the expected population growth will occur in the Southeast and the West, which is drier.

Technologies, including alternative cooling, wind power, and photovoltaics, to reduce water use in electric power generation are available, but they are expensive. Water use in the extraction and processing of current transportation fuels is small, but the United States may replace petroleum and natural gas with higher-water-using domestic fuels, including biofuels, synfuel from coal, hydrogen, and possibly oil shale.

The linkages between water and energy seem sure to drive up the demands for water and to increase the costs and difficulties in resolving conflicts. Electric power use seems certain to rise, especially if plug-in electric vehicles catch on. The major water impact is to cool thermoelectric plants, requiring massive quantities of water. The most recent USGS report (see Chapter 2) shows that thermoelectric water withdrawals are 49 percent of total withdrawals. For the most part, this water is diverted from streams and then returned with an added heat load after the water cools electric power plants. Some of this cooling water is from saline sources, such as bays, estuaries, and even seawater. Thermoelectric water use increased greatly to 1980, reflecting the rise in electricity production. It declined during the early 1980s recession, but now it seems on the rise again, although slower. Electricity production has continued to rise, even through the recent recession, so any reductions in water use will reflect greater efficiency and environmental rules.

Renewable energy sources will not alleviate the pressure on water. Production of biofuels such as ethanol is based on availability of crops such as corn. Other biofuel sources include sugar cane, which is a major source of energy in Brazil, for example. All of these crops require massive amounts of water. Irrigation water is already a major consumer of scarce supplies in the West, and if an added load is place on regional water supplies to produce crops for biofuels, it is apt to overtax an already fragile system.

Hydroelectricity is a major source of renewable energy (see Chapter 9) and seems destined for a resurgence, after many years of decline as a percentage of total national energy production. While wind and solar are promising sources of renewable energy, hydro offers the added advantage of storage, both in reservoirs and in pumped storage systems. Pumped storage can operate offline but regular hydro reservoirs are normally on stream and place large impacts on aquatic systems.

Coal bed methane is an emerging source of energy and its exploitation may lead to "produced water," which is groundwater that becomes available as a byproduct of gas production. Produced water may represent a valuable new resource in some arid areas.

Electric power and water have other interfaces, such as the strong dependence of water management on the availability of electric power for pumping and to operate control systems. Water systems serving critical facilities such as hospitals require backup power so they can continue to operate even when electric power goes down.

Groundwater heating and cooling systems have significant potential for energy savings by using the temperature of groundwater as a source of heating and cooling. The water is withdrawn and then returned to aquifers, which serve as large heat and energy reservoirs.

The major concern about energy water use and sustainable water management is the negative impacts that energy production has on water. While environmental and safety problems seem to suppress demand for coal, its use will not go away and coal mining has severe impacts on water systems, such as mine runoff toxicity to ground and surface water sources. Oil and gas production has a range of environmental impacts, which include runoff from drilling areas, road construction, and problems such as the blowout in the Gulf of Mexico in 2010. If oil shale ever becomes a significant source of energy, it will require massive amounts of water for processing and draw resources away from other users. Nuclear wastes threaten to pollute groundwater, while storage of fly ash on the sites of generation plants can be risky to surface water systems. In 2008, the Tennessee Valley Authority experienced a massive coal ash spill. Air emissions lead to acid rain, and nonpoint-source runoff from oil and gas operations threatens surface and groundwater sources. Uranium mining is currently a hot issue where I live, with possible pollution of groundwater. Natural-gas fracking has caused groundwater pollution in the East, and many other environmental concerns can be noted related to energy development.

Energy production has a higher political profile than water management, so water policy needs reevaluation because many energy-related water issues seem to be taken for granted. For example, people who are quick to promote biofuels might not be aware of the heavy impacts on water withdrawals, water quality, and ecosystems. It will be hard to come up with new water supplies for energy production, especially in headwaters regions that are vulnerable. Better data and indicators are needed. Looming behind energy issues is the specter of global warming and, while it is of global importance, attention to it lures policy makers away from state and local issues that determine success or failure of water management. That is, actions to respond to climate change are required more at the local level than at the national level, although national policy has some influence on local choices.

FUTURE ISSUES FOR INDUSTRIAL AND ENERGY WATER USE

It seems certain that industrial activity in the United States will continue to diversify and change from the old model of the basic industries that use large quantities of water to a newer model that responds to the global economy. This will not be bad news for the water business but will require it to respond to a greater variety of water needs, but perhaps not to increases in the demand for water volumes. The corollary is that many of the high water- and energy-using industries may locate themselves in developing countries where they can access resources more easily. This trend has been going on for decades, but what might be new is the realization that the trend will continue to evolve and it might even involve some rebounds. For example, the Milwaukee area is using its large water capacity to attract industry (see Chapter 23).

Energy water use for the future seems to be a larger issue than manufacturing water use, both in terms of actual water demands and of impacts on water resources. As the world moves toward a population of seven billion people, how will it meet rising expectations without rapid increases in energy production? Just one issue alone—the emergence of plug-in vehicles—could dramatically increase the demand for electric power, with its many demands and impacts on water.

Figure 7.2 shows trends in industrial and thermoelectric water use and electric power production, superimposed with manufacturing as a percentage of the economy. Data were plotted from USGS water use records (see Chapter 2), from USBEA (2010) GDP-by-industry data, and from historical records of the USEIA (2006). The water-use data show withdrawals, and the industrial data are for self-supplied water, which should be representative of trends in total industrial water use. The GDP data are manufacturing as a percentage of total GDP on the basis of value added. The electric power production was plotted by taking the beginning and end of the records (1950 and 2009) and connecting them by a straight line to show the trend,

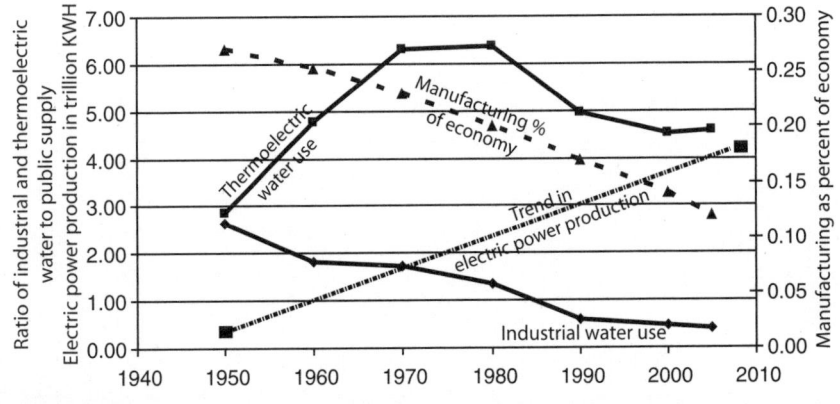

FIGURE 7.2 Historical trends in manufacturing and energy production

but the annual fluctuations are not shown. For example, there were four years of actual declines, 1982, 2001, 2008, and 2009.

The graphs require interpretation because they show ratios. The decline in industrial water use is actually more rapid than the drop in manufacturing as a percentage of the economy because it is an index of industrial to public water use. The thermoelectric water use is also an index to public water use, and it shows the rise, then fall in the use, followed by today's slower rise.

Both industrial and energy water users impact water quality dramatically. The impacts of industries such as food processors and paper mills is well known among water quality managers, but these are not apt to be the major issues for the future. Instead, new threats such as more hot water from energy cooling and unregulated nutrient runoff to gradually degrade ecosystems will be of concern. A principal example of the latter is the hypoxic zone off the coast of Louisiana caused by the nutrient- and sediment-rich runoff from the U.S. corn production zone.

Future risks in industrial and energy water uses will be similar to those for public water systems: that infrastructure failures will occur, that pollution will get out of hand to create regulatory risks, and that disasters—such as the mine waste failures—will happen.

CHAPTER 8

Water for Food Production

As the world confronts water scarcity and hunger at the same time, major changes must come to irrigation water management, which is the largest global user of water and a sector that has special issues of finance, social, and environmental impacts and management capacity. We tend to think of irrigation as a sector of large farms, massive quantities of water, and heavy environmental impacts, but the sector also includes small-scale systems, landscaping, and, in developing countries, a lot of subsistence farming. In fact, the field of irrigation water management is changing in its focus, and in ways it is experiencing an identity crisis as it moves to a new paradigm. This identity crisis is evident in the dichotomy that, while it is clear that irrigation is an urgent issue in feeding the world, technical fields such as irrigation engineering seem to be falling in popularity. This is not because they are not important. To the contrary, it is just that we are calling them by different names and integrating them with other issues.

In many cases it is difficult for irrigators at any scale to afford the infrastructure and management systems they require. As the same time, larger irrigators may be under attack from environmentalists and from water developers, who seek to buy out their supplies and dry up their farmland. These issues lead to different economic calculations in the irrigation sector than we find in public water and wastewater.

While the irrigation sector has some excellent and professional management institutions, it also has many small operators who must perform water management as a sideline. Improving the management capacity of irrigation institutions and water handlers is thus a critical issue, especially in developing countries, where most of the hunger problems are found.

The irrigation water management challenges are to make irrigation more efficient and to integrate it better with other water-handling sectors. In seeking these goals, the irrigation sector offers many opportunities for water products and services as well as to provide new supplies for municipal and industrial uses through cooperative ventures. This chapter explains the irrigation sector and provides a summary of its major issues and opportunities.

IRRIGATION AROUND THE WORLD

In traveling around the world on engineering projects, I have seen irrigation practiced in different forms. I experienced Colorado irrigation up close through engineering experiences that included relocating irrigation ditches for highway construction, avoiding using irrigation systems for stormwater conveyance, working with ditch companies to convert irrigation water rights to municipal uses, and doing stream-aquifer studies to implement a new Colorado groundwater law.

In 1969 I accompanied a group of students and teachers to Chihuahua, Mexico, and saw a dry region that is totally dependent on irrigation for economic and social development. This type of issue had been the basis for educational programs at Colorado State University, which developed programs to support pioneer irrigation farmers in Colorado and by the 1950s was working in other nations through foreign-assistance programs. My professors had worked on irrigation issues such as the big Link Canals in Pakistan, as well as large systems in the United States. In 1975 I participated in a water-planning mission to Egypt, where we studied irrigation along the Nile River and in the Delta. Later, I worked with professors and students to evaluate many water problems in the irrigation systems of Egypt, Pakistan, and Indonesia (Rijsberman, 1987; Sjarief, 1995).

My Colorado experience includes irrigating a small alfalfa field, which has a water right under a local mutual ditch company, where I learned to schedule the water, clean the ditch, operate the turnouts, and irrigate a whole field with a limited supply of water. Our flood irrigation system does not work very well, so I have been thinking about a sprinkler system, in an amateur way. Through these experiences, I've gained an appreciation for irrigated farming and how most people understand little about it. It's common for new arrivals in Colorado to look at irrigation systems and quickly conclude that irrigation is a waste of water. This seems shortsighted when the real issue is much more complex. It's true that the economic return from the application of a unit of irrigation water is normally less than in municipal and industrial uses, but this ignores many social and environmental issues, as well as how river and watershed systems work. The lesson is that those who govern irrigation systems require careful study before jumping to conclusions. The impacts are great and much is at stake around the world.

Irrigation around the world involves water systems and organizations that range in scale from large government-sponsored schemes to small farm and individual systems that may involve simply wells and local distribution systems. Irrigation is both a water-handling sector and a water-using customer. For the most part, the people who use water for irrigation are closely involved with their water-handling organizations and this attribute distinguishes irrigation from the water-handling sectors where the organizations that deliver water are separated from the water users.

Irrigation is directly connected to farm economies and is of great importance to people in many regions who struggle to increase their individual and collective food security, so it has many social as well as economic and environmental impacts. Global hunger and the aspirations of billions of people for better diets mean that the requirements for irrigation water will not diminish but will increase. The Food and Agriculture Organization (FAO, 2010) of the United Nations tracks statistics on world hunger. It estimates that 925 million people, or around one in seven on the planet, are undernourished. Most of these people live in developing countries, many of which are in irrigated regions. Better crop production is only one of the measures required to reduce hunger, but it is obvious that when you add growing population to the already-serious problem of hunger, it points to the need for expanding irrigation systems.

Given the large volumes of water that it uses, irrigation is controversial for its environmental effects, especially in the United States and other developed countries with extensive irrigation. It withdraws surface and groundwater from natural systems, adds pollutants and can ruin soils through salinization when drainage is poor. These impacts must be carefully managed through improved technologies for irrigation water management. When you add the need for more careful environmental management to the need for expanding irrigation systems that are more efficient, you begin to see a pattern of "smart irrigation" systems emerging, and that is in fact what is happening.

SECTOR CHARACTERIZATION

Irrigation and drainage services are generally linked through the diversion of irrigation water, which returns through channels and infrastructure that drain excess water back to water courses. Drainage can also be required in areas without irrigation, but with rainfed crops and systems that require the same kind of piping and construction work as irrigated areas. For this reason, the combined irrigation and drainage industry operates in many regions, but the irrigation part of it is more active in arid zones.

Large-scale irrigation is practiced in dry regions in the Middle East, Central Asia, the western United States, and South and East Asia (Molden,

2007). In the United States, irrigation occurs primarily in the West but it is increasing in some humid regions, such as Florida, Georgia, and the Mississippi Delta. Use of irrigation in humid areas is a way to add value to crops, create new cropping possibilities, and reduce risk of drought losses. It is a mistake to think that you have either irrigated or nonirrigated areas because there are advantages to irrigation in diverse types of farm areas.

At the large scale, the irrigation sector involves large systems that divert water to vast agricultural areas in dry regions. As examples, consider California's Imperial Valley, which contains a half-million acres of productive farmland, or the irrigated areas along the Indus River in Pakistan, which have lately been devastated by floodwaters.

In the United States, irrigation water users withdraw more than three times as much water as public utility systems. Only thermoelectric power utilities divert more water than irrigation users, but they return most of their water to the environment, although at higher temperatures. So, irrigation has a higher consumptive use than any other customer of the water business. Total irrigation withdrawals are flat or declining. In 2005, they were about 143 million acre-feet (MAF) per year, or about 2.4 feet for 60 million irrigated acres (out of a total of 440 million acres of cropland). This is about 8 percent less than in 2000 and near the water use level in 1970. Water is being used more efficiently through use of sprinkler and microirrigation systems, which were used for 56 percent of the total acreage irrigated in 2005. Use of microirrigation is increasing, and urban irrigation is also a significant user of water, and many local urban water officials report that outdoor water use is their most difficult problem.

In the United States, large irrigators may include farms with surface irrigation systems for corn, wheat, alfalfa, vegetables, or other crops; large farms with wells and center-pivot systems; golf courses with extensive systems to irrigate fairways and greens; and turf farms. At smaller scales, irrigation involves small plots, which may be watered by individual wells or from collective systems organized by groups of farmers. Smaller irrigators might include greenhouse operators or small farms with wells or pumps in streams. Greenhouse operators may be responding to increasing consumer demand for flowers and out-of-season plant varieties.

Irrigation is increasingly being extended to urban areas to provide water for local food production or neighborhood vegetable plots, which join lawn and garden irrigation as outdoor water uses in cities. The irrigation sector also includes aquaculture with its fish ponds and networks of channels and water-handling facilities. The sector is also closely aligned with water for livestock as farmers may use the same water-handling facilities for their livestock as they do for their crops. For example, a small to medium cattle operation might irrigate feed crops and use the same source of irrigation water to water cattle in the range or in feedlots. Adding in the growing use of irrigation water for landscaping and other amenities, such as golf courses, the full extent of the sector begins to come into view.

The interdependence of irrigation and city water use is increasing. Large-scale irrigators can partner with cities in city-farm water sharing, and farmers can idle land in dry years so cities can have water. Cities may have nonpotable water systems for urban farming.

IRRIGATION AND DRAINAGE ORGANIZATIONS

As with public water suppliers, the organizations that provide irrigation and drainage services are diverse in nature. Like other parts of the water industry, their organization is not described well by government statistics. The Census Bureau lumps them with water supply (NAICS category 221310, Water Supply and Irrigation Systems). The description is: "This industry comprises establishments primarily engaged in operating water treatment plants and/or operating water supply systems. The water supply system may include pumping stations, aqueducts, and/or distribution mains. The water may be used for drinking, irrigation, or other uses."

Around the world irrigation companies and authorities range from central government control, with lower-level districts, to various kinds of local government districts, cooperatives, and mutual companies. A farmer might be a member or customer of an irrigation company or district or other type of organization, but there is no reason (other than economics or legal restrictions) to prevent a farmer from developing his own system.

Given that so many types of irrigation organizations exist, they can be grouped according to their activities (Sagardoy, 1986). Integrated management organizations would include state farms, irrigation settlement projects, and irrigation cooperatives. State farms may occur where land is nationalized or land reform has taken place. Government irrigation schemes are found in Spain, Turkey, Bolivia, Iraq, Ecuador, and Kenya, among others. Irrigation settlement projects provide landless people or poor farmers with irrigated land and the means to farm. A cooperative will normally be by volunteer participation with a group of farmers forming associations with varied names such as irrigation and water districts, irrigation associations, and others. They are normally governed by an assembly of farmers and a board of directors.

In the U.S. West, local districts and ditch companies dominate the irrigation industry, and only about 15 percent of the water is provided by Bureau of Reclamation and some Bureau of Indian Affairs projects (Lea, 1985). Irrigation districts and companies range from small ditch operations to giant districts, with California's Imperial Irrigation District (IID) as the largest. IID's scope of operations will be explained in the next section. Organized irrigation districts are mainly in the western irrigated states, and states such as Texas and Florida have far fewer group delivery organizations (Interagency Task Force, 1979). California has a large group of them and the Association of California Water Districts (ACWD) provides information on them (www.acwa.com).

Federal agencies involved in irrigation are mainly the Bureau of Reclamation and the Department of Agriculture's Natural Resources Conservation Service, with EPA providing some oversight. The bureau operates projects in 17 western states, and the NRCS assists on smaller projects and conservation programs. State governments are not involved much in irrigation except for regulatory programs.

The bureau has regional offices to coordinate its activities across the western states. It is not building many new projects now, but it must maintain and manage its legacy of signature dams, such as Hoover Dam and Glen Canyon Dam on the Colorado River and Grand Coulee Dam on the Columbia River.

The Bureau is criticized by some for subsidies to irrigators. This longstanding controversy is based on the original terms of federal appropriations to build dams, which had varied payback provisions that were usually quite concessionary. So, if you have water rights that were enhanced by a subsidized Bureau of Reclamation project, you might have received a financial benefit from the project, but these are old now and have been absorbed into property values and other arrangements. For example, in northern Colorado water-right owners of the Colorado–Big Thompson project can sell their shares, which have been valued in an active water market.

The primary sources of data about U.S. irrigation water use are the five-year census of agriculture reports published by the U.S. Department of Agriculture (USDA) and the USGS reports on estimated use of water in the United States, which are also published every five years.

Associations that provide expositions and information transfer about irrigation issues include the Irrigation Association (IA) and the U.S. Committee on Irrigation and Drainage (USCID). To illustrate a case of an irrigation organization, the next section includes a description of a giant irrigation district in California. It has a number of unique features and issues, but it has the common attributes of an early history linked to development, federal involvement in water management, close links with food production and farming, environmental impacts, cooperation with cities, and the need for financial assistance. This section is followed by a brief description of smaller irrigation organizations, with examples from Colorado.

IMPERIAL IRRIGATION DISTRICT: A LARGE WESTERN WATER-MANAGEMENT DISTRICT

Nestled between the Lower Colorado River and the San Diego region, the Imperial Valley of California is the most productive food-production center in the world. More than 100 types of crops are grown, all dependent 100 percent on massive amounts of irrigation water.

The Imperial Irrigation District (2010a) is a focal point of the controversies over large-scale irrigation in the U.S. Organized in 1911, it has the largest water right on the Colorado River, which is now 2.6 million acre-feet as a "present perfected water right." The 1922 Colorado River Compact allocated 7.5 MAF to the lower basin is mostly because of IID's water right. This is the largest water right of this kind in the United States and perhaps in the world. IID was organized to acquire property of a bankrupt development company that was the result of entrepreneur plans that began back in the 1850s.

The IID water rights delivery system through today's All-American Canal is an essential element of the largest food-growing center in the United States, and now it is linked to two additional California issues: transfer of water to supply San Diego and sustaining a vital environmental system focused on the Salton Sea.

To grasp these issues, visualize the Lower Colorado River, a large diversion at the Imperial Dam, the All-American Canal, the IID service area, the Salton Sea, and San Diego (Figure 8.1). The Salton Sea was formed in 1905–1906, when the Colorado River jumped its banks and flowed unimpeded into a depression for about a year. As a landlocked sea, similar to the Great Salt Lake and the Dead Sea, it receives water inflows but has no surface flow outlet. The only way water flows out is through evaporation, which leaves the remaining water saltier. The Salton Sea supports a fishery, which sustains a migratory bird population; if the sea becomes too salty and the fish die, the bird population will be impacted.

San Diego is part of a growing population in southern California, which requires imported water supplies to augment local sources, which are inadequate. Providing water for southern California has required large efforts for decades and the transfer of salvaged IID water to San Diego is a big deal. The idea is to capture irrigation return flows that would seep into groundwater or drain into the Salton Sea and sell them to San Diego. The project came to be known as the All-American Canal lining project (AACLP), with partners being IID, the San Diego County Water Authority (SDCWA), the California Department of Water Resources (DWR) and the U.S. Bureau of Reclamation. It comprises the concrete lining of the mainline canal and paving of transitional structures, the conservation of an

FIGURE 8.1 Location map of Imperial Irrigation District area

estimated 67,700 AF per year, with the majority allocated to SDCWA for 110 years.

The business arrangements for such a large project are, of course, complex and huge. In 2003 a Colorado River Quantification Settlement Agreement was reached among multiple parties, who agree to conserve and transfer water so California will live within its entitlement of 4.4 MAF of Colorado River water per year. The AACLP will help IID meet the goals of Agreement and protect Colorado River Aqueduct supplies and extend supply, as restrictions on pumping from northern California cause shortages. California and the SDCWA share nearly $300 million in construction costs and IID provides construction management and operation and maintenance of the canal, while the USBR maintains ownership of the canal.

COLORADO IRRIGATION: DIVERSITY AMID GROWTH

Whereas IID remains a giant irrigation organization and will continue to consume large quantities of water, even after transferring salvaged water to San Diego, many smaller irrigation organizations operate around the West. For example, in Colorado, where crops will normally not survive without irrigation to supplement the 14 inches of rain and snow water that occur annually, a diverse set of small and large organizations has developed. The Colorado explorers did not envision that the state could develop as it has, but they did have the foresight to anticipate widespread adoption of irrigation. How Colorado developed its irrigation is explained by novelist James Michener in his book *Centennial,* which also became a television series. He explained how, in addition to irrigation, some Colorado farming is risky dryland farming, where farmers leave fields fallow to build up soil moisture, and then grow crops by combining soil moisture depletion with annual precipitation.

Colorado's water management system evolved from a system to supply water for farms, and irrigation made the difference between an area that seemed like a desert to the early explorers and the settled area we have now. Other parts of the world have similar experiences where the desert was made to bloom, but some irrigated societies go back many centuries earlier than Colorado.

The first irrigation organizations in Colorado were the ditch companies, where groups of farmers developed cooperative mutual companies under Colorado law. An example is the Water Supply and Storage Company, which was incorporated in 1891 to serve irrigators in Northern Colorado. Then, as the state developed, a number of special districts were organized. Some of the largest, such as the Northern Colorado Water Conservancy District, were necessary to accept responsibility for federal projects.

Today, Colorado has a diverse and influential group of irrigation organizations that share the common attribute of feeling under pressure from a combination of federal rules, encroaching cities, and the aspirations of new generations of real farmers and hobby farmers to make the most of their water rights. City-farm cooperative schemes are under consideration as well as new ways to earn more from limited irrigation supplies.

GOVERNANCE

The governance of the irrigation sector is a special challenge due to its close links to food production and local economies and societies and involves diverse agricultural interest groups. It differs from governance of utilities by regulators and involves ditch companies and irrigation districts that control withdrawals. Given the economic status of many farmers, effective irrigation policy and governance can improve incomes and increase food security in crop, fishery, livestock, and mixed systems (Molden, 2007).

In the United States, access to irrigation water is widely available, but cost, legal constraints, and environmental pressures present barriers. Given population growth, there will be opportunities for local farmers to raise vegetables and support urban food markets and a few irrigation projects may be considered to respond to demand for golf courses and other recreational venues. Use of reclaimed water for irrigation is also increasing.

In developing countries, rural development and alleviation of poverty and social unrest are dependent on access to irrigation supplies. For example, Egypt faces challenges to serve a rising population that lives on a limited land base and has a limited supply of water. India has a much larger population and a more distributed system based mostly on small landholder situations. Both countries have complex irrigation institutions that have evolved with state-controlled institutional arrangements superimposed over traditional small-scale community irrigation systems.

In the United States, the quality of drainage water is an important governance issue under nonpoint-source control. Farms discharge large volumes of sediment and nutrients, and runoff from animal production is a source of phosphorous and pathogens in lakes. In an ideal situation, farms would use best management practices and minimize loss of sediment, fertilizers, and pesticides, and most nutrients would be retained in the soil. In the real world, however, farmers are often challenged to manage difficult and variable conditions with financial limitations, and it would be impossible and impractical to regulate them closely. There is even a large hypoxic zone in the Gulf of Mexico that is caused by Mississippi River discharges that carry farm runoff from fertile lands in the nation's midsection.

IRRIGATION ECONOMICS

The economics of irrigation water are not purely market driven due to the many subsidies and social interventions in farm policy and practices. The provision of irrigation water is often by public projects or long-standing mutual irrigation companies that may receive preferential treatment, such as tax benefits and government assistance in infrastructure development.

Where water markets do exist, evidence is that as water becomes more expensive, irrigation water moves from lower-value crops such as hay and corn to higher-value crops such as vegetables and turf grass. Another higher-value crop might be urban lawns, as reallocated irrigation water in the West is often viewed as another source for public water systems. In some areas of Florida and California, reclaimed water is increasingly being used for lawn irrigation, and it is being used for industrial uses in several other states.

Given its economic complexities, it is difficult to explain the financial flows of the irrigation sector, but a few examples might shed some light on them. In terms of water volume, a high-profile example might be provision of irrigation water through large government projects. Take California's Imperial Irrigation District, for example, which is a special district. IID has more than 3,000 miles of canals and drains and provides water while also paying for ecosystem protection. Its Water Department operates and maintains a system that delivers up to 3.1 million acre-feet of Colorado River water to almost 500,000 acres. Ninety-seven percent of the water is used for agriculture, and 3 percent supplies municipalities and other water users. IID also developed an electric utility and is now the sixth largest electrical utility in California. Revenues for the electric utility are projected at $477 million, while the water utility side forecasts $122 million. Water sales are forecast at $20 per acre-foot in 2011, which is a low figure that probably reflects historical practices that favor agricultural production in the valley. While this is an increase from $17 in 2008, it is still lower than water prices in some agricultural regions and much lower than municipal prices. For perspective, if a municipal water rate were at a commonly experienced level of $3 per thousand gallons, that would amount to almost $1,000 per acre-foot.

Another example would be a mutual irrigation company in Colorado. A large one near where I live is self-supporting from fees and charges, but it owns a legacy of water rights that it could never afford today if it had to purchase or develop the water. It maintains a basic infrastructure of open channels and distribution facilities, and it serves a group of customers with services for water-ordering and billing. For example, an annual stock assessment for an acre-foot share of water might be on the order of $50, but assessments for deliveries and for surplus water might be very low, on the order of $5 per acre-foot. These low charges show that the ditch company will operate at a minimum level of costs, which reflects a very conservative agricultural culture.

As a final example, I will cite an example of a center-pivot irrigation farmer in southwestern Georgia, where use of irrigation increased dramatically in the recent decades. A large system might cost on the order of $300 per acre, not including the drilling of the well or associated pumping costs. Altogether, the full system might cost, say, $60,000 to irrigate 120 acres of a crop like soybeans or peanuts, which are common in that region. For this type of irrigation, a farmer will be pretty much on his own and not expect much direct government assistance, other than farm price supports. Credit is currently hard to come by due to the financial crisis, but if the farmer could get a loan for an interest rate of 6 percent and if the equipment will last 30 years, the annual capital cost is $4,360 or $36 per acre for the equipment, and the farmer will have to factor that into his business calculation.

CONSUMPTIVE USE AND AGRICULTURAL WATER ACCOUNTING

In the West some groups allege that agriculture wastes water because its percentage of use is high and often it appears that a lot of water is applied to land without much thought to conservation. It is true that large quantities of water are used for irrigation and that consumptive use is also high. However, agriculture gets a bum rap in accusations of water wasting. The fact is that as water travels downhill, water applied to crops is used over and over again as it moves down river and it is necessary to apply enough water to drive salts through the soil and downstream so that soil does not become too saline.

As a result of complexities like these, management of crop water use is becoming more scientific and the main issue with agricultural water use is to allocate the water to move it toward higher-value uses. As water becomes more expensive and the pressure to be efficient increases, it will require more focus on agricultural water accounting, which is complex, to say the least. The complexity is shown by lack of agreement on water accounting terminology, where confusing terms are used. These include terms such as *water application efficiency, water storage efficiency, water requirement efficiency,* and *conveyance efficiency.* These terms are attempts to explain the losses through various phases of the water transport and use systems, which cannot be simplified too much.

Agricultural water conservation for the sake of conservation is controversial. An expert task force concluded that there is lack of agreement about it and who benefits from it (Council for Agricultural Science and Technology, 1988). Water savings at the farm level occur from financial incentives, but basin or regional reuse possibilities are ignored. The task force wrote, "Low values of irrigation efficiency do not necessarily result in losses of water to further economic use by the public, and that changing irrigation practice to increase efficiency will not necessarily result in substantial savings of water."

IRRIGATION ISSUES FOR THE FUTURE

As we look into the future, it is clear that agriculture will continue to use vast quantities of water in irrigated regions. Given trends toward urban farming and rising standards of life, it is also likely that more water will be used in cities and the suburbs to irrigate landscapes and gardens. This trend might be offset, however, by rising prices for water that stimulate conservation among urban users. This movement might stimulate increased markets for water-efficiency products and services.

Although global hunger decreased slightly in the last decade, food production and alleviation of hunger will remain as critical issues and irrigation will continue as the largest water use globally, especially in regions that are dependent on it. Given the need to improve water efficiency in large-scale irrigation as well as in cities, it seems unlikely that in the aggregate total irrigation water use will increase much. This may result from the fact that new irrigation supplies are hard to come by as much as it does the impact of water efficiency.

In developing countries where irrigation is important to the social fabric as well as to food production, irrigation will continue as an essential local issue, and rural hunger and poverty will demand special government support for irrigation water, especially for farmers with small landholdings. The close economic connection between irrigation water and farm prices makes continued government involvement in irrigation inevitable.

In the United States, the development of large new irrigation schemes is unlikely, but incremental shifts will continue with urbanization and landscaping using outdoor water, new subdivisions moving into farm regions, and urban farming on the rise. So, it is likely that we will see continued flat or declining records of irrigation water use, but this will mask behind the scenes shifts in irrigation.

Rather than being included in the data of irrigation itself, urban landscape water use is embedded in municipal statistics. In dry areas, landscape irrigation is part of outdoor water use, which can account for a large share of total annual water use. For example, a three-person home in my town might use an annual average of 450 gallons per capita per day, but without outdoor use the figure might be 300 gallons or less. Extending the numbers shows that this home will use 0.17 AF of water in a year for landscape irrigation. For our population of nearly 150,000, this will amount to 8,500 AF per year.

In Colorado, the cost to buy rights to use an AF of water is highly variable, ranging from about $5,000 to $15,000 or so. Thus, the capital cost to the city to buy water for landscape irrigation might range from $40 million to $125 million or so. These costs are significant, particularly during times of fiscal stress, so cities are looking at alternative solutions. If the lower end figure applies, it would amount to a capital cost of some $800 per home in the city.

One alternative is to use less water for landscape irrigation by introducing xeriscaping. This is a method of using dry grasses and plants to replace high water-using varieties such as bluegrass. The term *xeriscaping* is believed to have originated with an employee of the Denver Water Department and has been around for at least 20 years. It is derived from the Greek word for *dry* and led to the English word *xeric,* for *dry* or *of a dry environment.*

Water utilities are giving rebates for conversion to dry landscapes. The utility in Cary, North Carolina, might pay $500 if a customer replaces 1,000 square feet of grass with a dry treatment of some kind. In Las Vegas, the Southern Nevada Water Authority pays an average of $1,300 for a xeriscape conversion (Chaker, 2010). These figures bracket the $800 per home value shown above for Fort Collins.

The rising demand for water from all sectors has created a new game for agriculture: the transfer of water from farms to cities to fuel growth. The highest profile U.S. transfer is from IID to San Diego, which was explained earlier in the chapter. Other plans for cooperation will continue to emerge from the grass roots and can be win-win arrangements.

Irrigation water quality will continue to be a difficult issue, as will solving the hypoxic zone in the Gulf of Mexico. Actually, water quality is one of the risk factors facing agriculture, along with failures in farm infrastructure systems, contamination of food, salinization of soils, and a bevy of economic threats, such as foreign competition.

Irrigation requires many reforms, but educators and public officials should ensure that urban public opinion is not misled about the value of water applied to irrigation. I think that in part the changed paradigm for irrigation water management that I described at the beginning is due in part to an image problem. Irrigation has a lot of work to do. Jan van Shilfgaard (1992) summed it up in a lecture at the U.S. National Academy of Sciences:

> *In the future, irrigation worldwide will gain further in importance, and better water management is essential for human survival. . . . There are clear limits to the insults the environment can absorb. . . . We should face up to the fact that equity has suffered, that third parties often have not been served well, and resolve to do better.*

CHAPTER 9

Instream Flows: Competing for Water in the Commons

While it is easy to understand water supply and wastewater as public services, the flow of water in streams is taken for granted. However, flows in public streams are actually a public responsibility and ought not to be neglected or left to chance. They comprise an important part of the water business, but their influence is felt more in regulatory and political pressures than it is in direct business activities.

Instream flows are the waters flowing in rivers and smaller streams after all the withdrawals, discharges, and losses have taken place. They are the result of nature and man at work as water traverses its path from atmosphere to sea and back again in the hydrologic cycle. No central authority regulates them directly but they are used by regulators of water withdrawals, discharges, and environmental water needs as guides to the upper limits of water uses. To engineers, they form logical management units, but these are confounded by the political boundaries that water must cross. In some ways their status is like an integrated indicator of the overall balance in water management, similar to body temperature is an index to the health of a person or animal.

Water in streams is a common resource, and water pioneers found a convenient way to explain the management of such common resources to serve varied stakeholders. They coined the phrase "multipurpose water management" to mean that water should serve different goals and people. Gilbert White (1969), a water-management visionary, broadened the phrase to the management of water for "multiple purposes" by "multiple means."

In essence these concepts seem to require a command-and-control authority to plan and execute water-management programs to serve needs that it has determined. While I would like to say that we now understand that the invisible hand of the marketplace can meet these multiple needs, I unfortunately cannot say that. The reason is that, as we have seen, our shared dependence on water resources mandates a partition between commodity services (mainly water supply) and public good services (environmental water quality, for example). Even the water commodities cannot always be sold through the private market, and the public goods certainly cannot be handled that way. At the center of the array of public water goods are instream flows, which are the subject of this chapter.

The management of instream flows was explained in Chapter 2 as being handled by a sector that is almost imaginary because it is not neatly organized itself but results from the largely uncoordinated but combined actions of groups who determine the flows in rivers and streams and the levels of lakes and reservoirs. You can think of it as a virtual sector, an indirect sector, or a sector that requires cooperation to deal with shared resources.

The sector is important because it is an arena where varied interests coordinate their actions toward individual and shared goals and the outcomes have a big effect on the triple bottom line. These interests pursue economic goals (electric energy and navigation), mostly social goals (water quality and recreation) and environmental goals (water for plants, fish, and wildlife). Instream flows do not form a business sector that produces and sells products and services so much as they represent a demand sector for coordination of business interests and government regulation. These can represent significant barriers to doing business, such as in the hurdle of relicensing hydroelectric facilities.

This chapter explains how the instream flow sector works, why it is important and how it affects water management decisions of a range of players, from hydroelectric generators to the recreational industry.

NAVIGABLE STREAMS—OUR COMMON PROPERTY

A good starting point for a discussion of instream flows is the concept of the navigable stream, which is a long-standing authority for instream flow water management. Under English common law, any person could navigate streams considered as navigable and also use them for incidental purposes, such as hunting and fishing (Getches, 1990).

This basic view of shared streams must be expanded to recognize this dilemma: Many of the customers for instream flows lack infrastructure and means to manage the instream water themselves, but they need it for commercial navigation, water-based recreation, sport and commercial fishing, floodwater passage, and other environmental or scenic purposes. The dilemma is explained by the Tragedy of the Commons concept, which explains why people look after their own interests but neglect the public interest (Hardin, 1968).

It is in the self-interest of diverters to take as much water as they can, and they have little incentive to conserve so that adequate flows remain in the stream for all to use. Therefore, unless some control mechanism is superimposed upon the uncoordinated stream and lake systems, everyone is likely to suffer.

The groups that can influence instream flows are the hydropower producers and the federal agencies that own and operate thousands of dams. So, before the full range of instream flow needs was recognized, these powerful owners of infrastructure could largely determine the flows themselves. In the case of private owners, such as power companies, no public authority might look after instream flows. In the case of public owners, such as the Corps of Engineers, the instream flows would be managed politically and through bureaucratic decisions.

Going back to the law of navigable waters leads us quickly into many complexities, but from a business standpoint it has several important implications. The first of these is probably the allocation of rights to use the water for competing purposes. This ranges all the way from use of big rivers—such as hydropower or navigation on the Mississippi-Missouri system—to use of small streams for uses such as rafting and fishing. In Colorado, for example, we have an ongoing dispute about state law that governs rights of rafters to traverse the fence lines that property owners string across mountain streams.

Federal law speaks to navigable waters in two important ways. First, if waters were judged navigable when a state was admitted to the union, then title to the bed of the stream passed to the state. Second, navigability determines the extent to which congressional regulation of the stream can be done under the Commerce Clause of the Constitution. Going beyond these federal controls, much of the authority over streams passes into the realm of state law (Getches, 1990).

While law about navigable streams is fairly clear, the governance of instream flows is more ambiguous. The competing uses of water along a stream require many decisions about withdrawals, discharges, dam releases, and protection of natural flows.

INSTREAM FLOWS FOR MULTIPLE PURPOSES

Instream flows provide a number of services for water users and the environment, and the following list captures the essence of their multiple purposes:

- Water conveyance—to provide "carry water" to points of withdrawal and use
- Water quality—provide dilution water for effluent discharges
- Environment—provide water for plants, fish, and wildlife

- Hydropower—provide flows to generate hydroelectric power
- Navigation—to provide minimum depths for commercial navigation
- Recreation—to control flows for swimming, boating, fishing, and aesthetics

To say that instream flows are needed to transport water may seem like double-talk, but this is known in some circles as "carry water" to help everyone's water along to their points of diversion. By aggregating water this way, we can share and overcome losses in dry streambeds, which is an especially important issue in arid regions. Streams normally cause water losses due to seepage into the ground and evapotranspiration from plants, and by aggregating their water in a stream the water users share the losses. If the flows drop too low, then the losses dominate too much, so it is important to leave enough water in the stream to spread losses equitably.

Carry water is normally a lesser issue in humid regions, where flows are usually greater than in dry regions and there is less need to share the stream losses. However, during severe drought, streams can dry up in humid areas as well.

The groups who control instream flows for carry water are dam owners and water-allocation regulators, who can allow or prohibit diversions through regulatory programs. In Colorado, for example, leaving enough water in the stream to ensure that downstream water rights are satisfied is a legal issue and controlled by courts and regulatory authorities.

Instream flows provide a service to wastewater dischargers because the flows dilute discharge waters from treatment plants and polluted runoff and help maintain higher levels of water quality in the streams. This is most urgent during droughts, when flows are the lowest and are controlled by state rules that govern minimum instream flows. These state rules, which are normally promulgated by state environmental and health agencies vary a good bit.

The Clean Water Act sets the basic policy for water-quality standards, which lead to the minimum instream flows for water quality. Water quality standards define goals for streams by designating their uses, setting criteria to protect the uses, and establishing rules to protect water quality. They have four basic elements: designated uses (such as recreation, water supply, aquatic life, or agriculture), water-quality criteria (numerical limits and other requirements), an antidegradation policy to maintain and protect existing uses and high-quality waters, and policies for implementation (such as low flows, variances, and mixing zones) (USEPA, 2010c).

The numerical value for low flows set by state governments is normally a risk-based hydrologic standard, which is determined from statistics of low flow. Their importance stems from the fact that they set a stringent standard for the dilution water to be expected when planning investments in wastewater treatment facilities. One approach is to set the low flow at the lowest seven-day average flow to be expected in a 10-year period (7Q10). Other statistical approaches can be used, such as Colorado's requirement where critical flow conditions are based on a the 30-day average low flow with an 1-in-3 year recurrence interval for chronic standards and on the 1-day low flow with a 1-in-3 year recurrence interval for acute standards (Colorado Department of Public Health and Environment, 2010).

Instream flows also serve the environment with an "ecosystem service" that nourishes fish and wildlife and maintains healthy stocks of vegetation and biota in streams. They shape streams through annual flood cycles, which have the beneficial effects of maintaining habitat in riparian areas and wetlands at the border between aquatic and terrestrial ecosystems.

Unless water is provided for essential environmental uses, the impacts will be drier habitats, fewer and different types of vegetation, and lower stream flows. These impacts are recognized by environmental impact studies, which are designed to identify the need to sustain environmental uses of water.

In contrast to direct water uses such as irrigation and residential water, it is more difficult to quantify environmental uses. Even biologists disagree on quantities of water required to support fish populations. A typical environmental study will involve specialists in different fish, bird, and animal species, as well as experts in hydrology, hydraulics, and plant life. By studying water needs from all views, a balanced view of water needs will emerge. Setting required environmental flows is not only a matter of requiring minimum flows, it requires that the flow regimes mimic nature in ways to enhance the survival of multiple species.

Of course, there is a link between environmental water and water for recreation and the pure enjoyment of nature. Water scenes provide some of the most compelling views that enhance the aesthetic qualities of social environments.

While dams fell out of favor with the public and water policy makers decades ago, interest in renewable energy is kindling renewed appreciation of their benefits. The interest is part of a national desire for sustainable energy from all sorts of water flows, from ocean waves to free-flowing streams and piped flows, whether water supply or even wastewater.

Hydropower is a big source of energy. Globally, hydropower provides 16 percent of electricity, according to the London-based International Hydropower Association. You would not know this from the low profile that hydro has in the United States. Hydroelectric plants generate electric energy from water flows through streams and reservoirs. The flowing water at high pressure turns the turbine blades to generate power, and the water is released to the tailwaters to continue its downstream travels. Hydropower accounts for two-thirds of U.S. renewable energy and 7 percent of all electricity generation. In some nations, particularly Latin American countries such as Colombia, Brazil and Venezuela, hydro accounts for more electric power generation than all other sources combined.

Hydropower is especially valuable for its capability to adjust output rapidly to meet fluctuating demands and to provide peaking power and help restore power after blackouts. When used with steam, natural gas, or nuclear plants, which operate at more constant loads, hydro can add power quickly to a system.

A run-of-river hydro plant has little water storage and generates power from the available streamflow. Storage reservoirs provide capacity to carry water over from one period to another and can operate like giant batteries. Pumped storage is like a rechargeable battery that enables the storage of excess electric energy from other sources. Water is pumped to a reservoir at a higher elevation to be released when the energy is needed. For example, Duke Energy's Bad Creek pumped storage plant, located in Oconee County, South Carolina, moves water from an elevation of 1,110 feet to 2,310 feet and has a capacity of 1,065 megawatts.

Small hydro plants can be adapted to special situations, such as the needs of a small town or factory. During industrialization in the United States, small plants were common and many still generate energy in local areas. As energy needs ramp up and technologies improve, small hydro plants may become popular again.

Hydroelectricity provided by nonfederal producers is regulated by the Federal Energy Regulatory Commission (FERC). Licenses to operate hydro plants are normally for 50 years, and FERC levies stringent water management requirements on the generators. For example, Duke Energy is currently seeking license renewals for its Catawba River system and has spent millions of dollars and several years of studies to explain and justify its water management plans. The lesson is that hydropower relicensing is already complex and expensive, and it is likely to become more so.

According to the National Hydropower Association (2010b), policies needed for hydropower would address: greater use of pumped storage, converting nonpowered dams, new capacity and modernization, hydrokinetic technologies for in-stream generation and ocean and tidal power, a strong renewable electricity standard, tax-credit parity for hydropower, and more efficient regulatory processes, especially for minimal impact projects such as converting nonpowered dams and closed-looped pumped storage projects.

The Electric Power Research Institute (EPRI), a utility industry research organization in Palo Alto, California, estimates that 40,000 megawatts could be added to the U.S. grid by 2025 even without new dams. Activity is picking up, including new research spending by USDOE, increased Federal

Energy Regulatory Commission permitting for small hydro projects, and new state mandates for renewable energy.

Hydro has advantages over wind and solar because streamflows are usually more predictable, you can store the water energy, and hydro is good for peaking power. The Department of Energy estimates the 2016 cost of a new hydro project at $120 per megawatt-hour, compared to $150 for wind and almost $400 for photovoltaic solar. Global potential is even better than in the United States. The estimate by the International Hydropower Association is that North America and Europe have developed most of their hydropower potential, but South America, Asia, and Africa have huge remaining potential.

Technical approaches include adding power plants to existing dams. Newer turbine designs can improve conditions for fish and help balance ecosystems. For example, American Municipal Power Inc. is adding power plants to three dams on the Ohio River at a cost of $2 billion. It believes that hydropower costs more initially than coal or gas but will have less maintenance for 60 or 70 years. Technologies can be tricky. A barge-mounted turbine in the Mississippi River worked but was not economical, according to developer Hydro Green Energy LLC. Low-head turbines seem promising but need more work. Pumped storage is increasing in favor and works like a battery to store electric energy. China, India, and Ukraine have many projects under way, according to MWH, an engineering firm with a business line in hydro.

Water-based navigation in the nation's system of intracoastal waterways and navigable rivers is another instream use of water. Historically, navigation was an important economic development tool. For example, the Erie Canal opened up markets in the Midwest and was responsible for New York's becoming the major port on the East Coast. The Panama Canal enabled East Coast shippers to compete in the Pacific Ocean, and in Europe, waterways such as the Rhine and Danube rivers are critical shipping lanes.

In the United States, water-based navigation involves about 200 locks and dams on the inland waterways system, river training structures, and the Great Lakes system (Schilling et al., 1987). New York State also has a Barge Canal System. The inland system involves the Atlantic Intracoastal Waterway, the Gulf Intracoastal Waterway, the Mississippi River System, and the Pacific Coast system (Columbia River system). Also, there are numerous subsidiary systems, such as the Ohio River, the Tennessee River, and the Black Warrior and Tombigbee rivers (Alabama).

This is a short list of organizations that manage ports along these systems and in some cases handle the interport transfer of navigation from inland to marine systems:

- Board of Commissioners for the Port of New Orleans
- Board of Harbor Commissioners of Milwaukee

- Inland and Intracoastal Waterway System
- New York State Barge Canal System
- Port Authority of New York and New Jersey
- Port of Seattle
- Virginia State Ports Authority

Almost since the country was founded, managing the waterways system has been a matter of national security as well as commerce. The USACE, which maintains most of the channels, has the Navigation Data Center at its Institute for Water Resources (2009), where statistics are kept for the coastal transport, Great Lakes, and inland.

On the basis of value alone, shippers would not support the full cost of maintaining the navigation system. Most of the cargoes are bulk commodities, such as coal and coke, crude petroleum and petroleum products, chemical and related products, forest products, pulp and waste paper, sand, gravel and stone, iron ore and scrap, primary manufactured goods, food and farm products, and waste and scrap. Subsidies are required, and sometimes charges of pork barrel are levied against the systems.

Navigation water needs cannot compete with others in terms of imputed value. For example, maintaining navigation on the Apalachicola-Chattahoochee-Flint (ACF) system could not compete with water supply for Atlanta on the basis of pure economic analysis. One problem with the ability to pay for navigation is a chronic shortage of funds for dredging and river maintenance. This occurred in 2010 as the Corps of Engineers found itself short of funds to fully dredge the Lower Mississippi River. This has attracted a lobbying group of shippers, state governments, port operators, farmers, and the Waterways Council to press Congress to add funds to the Corps budget for fiscal 2011. The main emphasis is funds to dredge ports and channels around New Orleans and Baton Rouge, Louisiana, to allow cargo ships to pass. The fiscal 2011 budget has $63 million for Lower Mississippi dredging, which is $6.3 more than in fiscal 2010; actual costs, however, average $85 million annually and exceeded $110 million in fiscal 2010. So, the funds available come from congressional appropriations and diversions from other parts of the Corps budget to make up shortfalls. This takes funds from repairs on locks, dams, and other projects. It is a rock-and-hard-place situation for the Corps, which is responsible for other ports and waterways and is looking at increased business when the scheduled 2015 expansion of the Panama Canal is ready. Cargoes on the Lower Mississippi are imported petrochemical products, construction materials, and other goods, together with export commodities such as grain, corn, soybean, and coal. Actually, more than 60 percent of U.S. agricultural exports are shipped through the Lower Mississippi. It is expensive to dredge the Mississippi, and costs rise with heavy rains and snow. If dredging is reduced, it will slow large ships and might require shippers to unload cargo to smaller ships, thus raising costs and hurting exports. Funding would be considered first by the House Committee on Transportation and Infrastructure, which is an authorizing committee without the power to appropriate funds. The Federal Harbor Maintenance Tax, which is an ad valorem tax imposed on importers, brings in $1.3 billion to $1.5 billion per year, but the government allocates only about $750 million a year to harbor maintenance (McWhirter, 2010). So, we see that waterway maintenance for navigation is funded mainly by government, not users. If the main source of funds appropriated by Congress is the maintenance tax, then importers are subsidizing our exporters, which is entirely fair within the context of public finance at the national level.

Given their attraction, rivers are attractive to communities for restoration and the creation of water-based urban developments such as San Antonio's River Walk or the recreation-based developments found in Denver, Cleveland, and Chattanooga, among other cities. Rivers and streams offer many possibilities for amenity-based developments such as bike trails. Floodplains, which are kept free of development as a protective measure (see Chapter 5), are environmentally attractive venues for mixed natural-area use in urban areas.

A diverse group of agencies and private interests promotes clean, abundant, and scenic water in streams, lakes, and reservoirs for boating, swimming, rafting, fishing, water skiing, picnicking, sightseeing, and general recreation. Environmental water managers also provide water for fish and wildlife, wetlands and riparian areas, vegetation, water-quality control, and water-sediment systems.

These providers usually work with other water management agencies to provide and protect water resources, but they may have their own water management programs to protect and manage streams and lakes. They may also own their own lakes and stream segments.

Federal agencies are active in water-based recreation, including the National Park Service, Forest Service, Army Corps of Engineers, and Bureau of Reclamation. The Forest Service permits dams and reservoirs on national forest lands and will take positions to protect instream flows. State parks departments maintain many lakes and streams, and they are vitally interested in their health and instream flows. Many county and city governments are also involved in management of lakes and streams located on their recreation lands.

Political leaders recognize that water-based recreation is important to their local economies and images. For example, Georgia has more than 70,000 river miles and sees them as attractive beacons for activities such as canoeing, kayaking, and fishing. The state is eying the America's Great

Outdoors Initiative of the Obama administration and has asked the administration to create the National Blueways Initiative to help communities create water trails, which are dedicated stretches of river with safe and legal access to the water and managed by a local government or similar organization. Georgia has a fast-growing water trail movement, with the Ocmulgee River Blueway, Chattahoochee River National Recreation Area Canoe Trail, Upper Chattahoochee River Canoe Trail, Southeast Coast Saltwater Paddling Trail, the Etowah River Blueway, and the Coosawattee Blue Trail, among others (Georgia River Network, 2010).

THE PULSE OF THE WATER ENVIRONMENT

Instream flows are the common responsibility of all the players in water management, including utilities, dam owners, regulators, power companies, irrigation companies, local governments, and other players. They provide water for water-quality management, environmental flows, navigation, recreation, and hydropower, and the stream channels provide capacity for flood control as well. The health of the water commons is continuously determined by dam releases, coordinated decisions, and unstructured actions.

Estuaries, lakes, and inland seas, such as the Great Lakes, are vulnerable for the same reasons as instream flows: overuse, pollution, drought, and eutrophication or aging of the water. The Aral Sea disaster in Central Asia is a globally significant case of failed instream flow management. There, central planning in the former Soviet Union diverted too much water for irrigation and all but dried up an inland sea.

Instream flow management can be risky. I served once in a court case in which alleged improper operation of a spillway caused damages for many miles along a flood-ravaged waterway. Poor management of environmental flows can lead to loss of habitat and environmental disasters, as well.

The main legal arenas for instream flows are state instream laws, state control of water withdrawals, low flow controls for water quality, FERC and other permits, federal reservoir authorizations, reservoir rule curves, and various agreements, such as the Law of the River, which controls the Colorado River.

As the nation learns to appreciate its rivers, streams, and lakes more, we can expect more attention to instream flows. They can be hard to manage, but they are the conscience of water managers. Because they involve many players, their main impact on the water business will be to control other activities, rather than to offer direct business opportunities themselves.

Driving Forces and Issues in the Water Industry

CHAPTER 10

Drivers of Change in the Water Industry

While the water industry is old and well established, it is being prodded by forces of change and modernization. Its main challenge is captured in the phrase *sustainable development,* which means managing resources so they will be available for future generations. Water is a renewable resource and will be available from nature in the future but many threats pose risks to supplies for humans and the environment. These include climate change, drought and scarcity, pollution, overexploitation of groundwater, eutrophication and pollution of lakes and estuaries, loss of species and other serious threats to health, the environment, and economic advancement.

These threats have many implications, and to anticipate them they must be interpreted across the sectors, scales and regions of a very broad water industry. On the one hand, the industry looks stable and slow to change. After all, water systems have been around since the beginning of recorded history. Indeed, the water industry sectors—water supply and wastewater, irrigation and drainage, stormwater and flood control, and instream flows with their dams and reservoirs—will always be required to meet human and environmental needs from the individual to national scales in all settled regions. This does not mean, however, that these water sectors will remain static.

This chapter identifies the main drivers of change across the subsectors of the water industry and discusses their probable impacts. It draws from the futurists and alarmists but also seeks to balance the discussion with looks into the realities of water supply, demand, and management.

ATTRIBUTES OF WATER

The attributes that make the water business susceptible to change begin with the fact that water as a natural resource is renewable. It has some common attributes with air and wind resources, mainly that they are all around us, hard to control, and like air needs to be protected. Water has few if any common attributes with forest resources, which are another key renewable natural resource. It is not like the animal world and has no real similarity to solar energy, so in many ways classifying it as one of the renewable natural resources can create a misleading impression that it shares attributes with the others. The distinctive attribute of water as a renewable resource is the way it flows from headwaters to the sea and is used over and over again. This makes it a shared public good, which is an essential element to a vital and sustainable future. Although water is everywhere, its services are mostly natural monopolies and not very amenable to economic competition.

As water flows along its path, people regard having access to it as a human right, and many believe the environment has an inherent right to it as well. These beliefs lead to government intervention and can throw a monkey wrench into well-developed investment plans. The media attention to human and environmental rights can be compelling. For example, the movie *Flow* alleges that large international water companies, development banks, and other corporate interests are exacerbating poverty and environmental degradation. The claim is that the movie investigates the "world water crisis" and "builds a case against the growing privatization of the world's dwindling fresh water supply with an unflinching focus on politics, pollution, human rights, and the emergence of a domineering world water cartel" (Oscilloscope, 2009).

Another important attribute is that the water industry is heavily regulated. This means that utilities are risk averse, and it creates tension in decision making. Categories of regulation are health and safety, environment, water use, fish and wildlife protection, and service levels. These are discussed in more detail in Chapter 14.

Decisions in the water industry are highly political because of conflicts caused by the misalignment of watersheds and political boundaries, the big money and stakes in water decisions and the fact that one city's sewage becomes the next one's water supply, among others. Water has so many uses that it is linked tightly to several economic sectors, including homebuilding, industry, and agriculture, among others. For example, as homebuilding slows, the need for new water connections goes down and suppresses the demands for equipment and services.

The water business is mostly stable, but it can surprise investors. Water agencies must spend billions of dollars annually on construction, equipment, supplies, and services, but growth spurts are rare, except in local cases. Investment surprises can involve deteriorated buried assets, declining revenues and other out-of-the-box events, such as vulnerability to disasters.

Water is difficult and expensive to move from points of surplus to points of need. The need to transfer water thus becomes a focal point for many of the industry's controversies. Water transfers go beyond fractious "interbasin" transfers and extend to many types of exchanges, trades, loans, water banking operations, conversions, and other modes of transfers.

The water industry is capital intensive, but its investments last a long time so annual capital investments for renewal are small. For example, the United States has more than a million miles of buried water-supply mains with a replacement value of around $400 billion, but the average replacement rate is only about once in 200 years.

Perhaps the most important attribute of water related to change is its nonstationarity. *Stationarity* is a scientific term that refers to whether systems are stable and constant, and scientists allege that they are not. This means that we cannot depend on our existing water systems to continue to deliver supplies year after year, and that sudden changes could occur. As a result, water handlers must take actions to manage risk and ensure that they can meet needs regardless of a future that might include climate change (Milly et al., 2008).

PAST SEA CHANGES IN WATER MANAGEMENT

In some ways change in the water industry will seem slow. Fifty years from now you will probably have a kitchen water faucet that looks a lot like the one you have now, although it may have different materials and mechanisms. This prediction is based on looking back over 50 years in which kitchen faucets changed some but not in fundamental ways. To verify that, just watch old black-and-white movies and check out the plumbing.

However, this apparent slowness of change masks important changes that have taken place and to illustrate, I'd like to cite one big change in each of the water-industry subsectors. Some of these extend back over a hundred years, and some are as current as today. The changes I have identified are shown on Figure 10.1, which reaches back into the 19th century to pin down developments such as the emergence of organized water utilities, new technologies in cast-iron pipe, discovery of the causes of waterborne disease, development of scientific formulas for water flow and energy loss, and construction of large scale irrigation systems.

Water Supply

One of the exam questions in my course on water resources management is: "What was the most important water-related public health improvement in the 19th century?" The stock answer, based on our class discussion, is the 1854 discovery by Dr. John Snow that a cholera outbreak in London was linked to a single source of water. When combined with the emerging field of microbiology, his discovery led to water treatment systems starting with

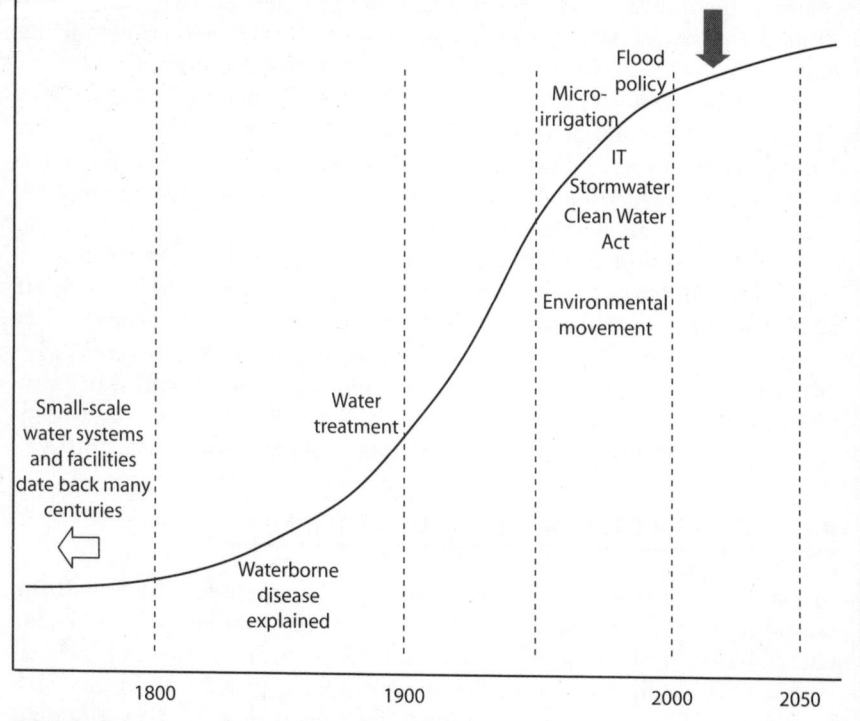

FIGURE 10.1   Sea changes in water management

filtration in 1887 and chlorination in 1909. By 1900, waterborne infectious diseases were on the decline and there was a dramatic reduction in waterborne disease outbreaks.

This innovation in water supply systems—microbiology to detect contaminant threats and treatment to remove them from public drinking water—was a sea change. As a result, water management has been responsible for greater improvements in public health than medical advances such as new pharmaceuticals or surgical procedures and, of course, protection of water is still an important public health responsibility to maintain vigilance against a host of waterborne diseases. More improvements are needed, of course, and the story of water supply treatment since Dr. Snow's work shows a continuing quest to remove additional threats from drinking water (see Chapter 13).

Wastewater and Water Quality

Although public demand for clean streams was building up anyway, the chosen signature event for wastewater changes is the burning of the

Cuyahoga River in Cleveland in 1969, leading to passage of the Clean Water Act in 1972. This legislation launched a new era in wastewater treatment and resulted in great improvements in stream water quality as well as a massive new system of infrastructure to be managed and financed.

Prior to 1972, the wastewater treatment infrastructure was much less than it is today. My own experience with it began in my hometown of Montgomery, Alabama, where we had no sewage treatment up to the 1950s, and all the wastewater from a town of more than 50,000 people was discharged untreated into a creek, which looked like a wasteland. This creek led to the Alabama River, and we fished in the river but never gave a thought to its enormous load of untreated wastewater. Today, Montgomery has advanced wastewater treatment and the river is much cleaner. That story is repeated in towns across the country, although many people are unaware of the great cleanup that occurred.

Stormwater

While we can think of many incremental improvements in stormwater systems, the sea change occurred when they became recognized as service-producing infrastructure systems that required planning, financing, and management. Rather than occurring as one discrete event, this change occurred between about 1960 and 1980.

In 1960, the nation was emerging from a great postwar land development phase that created subdivisions and new highways galore. With the urban sprawl that resulted, little thought was given to how to handle stormwater on a regional basis. Then, during the 1960s attention was given to how stormwater systems affected people downstream with flooding, pollution, and inconvenience. Cities such as Denver began to incorporate stormwater into their urban planning programs and to create ideas for how stormwater services could be used to create amenities such as open space, along with utilitarian water drains.

Then, with the Clean Water Act in 1972, the concept of stormwater quality emerged, to be combined with stormwater drainage into the integrated field of stormwater management. Today, this field is expressed in communities as a discrete program and is even organized as its own self-financed utility in many places. It has its own magazines, conventions, and body of knowledge, and it has become a recognized niche of the water industry (see Chapter 6).

Flood Control

A sea change in flood control occurred when the nation woke up and realized that building dams and levees to protect people and property really did not work the way it was intended. As with stormwater, this occurred over a few decades rather than suddenly. Flooding has always been a destructive and costly natural disaster and can occur from large river flows, flash floods, hurricane-induced floods, dam breaks, and urban storm events.

U.S. flood programs began with local efforts based on levee districts, conservancy districts, and individual landowners. After experiencing a number of serious floods, the nation entered an era of flood policy in which Congress authorized works through the Flood Control Acts of 1917, 1928, 1936, and 1938. As a result of public works during this era, the federal government, with the Corps of Engineers in the lead, had by the 1960s completed many projects with dams, levees, floodwalls, and flood channels.

In spite of these projects, losses mounted, and in the 1960s emphasis changed to nonstructural measures. This led to the Flood Insurance Act of 1968, which created a system of subsidized insurance and requirements for land use controls (see Chapter 6).

After the Great Mississippi River Floods of 1993, a national review committee affirmed the nonstructural approach and the need to recognize environmental management, along with flood control. The National Flood Insurance Reform Act in 1994 led to a report that identified a range of beneficial flood functions, such as natural flood and erosion control, water quality maintenance, groundwater recharge, biological productivity, and fish and wildlife habitats. As a result of these findings and experiences, it is unlikely that the nation will return to the old ways of relying on dams and levees as the main barrier to flood losses.

Irrigation

The sea change for irrigation is the emergence of microirrigation systems, which are defined as irrigation systems that use small devices to apply water to the soil surface or to the plants' root zone. These are used for precision water application and to save water in arid regions or to improve water efficiency in humid regions. They can be used for different cropping systems, orchards, urban gardens, greenhouses, landscaping, and nurseries.

It would be difficult to identify a single event that led to microirrigation, and the innovations were gradual. The occurrence that amounts to a sea change is the extent to which it has been incorporated in the name of water efficiency. Drip irrigation itself evolved from ideas such as using buried pots with water to gradually release water. Then, the use of perforated pipe and hose was introduced decades ago. Plastic pipes available from the 1930s introduced new possibilities for tubing and emitters. Israeli farmers were famous in the 1960s for introducing new systems, which spread around the world.

As an example of a U.S. company involved in microirrigation, Toro (2010) developed a drip tape in 1973. In 1996, Toro purchased the James Hardie Irrigation Company with the intent to create the largest microirrigation company in the United States, and later acquisitions led to today's Toro Micro Irrigation Company.

Instream Flows

The pivotal event for instream flows has been the emergence of the environmental movement and the legislation and controls that it brought with it. In my own lifetime I can remember times when no one thought of a stream as having inherent rights to environmentally sustaining flows. People tended to focus on economic uses of waterways, and environmental uses were a side issue in most places. A good example is that creek in Montgomery, Alabama, or the Cuyahoga River in Cleveland. About 1960 something happened, however, and the environmental movement and streamflows have received much more scrutiny since then, at least in the United States and other developed countries. In terms of how this sea change affected water management, you can say that no longer can streams simply be abused, but now you must consider their health from the standpoints of water quality and habitat as you ponder water-development options.

Dams and Reservoirs

The signature occurrence I point to for dams and reservoirs is the adaptation to their risks, limits, and negative consequences, to go along with the earlier recognition of their many positive benefits. This realization emerged along with the environmental and dam safety movements. Both of the developments fueled the emergence of a new ethic and understanding about dams on streams. They did not occur suddenly but gradually, beginning after World War II, when negative consequences of dams began to receive publicity, and after the 1960s, when environmentalists around the world started to attack them. Today, the idea of building a new dam in the United States is not totally out of the question, but it is considered to be a difficult measure to be used when other water management options do not work out.

Summary of the Sea Changes

These sea changes were driven by rising awareness and affluence, strong desires to meet basic human needs, and the political will that goes with a movement whose time has come, mainly environmentalism. Specifically, the rising expectations caused an awareness of the need for safer water and more environmental protection, a desire for urban amenities, and awareness of the importance of water efficiency and improved urban spaces. The political imperatives drove the need for rational approaches to solving complex problems, and this called for better data and calculations of risk, cost, and consequences. New and improved technologies helped all of this along but did not cause the sea changes themselves. So, if these were the drivers of the past sea changes, what can we look for in the future? Of course, it is hard to say, but as the futurists remind us, we can't predict the future but we can think about it.

TOWARD A WATER INDUSTRY FUTURE

Continuing Media Coverage

It is as certain as death and taxes that in the future there will be more headlines about water disasters and problems such as droughts and crop failures, flood disasters, broken pipes and flooded areas, disease outbreaks from polluted water, and conflicts over water rights or environmental issues. Climate change forecasts will fan our fears about threats such as sea-level rise, loss of ski areas, and advance of tropical diseases. From these many worries, we may think that water will be a growth industry and when you add it up, it most likely will be one.

The scary forecasts about water are part of the industry of speculating about the future, where futurists and lecture circuit speakers tantalize us with keynote speeches and high-profile books. The problem is that we really don't know what will happen, and we should be humble about our ability to forecast the future and be ready to adjust when things change.

I started tracking trends in the water industry in the 1980s after reading *Megatrends* by futurist John Naisbitt (2010). His 1982 book sold millions of copies and was on the *New York Times* best seller list for two years. He continues to track major global and social trends, such as globalism, economic change, and the rise of religious fundamentalism. In that period, large trends I was following included global economic and cultural integration, the triumph of democracy and privatization, ethnic and religious wars, the need for sustainable development, infrastructure deterioration and financial problems, acceleration of technology and communication shifts, explosion of scientific knowledge, social disintegration and terrorism, vulnerability to natural disasters, and exploration of outer space. All of these issues were valid and best sellers about them catch people's attention, but we know that the "x factor" will bring the real surprises of the future.

For example, in the last decade or two we have experienced major episodes that affect the water business such as fear over Y2K computer failures, September 11, the Great Tsunami, and Hurricane Katrina.

As a teacher, my approach to studying water has been to search for the facts to try to explain complex interactions. However, I have found that this approach to the water business has a low profile, which writers try to raise by highlighting social and environmental problems. This leads to continuing media attention to water such as former vice president Al Gore's book and movie, *An Inconvenient Truth,* which highlights an environmental issue and its consequences.

Glennon's 2009 book, *Unquenchable: America's Water Crisis and What to Do about It,* was explained in Chapter 1. He focused on economic, social, and environmental issues and emphasized government solutions, as well as societal interventions. In a focus on investing, Hoffman (2009) wrote *Water Planet: Investing in the World's Most Valuable Resource.* He covered topics that are similar to those in this book, including operation of water companies, fragmentation of the industry, and social issues.

These popularized views of the future may or may not hold water, but regardless of their reliability, major trends in society are evident and will have important effects on the water industry as drivers of change. By mapping these drivers of change onto the water industry, a short list of possible future trends can be created.

Pundit Forecasts about Water

The drivers and trends have been studied for the water utility industry by a team working for the Water Research Foundation (Means, Ospina, and Patrick, 2005). They classified them into categories that included population, political trends, regulations, workforce issues, technology, total water management, customer expectations, financial constraints, energy, and increased risk profile. To these can be added trends that affect the broader water industry, to include rising standards of living, environmental and climate pressures, rising water efficiency, financing systems, the water-energy nexus, water for food, and the unbundling of water services. The next few paragraphs are an attempt to classify these into a logical sequence of trends to watch in the water industry

Pressure on water and natural systems will intensify as global growth ratchets upward, including both population and rising standards of living. The U.S. population has passed the 300 million mark and world population is heading toward seven billion, with a large percentage in the rapidly developing nations of China and India. Within the global village, billions of people seek to escape poverty and enjoy rising standards of living, which demand better resources management and delivery of public services. With the Internet and increasing trade, globalization is affecting almost everyone. In the developed world, like the United States, Europe, Japan, and other wealthier nations, the frameworks of water management practices are mostly established. Meanwhile, billions in developing countries are seeking to escape from poverty or trying to cope with it. This means that while the water systems of developed countries may be mostly fixed and expect only incremental change, developed countries need to build entire infrastructures for water management.

Although water systems of developed countries are mostly fixed, access to new water supplies there and in developing nations will continue to tighten and water supplies will be more expensive. Solutions in developed countries will be found mainly in conservation, treatment, reuse, and technological innovation, but not in giant schemes to move water great distances. Local solutions such as rainwater harvesting may increase, and use of reclaimed water to supplant potable water makes existing supplies go further.

Supply pressures may open markets for water trading and investment mechanisms for raw water rights.

There will be tighter controls on municipal and industrial discharges and wastewater systems will use more monitoring and reporting and have greater information requirements. Green technologies such as use of biogas and recycling will be applied more in the wastewater industry. In developed countries, there will be more emphasis on controlling nonpoint sources, but this is a difficult problem that will be easy to ignore in the face of difficult societal challenges, such as fiscal deficits and health care. In developing countries, those with improving financial and political capacity will build wastewater treatment facilities. Those that continue to live in chaotic conditions will not make these investments until political conditions improve.

Environmental consciousness continues to evolve and is spreading from developed countries to the emerging nations that enjoy freedom of the press and the right to express opinions. As environmental awareness grows, it drives change in the water industry such as resistance to exploitation of natural resources, damming of streams and the like. For example, South Korea has developed a strong environmental movement, which has effectively blocked construction of new dams and requires sustained attention from the government to plan new projects.

The water industry has more impact on and control over the natural environment than any other industry. Environmentalism is mature but will remain a formidable force. While it is maturing, new emphasis on sustainability and worry about climate change have appeared on the radar screens of water utilities. Clearly, natural water systems cannot sustain much greater pressure, and there are limits on the availability of fresh water. Rising demands require more conservation and use of alternative sources, at least in many places. The emphasis on green infrastructure will increase, and we will see innovative programs such as wastewater resource recovery to take advantage of opportunities such as recovery of nutrients from wastewater streams.

While arguments about climate change continue, my sense is that the water industry has accepted it as a reality but will not make large investments that are based on uncertain forecasts so much as it will invest in adaptive strategies and security enhancements that make sense anyway.

The World Bank published a report titled "Cities and Climate Change: An Urgent Agenda," with a forecast that $80 billion to $100 billion will be spent per year in climate change adaptation costs. It reported that world cities, such as New York, Mexico City, Amman, and Sao Paulo, are already acting on climate change. Massive investments in buildings and infrastructure are helping them prepare for climate events like windstorms, flooding, heat waves, and sea-level rise (Stedman, 2010a).

The Carbon Disclosure Project (2010) reported that 39 percent of companies it surveyed are experiencing detrimental impacts related to water issues, which include service disruptions due to flooding, drought, and declining water quality. Eighty-nine percent of the companies surveyed had developed water policies, strategies, and plans, and 62 percent had identified potential business opportunities such as water efficiency systems and products. An example cited was a waterless urinal from Waterless Company. The report also identified sectors vulnerable to water risks as food, beverage, tobacco, metals, and mining. A report, "The Case for Water Disclosure," is available from the CDP web site.

The need for energy supplies for a growing world will add to the pressure on water systems, as explained through the water-energy nexus (see Chapter 7). The main way this affects water utilities is in the use of energy and the need to be more efficient, but the pressures on raw water for hydropower, biofuels, and cooling water will be felt in many other places. Small hydropower systems will be applied in many places as the value of energy rises. Electric power producers will see continuing demand increases, especially with the advent of plug-in electric vehicles, and this will increase demand for cooling water.

Several forces combine to cause the cost of water to continue to rise and it seems that it will rise faster than inflation for a long time to come. Cost drivers include dealing with the aging infrastructure systems and the need to keep old systems going, tighter regulations, more difficult access to water, and new security requirements.

Whereas the water industry has had many subsidies, future emphasis will be on full-cost pricing and enterprise management. Such market-oriented reforms, however, are difficult. It is easier to theorize about market reforms than to achieve them (see Chapter 12). However, it is hard to bring market discipline to regulated resources, and it is hard to move water from low-value to high-value uses and places. It will take a great deal of regulatory reform to use the market better to move water.

To overcome the difficulty in market and full-cost pricing new financing mechanisms will be introduced, particularly to help small systems. Higher tap fees are already charged in many places to pay the capital cost of water for new homes and businesses. These added costs are embedded in the infrastructure cost of the real estate.

While in the United States population growth will bring more development of land and urban spaces and urban farming and golf course expansion will increase demand for water, overall water use has been flat in cities due to conservation. Rapid growth of water demand from urbanization seems unlikely. The focus on water efficiency seems inevitable, meaning to get more from existing supplies and to meet emerging needs without always turning to new sources. Water use per capita seems likely to drop further and water will be more expensive, leading to more emphasis on efficiency and elimination of water losses.

On the other hand, there is a large pent-up demand for water and water services in the developing world, where many people lack access to even basic services and many more do not receive safe and reliable service. In the sprawling cities where millions live in informal settlements, new services are required but it is difficult to speculate about how they will be provided or financed.

The issue of water infrastructure is perhaps the most difficult to face, both because of the high cost and the difficulty in providing it in the face of obstacles such as environmental opposition, dense cities and disorganized governance systems.

U.S. water handlers face difficult and expensive renewal issues for their large and complex infrastructure systems. The dam-building era will not return in the United States, and emphasis will be on management and even in some cases on removal of existing dams. In developing countries, new dams will continue to be built. Infrastructure renewal for all water systems will remain important but only experience slow growth.

At the level of individual buildings, millions of service lines are aging and some of them are made of lead and need replacing. Relining them is an emerging market area.

Residential and commercial fire protection systems will increase in sophistication. The importance of premises plumbing systems as a health issue will rise on the radar screen. This will generate demand for new products and materials for baths, kitchens, and outdoor uses.

In response to infrastructure issues, water-supply systems might switch toward more innovative approaches, but they could remain static and continue to deliver treated water at current levels of quality and leave it to customers to take more responsibility for enhancing water-quality levels. Large self-supplied industries will need to apply efficiency and system renewal in the same way as utilities. Stormwater and flood-control systems must adapt to global climate change, even as they address legacy problems such as severe flooding in large urban areas and nonpoint course control.

In developing countries it will be difficult to solve infrastructure issues in disorganized rapidly urbanizing areas. A graduate student from Africa related to us how the water system in his large city works. The old central city has underground pipes, but they are neglected and in poor condition. In the suburbs, people have built houses wherever they could get a piece of land, and there is no city planning nor any organized utility system. People take matters into their own hands. They install illegal taps and cause large water losses. They dispose of wastewater however they can. You get the picture.

Perhaps the solution for these problems is like the one that is occurring with cell phones. There would be no way to run copper wire into these settlements, but technology solved the problem with cell phones. Why not introduce such innovations for water services?

Proposals for water system innovation include going off of the water grids, using bottled water, using gray-water systems, distributing reclaimed water through dual distribution systems, requiring much higher water efficiency, using different plumbing materials, and increasing use of point-of-use systems, among others. Some of these proposals carry with them public health and liability issues, and some of them might lead to greater business opportunities, such as service contracts with regular testing and maintenance.

In the United States, dual distribution of water supplies, with reclaimed waters used for nonpotable applications, seems certain to increase, but the public will remain concerned about drinking reclaimed water. Decentralized treatment, use of smart pipes, and much more monitoring and control might happen. Innovative storage systems, such as aquifer storage-recovery systems, will be used more. There is interest in going off-grid to create zero-net-water-use zones, but the future is likely to be one of continued connection to grids. Point-of-use treatment systems and bottled water will continue to grow in popularity. Desalting and other treatment technologies will improve. Technologies to renew old infrastructure, especially dams and conveyance structures, will be in demand. There will be more trenchless construction of water pipes, or construction and replacement without digging the surface.

Technology will be an important driver for the water supply industry, led by information technologies for data collection and management, meter reading, and control systems. The use of IT to help wheel water from one place to another will help to move information instead of water. The Internet has also created new ways to cooperate in water management.

There is much activity in developing new and smart meters for automated meter reading and advanced metering infrastructure systems. In these applications, water and electricity have similarities. Electric power companies coordinate to share power reserves, and reliability of the system stems from the interconnected structure known as the grid. Competition and deregulation in electricity have brought expanded use of the grid, with interconnections allowing utilities and users to make power transfers. However, whereas electricity can be transported through a grid system, possibilities for transport of water are more limited because water is a heavy commodity. Thus, information can play an even more critical role in sharing water than in sharing electricity. Many applications for IT are emerging to improve management and security.

Security concerns are driven by the fact that water is interdependent with other networked infrastructure and service sectors. Terrorism is an important issue, but natural disasters are also important threats. Critical water facilities will have fences and security monitors installed and be less accessible in the future. Dam safety will increase as a concern. All of these cry out for better IT monitoring systems. As an example, the Taum Sauk pumped storage plant in Missouri suffered a catastrophic failure due to overtopping in 2005. As reported in my graduate class in water resources, the problem could have been prevented with an effective monitoring and control system.

Given rising populations, standards of living, and the current extent of hunger in the world, the use of water for agriculture must grow, even as traditional irrigation systems fall from favor. When I started to practice engineering in the 1960s, the fields of agricultural and irrigation engineering were relatively robust, but now they seem outdated. The problem is not that they are outdated, but it is one of labeling. The same skills are even more in demand, but where they are applied is more diffused that it used to be. Water efficiency will also be applied to the irrigation sector. In places with high demands for water for all uses, irrigation water use will be flat and move toward higher-value crops, as in the U.S. West and in the Middle East. Irrigation systems will continue to see growth in microirrigation as the rising value of water creates change in use of water to grow food.

Organizational change in the water industry has been dramatic and it continues. One result has been the unbundling of what were integrated water services into components. Outsourcing and privatization will increase and industry consolidation will continue. This is the latest chapter in a long story about organizational change, one that goes back to the birth of the modern organization and corporation.

Water-industry consolidation will occur gradually, and any enthusiasm for privatization in the water industry and its regulatory and political aspects will be approached with caution. Professional service organizations stand to increase business as utilities downsize and seek to outsource.

Water-industry workforce diversity will increase in the United States. Workers will be challenged by greater workloads, complexities, and new technologies. Utilities will be challenged by loss of key employees and knowledge. The employee count will not increase much, but a new workforce is required to replace retiring baby boomers. Managing the thousands of small water systems will continue as a challenge, mainly due to lack of funds to pay for managers, equipment, and support services.

As industrialization becomes more diversified and complex, new water-quality challenges will continue to occur. So far, they have been manageable in the United States, but contaminants of emerging concern are worrisome and many chemicals are found in surface and groundwater supplies. The POU industry would like for these concerns to drive demand for its products and services, but how much demand will occur is unknown.

The politics of water were introduced in Chapter 1, and no solutions are in sight for tough issues such as regional competition for water, as in Georgia where Atlanta has been trying for 20 years to secure its future water supply. Similar scenarios play out in other parts of the United States, where scarcity may exacerbate future conflicts, such as in the Colorado River Basin. China is trying to solve similar problems by mandating projects such as the south-to-north water transfer scheme, but such solutions are unlikely in the United States.

Where the Industry Is Heading

The media coverage of the "world water crisis" will continue, as it has for nearly four decades. This can translate into business growth in some areas—such as building infrastructure—but it also can thwart business ventures in other areas, such as investing in water rights. The water industry has many political and social aspects that can override business principles. It mixes the themes of poverty, human rights, public health, access to safe water, climate change, environmental degradation, privatization, and roles of international corporations and development banks, among others. These valid and compelling concerns have been on the radar screen for a long time and are difficult to fix. Part of the issue is how to lift people from poverty and accelerate international development. Another piece is justice, in this case the obligation and equity involved in providing low-cost and safe water. Another piece is socialism versus capitalism. Then, there is the issue of corporate social responsibility. It is a stew of many complex issues, and it seems nonsensical to single out a water company as a culprit or to allege that a soft-drink bottler is somehow guilty because it wants to locate a bottle plant in a town somewhere. Publications and media accounts about the water crisis do us a favor by sounding the alarm, but they seem sometimes to go off the deep end in describing the issues. As an engineer and manager, I may see solutions where others see just problems, but I have to temper my optimism with the same statement—a lot of the problems require political will and changes in human behavior that won't come easily.

CHAPTER 11

Government and Politics
in the Water Business

If there is any message in Tony Blair's 2010 book, *A Journey: My Political Life,* it is that policy takes a backseat to politics. It is not that good policy is not important, because it definitely is necessary. It is just not sufficient because, without successful politics, you can't do policy. That's a hard message for policy wonks, who think there are rational solutions to hard problems like water management.

Policy and politics go together, but they are different. Many of the likely changes identified in the last chapter require policy responses from the water governance system, which is the collection of society's control levers that determine how water is managed to meet human and environmental needs. Governance is a shared responsibility among the levels of government and water management organizations, and it controls water management to make sure it does its job (Grigg, 2011). Politics is a requisite to making sure that effective governance occurs.

Looking at the likely changes, we can identify those that require the most from governance as:

- Responding to aspirations among billions of people for up-to-date water systems.
- Regulating and enabling the water industry to protect environmental systems and respond to climate change.
- Providing incentives and controls to encourage water efficiency.
- Filling the gap between the old models of subsidy and the new models based on full-cost pricing, while not backing away from essential public purposes.
- Enabling water supplies to meet demands of energy production and to assist with hydropower production when possible.
- Enable systems of irrigation to help meet food production targets.

- Enable industry transformations to encourage unbundling and de-regulation of water systems.
- Provide a stable and transparent public presence for water policy in response to the media's need for public interest stories.

It is important to understand the role of governance in the water business because opportunities and situations that might seem mostly to be business scenarios often turn out to be decided by governance-related controls, rather than market forces. This chapter explains how governance affects management across the sectors of the water industry.

WATER GOVERNANCE

Water governance involves policy, capacity-building, and control. While governance involves the private sector as well as government and other public-sector institutions, government sets directions and gives policy guidance for water decisions and actions. Its activities include policy, programs, government agency operations, and the political process itself. Since government drives so much of the activity in the water industry, it is important to know what it has done and will do in the future to influence water management.

Government programs are activities such as the flood insurance program or the dam safety program. They involve agencies such as the Corps of Engineers, Environmental Protection Agency, Federal Emergency Management Agency, and the Bureau of Reclamation. The workforces of these agencies are the bureaucracies, a word that derives from *bureau*, which is just another word for *office*. Although the word *bureaucracy* has the negative connotation of suggesting overly complex procedures, its root meaning is about government structure and processes. It is important to understand how politics affect the water industry, what is meant by water policy and how it is made, which government water programs are dominant and how they work, and how government water agencies work at the three levels of government.

The three levels of government control most of the water industry's decisions, and politics involves both the art of government and working with others to make government work. While government can achieve a great deal, citizenship is key to water stewardship, which relies on people doing the right thing and not always having to be regulated. For this reason, the work of non-governmental organizations is of enormous importance in water management.

The executive branch of government is most important in water management and its regulation, but the legislative branch passes laws and makes financial appropriations, and the judicial branch is extensively involved in interpreting laws and resolving conflicts.

POLICY AND POLITICS

Policy and politics drive the water decision-making process, and government and relationships between people create the framework of institutional controls for work in the water industry. While *policy* and *politics* sound similar, they are different. Policy is a plan or course of action that influences and/or determines decisions and actions of government or nongovernmental organizations. Politics is the art or science of government or participation in political affairs. So, politics includes all participation in any aspect of government, and given the role of government in water management, these are very important to the water manager.

In the past, a few powerful decision makers controlled many water-management decisions. As an example, a dam might have been constructed with federal funds without much public disclosure of congressional proceedings. Now, there is a much greater requirement for public involvement within the framework of democratic government.

Public involvement in water management seeks to draw in all appropriate stakeholders and includes task forces and advisory groups, public meetings, mediation sessions, and collaborative problem solving.

Water policy is a crosscutting topic that draws from sectors that include natural resources, health, environment, and the economy. At the national level, it is distributed among various cabinet-level departments, with individual departments having lead roles in policy categories such as USEPA in safe drinking water. Policy categories are distributed among congressional committees, which accounts for some of the fragmentation in water policy.

Although water management is basically a local service, most policy is made at the state and federal levels. Water issues are multifaceted, which makes it difficult to have a unified water policy. Water-industry regulators have authorities in health and safety, environment, water use, fish and wildlife protection, and service levels, and these express areas of policy, which are normally focused in separate legislation such as the Clean Water Act and the Safe Drinking Water Act.

Water politics involves working out issues and conflicts among stakeholder interests. Speechmakers often quote President Kennedy, who is reported to have said: "Anyone who solves the problems of water deserves not one Nobel Prize but two—one for science and the other for peace." This quote illustrates the complexity and conflict that occur in water decisions. A simpler quote is attributed to Mark Twain: "Whisky is for drinking, but water is for fighting."

Water managers participate in politics as "the art or science of government" but they must refrain from politics as the conduct of or participation in political affairs because the essence of water management is balance, not partisan or interest-group politics.

The iron triangle of water politics involves congressional authorizations and appropriations, along with government agencies with roles in water; a broad band of interest groups; and the industries that support products and services to water handlers.

At the local government level, a great deal of the water politics deals with issues such as rate increases, floodplain zoning, and water conservation.

The ranges of interest-group politics illustrate the traps that can develop when advocating a water project or program. Perhaps the strongest group is the environmentalists, who are central players in water management. They generally push against growth, promote instream flows over water diversions, oppose dams and lakes, promote habitat, and oppose use of water for green lawns in cities.

Intergovernmental and regional politics occur among governments at the same level and between layers and jurisdictions. These involve federal versus state and local interests, interlocal conflicts, conflicts between uses such as water supply and recreation, conflicts between metropolitan areas, interbasin transfer, cities versus suburbs, and conflicts between states or nations.

Some of the conflicts occur from value differences and even personalities. These include conflicts between experts from technology, law, finance, policy sciences, and life sciences; conflicts involving staffs, legislatures, interest groups, and the public; public- versus private-goods arguments; and conflicts during emergencies, such as allocating water during drought. One expert, when asked what it would take to resolve conflicts among groups of farmers, said, "It is going to take some funerals."

The political goal for water managers is to resolve conflicts. This requires them to know who the stakeholders and decision makers are and to recognize the divergent agendas. Planning organizations are supposed to harmonize water management, but they may have biases toward one goal or another, and even public-interest organizations have diverse goals.

Balancing water decisions requires cooperation as in regional cooperation or integration. This might include such things as a regional management authority, consolidation of systems, a central system acting as wholesaler, joint financing, or coordination of service areas. Use of such win-win approaches in water management increases as the limits of what government can achieve become more apparent. Water problems require more than the earlier autocratic style. They require a special type of leadership highlighted by cooperation.

EMPOWERMENT AND CAPACITY-BUILDING

The water business requires more than simply government control through laws and regulation. It also requires capacity-building for its many large and small organizations. Capacity-building through financial assistance, organizational efforts, technical assistance or human resource development opens many opportunities for private sector actors to do business with water handlers.

Capacity-building enables water organizations to function effectively so they can provide the required services and controls. Capacity involves institutional issues that are internal (within the water management organization) and external (outside the water organization). Financial, technical, and workforce capacity apply to internal and external cases, and organizational capacity focuses on the development of the individual organizations.

In the case of safe water and sanitation, the situations around the world illustrate the need for capacity-building from the bottom up and the need to include planning, financing, designing, constructing, and, most important, maintaining. An external motivator such as a consultant or a donor might help establish the need, but to spark the service requires leadership to initiate action and overcome obstacles. In some cases, community organizers might get things done, but in other cases private investments might be required. In all cases, resources in the form of money, equipment, energy, water, and infrastructure are required.

Irrigation and drainage water services may require different approaches to organizing because they involve individual farmers rather than water supply customers. The farmer is engaged in bringing water and other inputs at needed times to optimize his income and may need to cooperate with others to manage irrigation systems. Mutual irrigation organizations exist around the world as business organizations to provide management and coordination. Irrigation farmers also need advice from extension agents and access to credit.

GOVERNMENT ACTIONS AND REGULATION

Regardless of the need for policy and empowerment, the real governance action in the water sector is regulatory control. At least this is the case in developed countries like the United States. However, the governance takes place in a system of balance of powers and the water industry operates with its own iron triangle, as shown in Figure 11.1. The figure shows how the water handlers are utilities and service providers, how the government operates at three levels in its various roles, and how the support sector is diverse and has vested interests in the industry's operations.

Chapter 14 explains regulations and how they are implemented and enforced. Another control mechanism is the coordination process itself, which can break down into litigation and/or political strife. Actually, the

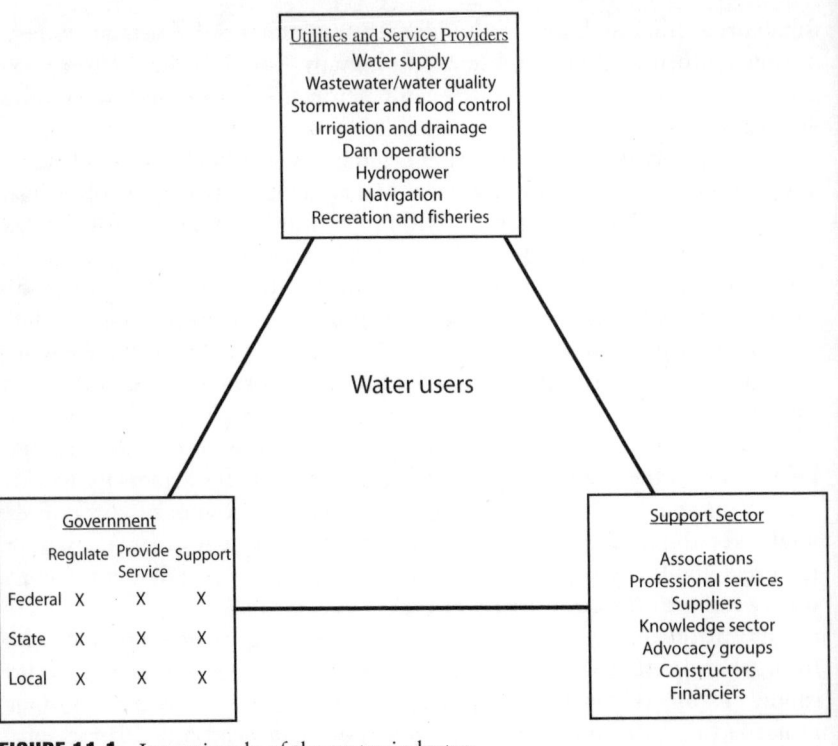

FIGURE 11.1 Iron triangle of the water industry

regulatory process that accompanies environmental impact statements serves as a coordination mechanism, and it can be long and costly.

Government agencies at the national, state and local levels are active in the water business, both for regulatory and programmatic actions. They operate in government-owned utility or service programs, which are mainly enterprises of government and mainly at the local government level or they can engage in direct government water programs, such as regulatory, data collection, disaster response, and others at all three levels of government. There is also some quasi-government activity, such as public universities with some water-industry involvement.

Federal Agencies

Direct government programs can be classified by federal, state, and local level and by function, such as mission agencies, regulatory agencies, and support agencies. Federal water "mission agencies" build and operate water facilities. They are the agencies with engineering staffs and budgets to build or maintain dams and related facilities. Two agencies, the U.S. Army Corps of Engineers (USACE or Corps) and the Bureau of Reclamation (Burec), have built the major share of large dams in the United States. The bureau operates in the 17 western states and the Corps operates nationwide, as well as overseas. The Corps is in the Department of Defense and the bureau is in the Department of Interior. In addition, the Natural Resources Conservation Service (NRCS), part of the Department of Agriculture, assists others with dam and watershed projects, but is not a dam owner like the Corps and bureau.

The Tennessee Valley Authority is another federal agency that built dams in the past. However, it is an independent government-owned utility. TVA is the nation's largest public power company, with 33,000 megawatts of generating capacity, and it works on integrated management of the river system and environmental stewardship.

The USACE is a source of business and jobs in the water industry because it has built several hundred dams and maintains water facilities for navigation and related functions. It has its own large workforce of civilian and military employees, many of whom provide engineering services that focus on water resources and other civil works projects, military construction, and design and construction management support for other defense and federal agencies. The Bureau of Reclamation has constructed more than 600 dams and reservoirs, including Hoover Dam on the Colorado River and Grand Coulee on the Columbia River. It is the largest wholesaler of water in the country, the water supplier to more than 31 million people and provider of water to 140,000 western farmers on 10 million acres of farmland that produce 60 percent of the nation's vegetables and 25 percent of its fruits and nuts. With 58 power plants, it is also the second largest producer of hydroelectric power in the western United States (Bureau of Reclamation, 2010).

The Environmental Protection Agency (USEPA) is the main water and environmental regulatory office of the federal government. Its headquarters programs are carried out in the Washington, D.C., office, where an assistant administrator directs the Office of Water. Programs are delivered through 10 regional offices, each of which has a unit dealing with water regulations. USEPA maintains extensive statistics about water and wastewater finance and has publications available with guidance about state revolving loan programs and other avenues of financial assistance. It was the main federal agency to oversee the original wastewater construction grants program, which dispensed $50 billion in grants from 1972 to the mid-1980s. These provided the subsidies to build much of the existing infrastructure of wastewater plants, which are now aging and needing renewal.

Other federal agencies have significant programs in water. Within the Department of Energy, the Federal Energy Regulatory Commission is an independent agency that regulates nonfederal hydropower projects. The Department of Health and Human Services exercises regulatory powers related to health and has responsibilities for bioterrorism and public health emergencies, waterborne disease outbreaks (Centers for Disease Control and Prevention) and regulating bottled water (Food and Drug Administration). Also, the Indian Health Service promotes health and sanitation among tribes. The Department of Justice has an Environment and Natural Resources Division, whose mission is "through litigation in the federal and state courts, to safeguard and enhance the American environment; acquire and manage public lands and natural resources; and protect and manage Indian rights and property." A number of courts within the federal courts system are involved with water cases. They are not identified with water specifically, but some judges have expertise in water matters. Two federal agencies, the U.S. Geological Survey and the National Weather Service, provide most of the streamflow and weather data used in water management.

Federal natural resources agencies in the Department of Interior and Department of Agriculture include the National Park Service, the Fish and Wildlife Service, the Bureau of Land Management, the Natural Resources Conservation Service and the Forest Service. Each of these has an important mission related to natural resources management and deals significantly with environmental water issues.

Other federal agencies with significant programs include the Department of Homeland Security, with a mission that includes the protection of infrastructure and water resources, and the Federal Emergency Management Agency, which is responsible for advising on building codes and flood plain management, disaster management, and the national flood insurance program.

The Department of Energy has strategic goals relating to water and has been studying it recently as part of the water-energy nexus. The Department of Defense addresses water issues for the armed forces, such as base logistics, providing water security, and providing drinking water to troops on operational missions. The Department of State works on water diplomacy, global environmental issues, and other water topics. Its Agency for International Development includes water-related international development. The Federal Highway Administration mission includes work on flood control, water quality, and stormwater management.

The Government Accountability Office (GAO), the Congressional Budget Office, and the Office of Management and Budget (OMB) provide oversight into water finances. The GAO has sections on natural resources and environment and on physical infrastructure. Closely related, the OMB has water-related programs, including the Energy, Science, and Water Division and the Natural Resources Division.

As the legislative branch, Congress has important committees with missions related to water: These include the House Resources Committee (Water and Power Subcommittee); the House Transportation and

Infrastructure Committee (has subcommittees for Water and Power; and for Highways, Transit and Pipelines); and the House Appropriations Committee (has subcommittees for Energy and Water Development, and for Interior, Environment, and Related Agencies). The Senate Environment and Public Works Committee has subcommittees for Clean Air, Climate Change, and Nuclear Safety; Fisheries, Wildlife, and Water; Superfund and Waste Management; and Transportation and Infrastructure; and the Senate Energy and Natural Resources Committee has the Water and Power Subcommittee. The Senate Appropriations Committee has the Subcommittee for Energy and Water Development.

State Agencies

State governments are the main units for regulating water systems. In a few cases, regulatory authority has not been delegated to them from the federal government but for the most part, as rules and regulation of water resources and health have increased, state governments have developed sophisticated regulator departments to administer them and legal staffs to handle issues in court or requiring legal work. The main regulatory agencies are state environmental protection agencies or health departments, which often perform the same tasks, state engineer or water resources offices to administer water use permits or water rights, public utility commissions (PUCs), attorney general offices, and special courts to handle water matters.

Regulation involving state agencies can occur in six categories, as indicated in Table 11.1.

State programs for administration of the Clean Water Act and Safe Drinking Water Act are usually combined in state agencies. Some states have state EPAs, and some have water pollution and drinking water programs in health departments. The recent trend has been to move these programs from health departments to state EPAs, although not all states have made that change.

TABLE 11.1 Categories and Examples of Water Regulation

Area	Regulatory Programs
Health and safety	Safe Drinking Water Act, dams and flood plain regulation
Water quality	Clean Water Act
Fish and wildlife	Endangered Species Act, other federal environmental statutes
Quantity allocation	State water rights or permit programs
Finance	State public service commissions (private water companies)
Service quality	Standards and codes of state and local governments

There are, of course, many more state than federal water agencies. Examples include the Arizona Department of Environmental Quality, the Illinois Environmental Protection Agency, the Kansas Division of Environment in the Department of Health and Environment, and the New Jersey Department of Environmental Protection. Officials of these agencies can associate with their peers in the Association of State and Interstate Water Pollution Control Administrators and the Association of State Drinking Water Officials.

Regulation of private water companies for water rates and business matters is handled by state public-utility commissions, which also regulate electric, natural gas, telephone, and related systems. These units have an NAICS code (926130) for "Regulation and Administration of Communications, Electric, Gas, and Other Utilities." It specifies: "This industry comprises government establishments primarily engaged in the administration, regulation, licensing and inspection of utilities, such as communications, electric power (including fossil, nuclear, solar, water, and wind), gas and water supply, and sewerage." (Note that "Government establishments primarily engaged in operating utilities are classified in Subsector 221, Utilities.")

Examples of PUCs are the Connecticut Department of Public Utility Control, the Massachusetts Department of Public Utilities, the North Carolina Utilities Commission, and the Public Utilities Commission of Nevada. The regulatory commissioners can associate with their peers through the National Association for Regulatory Utility Commissioners.

Normally, state governments locate their water legal staffs in the attorney general's office. In western states, several attorneys may staff these offices, while an eastern state will normally assign both environmental and water matters to the same legal staff. Some state courts, particularly in Colorado and Montana, are dedicated to water matters. In other states, special courts may be organized for particular problems. For example, a locality with drought problems might have a special court to enforce drought rules.

In state government, these two water resources management functions may or may not be located together: regulatory control of water diversions (water rights and permits), and coordination and promotion of water development and management. Control of water diversions is usually by water rights or water-diversion permits. Systems of water rights are common in the drier, western states, while eastern states have systems based on permits. In some cases, water use permits are handled by state EPAs. However, water diversion permits may be handled by a separate division or branch in those states.

The national association that serves these offices is the Interstate Conference on Water Programs. The unit to regulate dam safety is usually located in the state water resources department, and it is usually affiliated with the Association of State Dam Safety Officials. The flood plain unit may be located here, and it is coordinated through the Association of State Flood Plain Managers.

State water resource management agencies have different objectives than "regulatory" agencies. The primary agencies of this type are water resources departments (or divisions, branches, offices, etc.). Departments or divisions of water resources are more prominent in western states with systems of water resources development and/or management. Perhaps the leading example is the California Department of Water Resources, which is much larger than most comparable units in other states. In some cases, the water-resources management program is within the department, and the secretary of Natural Resources is the actual water-resources chief for the state.

Examples of water resources agencies and offices include the Alabama Office of Water Resources (Department of Economic and Community Affairs), the California State Water Resources Control Board (Environmental Protection Agency) and California Department of Water Resources, the Colorado Division of Water Resources and Colorado Water Conservation Board (both in the Department of Natural Resources), and the Division of Water Resources, North Carolina Department of Environment and Natural Resources.

State governments also have a group of resource management agencies with interests in, but not direct control of, water resources. These are usually housed in departments of natural resources (DNRs) or conservation. Regardless of the title or organization, DNRs usually contain several departments with water-related missions. These mirror the organization of the U.S. Departments of Interior and Agriculture. The agencies include: natural resources staff offices, forest services, mining boards, land-use commissions, fish and wildlife, parks and recreation, and coastal management. In addition, climate offices and state finance offices are important in water management, as are state water institutes and Sea Grant programs.

Some states have special finance offices to support water resources development or they have state finance offices that include water projects in their loan or grant portfolios. In most cases, these offices are located within larger groups. USEPA has an office of water and wastewater infrastructure financing, and states have created subsidiary offices to coordinate with it. In many cases, these offices will be within the state EPA. Examples are the California Division of Financial Assistance, State Water Resources Control Board; the Colorado Water and Power Resources Development Agency; the Texas Water Development Board; and the Rhode Island Clean Water Finance Agency.

As examples of the range of programs that a state agency might offer, the Texas Water Development Board coordinates the following financing programs. This might be the broadest portfolio in the nation, and similar agencies might offer only one or two such programs:

- Agriculture Water Conservation Grants and Loans.
- Clean Water State Revolving Fund Loan Program.
- Colonia Plumbing Loan Program.
- Community Self-Help Program.
- Drinking Water State Revolving Fund Loan Program.
- Economically Distressed Area Program.
- Federal Emergency Management Agency Flood Mitigation Assistance.
- Flood Protection Planning.
- Groundwater Conservation District Startup Loan Program.
- Regional Facility Planning Grant Program.
- Regional Water Planning Group Grants.
- Rural Water Assistance Fund Program.
- State Participation in Regional Water and Wastewater Facilities Program.
- Water and Wastewater Loan Program.
- Water Research Grant Program.

When water is an important political issue, a state governor may have a staff office or special assistant related to water. Governors also work together on joint issues and have representatives. For example, the National Governors Association has its Natural Resources Committee and the Council of Great Lakes Governors has its Water Management Working Group. Legislatures may also have committees to focus on water matters, such as the Colorado Senate Water Committee.

Local Government Water Programs

Because many water matters are handled at the local level, city and county governments may have water boards to advise on or manage water issues. Regional governments may have water planning offices or advisory boards. Special districts and soil and water districts are also involved in water-management activities.

Municipal policy groups or water boards may advise or work with local government water utilities, and in some cases, the water boards may govern the water utilities. For example, the Denver Water Board is a quasi-independent appointed board of citizens that governs the Denver Water Department.

The United States has 3,068 county governments. County governments may be involved in water-resources planning and coordination, and their engineers and natural-resources staffs may handle water matters. These water matters may include drainage and flood control, solution of countywide water problems, and watershed matters. County commissioners or governing boards may appoint citizen advisory boards to handle or advise on these issues. The National Association of Counties (NACO, 2010) has an ad hoc Watershed Management Advisory Committee.

Regional government and councils emerged in the United States from the 1960s and have become an important governmental force. Examples of regional government focus on councils of government, which may have multijurisdictional water planners. Service authorities and city-county mergers are other examples of regional government.

Regional government and councils have diverse responsibilities. Councils focus on planning and coordination. For example, the Atlanta Regional Council deals with diverse matters that include regional water supplies.

Special districts and resource or soil and water conservation districts provide multiple-purpose management services, including water services. Special districts manage water, sewer, or irrigation water services, especially in California and other western states. For example, the Irvine Ranch Water District provides water and sewer services across a broad area of southern California. Other special districts may serve multiple purposes in water management, such as areawide water management or conservation. Soil and water districts (or resource conservation districts) are special examples of areawide management entities. For example, the Randolph Soil & Water Conservation District in North Carolina advises on water quality for confined animal feeding, soil and water plans, and assistance to farmers.

GOVERNANCE CHALLENGES IN WATER MANAGEMENT

Neither government nor the private sector has been able to solve institutional obstacles in water management. These were listed by Viessman and Welty (1985) and by Rogers (1993):

- Ineffective law (patchwork of law, failure of law to integrate surface and ground water, separation of water-quantity and -quality law).
- Regulatory gridlock and proliferation of regulations.
- Fragmented authority and difficulty in coordination (diffusion of jurisdictions and split committees).
- Market failure (not recognizing that water is not a free commodity and difficulty in setting prices).
- Conflicting priorities (nonuniform evaluation criteria and difficulty in setting investment priorities and implementing projects).

This list explains why many rational approaches to solving water problems founder on problems such as those listed.

Advocacy and Interest Groups in Water

Any of the stakeholder groups explained in Chapter 2 can have its own interest or advocacy group, and most of them do have some type of organization. In water politics, environmental and other advocacy groups seem to have more influence than most others, however. These groups actually have NAICS categories for Civic and Social Organizations (NAICS 13410) and Environment, Conservation and Wildlife Organizations (NAICS 813312). The groups are generally known as environmental, watershed, conservation, and civic organizations. Examples of environmental groups are the Sierra Club, American Rivers, and the Environmental Defense Fund. Prominent wildlife and conservation groups include Ducks Unlimited and Trout Unlimited.

Civic groups can include organizations such as the League of Women Voters and various consumer groups that advocate for effective government and financial responsibility, among other causes.

Search for Integration

To address political differences and achieve balance in water management, concepts such as "integrated water management" have become fashionable. During the 1990s a concept called "integrated resource planning" was studied by water communities to improve the balance in supply planning. It was a framework to give equal attention to supply and demand, considering competing demands on source of supply, environmental considerations, plans of neighboring utilities, and stakeholder opinions (Vista Consulting Group, 1997).

The triple bottom line is a helpful integrative concept to frame the issues. Utility managers have explained it in terms of a comprehensive approach, or "total water management," which is defined as "stewardship of water for the greatest good of society and environment" (Grigg, 2008). The water business can actually be seen as in tension between ideals such as this and realities that involve a lot of politics and problems that need fixing.

Pivotal Roles of Government and Politics in Water Decisions

The chapter started with an anecdote that policy takes back seat to politics, and a quote attributed to John F. Kennedy about conflicts over water.

The conflict over water will continue to provide grist to feed the public's hunger for sensational stories, and it will require a stable and transparent public presence for water policy in response to the media's need for public-interest stories.

Global politics addresses the aspirations among billions of people for up-to-date water systems and the need to improve public health in developing countries. Other issues of global recognition include the rising demands of energy production, especially to meet the needs of emerging countries, and the need to sustain irrigation to help meet food production targets across the globe.

Advocacy and interest groups in water will continue to push for change, and political leaders recognize the need to regulate and enable the water industry to protect environmental systems, including a response to climate change. Water-efficiency programs are favorites of environmentalists, who see them as a way to avoid exploiting natural systems further. They also favor enabling the water industry to be more efficient by unbundling and deregulating water systems, but this goal sometimes seems to conflict with social objectives.

While water is a business, it is clearly more of a public business than a private business. No matter how much we want to unbundle its different parts, at the end of the day government must act as an arbitrator and coordinating mechanism among the many competing interests. This requirement for government action tends to throw a monkey wrench into entrepreneurial ideas such as privatization (see Chapter 16) and selling commodity water (see Chapter 20). This does not mean the ideas cannot succeed, but it does mean that proponents of projects and programs must be prepared to slog through long processes of government actions. It also means job security for many government workers in agencies at the federal and state levels, where regulatory and programmatic activities prevail.

The political orientation of water decisions means there is a tendency to defer capital and maintenance needs, especially those that are not so visible such as pipeline repairs. Water finance cannot avoid the need to subsidize some water services, even when conservative financial managers would like to move to full-cost pricing.

It would not make sense on a rational basis, but pork-barrel projects might receive precedence over more-needed basic maintenance projects.

CHAPTER 12

Financing the Water Industry

Given its diversity and public-private makeup, it is a challenge to find the right formula to finance the water industry. While none of its individual parts seems that large, the aggregate of water services rises to compete with electric power and natural gas among utility industries.

This chapter explains the sources of capital and operating funds in the water industry and where expenditures occur. It begins with the general framework for financing water management and traces the dividing lines between public and private responsibilities and between government and business activities. For example, you can have private responsibility, such as to pay for your own drinking water, but government operation of the service. The chapter also explains how rates and charges are set and how projects and programs are financed. It explains why the water industry is capital intensive and the problems of aging infrastructure and deferred maintenance occur. The conclusion of the chapter explores future financing scenarios.

PUBLIC AND PRIVATE RESPONSIBILITIES

The water business involves a mixture of public and private responsibilities and it is often difficult to draw the line between them. There are two dimensions to this problem. First, we have to decide on the responsibilities that involve public goods and should belong to the public sector. For example, should government be involved in health care? Not everyone agrees. Water supply is even more basic, but should it be a responsibility of government? The nation has agreed on some roles for government—such as regulating water safety and subsidizing water supply systems on a very limited basis— but many other questions remain unanswered.

The second dimension to the question is whether services ought to be provided and managed by the public or private sector, and this can involve different questions than the public good issue explained above. For example, the nation can decide that health care is a responsibility of government, but still have a management model that involves private-sector management.

In some ways, water services fit the definition of a public good, which is a concept from economics that means if a person consumes the good, there is no less for everyone else, such as air to breathe. The concept also includes the requirement that no one can be excluded from using it, that is, no corporation can gain control of it and sell it as a commodity. While this concept is idealistic and no good fits the definition completely, it leads to important questions of government responsibility. For example, it leads to important questions of whether it is a public responsibility to provide essential goods as human rights, such as clean air or drinking water. These questions have been answered by governments as they step in with social and environmental legislation to address human needs.

As a result of these questions, the field of public finance has had to address many issues about paying for goods provided to the public, including the range of water services.

Some water-sector costs are financed through user charges, but water management also requires tax financing through government agencies to pay for public purposes and to compensate for the reality that the cost of water services sometimes exceeds people's ability to pay.

As an example of public purposes, let's consider an environmental example. Assume that a government regulation requires a $1 million modification to a small dam to improve fish migration. Experts estimate that this will increase recreational catches by 2,000 pounds of fish per year. Using a cost of money of 5 percent and a project lifetime of 50 years, the annual capital cost of the improvement is $54,777 or $27 for each pound of fish caught. This cost will only increase because operating costs of the dam are not included, and the net weight of fish will be less after cleaning. So, the cost to compare with the grocery store cost might be $30 to $50 per pound. Opponents of environmental spending often seize on economics like this to bolster their case against public investments, but political leaders might decide to make this investment anyway. In making their decision, they will be looking at broader purposes, which show that the values of the water improvements are greater than that shown by this limited economic analysis. This is an example of a widespread challenge in public finance, how to allocate funding for water and related services toward their true values.

Ideas about the issue of public versus private management of public utilities seem to swing like a pendulum. In the 1920s and 1930s, support for publicly owned utilities grew, and then privatization became popular again during the 1980s due to backlashes against government programs. Now, the water industry operates as a mixed model, somewhere in between a government-owned and a privatized model.

As a result of the many years of argument about privatization of water services, the picture seems clear and to depend on a case-by-case analysis. On the basis of ideology, the argument is that water is an economic good and ought to be managed by the private sector and that smaller government is best because government is not reliable and people do not trust it. The counterargument is that water is a public good and ought to be managed by government to prevent private-sector exploitation, loss of political control, loss of jobs, and loss of public benefits of water.

On the basis of efficiency and business matters, privatization advocates argue that the private sector is more competent than the public sector and can deliver cost savings in construction, procurement and management, and in hiring and training. Also, private-sector management delivers tax revenues that do not occur from government control. They say that private operators can provide access to capital in private markets and government debt limits will not be imposed and that private firms can reduce risk by guaranteeing performance.

Advocates of public-sector management say that it is efficient, that cost savings from privatization are fictional, that tax benefits are a shell game and that long-term contracts create negative results and the potential for excessive rate increases. They argue that the public sector should generate capital for infrastructure and that effective management by government minimizes overall risk.

FINANCIAL FRAMEWORK

The water sector's overall financial framework is shown on Figure 12.1, which shows how revenues originate as fees, purchases, or tax payments from households and businesses, which include all funding, even government grants. The funds flow from the income and savings of households and businesses to the water handlers, which are utilities, industrial water managers, government agencies, and the facility managers of residential and commercial units.

The financial flows on the left are the total revenues required to support the full water industry, or $150 billion per year according to my estimates. The utility-sector revenues are the largest portion to pay for the work of organized utilities and the products and services they require. The industry-sector portion is difficult to quantify, but would comprise the total allocated portions of industry budgets for water-related services. Government-sector revenues would be tax receipts that go toward its water-related programs. Facility manager expenditures, other than industry water management, would be the total allocated portions of facility budgets to water-related services.

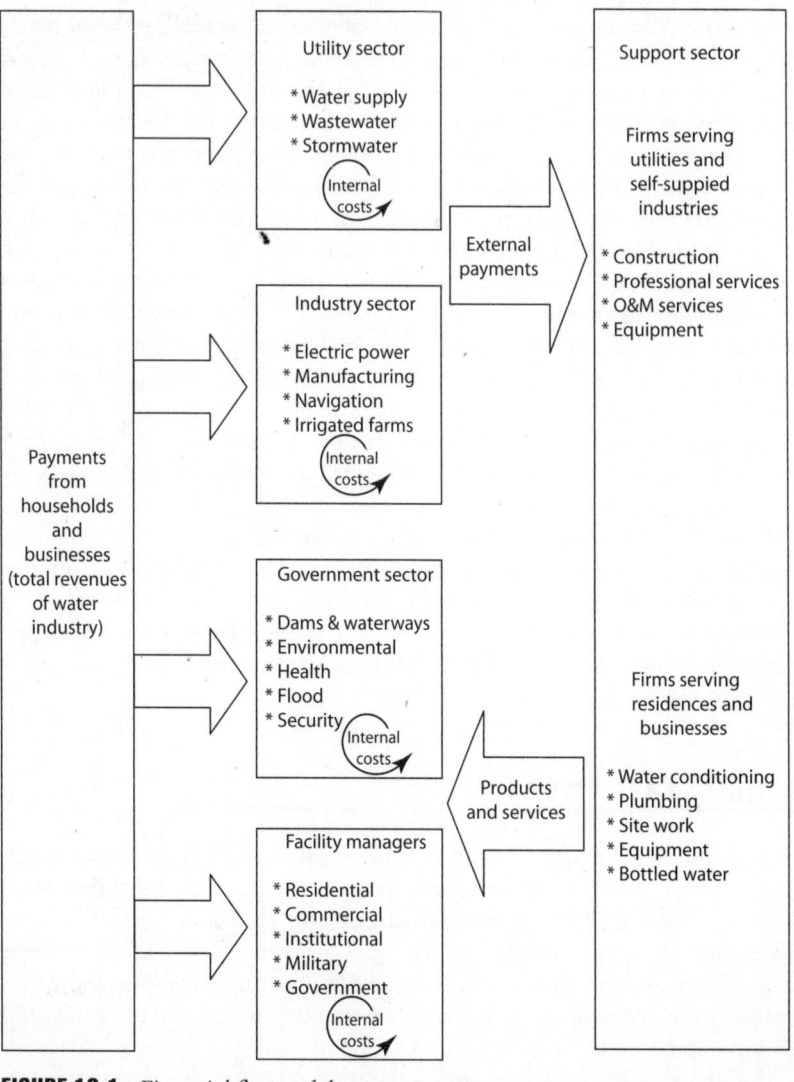

FIGURE 12.1   Financial flows of the water sector

Some of the funding is spent in-house by the water-management units, such as wages to the workforces. Other funds go toward external payments to firms providing products and services to large-scale or smaller water management units. At the larger scale, this might involve, for example, funding to engineers, contractors, and suppliers for construction of a pump station. Also, an industry might operate a water system that requires a good bit of outsourcing, but it might also have a staff to operate and maintain parts of the system. At the lowest level, the facility manager for a residence is actually the homeowner, who manages the household water system. The homeowner pays himself for work he does to repair the system or the funds flow through the homeowner's budget to hire a plumber.

Water supply, wastewater and stormwater are the three water-related utilities. The water-supply utility is the cornerstone of the sector, wastewater is almost as universal, and the concept of stormwater service as a utility is gaining traction, but it has a long way to go.

The flowchart shown on Figure 12.2 illustrates how money moves through water and wastewater utilities. This diagram was initially

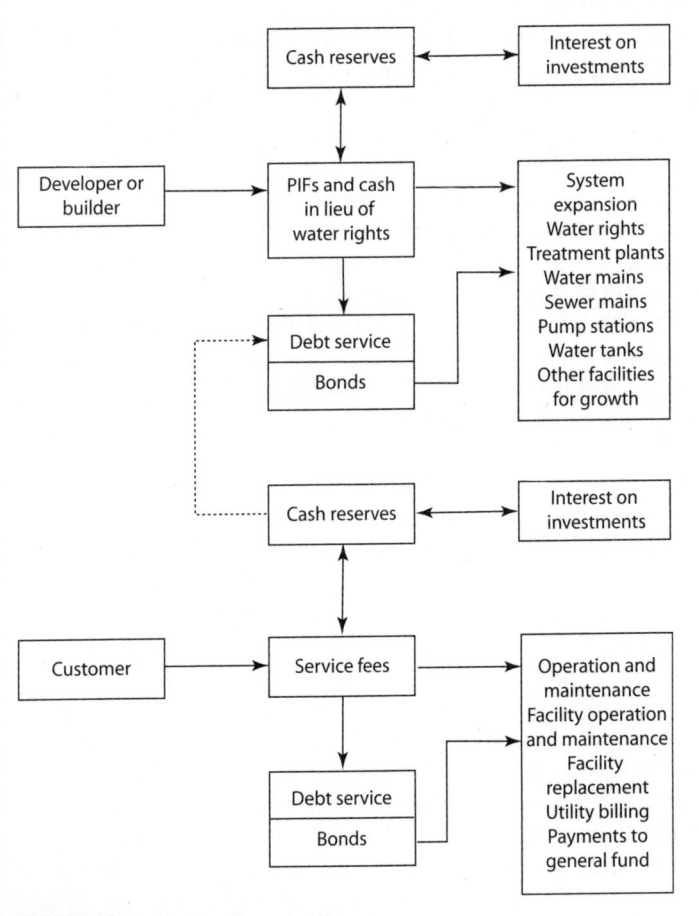

FIGURE 12.2 Utility financial flows

developed by Michael B. Smith, who was the director of the Fort Collins Water Utility, and he used it to explain to the Water Board (which I was on) and City Council how the utility funding worked. The diagram is dated but it still explains utility finances.

At the top of the diagram you see how developers and builders contribute capital funding in the form of plant investment fees (PIFs) and/or cash in lieu of water rights. The PIFs are intended to pay for infrastructure, and the water-rights funding pays for the raw water. In an eastern state, you might not have water-rights purchases but still have to pay for additional infrastructure to obtain raw water, so the concept applies across the board when you look at it like this. Of course, when the customer purchases or rents a property, the purchase or rental price includes a component to repay the developer or builder for the initial capital investment. These funds become part of the capital assets of the utility and may be used to finance system expansion or purchase water rights, to service bonded debt that was used for the same purposes, or to go into reserves.

At the lower part of the diagram, you see how customer payments in the form of service fees are used for operation and maintenance (O&M) and facility replacement. O&M funds pay for salaries, energy costs, materials and supplies, and other ongoing expenses. Facility replacement refers to the capital funding that is required to set aside to deal with depreciation, deterioration, and upgrading to maintain the integrity of the system.

Notice that facility expansion and facility replacement occur in different parts of the diagram. This illustrates an important principle of public finance that it is inappropriate to divert PIF funding to replace aging facilities because it is contributed to build new facilities for expansion. By the same token, it may be inappropriate to charge existing customers for the capital cost to add new customers. The exception is the situation where a city and its utility follow a policy of subsidizing new growth for purposes of economic development. This is the case where developers and builders pay less than the cost of expansion, thus requiring subsidies from existing customers. This is actually the case in many slow-growing communities that do not want to run off potential new businesses by charging high entry fees to the community.

The diagram also illustrates the need to collect enough money in service fees to pay for facility replacement. If enough funding is not collected, then the problem of deferred maintenance starts to build up, which is in fact what happens in most places. You can also see from the diagram the diversion of service fees toward utility billing services (located in a different part of the city government) and payments to the general fund, which include both administrative fees and payment in lieu of taxes (PILOT). In the best of cases, these represent valid ways to pay for public needs through transparent accounting, and in the worst of cases they are ways for general government to siphon off funding from utility fees to avoid raising taxes.

WATER-SUPPLY REVENUES

We can estimate the total of water-industry expenditures by adding up the individual water sectors. I assessed these in 2005 for water supply at $40 billion per year, which might need to be increased slightly now due to rate increases and growth. The 2005 estimate was based on data on water sales, which is maintained in AWWA's (1996) Water://Stats electronic database. Although this is dated, it is still in my opinion the best comprehensive data base available about the U.S. water-supply industry because it received information from more utilities than subsequent surveys.

The $40 billion estimate is corroborated by USEPA's (2010) Community Water Systems Survey (CWSS), which showed revenues of $39 billion for 2000 and provides details on sources of revenues and on expenditures. The 2000 CWSS is the latest available from USEPA, but the 2005 study is currently (in late 2010) being processed. The AWWA data is based on mailed-in surveys from utilities named in the survey data. The CWSS is based on sampling, which is conducted for USEPA by a contractor, who maintains the data in its files and does not disclose the names of utilities.

The AWWA data represent about 800 utilities serving a 1996 population of around 123 million. Some 744 utilities responded to the question about volume of water sales. A summary of the AWWA data is as shown in Table 12.1.

The total of all sales shown by AWWA was $10 billion, but the detailed data do not always sum to the total due to reporting inconsistencies. Other

TABLE 12.1 Water-Supply Sales from AWWA 1996 Survey

	Sales ($ millions)	Delivery (Billion gal/year)	% Sales	% Delivery
Residential	$4,838	2,266	0.52	0.42
Commercial/ Industrial	$2,304	1,360	0.25	0.25
Municipal	$ 225	110	0.02	0.02
Agricultural	$ 42	47	0.00	0.01
Wholesale	$1,462	1,383	0.16	0.25
Other	$ 461	260	0.05	0.05
Total above	$9,333	5,426	1.00	1.00

Data source: American Water Works Association, 1996

revenue (tap charges and other fees) was $1.3 billion. If you total these and increase this by population to 2005 levels, with an annual revenue increase of 4 percent from 1996 to 2005, the national total for the 2005 population of 295 million was $38.5 billion. The actual water charges may increase faster than inflation, so the total might be higher. However, a problem with the extrapolation by population is that not everyone is served by an organized utility and charges may be lower in some of the smallest utilities. For these reasons, the $40 billion estimate seems accurate only within about 10 percent, but as it was corroborated by the CWSS, it at least has some validation.

The operations and maintenance expenditures in the 1996 AWWA survey were $5.5 billion, of which most was for labor. Electric power and outsourcing were other significant categories of expenditures. Most expenditures were for source of supply, pumping and transmission, and next was for distribution of water, followed by treatment and laboratory expenditures. Billing, metering, and administration were also significant but less. The data were not always reported consistently, so it is not feasible to give exact breakdowns.

Total capital expenditures were reported as $4.5 billion, with source of supply, pumping, and transmission again being the major category at 30 percent, followed by distribution, pumping, and meter maintenance at 29 percent and water treatment and laboratory at 17 percent.

WASTEWATER AND STORMWATER REVENUES

Although we lack a comprehensive survey such as AWWA's for wastewater, the revenues are on the same order of magnitude as water supply. In a smaller survey, AMSA (2002) found 2001 revenue of $12 billion for 126 agencies serving 85 million people. By ratio according to population and by inflating the revenue by 4 percent per year as we did for water supply, we arrive at $48 billion, slightly larger than the water-supply estimate. However, AMSA mixed bond proceeds in with revenues, distorting the difference between recurring and one-time revenues. USEPA does not publish a survey comparable to the CWSS for wastewater, although it collects extensive data on investment needs. Lacking other data it seems reasonable to estimate that annual revenues for wastewater are the same as for water supply. Water and sewer rates are highly variable, but in my own community they are about equal on monthly bills.

Stormwater revenues have not been surveyed in any systematic way, but they are significant, as shown by the large construction activity to catch up with drainage needs and Clean Water Act rules, whether they are paid by fees or by taxes. In my community, stormwater fees are more than half of wastewater charges, but this may not be representative of the national picture. Based on my studies, I estimate that national revenues for local stormwater and flood control are about half the cost of water supply and wastewater, or $20 billion per year.

A number of industries provide their own water and wastewater services, but some would be connected to utility systems and their charges would be reflected in the utility totals. In some cases an industry might receive its water supply from a utility but have its own wastewater system. We lack an estimate of total water and wastewater costs for the industrial self-supplied sector, but in Chapter 2 it was shown that industrial self-supplied water was about 40 percent of public supplies. Industries normally do not finance the extensive and expensive distribution and collection systems required by public utilities, so we cannot estimate the costs by direct ratio. While there seems to be no accurate way to estimate a national total, it seems plausible that self-supplied water and wastewater costs of industry are on the same order of magnitude as utility revenues but should be reduced to account for the lack of collection and distribution system costs. Based on this, I estimate them at $20 billion each for industrial water supply and wastewater, or a total of $40 billion when combined.

Government water expenditures are estimated at $20 billion, mainly at the federal and state levels. These include agency budgets for resource management, environmental protection, regulatory controls, large-scale flood control, and security and would be in the budgets of agencies such as the Corps of Engineers and Bureau of Reclamation, as well as the smaller budgets of some federal agencies, such as the U.S. Geological Survey, and many state agencies. This sector receives mostly taxes and appropriations because its services are difficult to charge for.

An accurate estimate of revenues of other water industry sectors is difficult to make, and we need to distinguish between water management, water use, and ancillary activities. For example, if a parks and recreation department collects fees to manage a reservoir, some might go toward water management but others might be to manage facilities such as docks.

The activities included in this category are shown, along with my estimates, in Table 12.2.

In the household and business sector, payments from individuals or small businesses are applied toward water-system improvements, such as plumbing construction and renewal, site landscaping, water conditioning and purification, bottled-water sales, and boating and sport fishing. It is hard to analyze and estimate expenditures in this sector, but the sector is large. For example, the Bureau of Labor Statistics estimates that in 2007 there were 435,010 plumbers, pipefitters, and steamfitters working at a mean annual average wage of $47,350. This totals over $20 billion in wages and does not include

TABLE 12.2   Estimated Revenues of Water-Industry Sectors

Sector	Activities	Estimate
Irrigation and drainage	Budgets of irrigation providers and expenditures for irrigation and drainage. Landscape industry	$20 billion
Hydropower	Water-related expenditures of hydroelectricity producers	$20 billion
Navigation	Water-related work of private navigation providers, including channel maintenance, port authorities, docks, and marinas	Not estimated
Recreation and fisheries	Water augmentation and improvements for fisheries and water-recreation facilities	Not estimated

costs of their support systems. Based on this number, I am estimating this sector at $20 billion per year, but the number does not include many equipment items, such as costs for new homes, and it may be way low on household and business landscape irrigation expenses and drainage.

The bottled-water and point-of-use (POU) treatment sectors can be included here as well. Chapter 21 provides details of the bottled-water and point-of-use treatment industries. The only firm number available for bottled water was $12 billion for wholesale revenues. Revenues of POU providers are not known exactly, so a ballpark figure of $20 billion is adopted for the combined category of POU providers and bottled water.

Aggregated water-industry revenues are shown in Table 12.3.

TABLE 12.3   Estimates of Aggregated Water-Industry Revenues

Water Sub-Industry	$, billions
Water utilities	40
Wastewater utilities	40
Stormwater and flood control	20
Industrial self-supply water and wastewater	40
Government	20
Irrigation and drainage	20
Hydropower	20
Navigation	NA
Recreation and fisheries	NA
Residential and commercial plumbing and irrigation	20
Bottled water and POU services	20
Total water-industry revenues	240

As you could see from the explanations, the estimates in Table 12.3 are approximate and the accounting system is not rigorous, but it does give some idea of the expenditures across the water industry.

The financial sector that supports the water industry includes consultants, commercial and investment banks, equipment financiers, and insurers. Financial consultants help perform rate studies and advise on financing packages. Most of the banking is through what you might consider as development banks, and the state infrastructure funding agencies are perhaps the most visible among the banks. Although the New York City water system was started under the auspices of a bank scheme, commercial banks are not very involved in financing major utilities, but they might finance small utilities and water-industry support businesses. For example, firms such as GE Capital will finance industrial water-related equipment. Investment banks are involved to the extent of underwriting bonds, and bond rating agencies, such as Moody's and Standard & Poor's, are involved in water and sewer bond ratings.

Private equity companies purchase water systems and operate in other ways to increase capital funding. In fact, the Asian Development Bank (ADB) announced in 2010 that it would invest up to $20 million in a private equity fund to support the development of water-related infrastructure in Asian countries. The fund is named the Asia Water Fund, and it will invest in water and wastewater assets in China and Southeast Asia. The fund is owned by a subsidiary of the AmInvestment Group and has a target fund size of $100 million, which will be disbursed in $5 million to $10 million investments. ADB noted that the opportunity for private investment in water has increased with government finances being constrained by the global crisis and the regulatory environment in Asia moving toward full-cost recovery (Stedman, 2010). The water industry financial sector involves various government agencies, such as the Flood Insurance Program that is run out of the Federal Emergency Management Agency. Private companies are also active in flood insurance, and they also insure various aspects of utility operations.

RATES AND CHARGES

Based on the estimates given above, the utilities are on the order of half of all water-industry expenditures and they are the sectors where finances are raised by rates and fees. The rest of water handling is financed by government or by industry and homeowners as part of their ongoing expenditures.

The procedures for setting fees and user charges vary among the three urban water services. Water-supply rate-setting is based on well-established procedures, and AWWA has published a manual for many years about how to set fees. Rate procedures for wastewater are not as well established, but in most large utilities they are based on cost-of-service principles. In the past, stormwater systems were mainly financed from property taxes, but a number of cities have initiated stormwater utilities that charge users based on parameters such as lot size and runoff coefficient.

Water utilities are businesses and require charges to pay for services provided. This is the essence of the "enterprise" basis of water services, where charges are imposed for services delivered. Under the enterprise basis of operations, most revenues should come from rates and charges so that you pay for what you use. In other cases, taxes, fees, grants, and intergovernmental transfers are used as revenues.

Setting charges for water services falls into the realm of utility rate-setting. Principles for setting them include (Vaughn, 1983):

- They should be levied on the beneficiaries of the services.
- Prices or fees should be set at the marginal or incremental cost of providing the service, not the average cost.
- Peak load pricing should be used to manage demand.
- Special provisions should be made to ensure adequate access to services for low income residents where burdens will result from marginal cost pricing.
- User fees should be responsive to inflation and to economic growth.

In addition, rates ought to promote wise use of resources, generate the funds required, be stable so as to avoid shocks, and be simple to understand.

According to AWWA (2000), the rate-setting process consists of the determination of revenue requirements, the determination of the cost of service by customer classes, and the design of the rate structure itself. The AWWA manual specifies two basic approaches: the commodity-demand method and the base-extra capacity method. The difference between these two methods is essentially the way to classify the costs.

The principle that prices or fees should be set at the marginal or incremental cost of providing the service, not the average cost, leads to the "cost of service approach," which has been used in the water-supply industry for many years. Howe (1993) explained that, although determining the correct price for water is complex, the correct price ought to be "the amount paid per unit of water withdrawn from the supply system, for the next (or marginal) unit withdrawn." With this cost, "a rational user will compare with marginal benefits in deciding how much water to apply" to different uses such as domestic, industrial, irrigation, and other water uses. Howe reasoned that "water prices, appropriately set and applied at different points of the water supply and use cycle, perform many valuable functions, namely to confront water users with the costs of providing water, to help signal water suppliers when supply augmentation is needed, and to help shape a rational approach to a healthy water environment."

While the cost-of-service approach to setting rates is valid for business objectives, it is a problem to include social costs into the equation. An approach to achieve social or political objectives is sought by many cities, and it might change from a declining block rate to an increasing block rate to promote conservation. It might also organize rates among classes of users to promote social equity by lowering the cost of water for low-income customers.

To know how something really works, you must follow the money, and we can do that by analyzing a water bill. These are based on rates set for water use, and as I was writing this in late 2010, a proposed rate increase by Denver Water was in the news. One news report was titled: "Denver Water raising rates for 20th straight year" (Finley, 2010). The Denver Water Board explained that it had to maintain more than 3,000 miles of pipe, 12 reservoirs, 22 pump stations, and 4 treatment plants. The infrastructure is aging and requires upgrades, which must be financed from the board's $340 million annual budget, which receives no subsides to augment rates and tap charges. The rate increase is expected to generate about $21 million per year to use for improvements. The in-city rates are still low, at about $330 per year per connection, or about $27.50 per month. This is for water supply only, as wastewater service is provided by another city agency.

To put these figures into perspective, let's look at the need for water funding from 30,000 feet, as they say. Denver Water's 3,000 miles of pipe is about 0.3 percent of a national total of about one million miles. On the basis of its pipe inventory, Denver Water apparently serves 900,000 people. Based on its full customer base of 1.3 million people, this is in the ballpark because many suburban customers are served with wholesale water where most of the pipe of the infrastructure is owned and maintained by other utilities.

National figures such as the ASCE Report Card peg the unmet drinking-water infrastructure needs at $125 billion over five years. This tracks with national estimates of replacement costs of drinking water that run upward of $500 billion, and it is consistent with numbers I use for my classes that suggest that to build new drinking water infrastructure costs about $1,500 per capita. This is the total cost for source of supply, treatment, and distribution and suggests a tap fee of $3,000 to $4,000 for a three-person house, which would be added to tap fees collected from commercial and industrial customers to pay fully for the infrastructure. The current tap fees in my city and nearby Colorado cities range higher than this, but the cost of raw water here is higher than in many parts of the United States, and many cities have not implemented these types of infrastructure charges, so it is difficult to compare.

TABLE 12.4   Rate Codes and Examples for Fort Collins

	Rate Code	Usage, Gallons	Charge, $
Base charge	WB20		13.21
Tier 1	W220	7,000	14.31
Tier 2	W220	6,000	14.09
Tier 3	W220	8,980	24.26
	Total	21,980	65.87

Data source: www.fcgov.com/utilities/

If you amortize a $1,500 per capita capital charge over a 50-year example period at an interest rate of 3 percent, the annual cost is $58.30, or about $14.50 per month for a three-person home. If you add in operational and maintenance costs, you will very quickly justify a monthly water bill of more than $30, which is higher than in many parts of the United States. Bear in mind that amortizing the capital over 50 years at 3 percent is very low-end and that the $1,500 infrastructure cost is also low, so you might easily estimate a water bill of double the $30 per month.

Lest the loose ends of this financial analysis begin to look like an analysis of the Social Security deficit, the goal was simply to point out the fundamentals of how a water bill is determined. Now, let's analyze an actual bill to see some of the numbers.

Table 12.4 shows charges from one of my utility bills from the city of Fort Collins, which has water, wastewater, stormwater, and electric energy on it. As you see, the total bill for the month between August–September 2010 was $180.01, of which all but $68.50 in electric energy is for water-related services.

Reading from the top down, you see the four services listed, and each has a rate code next to it. The only water service with a meter reading is water supply, with the readings being 15,886 and 18,084 for a difference of 2,198. The bill states that there is a multiplier of 10, so the usage is 21,980 gallons. The bill does not say that these are gallons, but you can figure that out from the data below, which do state GAL (or gallons) as the unit.

The four rate codes for water supply, corresponding to different levels of use, are shown, along with the charges, in Table 12.4.

This is actually a high per-capita use, and for the three-person home it indicates 236 gpcd. The main cause of the high usage was outdoor watering, which peaked in August due to a dry month of one inch or less of rain. Like most Fort Collins homes, ours has a yard of bluegrass that requires a lot of water to prosper. If bluegrass needs two inches of water per week to prosper, then from rainfall our yard was short about seven inches for the month,

TABLE 12.5 Basis for Fort Collins Water Rates

	Base charge for water regardless of use	$13.21
	Use levels	Volume charge per 1,000 gallons
Tier 1	0–7,000 gallons	$2.04
Tier 2	7,001–13,000 gallons	$2.35
Tier 3	Over 13,000 gallons	$2.70

Data source: www.fcgov.com/utilities/

and if that was applied to 5,000 square feet of grass, it would require the full 21,000 gallons on our bill. We must have applied less, such that if we used 100 gpcd for in-house use, then our irrigation use was about 12,000 gallons. These approximate calculations illustrate how outdoor water use affects a water bill.

The Fort Collins Utilities web site explains how the rate codes work (Table 12.5).

The rates include the PILOT charge (payment in lieu of taxes). By multiplying the usage times the rates, you obtain the totals shown in utility bill.

Notice the increasing rates with level of usage, from $2.04 to $2.70. This is known as an "inclining block rate" or "conservation rate," which is intended to encourage conservation of water. This is considered an innovation in water efficiency, along with other approaches, such as water budgeting for homes, with higher rates after you pass a threshold of water use.

Notice the wastewater charge on the bill at $27.49 with a Rate Code Q221 and a usage of 5,280 as the winter quarter average (WQA) for January–March. This reflects the fact that water use in the summer is variable (as shown by how the August–September bill reflects lawn irrigation), but wastewater discharge will be more constant and reflect in-home use mostly. Therefore, the winter quarter average use of water is more representative of your wastewater load. If the average winter month is 30 days and the average use is 5,280 gallons, it would work out to 88 gallons per capita per day for two people in a residence. This is a common level of in-home water use for the United States. Our utility reports that 5,200 gallons is the median winter quarter use in the city. Your WQA use is recalculated every April.

The base single-family wastewater charge is $13.57 and the volume charge per 1,000 gallons is $2.64, figured on all use above 3,000 gallons. Therefore, our charge of $27.49 is computed as $13.57 + 2.64*(5,280)/1000. A minimum WQA of 3,000 gallons is assumed for all residences.

TABLE 12.6 Stormwater Rate Factors, Fort Collins

Rate Factor	Percent of Impervious Area	Rate Factor Category Based on Land Use
0.25	0–.30	Very light
0.4	.31–.50	Light
0.6	.51–.70	Moderate
0.8	.71–.90	Heavy
0.95	.91–1.0	Very heavy

Data source: www.fcgov.com/utilities/

Notice the stormwater charge of $16.21 with rate code H116 but no further explanation. The Fort Collins web site explains how rates pay for construction and maintenance of the stormwater system and rates are based on lot size (perhaps including a share of open space), on a base rate of $0.0041454, and on a rate factor that is determined from the percentage of impervious area.

For single-family lots under 12,000 square feet, the monthly rate is lot size x $0.0041454 x rate factor. For lots over 12,000 square feet, the charge is the same for the first 12,000 square feet and 25 percent of the charge for areas larger than that. The logic is that larger lots are more rural in character and produce less runoff.

The rate factors used by Fort Collins are shown in Table 12.6.

Our lot is in the range of 10,000 square feet (0.23 acres), and the city has apparently applied the "light" designation, assigning a rate factor of 0.4 to compute our monthly bill. The stormwater bills in the city are somewhat controversial because people are not always sure about the service they receive, as explained in Chapter 6.

To illustrate where this money goes, we look at Fort Collins' utility budget and a flow chart of the funding streams. The utility budget is shown in the Fort Collins city manager's recommended budget, which provides a link to previous and future recommended budgets (City of Fort Collins, 2010b). As an example, we find the water fund statement in the budget (page 297), and it shows the following income and expenses (summarized from the detailed version) from the actual 2009 budget (Table 12.7):

The statement was simplified to give a focus on the major income and expense items. As you can see, personnel are the major expense, with internal administrative services being a close second. In Fort Collins, billing is handled by other city departments, so we assume that most of the charges are for billing.

TABLE 12.7 Income Statement of Fort Collins Water Fund

Revenues	
Water sales (all water fee income)	21,752,118
Interest (allocated interest on water fund balance)	1,553,797
Contributions and donations (miscellaneous income)	2,115,681
All other	279,549
Total income	$ 25,701,145
Expenses	
Personnel (utility personnel)	6,391,492
Professional and technical (outsourced professional services)	1,856,081
Utility services (electric, gas, and telecommunications)	400,805
Repair and maintenance	1,539,790
Internal admin services (funds allocated to other city departments)	5,804,701
Depreciation	4,853,325
All other (vehicles, supplies, facility costs, and other miscellaneous)	4,423,014
Total expenditures	$ 25,269,208
Debt service	5,854,267
Ending fund balance	$240,702,356

Data source: City of Fort Collins, 2009

AGING INFRASTRUCTURE AND DEFERRED MAINTENANCE

The United States has a problem with aging infrastructure, and it can be seen from utility finances. The ASCE Report Card shows five-year investment needs for water and wastewater at $255 billion, and other needs estimates are for the same order of magnitude.

To understand the problem, let's compare management of our water infrastructure with management of our personal vehicle. If you care about your safety and the performance of your vehicle, you will maintain it to keep it in like-new condition, and when the time comes, you will replace it. You will monitor its condition and performance, and if they drop below what you need, you will take steps to remedy the situation. You do these things because you care about your safety and your vehicle's performance and you choose to take responsibility.

In contrast to this, most water infrastructure is out of sight and out of mind. It belongs to us collectively, so none of us has the same stake in managing it that we do for our personal property. It is difficult to monitor condition and performance, so we may assume all is well until we get a wakeup call from a failure, such as a blown-out water main. When experts tell us that certain funding levels are required to bring the infrastructure up to like-new condition, we say, "Why should we?" People are having a hard time and cannot afford higher water bills.

To some extent you can see this in the Fort Collins fund statement (Table 12.7). The city has a relatively new system, and it earmarks $4.8 million for depreciation of a water system that has a replacement value on the order of $150 million. Those funds reduce the indicated surplus that can be used to increase the fund balance, so the fund balance is reduced by the amount of the depreciation. All of this sounds good, but the main issue is the willingness of the organization to set aside the funds.

CAPITAL STRUCTURE OF THE WATER INDUSTRY

Capital for water infrastructure projects comes from government grants, debt financing, and reserves of water organizations. As we explained at the beginning of the chapter, the public-private nature of the water industry requires a blend of financing. This means that government financing actions are required, but user-pay and private-sector financing is also needed, especially for enterprise management of utilities.

The water-industry infrastructure that was explained in Chapter 2 has an asset value in the range of $1 trillion, and the major share is in water-supply and wastewater systems. My estimates for these sectors are shown in Table 12.8, which also provides comments on the need for capital investment in the sectors.

The categories shown are the mostly large and public systems that require the greatest capital investments. Industrial, commercial, and small-scale systems are not shown in the table. See Chapter 2 for more detail on them.

Looking at the totals in the table, we see that the major capital needs are for the supply, treatment, and distribution systems of water-supply utilities and the collection, treatment, and disposal facilities for wastewater utilities. In general, these are financed by bonded debt, government revolving programs, pay-as-you-go, and government grants. A good overview of these modes of financing can be developed by consulting the *Municipal Year Book*, which is published by the International City and County Management Association (ICMA). While it does not contain an actual database, the *Year Book* publishes reviews of various municipal finance issues, and by consulting a number of volumes you can compile a good picture of water-related capital financing.

Debt financing through tax-exempt bonds is the favorite way to raise capital funding for water and wastewater. Municipal bonds can be general

TABLE 12.8 Infrastructure Investment Needs in Water Sectors

Sector	Assets $ billions	Need for Capital Investment
Water supply	400	Aging infrastructure creates growing backlog, expansion follows land development, and there is an ongoing need for upgrades to meet regulations and to reduce risk
Wastewater and water quality	400	Similar to water supply, with focus on rapid deterioration of wastewater-treatment systems and on upgrades to reduce pollution and failures
Stormwater and flood control	100	Stormwater systems require upgrades to meet nonpoint source controls and to fix inadequate systems. Urban flood control emphasizes land use control.
Dams, reservoirs, and levees	100	Major unmet needs exist for levees and for dam safety upgrades. See Chapter 3.
Irrigation and drainage	100	Difficult to generalize about investment needs, but farm-to-city water deals will require major projects, see Chapter 8.

obligation (GO) or revenue bonds, with GO bonds backed by taxes and revenue bonds backed by government authorities on the basis of revenues of an enterprise. The generally reliable water and sewer fees seem ideal to service revenue bonds and, in fact, the number of bond financing issues for water and wastewater is quite large.

Revenue bond financing is through tax-exempt municipal bonds, which are debt obligations issued by states, cities, counties, and other governmental entities to provide capital for construction. The tax-exempt feature of municipal bonds creates a subsidy from the federal government and in some cases from state governments. Current (2010) total bond indebtedness in the United States is $35 trillion, of which $2.8 trillion is in municipal bonds. The larger categories were mortgage related bonds, corporate debt, and Treasury-backed bonds.

Bonds offer the choice to use "pay as you use" rather than "pay as you go" financing. This means that customers who use the infrastructure pay for it directly, rather than customers contributing to a fund for future investments. I explained this in more detail in (Grigg, 2010). This approach to bond financing has held up in the legal arena and complies with federal law and policy.

Water and sewer is just one of the categories of municipal bonds, which also finance airports, schools and universities, hospitals, public housing, public power, toll roads, and special districts.

I consulted the Securities Industry and Financial Markets Association (2010) web site to see if I could determine the total of water and sewer debt, but no one seems to compile these statistics. Total debt is reported, but the statistics do not break down the categories of municipal bonds.

When you look at the categories, it seems reasonable to assume that the percentage of bonds would correlate with asset values and construction spending. In spite of that assumption, I have been so far unable to estimate the total water and sewer bond issues.

News releases for large city water and sewer bonds show indebtedness of as much as $2.6 billion in water bonds, for the Los Angeles Department of Water and Power (Yahoo Finance, 2010). The Fort Collins (2009) Comprehensive Annual Financial Report does not list the total outstanding bond issues, but it shows that the city issues about $8 million in water refunding bonds and about $30 million in sewer bonds to rehabilitate a wastewater treatment plant. Total city revenue bond indebtedness for business-type activities ranged from $100 million to 120 million over the last 10 years. Water debt service requirements were $3.8 million, sewer requirements were $6 million and stormwater requirements at $5 million, or total water-related debt service required at about $15 million per year. This compares to revenue of $16 million for water, $10 million for sewer, and $8 million for stormwater, such that total revenues of $34 million provide a coverage ratio of just over 2.0. I asked the Water Utility for the latest totals, which were water fund, $25.9 million; wastewater fund, $42.9 million; and stormwater fund, $33.9 million, for a total of $102.7 million. Total interest payments were about $5.34 million, which suggest that the city is paying an average interest rate of about 5 percent, which creates an incentive to re-fund the bonds toward lower interest rates.

Based on the total of all municipal bonds and the level of activity shown here, it seems reasonable to speculate that all water and sewer bonded indebtedness in the Unites States is in the range of $300 billion, or 10 percent of all municipal debt, and in the neighborhood of 30 percent to 40 percent of total water and sewer asset value.

Although the revenues of water and sewer utilities should be reliable, revenue bonds are not without risk. For example, sewer bonds of Jefferson County, Alabama, were given "junk" status in 2008 and since then it has been unable to resolve its financing issues. If Jefferson County, which includes Birmingham, goes bankrupt, it will be the largest U.S. municipal bankruptcy. A sewer refinancing deal arranged in 2002 and 2003 ran into difficulties during the credit crisis. In 2008, the bondholders' trustee sued to improve system operation and raise rates to repay

$3.2 billion of bond debt. In 2003, the county received a consultant's recommendation to raise sewer rates by 89 percent over six years to service the debt. In early 2010, Raftelis Financial Consultants recommended a rate increase of 6.8 percent, but the typical bill was already more then $50 per month (Edwards and Braun, 2010). This problem continues at this writing, and it will be interesting to learn of the eventual outcome, which is certain to tarnish the image of water and sewer bonds, at least in some quarters.

Actually, government revolving loan programs are another form of debt, and they may be partially financed themselves by more debt. For example, a revolving loan program is like a development bank, which might be capitalized by contributions and bond sales, with loan repayments going to service its own debt.

The best-known revolving loan programs are based on government grants to state organizations, which are used as capital to loan to local governments. These are the USEPA-managed Clean Water State Revolving Fund (CWSRF) for wastewater and the Drinking Water State Revolving Fund (DWSRF). These funds were created to assist state and local governments with their financing needs, with the CWSRF in place since 1987 and the DWSRF in place since 1997.

The CWSRF replaced the construction grants program, which provided matching funds as subsidies to help local governments construct wastewater facilities. The DWSRF was created to respond to the unfunded mandate issue and underinvestment in drinking-water facilities.

To illustrate magnitudes of funding, the CWSRF has recently (as of 2010) funded more than $5 billion annually for wastewater treatment, nonpoint source pollution control, and watershed and estuary management and has provided $74 billion through 24,688 low-interest loans. The newer DWSRF has financed more than 5,000 loans and disbursed $10 billion (as of 2007) (USEPA, 2010).

The development bank concept, based on revolving loans, has found its way into many state governments, who have programs to assist in construction of public facilities, including water infrastructure.

For example, the Colorado Water Resources and Power Development Authority (2010) operates the CWSRF and the DWSRF for the state, but it also has programs for small hydropower, small water-resources projects, and water-revenue bonds to supplement the other water and wastewater programs. In some other states, such as Illinois, the programs are run out of state water agencies.

Other examples of state funding programs (which were discussed in Chapter 11) include the Oklahoma Environmental Finance Authority, the Texas Water Development Board, and the Rhode Island Clean Water Finance Agency.

Pay-as-you-go is simply a way to save money into a fund, then use it when capital investments are needed. It is different, timewise, from pay-as-you-use, which is the approach when bond financing is used. In pay-as-you-go financing, the current ratepayers may be contributing for future needs, although you could look at it as they are paying for current depreciation. In any case, it is a valid way to finance some infrastructure needs, although debt financing is, in general, more popular.

Government grants for water-related programs occur from political decision-making. The 1970s and 1980s Construction Grants Program infused more than $50 billion into wastewater facilities, and under the current stimulus program the CWSRF received $4 billion from the American Recovery and Reinvestment Act of 2009 and the DWSRF received $2 billion. Additional spending has occurred through earmarks and other appropriations. To recipients, government grants are a welcome source of financing, but they are not a predictable source on which to base enterprise financing.

Stormwater and flood control capital financing is a mixed bag, which involves all three levels of government and types of facilities. As explained in Chapter 5, flood control programs are largely based now on land-use controls, although the need to upgrade levees has created a large financing gap that must be faced. The stormwater utility concept, discussed in Chapter 5, is the main financing innovation for local stormwater and drainage facilities.

When cities lack stormwater utilities, they must turn to methods of financing they might use for other municipal improvements, which can include the range of debt, pay-as-you-go, and government grants that are available for other municipal improvements. Once a city joins the stormwater utility game, it can finance facilities in the same way as water and wastewater, and this enables the utilities to move away from total reliance on development contributions, taxes, and general obligation bonds. Fort Collins currently has $34 million in outstanding stormwater revenue bonds, for example.

Capital financing for dams, river controls, and navigation is largely from government, such that it occurs in today's environmentally sensitive climate. Repairs to dams that are owned by utilities, local governments, and others must be financed through revenues available to them, of course. As major dam owners, the Corps of Engineers and Bureau of Reclamation largely use government funding to repair and manage their inventories. They receive annual appropriations for ongoing activities and the corps also manages a trust fund for inland waterways improvements, with funding from user fees, following the same concept as the Highway Trust Fund, which provides major funding for federal highways.

When special issues arise, such as a dam failure or other special need, Congress and federal and state agencies will step to the plate to provide funding. For example, when Hoover Dam required a bypass bridge to improve its security, funding came entirely from the U.S. government. While this is a large and unusual project and it was treated as a transportation project, it involved the dam and its security. Funding in the range of $250 million was provided through federal and state grants and loans (U.S. Federal Highway Administration, 2010).

Capital funding for irrigation systems is not at high levels, and when it occurs it will respond to local needs. For example, in Colorado, which is a major irrigation state, little capital project funding is underway. There is discussion of major projects, which might include some irrigation funding, but none is in the pipeline. Irrigation agencies may be involved in project development for other purposes, such as to convert supplies to municipal use, but the capital funding will come mainly from utilities. This is the case, for example, for the Imperial Irrigation District's large project to transfer water to San Diego (see Chapter 8). In developing countries, assistance to irrigation projects may be part of national development schemes, which might participate in development bank loans or government programs.

Capital for industrial water facilities will generally be provided from corporate sources and be considered as part of the cost of doing business. This would also be the case for energy-related investments, whether for cooling water or hydroelectricity. Capital for water facilities as part of residential and commercial developments will be provided with the funding for the facilities themselves.

Tap fees and development—this refers to the cost of water infrastructure—is added to the cost of houses and commercial/industrial developments.

FUTURE FINANCING SCENARIOS

It seems certain that water industry costs will continue to rise. According to Means, Ospina, and Patrick (2005), drivers of the water industry will be water shortages, climate change, demand for high-quality water, environmentalism, aging infrastructure, security, and new information technologies, and all of these will tend to raise the cost of water services. New water supplies will be hard to find in the future, which means that larger expenditures must be made either to develop more marginal sources or to transform alternative sources, such as desalted seawater, into viable new sources.

The aging infrastructure of the water industry will drive future capital expenditures because the asset base is huge but deteriorating, due to many unseen factors and building up unmet needs year by year. This includes water and wastewater piping and many other facilities, including 85,000 dams in the United States alone.

At the same time, the public demands higher-quality water for an aging population that is becoming more vulnerable to illness and consumers who are paying attention to health alerts and the quality of their food and drink. Environmentalism is another force that adds to the cost of water. Planning for new supplies, treatment plants, and other construction projects is much more expensive than in the past, and construction requires more mitigation and protective measures.

The aggregated water industry is large and will grow at greater than the rate of inflation and population growth because of the backlog of unmet needs. Reports of the size of the industry will continue to be inconsistent because of a lack of standard definitions. Generally, they will depend on whether the report is about revenues or about capital expenditures and on the subsectors included in it. The *Wall Street Journal* characterized the water sector as a $400 billion business globally (Zuckerman and Kranhold, 2005). The global market for water and wastewater equipment and chemicals was estimated by the U.S. Department of Commerce (2002) at $47 billion, with the United States, Western Europe and Japan at about 80 percent of the total. This figure is consistent with the estimates in this book. Emerging markets will grow faster, but they are hard to estimate.

People should get used to paying more for water, but the ability of water pricing to advance social objectives is limited. Some advocates think all water uses can be priced in the market, but most economists know this won't work. The argument for such pricing was made by an editorial in the *Wall Street Journal* (1991), which thought that "if a judge and his trusty biologist think salmon-species salvation is worth any price," it ought to note that "Utilities . . . warn that protecting the salmon could deprive the region of several times the annual megawatts it takes to keep Seattle lighted." The *Journal* then opined that if the "broader public cared enough to protect the fish ahead of some other perceived need, legislators could appropriate funds to buy water flow at a marginal price higher than the power companies and the farmers are willing to pay." It did acknowledge the difficulty in charging customers directly for such water services as salmon preservation: "Approximating a free market in natural resources isn't going to be easy—especially when so many parties have careers and causes at stake. But it's hard to think of any other mechanism capable of arbitrating the myriad demands of millions of people in an economy. . . . Without a pricing system to mediate the process, the swings of human nature can be violent."

Paying to pollute, a concept of paying for water pollution infrastructure by charging for the "right to pollute," is not practiced much in the United

States, and it appears that it won't be for the foreseeable future, but we should not forget about this concept altogether because it has the capability to introduce more rationality into water-quality management programs.

Security is also a cost driver in the water industry, which has already fenced its treatment facilities and added many security enhancements. In the future it will require more redundant facilities, hardened control systems, and more fail-safe systems. The 300-pound gorilla in the closet on security financing will be disaster financing for recovery from events such as Hurricane Katrina.

The water sector will continue to be difficult to finance with only user charges because it manages both public goods and private commodity-type goods. Given the propensity today by both ends of the political spectrum to limit taxes, this will place obvious pressure on water-industry financing sources.

The water industry needs a lot of capital investment. The potential of private equity to meet needs in the water business is untapped but promising. The Asian Development Bank (ADB) will invest up to $20 million in a fund supporting water and wastewater systems in China and Southeast Asia. ADB hopes to stimulate private investment in the water sector in Asia to support sustainable growth and improve living standards. The fund will be owned by a subsidiary of the AmInvestment Group, and about 70 percent of its portfolio will be in China. It plans to contract with effective engineering groups, invest in companies with good corporate governance and financial management, and seek a majority ownership stake in each investment. It will also expect engineering companies to invest their own equity (Stedman, 2010b).

The water industry faces several conundrums in its attempt to finance itself. One is that if you implement conservation pricing, the customer pays more and gets less. This will be difficult for some customers to swallow, of course. Another conundrum is that you cannot recover full costs for system deterioration without driving rates up beyond politically acceptable thresholds, so the buildup of deferred maintenance seems inevitable. Another one is that it is difficult to recover costs for distributing reclaimed water. Also, while irrigation water is essential for many reasons (see Chapter 8), it normally cannot pay the full costs of water infrastructure and operations.

CHAPTER 13

Public Health as a Water-Industry Driver

The link between drinking-water quality and health is a strong driver of the water business because people are vitally interested in their health. Also, the quality of recreational water and even water in baths and showers affects our health. As people gain access to more knowledge about health, they become more interested in the quality and integrity of their drinking water. This factor, along with the aging of populations in many countries, has fueled the expansion of a water-quality industry that serves markets from large systems down to individual users.

The water-quality industry provides treatment systems, monitors, chemicals, and a wide range of devices to meet every need, whether residential, commercial, or industrial. Like the other parts of the water business, it has sectors for large and small systems, but its basic principles and processes are the same. Its large parts are explained mostly in Chapters 4 and 5, which cover water supply and wastewater. Chapter 14 explains the main regulatory laws. The smaller parts are explained here and in Chapter 21, which explains the point-of-use treatment industry.

The focus of this chapter is on water, health, and consumer behavior and how these drivers affect the overall water business. Part of the issue is about science and its increasing capability to monitor and detect contaminants and to measure health effects, and part is about psychology and what people choose to believe about their water.

WATER QUALITY AND HEALTH

Among engineers and health professionals, the close relationships between water quality and human health are well known. The story goes back many centuries to when people began to suspect a close link between water and infectious and chronic diseases. Somehow, they lost this chain of knowledge, and water quality remained in the background until the 19th century. As Chapter 10 explained, the watershed public health discovery came when Dr. John Snow linked an 1854 cholera outbreak in London to a single source of drinking water. From that time, knowledge of drinking water quality has increased greatly with development of microbiology and chemistry, and today the water-quality industry is large, robust, and growing.

Water-treatment systems started in the 1880s, when filtration was begun. Disinfection with chlorine was initiated in 1909, and many subsequent treatment methods were developed. Not all problems have been solved, however, and in recent decades waterborne disease outbreaks have occurred about 30 times per year in the United States (Craun et al., 1998). Many more occur in developing countries that lack effective drinking-water control systems; when disasters occur, problems become much worse.

Although waterborne infectious diseases declined sharply after 1900, chemical problems increased with industrialization. New and insidious chemicals were introduced into the water cycle, and today trace amounts of even pharmaceuticals and endocrine-disrupting compounds are found in the water in many locations. None of this means that waterborne disease has ended, of course. As this is being written a large outbreak of cholera is occurring in Haiti, and more than 1,000 deaths have been reported already. The 2010 Pakistan flood disappeared off the public's radar quickly, but its impacts on public health were severe and affected millions of people.

The history of water quality and health is aligned with development of the Safe Drinking Water Act (SDWA), which is the basic U.S. law to safeguard drinking water supplies (see Chapter 14). Most countries that operate under the rule of law have a law to regulate drinking-water quality, and guidelines of the World Health Organization have been adopted or suggested as standards around the world. Development of the U.S. SDWA illustrates the progression of new thinking about protecting drinking water quality and health.

The SDWA applies health-based standards to protect drinking water against threats from improper disposal of chemicals, animal wastes, pesticides, human wastes, wastes injected underground, and natural substances. The act was originally passed in 1974 as the successor to earlier regulatory programs of the U.S. Public Health Service, and it was amended in 1986 and 1996. It provides a framework for USEPA, states, tribes, water systems, and the public to work together to provide safe water. Originally, it focused on water treatment, but the 1996 amendments added source-water protection, operator training, funding, and public information. Currently, much more focus is placed on the quality of water in distribution systems.

States can be delegated the authority to operate the SDWA program, and implementation of its regulatory provisions is mainly through state environmental or health agencies. Programs include testing, reviewing plans for improvements, inspections and surveys, training and technical assistance, and enforcement actions. The principle of the SDWA is to apply multiple barriers to protect drinking water. These include source water protection, treatment, distribution system integrity, and public information. If the water does not meet standards, the water system's operator is obligated to inform the public. Water-system operators are also required to issue annual consumer confidence reports. These report the source of the water, detected contaminants, and possible health effects. The SDWA also provides for watershed and wellhead protection and Underground Injection Control program, which controls the injection of wastes into groundwater.

Standards are set by USEPA, which uses scientific research to assess risk to health from exposure to various contaminants. It considers risk to the most sensitive populations, such as infants, children, pregnant women, the elderly, and people with weak immune systems. Primary standards govern contaminants that threaten health and secondary standards address those that threaten welfare. The National Primary Drinking Water Regulations include mandatory maximum contaminant levels (MCLs) and nonenforceable health goals for each included contaminant. Secondary drinking-water standards were set in 1979.

RISKS FROM DRINKING WATER

Risk assessment is used to set drinking-water quality standards to protect people from exposure to disease-causing agents, mainly microbiological and chemical. For example, when assessing the risks from exposure to a chemical in drinking water, the first step is to measure how much of the chemical is in the water. Next, scientists estimate how much of the chemical the average person is likely to drink, or the exposure. In developing drinking-water standards, EPA assumes that the average adult drinks 2 liters of water each day throughout a 70-year life span. Finally, an estimate will be made of the likelihood that disease will occur from the exposure.

For cancer effects, a risk assessment measures the chances that someone may get cancer because they have been exposed to a drinking-water contaminant at a risky level. USEPA generally sets maximum contaminant levels to limit an individual's risk of cancer from that contaminant to between 1 in 10,000 and 1 in 1,000,000 over a lifetime. MCLs are based on anticipated adverse health effects, the ability of technologies to remove the contaminant, and cost of treatment.

Water-related risks to health are estimated from threats, vulnerabilities, and consequences of infection. Threats refer to paths where people are exposed to contaminants, mainly drinking, swimming, inhaling, and eating products affected by contaminated water, especially fish. There are many health threats from exposure to contaminated water, whether by drinking or exposure through swimming or aerosols from showers and from insect populations that breed in water and then spread disease (U.S. Centers for Disease Control, 2010). Threats to public health focus on outbreaks, although toxicological agents from spills and accidents also affect health. All drinking water contains some naturally occurring contaminants, but at low levels, the contaminants are generally not harmful in drinking water. Removing all contaminants would be extremely expensive and not very effective.

Vulnerabilities differ among people. Normal people and people with weak immune system respond differently to threats. Youth are in a growth phase, while the adult population is in various phases of maintenance and aging. As you would expect, poor people are more exposed than those who can afford safe water and sanitation.

Figure 13.1 illustrates some of the contaminants, pathways, and health effects of water use and contact. A great deal of study has been given to these threats, but they mainly occur in local situations which are sometimes hard to diagnose.

Consequences of water contamination vary according to severity of impacts, from mild illness to death. CDC listed the many disease threats by

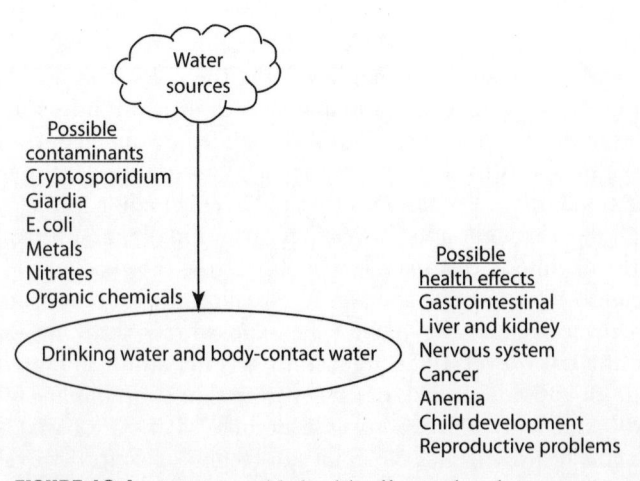

FIGURE 13.1   Some possible health effects related to water

type of disease or by symptom or body location. Examples of types of disease are cholera (bacterial), giardiasis (parasitic), enterovirus (viral), lead poisoning (chemical), and ringworm (other).

Examples by body location or symptom include diarrhea and acute gastrointestinal illness, ear, eye, nervous system, skin, wound infections, hepatitis, leptospirosis, respiratory illness, impaired nutritional status (such as schistosomiasis), and other types of illness/infection or contaminant, such as mercury poisoning.

Table 13.1 gives examples of the many health effects listed in USEPA's (2010) presentation of primary drinking water standards.

TABLE 13.1 Examples of Health Effects of Water Contaminants

Contaminant	Potential Effects
Microorganisms: Cryptosporidium, Giardia, and enteric viruses from human and animal fecal waste.	Gastrointestinal illness (e.g., diarrhea, vomiting, cramps).
Disinfection byproducts: bromate or total trihalomethanes (TTHMs).	Increased risk of cancer (bromate and TTHMs). Liver, kidney or central nervous system problems (TTHMs).
Disinfectants: chlorine and chlorine dioxide.	Eye/nose irritation; stomach discomfort, anemia (chlorine). Anemia in infants and young children, also nervous system effects (chlorine dioxide).
Inorganic chemicals: Arsenic from erosion of natural deposits or runoff from some wastes.	Skin damage or problems with circulatory systems, maybe increased risk of cancer.
Inorganic chemicals: Lead from corrosion of plumbing systems.	Kidney or high blood pressure problems in adults. Infants and children may have delays in physical or mental development.
Inorganic chemicals: Nitrate as runoff from fertilizer use; leaching from septic tanks, sewage, or natural erosion.	Infants may suffer shortness of breath and blue-baby syndrome; could become seriously ill or die if untreated.
Organic chemicals: Benzene as discharge from factories or leaching from gas storage tanks and landfills.	Anemia, decrease in blood platelets, increased risk of cancer.
Organic chemicals: Polychlorinated biphenols (PCBs) as runoff from landfills or discharge of waste chemicals.	Skin changes, thymus gland problems; immune deficiencies, reproductive or nervous system difficulties, increased risk of cancer.

Sudden outbreaks of waterborne disease can occur anywhere, especially in developing countries and after disasters. Even during normal conditions, localized outbreaks of waterborne disease can be linked to contamination by bacteria or viruses, most likely from human or animal waste. Haiti is suffering from a cholera outbreak after flooding. Environmental epidemiology is used to study how these outbreaks occur, usually from disasters such as floods, hurricanes, or earthquakes that lead to problems with sanitation, water supply, shelter, and mental health.

Famous recent episodes of water-borne diseases include a 1993 outbreak of Cryptosporidium in Milwaukee that caused illness in 400,000 and many deaths. The water supply was from Lake Michigan, and before the outbreak, severe spring storms may have increased disease-causing particulates to pass through the treatment plant (Fox and Lytle, 1996). In May 2000 an E. coli contamination incident in Walkerton, Ontario, led to seven deaths and more than 2,000 cases of illness. Floodwaters over cattle-grazing lands and possible problems in utility operations and training were said to be the causes (AWWA Mainstream, 2000).

Outbreaks occur frequently in the summer at treated-water venues and cause gastrointestinal illness. Deficiencies were water-quality, venue design, usage, and maintenance. During 2005–2006, a total of 78 waterborne-disease outbreaks associated with recreational water were reported, with illness occurring in 4,412 persons and five deaths. Most of the outbreaks (61.5 percent) were gastroenteritis from infectious agents or chemicals. Other types included acute respiratory illness, dermatitis or other skin conditions, leptospirosis, and primary amebic meningoencephalitis. Among the gastroenteritis outbreaks, Cryptosporidium caused 64.6 percent of the cases and all except two occurred in treated water.

Fourteen states reported 20 outbreaks for 2005–2006 that were associated with drinking water. Six of these were associated with water not intended for drinking and two more with water of unknown intent. These 20 outbreaks caused illness among an estimated 612 persons and were linked to four deaths. Most were associated with bacteria and fewer with viruses and parasites. Illness types included acute respiratory illness, acute gastrointestinal illness, and hepatitis.

About half of the drinking-water deficiencies occurred outside the jurisdiction of a water utility (such as regrowth of Legionella in hot-water systems), and the majority of these were associated with Legionella. This suggests improved education of consumers and plumbers to address the risk factors. Also, systems using ground water caused problems, suggesting that EPA's potential Ground Water Rule might prevent similar outbreaks.

CONSUMER PERCEPTIONS OF WATER AND HEALTH

Before starting on this book I thought that people's deep interest in their health would drive an active market for consumer water systems, but I found the market is smaller and less active than I thought. Chapter 21 explains the bottled water part (which is large) and the point-of-use treatment part (which is smaller than I thought). Part of my interest was sparked by books about exotic health threats (and benefits) from drinking water. Some of the attributes of water they point to are mineral content, additives, and even the orientation of molecules in the water. I'm no expert in these things, but I wanted to add some information here about this industry niche that makes claims about drinking-water threats and benefits.

The books illustrate the range between writing about water from a medical standpoint and writing to make more spectacular claims about its effects. On the spectacular end, the advice will range from explaining how adequate hydration is important for health to wild claims about cures for diseases from drinking water with various attributes, even including how the molecules are aligned at the molecular scale.

From the medical end of the spectrum, Barzilay et al. (1999) explained how even in Roman times a lot was known but then forgotten about water and health. They described how, even in the Bible (Genesis 29:8) there was wellhead protection as Jacob removed a stone from the well so Rachel could drink. Now, with the scientific method and microbiology we can understand these issues much better.

They explained links between minerals and cardiovascular and bone health, between metals and the nervous system, including Alzheimer's disease, between industrial chemicals and cancer and infertility, and between infectious diseases and immune systems. In the case of water hardness, it seems that harder water is correlated with lower incidence of strokes and heart attacks. In particular, they wrote that magnesium and calcium might be important. Diseases such as osteoporosis and kidney stones can be related to water hardness. Fluoride addition to water is a very controversial issue. Metals such as lead, copper, aluminum, and mercury have varied negative effects. The Lead and Copper Rule is explained in Chapter 14.

The response to threats can be point-of-use treatment systems, such as filters, ion exchange, distillation, ozonation, and reverse osmosis. The authors gave practical advice for treatment systems as shown by Table 13.2.

TABLE 13.2   Treatments for Water Contaminants

Contaminant	Treatment
Chlorine	Carbon filtration
Nitrates	Reverse osmosis
Fluorides	Reverse osmosis
Iron	Carbon filtration
Lead	Carbon filtration
Sodium	Distillation
Volatile organics	Distillation, reverse osmosis
Turbidity	Filtration
Arsenic	Carbon filtration, reverse osmosis
Bacteria	Filtration, ozonation
Cryptosporidium	Ultra-filtration, ozonation, reverse osmosis
Giardia	Ultrafiltration, reverse osmosis, ozonation
Odor	Carbon filtration
Radon	Carbon filtration
Organics	Carbon filtration, reverse osmosis, ultrafiltration
Pesticides	Carbon filtration, reverse osmosis
Radium	Reverse osmosis

THE BUSINESS OF WATER QUALITY

In responding to concerns about threats to water and heath, a broad water-quality business has emerged. It is a concern from the largest river basins—actually from the oceans—to the consumer's tap. This wide span of concern draws in many people, stakeholders, and organizations around the globe. At the macro level (state, national, international) discussions of water quality take place among professionals and government officials. Topics of concern are the health of rivers and aquifers, monitoring and enforcement systems, and the regulatory scheme in general. At the micro level people are more concerned about the water they drink and how it affects their health. This has given rise to the point-of-use water-quality industry that is explained in Chapter 21.

A good place to see how this industry fits together is the Water Quality Association (WQA), an international trade association representing the residential, commercial, industrial, and small community water-treatment industry. The association (2009) lists 16 independent member associations in the United States and regional offices in China and India.

The WQA organizes the Aquatech tradeshow, which is for multiple water-industry groups including process, drinking water, and ultrapure water for residential, commercial, and industrial users. At the 2010 show, there was much focus on how to market a new study by the Battelle Institute that showed benefits of softened water on energy efficiency. The keynote speaker was Marc Edwards (2010), who some people call the "plumber professor." He is a distinguished professor at Virginia Tech University and has become an internationally recognized authority on corrosion and related issues of water-distribution systems.

Edwards explained that premises plumbing is complex and much more extensive than big systems. He thought that premises plumbing is the next major water-quality and infrastructure challenge, after distribution systems. In them are many sources of metals with high potential reactivity with chlorine, chloramine, and bacteria, thus causing many corrosion and health issues. In particular, hot-water systems can create problems due to rapid regrowth of bacteria and accelerated chemical reactions.

Corrosion costs in premise plumbing systems are gigantic and copper pipe failures show how little understanding there is of the issues. For example, pinhole leaks can appear quickly in copper piping due to corrosion. Edwards explained that premise plumbing systems involve split responsibility among utilities and homeowners, and he gave major credit for public health advances to engineers and plumbers.

THE FUTURE OF THE WATER-QUALITY BUSINESS

Water quality and health will continue to be strong drivers of the water industry, but their influences have to some extent already been factored into people's beliefs and habits. The managers of public water systems are risk averse when it comes to tolerating regulatory violations that lead to disease outbreaks. They consider it as a real failure if they have to report excessive violations and issue boil water notices.

While media accounts of water quality and health are frequent, the public is to some extent used to them, and many reports of water-quality violations are from very small places and sites, which are difficult to regulate in any case. During 2010 in my water class we discussed reports of drinking violations, and you almost have to follow small-town newspapers or read the online water newsletters to track them. That does not mean that violations do not occur, because they do. In fact, you can search USEPA's Safe Drinking Water Information System to locate violations by area or water system, if you know the identification number of the system. I searched Gaston County, North Carolina, Town of Cramerton, which serves 3,212 people. A list of its violations showed that in 2007, it had a violation of TTHM. Compliance was achieved in 2009. Several other violations were listed, and followup information on each one was included.

Books and products that make wild claims about water and health are at the deep end of the chart, and they seem to apply more to niches of the nutrition business than they do in the mainstream of consumer demand. We have to be careful about what we label as snake oil, but it seems that no one really regulates many of these claims.

The treatment systems, monitors, chemicals, and small and large devices will be provided by a broad band of suppliers, but no one will have anywhere near a major share of the business. The point-of-use business is not as large as you might expect and not growing fast. It thinks it might need an "event" to increase business (see Chapter 21). Bottled water is already big as a business, but it might be leveling off, especially with adverse publicity about plastics and their impact on the environment.

While these observations are prepared about the United States and similar countries, the billions of people who need better access to safe water are another market altogether. However, it will be many years before their incomes can support discretionary purchases for safer water, if they can get it at low cost. This topic is explained in more detail in Chapter 22.

CHAPTER 14

Law and Regulation in the Water Industry

By now it should be clear to readers that the political and social elements are huge in the water industry, which is hard to finance in any case. This chapter explains the main responses to these realities: the application of law and regulations to water management. It is about water law and the regulatory structures that the law creates. The chapter is not meant to be an exhaustive treatment of water law but to identify its main features and how they apply to water as a business.

ABOUT WATER LAW

Two of the main legal controls on the water business are on allocating the water and its cost and about balancing the rights of competing users. In Chapter 1 these were illustrated with an anecdote about a nun who thought water should be free and another one about how people make money in water by litigating over it.

Water is a highly regulated industry, and law and regulations exert strong influences on business decisions. Regulatory decisions determine how much money is required to meet standards. Capital decisions require that projects pass through hoops established by environmental laws. Operating decisions require compliance with health and safety, and financial decisions are based on legislation passed by the three levels of government.

The legal structure of the water business and the fact that it is heavily regulated explain many of the difficulties that surprise entrepreneurs seeking a toehold in some niche of it. On the other hand, the heavy regulation creates many business opportunities for the professional firms and other suppliers who help utilities meet their regulatory requirements.

All parts of the water business are deeply affected by law and regulations, perhaps more than many other business sectors. In many ways, the businesses of the sectors engaged in handling water are defined by regulatory controls on water handling. If the business is water supply, it requires the right to divert water or pump a well. This applies to water supply for domestic, commercial, industrial, or irrigation purposes. In the case of thermoelectric cooling, the requirements are very stringent due to the massive quantities of water required.

The water-supply industry is regulated strongly for public health. Water-supply utilities must comply with provisions of the Safe Drinking Water Act (SDWA). In the case of bottled water, the provisions of the Food and Drug Administration apply. In all cases, various environmental laws apply to your activities. If you build a diversion structure or dam up a waterway, you must have a permit under the Clean Water Act (CWA). Hydropower generators are regulated by the Federal Power Act, with most of the focus on environmental issues. If your business is wastewater management, you must comply with the CWA. Irrigators and stormwater dischargers are also regulated under the CWA. Stormwater management and flood control follow various local codes and the flood insurance act for land use control.

Water law refers to all law relating in any way to water and it cuts across types of law, including resource allocation, environmental control, public health, energy, and land use. Some controls that it exerts in these categories include permits for water use, limits on instream flows, health concerns for safe water, hydropower licenses, and drainage controls.

Water law appears in constitutions, statutes, administrative rules, and court decisions for all three levels of government. For example, in Colorado, the state constitution establishes the appropriation doctrine to allocate water and forms the basis for water markets. Federal statutes establish the authority for most environmental laws, and the Supreme Court and other courts set important decrees to control how some water systems must operate.

LAW AND WATER USES ALONG THE HYDROLOGIC CYCLE

The first striking feature of water law is how it applies to water's travels from atmosphere to sea. Figure 14.1 illustrates controls on water as it moves along its path from upper reservoirs through various uses and on to downstream locations.

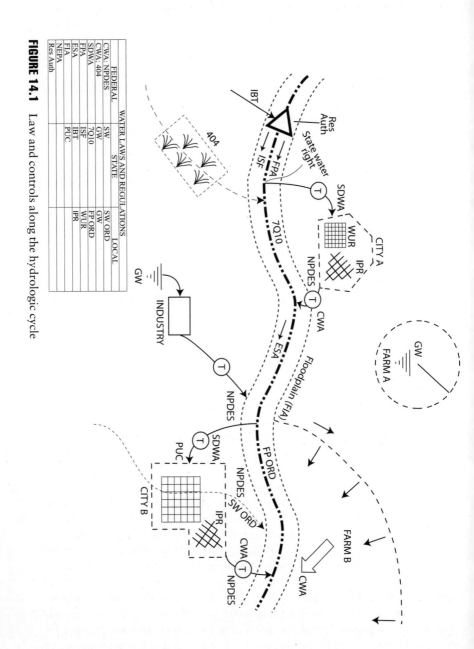

WATER LAWS AND REGULATIONS			
	FEDERAL	STATE	LOCAL
CWA: NPDES		SW	SW ORD
CWA: 404		GW	GW
SDWA		7Q10	FP ORD
FPA		ISF	WUR
ESA		IBT	IPR
FIA		PUC	
NEPA			
Res Auth			

FIGURE 14.1 Law and controls along the hydrologic cycle

At the upper end of the diagram you see how reservoir authorizations and rules on interbasin transfer (IBT) take effect. Reservoir releases will be subject to laws such as for instream flows (ISF) and the Federal Power Act (FPA), and state law will govern diversions from the stream. Then, as water moves downstream, the Clean Water Act's Section 404 regulations will affect wetlands in a tributary area. Also, low-flow rules govern streamflow for water quality and environmental purposes. The local floodplain ordinance will govern land use in the floodplain.

The Safe Drinking Water Act (SDWA) will govern water treatment, and water-use restrictions will govern operation of the distribution system. Industrial pretreatment rules govern discharges to the collection system, as well as local ordinances. The wastewater treatment plant (WWTP) complies with the National Pollutant Discharge Elimination System (NPDES) permit program of the Clean Water Act (CWA).

An industry and farm are pumping from wells and must comply with state or local groundwater restrictions. The farm and the city must also comply with CWA rules on irrigation and stormwater return flows. City B has a private water company that is also regulated by the state's Public Utilities Commission (PUC). These acronyms make an alphabet soup, but their occurrence is a reality of the highly regulated and government-dominated world of water management.

PERMITS AND RIGHTS TO USE WATER

For a city or industry, getting a permit or right to use water is the first step in starting a water-supply system. In many places, you need a permit even to drill a residential water well. Permits to use water, along with the necessary pipes, pumps, and other equipment, can be expensive. The trend among many local utilities is to pass along the full cost of water rights to developers, who pass the costs in turn to home buyers. Here in Colorado, the piped water supply can add $10,000 and more to the cost of a home.

Permits and water rights are controlled by water-allocation law, which deals with the right to use a quantity of water. While water-allocation law has been a central focus in dry, western states for decades, it is becoming much more important in humid states as well due to increasing population and competition for water.

In the United States, the eastern states mainly follow the riparian doctrine, which evolved from European common laws. The idea is that a person whose land abuts the water (a riparian land owner) has rights to the flow of the stream and to make reasonable uses of the water body. This is not a very practical doctrine anymore, and it has evolved into a set of administrative systems, which are patchworks of riparian doctrine and practical, politically acceptable methods for allocating water through administrative systems.

Administrative systems normally use permits, which are like water rights in that they entitle the holder to use the water but are not property rights that can be traded. Permits usually entitle the holder to withdraw a quantity of water; an example would be a permit to withdraw water for a city of 50,000 or for an industry requiring 100,000 gallons per day. Conditions on such permits would be negotiated between the administrative agency and the diverter. Along with these permits, questions that arise during shortages are dealt with in drought response plans. Security for the permit holder is important because, if you are going to make an investment, you want to be sure your water will be there.

The drier states in the West use the prior-appropriation doctrine or variations of it because there is often not enough water to satisfy all users, so a system of allocation by priorities is needed. This doctrine provides that the water belongs to the public but the water-right owner has the right to use the water, in order of priority, as long as it is being applied to a beneficial use. An appropriation of a water right includes the intent to apply the water to a beneficial use, an actual diversion, and demonstration of application to the beneficial use. Water rights are administered by a system of rules and regulations, including calls on the river.

In administering the appropriation doctrine, numerous practical problems arise. Imagine trying to precisely determine each water-right owner's entitlement in a stream that rises and falls according to hydrologic variation, with uncertain routing of flows from one point to another, unknown return flows, variable weather, and everyone diverting and releasing water according to schedules not under control of the administrators. While the appropriation doctrine has flaws like this, it seems destined to continue in use in the West, with periodic tuneups to respond to pressing needs.

One contentious issue in water allocation is the interbasin transfer, in which one basin is forced to give up water to another. In these, water is removed from its natural watershed and transferred to another basin, usually on a permanent basis. This can have the effect of permanently changing the economy and ecology of both the basin of origin and the receiving basin. In riparian states, they are usually handled under the rules of a permit system or authority of the state government. In appropriation states, these are handled under the water-rights system.

The riparian and appropriation doctrines apply mainly to surface water, and groundwater allocation law is a hybrid of state water-allocation law, resource law, and land-use law. In some states, little control is exercised over groundwater pumping. In other states, sensitive areas are brought under control to respond to public pressure and water-table declines. For example, an area that develops water-table problems might be considered for regulation of pumping, as, for example, in coastal zones where saltwater intrusion might occur. In other cases, regulation might be imposed where groundwater levels drop so fast that pumpers are threatened. This is the case in some groundwater management districts. Local groundwater ordinances may be implemented by county governments or management districts with authority to limit pumping. This might occur under the authority of state law, in recognition of the need to regulate groundwater use for the common good.

PUBLIC HEALTH AND THE SAFE DRINKING WATER ACT

Whereas water allocation law is normally a main concern of larger water users, such as utilities and farms, everyone is concerned about the safety of drinking water, and this public concern, which was the subject of Chapter 13, drives much of the water-supply business.

This public concern about water quality and health has required a heavy dose of regulation, which is expressed mainly through the Safe Drinking Water Act. This law applies health-based standards to protect drinking water against threats from chemicals, animal wastes, pesticides, human wastes, wastes injected underground, and natural substances. Now, it is also becoming the barrier to protect us against endocrine disruptors, such as pharmaceuticals dumped into drinking water.

Like its sister law, the Clean Water Act, the SDWA has had widespread and dramatic effects on cities and on the water management industry. As explained in Chapter 4, it applies to all public water systems in the United States that provide piped water for human consumption and have at least 15 connections or regularly serve at least 25 people.

The strategy of the SDWA is to apply multiple barriers to protect water at the points of source water, treatment, distribution, and consumption. If the water does not meet standards, the water system operator is obligated to inform the public through consumer confidence reports. These report the source of the water, detected contaminants, and possible health effects. The SDWA also provides for watershed and wellhead protection and for the Underground Injection Control (UIC) program, which controls the injection of wastes into groundwater.

Standards are set by USEPA, which uses science to assess risk to health of the contaminants. It especially considers the most sensitive populations, such as infants, children, pregnant women, the elderly, and people with weak immune systems. EPA is currently assessing risk for microbial contaminants (such as Cryptosporidium), byproducts of disinfection, radon, arsenic, and groundwater without disinfection.

Standards are classified as primary and secondary standards. Primary standards govern contaminants that threaten health, and secondary standards address those that threaten "welfare." The National Primary Drinking Water Regulations include mandatory levels and nonenforceable health goals for each included contaminant.

USEPA adopted the Primary Drinking Water Regulations for microbiological contaminants, radionuclides, volatile organic chemicals, fluoride, surface-water treatment, synthetic organic and inorganic chemicals, lead, and copper. Secondary drinking-water standards were set in 1979. Later, monitoring requirements for corrosion and sodium were set, and rules for disinfection byproducts were developed.

The primary regulations are implemented by various rules, as well as by the maximum contaminant levels. For example, in 1991 the Lead and Copper Rule (LCR) was passed to regulate the levels of lead in water at the tap. If a utility has high lead levels caused by metal leaching, it must implement corrective measures and prove that they work by testing water at the customer's tap. It took a long time to develop this rule. An interim standard was established in 1975, and the 1986 amendments to the SDWA banned lead in new solder and use of leaded pipes in public water supply systems and plumbing, and it also directed EPA to review lead and copper regulations. The 1991 LCR required water suppliers to optimize treatment to control corrosion in customer plumbing and to sample water at the tap. The rule making showed how institutional issues were faced, including to protect customers but not to have utilities be responsible for plumbing systems they could not control. The science debates were about health effects due to lead exposure and analysts thought that estimating exposure was too complex because data on water at the tap and on consumption patterns were poor. In the end, the rule makers had to deal with complexity in water chemistry, how aggressive water is in attacking lead, and uncertainty about exposure and health effects data.

Secondary standards are for contaminants that are not health threatening. Problems might cause undesirable tastes or odors, have cosmetic effects, or damage water equipment. Public water systems test for them on a voluntary basis.

The Secondary Standards can drive interest in water-conditioning equipment (see Chapter 21). Odor and taste indicate water quality, but methods to measure them are subjective. Color may indicate dissolved organic material, inadequate treatment, high disinfectant demand, and the potential to produce excess disinfectant byproducts. Foaming may be caused by detergents. Skin discoloration may result from silver ingestion, and tooth discoloration may be from excess fluoride exposure. Corrosion can affect the aesthetic quality of water and have economic implications from corrosion of iron and copper and staining of fixtures. Corrosion of pipes can reduce water flow. Scale and sedimentation can also have economic impacts. Scale deposits build up in hot-water pipes, boilers, and heat exchangers, restricting water flow. Loose deposits in the distribution system or home plumbing cause sediments to occur (EPA, 2003c).

The 1996 amendments to the SDWA were important for their requirements for the consumer confidence reports, cost-benefit analysis, a drinking-water state revolving fund, protection against microbial contaminants and disinfection byproducts, operator certification, and help for small water systems.

Oversight of the SDWA is mainly through state drinking water programs, and states can receive primacy to operate their programs through what amounts to a license from the federal government. This involves testing, reviewing plans for improvements, inspections and surveys, training and technical assistance, and enforcement actions.

The SDWA will continue to have strong and permanent effects on the U.S. drinking water industry. It drives the industry's regulatory structure, finance, research, and product development.

ENVIRONMENTAL LAWS

Next to the SDWA, the laws with most impact on the water industry are those in the environmental category, with the Clean Water Act (CWA) as the most far reaching.

Clean Water Act

The 1972 Clean Water Act has had dramatic effects on water management, on industry, on cities, and on the environment. It regulates discharges of municipal and industrial pollutants into streams, and it indirectly affects the protection of wetlands and regulation of dredging in streams. Although it was passed during a Republican Administration, it chose a command-and-control regulatory system over an economics-based system and created an expensive subsidized national system of wastewater treatment infrastructure.

The early efforts under the CWA were focused on point source dischargers where pipes discharge effluent back to streams. This program operates through the National Pollutant Discharge Elimination System (NPDES) permit program, which covers point sources of pollution discharging into surface waters. Today, all wastewater plants (see Chapter 5) must have permits and hundreds of thousands of industries and small dischargers also have permits. Now, more attention is given to polluted nonpoint runoff from urban areas, farms, and construction sites. In particular, its new emphasis on stormwater controls has widespread effects on land use and city planning.

Section 404 of the CWA regulates the placement of dredged or fill materials into wetlands and other waters of the United States and has strong effects on land development. Authority to operate it was delegated from USEPA to the Corps of Engineers.

In contrast to drinking water, where people are mostly willing to pay for safe water, there is a built-in public reluctance to fund sewage treatment, which is seen to benefit others downstream. Thus, under the CWA financing and construction of sewage treatment plants was initially subsidized under a construction grants program that spent $50 billion in the 1970s and 1980s. This subsidy was curtailed in the 1981 amendments, which reduced federal financial support, and the 1987 Water Quality Act replaced the grants program by authorizing capitalization of the Clean Water State Revolving Fund. Today, local authorities are mostly responsible for maintaining and renewing the complex infrastructure of wastewater management.

In the nonpoint source control program, Section 319 of the CWA addresses sources such as farming and forestry, mostly through grants. The 1981 amendments required USEPA to develop regulations for stormwater, and this has evolved into a complex program that requires cities and many industries to have plans.

The condition of the nation's waters is reported every two years in a USEPA release called the 305(b) Report, which identifies healthy, threatened, and impaired waters.

National Environmental Policy Act

Another far-reaching environmental law, the National Environmental Policy Act (NEPA), was passed in 1970 to establish policy and set requirements for environmental impact statements (EIS) for major federal actions. NEPA also established the Council on Environmental Quality, which prepares the president's annual environmental report to Congress. This report is to describe the condition of the nation's air, aquatic, and terrestrial environments and the effects of these environments on the social, economic, and other requirements of the nation.

Since NEPA was passed in 1970, the EIS process has influenced many projects and actions. On the positive side, it provides for coordination of the inputs of diverse interests and thus improves planning. On the negative side, the process can be bureaucratic, time consuming, and very expensive.

In the water industry, the effects of the EIS requirement can be seen in its controls over proposed actions such as adding capacity to reservoirs, diverting water from streams, and even building water-treatment plants. Currently in my area, plans of a water-conservancy district to build an off-channel reservoir to provide municipal water supplies along Colorado's Front Range are bottled up in a long EIS process managed by the Corps of Engineers. While it is fair to say that the project's merits must be thoroughly proved before it should be built, the EIS requirement adds slow and expensive study processes to a decision process that is already quite complex.

Endangered Species Act

Compared to NEPA, which is essentially a planning act, the Endangered Species Act (ESA) offers the authority to stop projects and programs in their tracks and has arguably had the greatest effect on water management of any of the environmental laws. Under the ESA, when fish, wildlife, or plant species are listed as threatened or endangered, recovery plans are required in order to protect them.

The secretary of Interior is required to use scientific data to list the species as endangered or threatened, and the Fish and Wildlife Service (FWS) implements the act for all species except ocean species, which are the responsibility of the National Marine Fisheries Service (NMFS). Factors to be considered include habitat destruction, overuse, disease or predation, inadequacy of regulatory mechanisms, and other natural or man-made factors.

Section 7 of the ESA outlines procedures for interagency coordination to conserve listed species and designated critical habitat. It seems like a heavy dose of authority to water managers, because it changes the game and initiates a control environment that subjects them to stringent controls. Naturally, a number of jokes have circulated about how government biologists exercise an enormous amount of power by listing species as threatened or endangered.

Electric Power and the Federal Power Act

Water and energy have many interfaces and one that has its own law is the licensing of energy generation facilities through the Federal Power Act (FPA), which dates from 1920. The act is administered by the Federal Energy Regulatory Commission (FERC), which was formerly named the Federal Power Commission. It has responsibility to license nonfederal hydroelectric power projects up to 50 years and to regulate interstate sale and transmission of power.

The FPA requires water planning because projects must be adapted to comprehensive plans for improving or developing waterways. In permit actions, FERC is required to consider recommendations of relevant federal and state agencies and Indian tribes and how the project is adapted to the comprehensive plan. It must consider interstate or foreign commerce, water-power development, fish and wildlife, and beneficial public uses, including irrigation, flood control, water supply, and recreation.

The FPA requires FERC to give equal consideration to environmental issues. Licenses must contain conditions that adequately and equitably protect, mitigate damages to, and enhance fish and wildlife affected by the development, operation, and management of projects.

Hydropower relicensing will continue to be an important part of water management, and many projects will be subjected to it in the years ahead. In 1994 the Supreme Court expanded the regulatory authority over hydro projects to state governments. The court ruled that under the Clean Water Act states can accomplish goals such as preserving fish habitat (Barrett, 1994). In that case, a state's Department of Ecology had set a minimum stream-flow requirement higher than the project design would allow, arguing that the higher flow was necessary to protect fish.

FERC may exempt from the licensing provisions facilities that use only the hydroelectric potential of man-made water transmission and distribution conduits if they are not primarily for generating electricity (University of New Mexico School of Law, 2003).

FLOOD INSURANCE ACT AND LOCAL LAND USE

As explained in Chapter 6, the nation's response to flood risks has shifted from building dams and levees to a nonstructural approach based on the National Flood Insurance Act of 1968. This law made flood insurance available and created the Federal Insurance Administration, which now resides within FEMA.

The law evolved after a long period of increasing federal attention to flood problems. As far back as the 1850s, the federal government was surveying the Mississippi River to determine options to control floods. By 1890, the lower river was divided into state and local levee districts, which are the basis for the flood walls around New Orleans. In 1913, a flood in the Ohio River Valley killed more than 400 people, and the House Committee on Flood Control was created by Congress, leading to the 1917 Flood Control Act. Over the years, the limits of structural concerns with flooding became more apparent and the government began to consider a different approach to flood policy. By the 1950s, the government was considering a flood insurance program and this led to the 1968 act (FEMA, 2004).

The flood insurance program has important effects on real estate, the insurance industry, and responses to disasters, both in river and coastal environments. Local floodplain ordinances are required to implement the flood insurance program. These typically regulate land use in the 100-year floodplain and have significant effects on property values and land development options.

Local stormwater programs are closely related to flood control programs. These may include stormwater standards, subdivision regulations, stormwater quality, erosion control, and land quality, and programs such as stream restoration, greenbelt construction, recreation, and environmental education. For the most part, these rules are set by local governments, but a few states, such as Pennsylvania, Maryland, and Florida, have stormwater statutes.

Locally set stormwater standards usually apply risk analysis to system requirements. This translates into standards and requirements on land developers, including development standards that impose requirements for amenities such as greenbelts, walkways, and ponds. The stormwater quality program must respond to CWA requirements.

Legal doctrines in the law of drainage and hydrologic modification are the common-enemy rule, the natural-flow rule, and the reasonable-use rule (Goldfarb, 1988). Under the common-enemy rule, you can do anything to protect your property, regardless of how you affect your neighbor. The natural-flow rule is the reverse; you must not change anything that would affect natural flows. The reasonable-use rule is more practical. Under it, you may modify your land, even if you affect your neighbor, but there is a test of reasonableness. This rule recognizes that development will occur, but also that there is a community obligation to work together to accommodate it. A requirement for detention storage is an example of a reasonable-use doctrine.

AUTHORIZATIONS FOR FEDERAL WATER PROJECTS

Water Resources Development Acts (WRDAs) provide the basic authorization for federal projects, and other water-management provisions added by Congress. In recent years, the WRDA of 1986 introduced new reforms for project planning and cost sharing. As it relates to Corps of Engineers programs, the WRDA of 1990 created an interim goal of no overall net loss of the nation's remaining wetland base and a long-term goal of enhancing all of the nation's wetlands. It also directed the secretary of the Army to include environmental protection as a primary mission of the Corps. The 1996 and 2000 acts included provisions for the comprehensive Everglades Project.

WATER-USE RESTRICTIONS AND WATER EFFICIENCY

Local water-use restrictions may be imposed during drought or other emergencies. Authority for these varies and depends on systems of water-allocation law. For example, under the appropriation doctrine, local governments cannot impose any restrictions on water users who own water rights. However, they can impose restrictions on customers who draw water from a central system. Water use in the United States is essentially stable (see Chapter 6), so no dramatic change in these rules is expected. However, growing populations that are concentrated in urban regions may trigger water-use restrictions as a result of overtaxed local supplies.

INSTREAM FLOW LAWS

The purpose of instream flow law is to set aside water in streams for the protection of wildlife and public health. This body of law responds in different ways to stream water quality and the needs of environmental habitat. Also, instream flows can be required as carriage water to ensure that downstream water right owners get their entitlements of water. Taken together, this results in three reasons to regulate instream water: to provide dilution water for wastewater, to provide enough water for habitat, and to deliver water supplies to downstream users.

Instream-flow law is mainly at the state level. States may require that the 7Q10 flow remain in the stream to dilute wastewater returns and that minimum levels be left in the stream for fish and wildlife.

While there is no federal instream-flow law, other federal laws can be used to protect instream flows. For example, a permit holder might be required to bypass flows around a federally permitted lake to ensure that fish in the stream have enough water.

TREATIES AND INTERSTATE COMPACTS

Water flowing across state or national lines requires treaties, or interstate compacts, and can lead to transboundary conflicts. The University of New

Mexico School of Law has a special center dealing with them. Problems of interstate or international streams can involve both water quantity and quality. Water quantity has traditionally been the most urgent, because of supply issues for cities and agriculture. In the United States, interstate water-quality problems are covered by uniform federal stream standards. However, stream standards are set by states, so the potential for problems exists.

Normally, transboundary issues should be handled in the context of river basin management, and when more than one state is involved, the complexity grows. If voluntary agreement breaks down, formal compacts may be required. These are common in the West, but also occur in the East, as in the case of the Delaware River involving New York, Pennsylvania, Delaware, and New Jersey. In the West, the most famous compact is for the Colorado River, which involves seven states and Mexico.

REGULATORS OF THE WATER INDUSTRY

The controls of water law are implemented mainly through the process of regulation, which means to control behavior in accordance with a rule or law and is used to protect the public interest where private markets do not. Familiar examples of regulation are the sale of alcohol, highway speed limits, and the practice of medicine. Regulators in the water industry enforce rules about health and safety, water quality, fish and wildlife, quantity allocation, finance, and service quality.

Water-industry regulation applies a combination of federal, state, and local laws and regulations to govern water-service providers and individual water users. At the federal level, the Administrative Procedures Act gives coherence to rule-making under laws such as the Safe Drinking Water Act. For example, the Lead and Copper Rule is a regulation issued by EPA under the authority of the SDWA and is included in the Code of Federal Regulations. Regulation of local water agencies comes from state and federal laws, implemented mainly by state agencies. Other regulation is informal, through the political process. For example, rate setting by local governments normally requires no approvals, whereas rate setting by private utilities is regulated by public service commissions.

Regulation of all public services started with railroad controls in the late 19th century, but water industry regulation began even earlier with water-allocation systems in the West. Later, it was extended to public health laws related to drinking water. Now, new laws have extended it to environmental issues such as endangered species. Finance of water-agency operation is regulated less, although private water companies are regulated by state public service commissions. Service quality is regulated indirectly through other programs, but regulation of it might increase in the future, such as to regulate water pressures for water-quality integrity. Fire protection, an important service, is regulated under design codes that respond to insurance requirements.

Each sector of the water industry has its own regulatory programs, based on the Safe Drinking Water Act, the Clean Water Act, stormwater rules, floodplain regulation, hydropower licensing, and environmental regulations.

In the categories of regulation, health and safety of drinking water is regulated under the Safe Drinking Water Act, and most regulators are in state EPAs or local health departments. Water quality to ensure clean streams is regulated under the Clean Water Act, and most regulators are in state EPAs, often in the same departments as those overseeing the SDWA. Water allocation to recognize legal water rights or to issue permits for water use is regulated by state government departments. Fish and wildlife protection require instream flows for fish, but authority is weak and distributed among environmental laws and enforced through state government departments, when it is in place and enforced at all. Financial regulation of rates of private water companies is by state public utility commissions. Government water companies are mostly self-regulated for financial operations. Some regulation for service quality by private water companies occurs in public service commissions but only indirectly for government-owned utilities.

Principles for regulatory programs have been developed over the years, and they were articulated by Rouse (2007) from experience in the United Kingdom. They include the need for government structures and capacity to facilitate sound integrated policies; separation of policy, regulation, and delivery of water; having independent regulators empowered to act transparently; having effective monitoring and enforcement of regulations; providing transparent information and reporting to combat corruption; organizing public participation for transparency, buy-in, and commitment; and enabling empowered utility operators to be free from politics so they can provide efficient services.

Regulatory programs should especially follow the principle of not allowing the fox to guard the chicken coop, or not allowing persons to regulate themselves. As agencies that write rules also enforce them, their regulators need oversight as well as an illustration of the principle of separation of powers in government.

A regulatory program must have an enforcement mechanism to be taken seriously. Most of the experience in the water field is from enforcement of the Clean Water Act, which gives authority to USEPA to enter and inspect premises, review records, test monitoring equipment, and take samples. USEPA can issue compliance orders or take action in civil courts. Enforcement officials must have reliable information to base decisions on and they should try to obtain compliance before levying penalties. The system of enforcement must be efficient and fair, and appeal panels must be available to provide due process, as well as to back up the regulatory goals.

Working for regulators does not appeal to everyone. I sometimes think that regulators need a "police orientation," but the regulatory process includes many parts other than issuing tickets, such as studies, issuing permits, policy, public involvement, and outreach.

Most water utility services are natural monopolies, and it is hard to organize competition. Beecher (2000) wrote:

> *Water service is unique among the public utilities, and water supply is perhaps the most monopolistic of the utility enterprises. . . . Water technologies and economies also cannot be restructured along the lines of the telecommunications and energy industries. The water industry has not experienced major technological break-throughs or come close to exploiting economies of scale in management and operations, as did other utilities before restructuring. Long-distance and open access transmission are particularly problematic for water. A de facto form of deregulation occurs when private water systems are taken over by cities or when substantial operations responsibilities are placed in the hands of unregulated contractors. Arguably, the water industry—with rising costs and weak competition—needs more, not less, regulation.*

She also wrote:

> *The title of the "last monopoly" has been transferred from the electricity to the water sector . . . perhaps the most monopolistic of the utility enterprises. . . .*

Chapter 1 explained that water utilities and the water industry have lower profiles than the electric and gas industries. This effect is also apparent in the actions of public utility commissions, which are dominated by regulatory scenarios of other public services.

State law empowers public service commissions to regulate costs of water service for some utilities. These commissions, where they are concerned with water at all, regulate only private water companies. The public is largely ignorant of whether they are receiving the most cost-effective water-supply service possible. Electric, gas, and telecommunications utilities have their rate decisions made public and comparisons of costs are easier for the public to make. The National Regulatory Research Institute (1983) publishes reports on how states regulate water utilities.

The regulatory arena is where conflicts over business versus environment are worked out. In this sense, regulation is a "coordinating mechanism" for the water industry, as well as a control mechanism. Calls for "regulatory relief" and "regulatory reform" are common because people and businesses don't like being regulated, but water industry regulation is not likely to ease. Rather, existing regulations are likely to remain and we can look for new ones to respond to issues such as contaminants of emerging concern (see Chapter 5).

WATER LAW IN THE FUTURE

Water law is the authorizing vehicle for water management, and it should enable continuous improvement in management. For example, inflexible supply systems result from lack of water markets and difficulty to lease, borrow, or cooperate in the development of water supplies. Water law should encourage the move toward market solutions and encourage people to cooperate. This is a challenge because of the inherent conflicts in water management and the large body of water law already on the books.

The inherent conflicts lead to a surprising finding about how much the third branch of government—the justice system—is involved in water-resources management. I have learned this in several roles: as expert witness, as advisor to litigants, and as an agent of the court.

The justice system involves federal, state, and local courts, as well as the administrative law system. While the main part of water law is statutory, much of it is case law, in which complex situations have been tried and precedents have been set. Attorneys search hard for cases to prove their points and to build arguments based on precedents. Lawsuits are used to gain decisions about complex issues. When an action gets to court, it means the voluntary, coordinated approach has broken down, and court decrees and decisions may take the place of agreements and programs.

CHAPTER 15

Water-Industry Workforce: Crisis and Opportunity

Although the private sector has an important part in the water business, its core is formed by public-sector utilities and agencies. Employment conditions in these organizations have changed significantly during the past two decades, and water utilities report a workforce crisis that has two facets. On the one hand it threatens the capacity of utilities to do their jobs in delivering safe water and managing the environment, but on the other hand, the crisis might open opportunities for outsourcing and use of knowledge-management systems to mitigate the adverse effects of rapid change in the workforce.

This chapter explains these workforce issues and how knowledge-management systems may help to mitigate them. It draws from a paper I published about workforce and knowledge-management issues of water-supply utilities (Grigg, 2006) and a book I published with Mary Zenzen on the general aspects of workforce management (Grigg and Zenzen, 2009). It also includes an up-to-date review of research performed by the Water Research Foundation on workforce and knowledge management.

DIMENSIONS OF THE WATER WORKFORCE CRISIS

While we have a lot of statistics about the crisis in the water workforce, my analysis shows that the problem is caused by a few underlying factors that are not unique to the water industry. First, I would point to increasing complexity of work and more stringent requirements for safe and reliable water. Then, it seems evident that work practices and incentive systems in the mostly public sector water industry do not promote the greatest effectiveness in using employees, and water utilities are not generally regarded as "employers of choice." These problems are exacerbated by ubiquitous undercharging for water services, which creates funding problems for utilities. Finally, I would point to the general education levels and preparation of new employees. This final issue is captured in this quote from a book by Edward E. Gordon: "By 2020 there will be 124 million jobs requiring higher skills and only 50 million qualified Americans."

For about a decade the water industry has been talking about this "workforce crisis." Water and wastewater utilities that experience a rapid rate of baby boomer retirements must stem the loss of institutional knowledge and even improve their performance by becoming learning organizations. The problem is not limited to water utilities but afflicts many industries and has complex causes. As it emerged over the past three decades or so, it resulted from demographics, competitive pressures, the rapid change and complexity of work, and introduction of new technologies.

The demography of the water industry is driven by the aging of baby boomers, the generation that was born after 1946 and is now reaching their sixties. Retirements of workers who joined utilities 30 years ago are occurring rapidly, and new workers were born mostly after 1980 and have distinctly different experiences and attributes. A baby boomer technical worker in a water utility would tend to be male and white and expect a stable 30-year career based on lifetime employment. This tends to make water-utility employees older than those in more turbulent industries and less gender diverse. Water utilities have found it hard to attract women to engineering and technical jobs and, while water utilities have ethnic and racial diversity profiles similar to other organizations, white men still hold the key jobs.

Water and wastewater systems have become more complex and they use far more information technologies than in the past. To operate and maintain them, utilities will need additional skilled technical employees as well as to replace the departing ones. The Bureau of Labor Statistics reports the need for plant operators, distribution and collection field maintenance, administrative (nonmanagement), customer service, line supervisors, meter readers, engineers, and plant maintenance (DeNileon and Stubbert, 2005).

Today's overall employment environment is more turbulent than when baby boomers began to work in the 1970s with more global competition, outsourcing, mobility, and uncertainty. Advances in technology, along with shifting demands on workers, make work more complex for everyone. In water utilities, the core processes of providing safe water—source, treatment, and distribution—use many of the new technologies and require water-utility workers to adapt new methods constantly.

The water industry explained in this book has an employment base of around one million jobs, including several hundred thousand technical jobs in which employees are at risk for knowledge loss. When supervisors and workers walk out the door after many years of service, they take a great deal of institutional knowledge. During my research for an article about workforce issues, a manager in a large water utility told me that two of his three technical supervisors were retiring that same day after 30 years. This problem is exacerbated when, due to cost pressures and downsizing, training is often inadequate.

One water industry report explained that water utility workers can be slow to change, can rely on paper operations and maintenance (O&M) documents instead of computer-based data, can suffer organizational amnesia, and often lack plans for succession (Olstein et al., 2005; Moss et al., 2005).

The problem of becoming an employer of choice is hampered by a changing social contract with water-utility workers, one in which utilities may not be able to offer the same job security as in the past. Factors working against water utilities include defined-benefit retirement programs, lack of advancement potential in technical positions, and pressure to hold costs down (Herman et al., 2003).

These complexities are evident in concerns of water-utility managers. In a 2005 survey, workforce factors cited were aging workforce and loss of brain trust, rising skill requirements, and inadequate industry incentives (Runge and Mann, 2005). These concerns have continued in later surveys, and workforce has risen in the list. This also applies to wastewater utilities, of course. These problems are accompanied by concerns about regulatory issues, business factors, source water supply, security, and water storage/infrastructure.

In conclusion, the water-industry workforce problem is characterized by aging professionals, a need for new leaders, and by the need for capacity increases among water-industry workers and organizations. Water and wastewater utilities are microcosms of other small to large business organizations, which have similar problems, at least in some industries. Kathryn McCain (2007), a president of the American Water Works Association (AWWA), summed it up:

> *It's hard to overstate the significance of this challenge. At the end of the day, we're all in the business of public health protection. The day-to-day decisions made by plant operators, water quality engineers, chemists, mechanics—all the people involved in treatment and transportation of water—have profound impacts on the health and safety of your customers. So we have a real obligation to address this situation, not just for the health of our business, but for the health of our citizens.*

It is fair to ask: "Did the great recession beginning in 2008 end this workforce crisis? The answer is no. While the recession increased the number of people looking for jobs and decreased the number of vacancies by cutting funding for utility personnel, it did not end the crisis at all. The loss of institutional knowledge and other issues of the crisis remain in place and may in fact get worse.

RESPONSES TO THE WORKFORCE CRISIS

The responses required to the workforce crisis should align with its main causes. The increasing complexity of work and more stringent requirements for safe and reliable water will not go away. There is no way to respond except to step up to the plate and confront these challenges, which are common in other business sectors. So, this becomes an input to the other required measures.

To become employers of choice, water utilities must reform their organizational practices to adopt the best practices among businesses and to do this, they must be funded better. This does not mean that they should be shielded from competitive pressures, but it means that they are not starved for budget resources and artificially manipulated by politically motivated budget cutters. The common undercharging for water services creates a challenge to justify the needs for funding across the board and look in every corner for savings and efficiencies.

The larger societal problem of education levels and preparation of employees is a shared issue, and water utilities can take their places with other businesses to respond by doing what is required to insist on a solution to this general problem.

From a business standpoint, the overall challenge is to implement these reforms within organizational management systems that empower employees to do their best, succeed, and create value. In this information age, older forms of hierarchical organizations are out of date and organizations that are flatter, leaner, and more responsive are required.

One useful organizational development tool is AWWA's QualServe program, which offers self-assessment, peer review, and benchmarking (American Water Works Association, 2010). In QualServe, organizational development is one of four business systems, along with business operations, customer relations, and water operations. For benchmarking, four categories of performance indicators were developed and an organizational best-practices index measures seven management practices: strategic planning, long-term financial planning, risk management planning, optimized asset management, performance measurement, customer involvement, and continuous improvement.

One of the organizational performance categories deals with information management and whether the systems capture knowledge and make it accessible to overcome organizational amnesia. Training and workforce capacity building programs should be provided as well, and these offer business opportunities that will be discussed later in the chapter.

Although workforce issues involve the whole organization, human resources officers have a big role in them. They deal with work design, employee recruitment, training, compensation, evaluation, and retention. As the National Human Resources Association (2010) states, "In addition to managing traditional human resource functions, HR is expected to . . . continuously improve the company's return on its greatest asset . . . its people." To respond to organizational change, it may be necessary to redesign jobs and create new communication patterns to facilitate knowledge capture.

KNOWLEDGE-MANAGEMENT SYSTEMS

Computer-based knowledge-management systems are emerging as tools to help fill the gaps caused by dramatic changes in organizations. While information systems are involved, a utility's knowledge-management system includes more functions and extends to a range of tools and techniques that include methods and software. Knowledge management is a process to make important information and experience available for utility employees to use in their jobs. Knowledge-management systems are merging with information science, and management information systems and decision support systems are being added to it. Knowledge-management participants include researchers, managers, management consultants, and vendors.

Opinions on the definition of knowledge management are still being formed because the field is changing rapidly (Rosen et al., 2003). One definition is that knowledge management is "a business strategy by which a water utility consciously identifies, captures, indexes, manages, and stores experiences, data, and information and provides methods for easily accessing and acting upon these collective assets (corporate history) in a collaborative environment (learning culture) optimizing the use of (leveraging) people, processes and technology in support of: effective decision making, assuring compliance, improving performance, innovation, and business continuity, all on a timely and sustainable basis" (Moss et al., 2005).

We evaluated the portfolios of several firms that practice it and developed a list of seven categories of systems, methods, and tools (Grigg and Zenzen, 2009):

- Analysis and synthesis tools (case based reasoning, meta analysis, scenario planning, social network analysis, knowledge mapping).
- Communications and relationships (peer mentoring, brainstorming, collaborative technologies, communities of practice, conferencing).
- Information systems (document management, records management).
- Learning systems (distance learning, eLearning).
- Management systems (intellectual property systems, best practices, project management, workflow management, digital asset management).
- Software (artificial intelligence, expert systems, knowledge based systems, knowledge based decision support, creativity software, data analysis and management, groupware systems).
- Web knowledge portals and systems (web systems, digital dashboards, intranets, knowledge portals).

Management in utilities is becoming data centered, and this opens the opportunity to develop and market software packages for various functions, including work management to guide employees in structured tasks, such as scheduled maintenance management or work orders. The technical functions of a water utility require an information architecture with: facility and system maps, inventory data, engineering drawings, system O&M manuals, equipment manuals and shop drawings, preventive maintenance schedules, maintenance histories and inspection data, operating and performance records, case and incident files, technical studies, regulatory and legal documents, and other technical background documents.

Practical approaches to knowledge management are required. A project for the Water Research Foundation identified strategies for knowledge retention, integrating them with core management processes, piloting a community of practice web site, and advancing organizational development (Moss et al., 2005). In one of my projects, I organized water utility focus groups on workforce capacity and knowledge management and the participants focused on how support from leaders is needed to set priorities, implement budget and training, and overcome obstacles. The groups emphasized how utilities must be well organized and that there should be up-and-down understanding, as well as cross-functional understanding.

Incentives attracted the most attention as being important to get employees to do required work, share information, and do cross training. Incentives, such as training on new equipment and technologies, should raise the capacity of employees. Certifications were seen as important. Employees also thought they should feel good about their work and that utilities can do a better job on recruitment, such as showing work of the water utility on CATV and interviewing happy customers.

Everyone agreed with the need for training and methods, equipment, and standards, but lack of time and money were seen as issues. They saw attitude as very important, and that incentives for employees, such as getting off of work early, are important. Methods of training such as extending knowledge of older people, use of apprenticeships and mentoring, cross training, and vertical training were mentioned.

Knowledge-management tools and techniques attracted less attention because the participants were not familiar with them. They did emphasize the utility's information systems, software, mapping and data systems, and having funds and management systems, including training, to use them.

BUSINESS OF WATER-INDUSTRY TRAINING

Training of water industry staff is a good candidate for outsourcing. How it is categorized is reflected in the tasks by activity within the American Society for Training and Development (2010), which has the vision to be a worldwide leader in workplace learning and performance. The society's "manifesto" is:

> *The ability to learn, and of those who know how to convert that learning into practice (performance), creates extraordinary value for individuals, teams, and organizations. Smart organizations recognize that a learning and performance plan is as much a strategic tool as a marketing or finance plan and that it should get the same kind of tough love from the top: insistence on results and full support if it can deliver.*

Visionary concepts about training are appealing, but the challenge is how to implement them in the real world of utility operations. Training extends across the entire spectrum of employee needs. For example, the East Bay Municipal Utility District in Oakland, California, developed an academy to train its future leaders. It focused on basic skills, such as leadership, project management, communication, business writing, decision making, and supervision. For more technical subjects, certification and licensing courses can be offered internally or through other organizations. An example can be seen from courses offered through the Texas Engineering Extension Service that include basic calculations, field and laboratory operations, and customer service.

It is not practical even in large utilities to organize all aspects of training through one centralized office. In the tens of thousands of small utilities, training responsibilities fall on managers who have other duties and training might be on a hit-and-miss basis unless a deliberate approach is taken.

Categories of required training begin with fundamental management issues, such as finance through purchasing and other controls. Another important example is in legal, risk, and regulatory responsibilities. Equal opportunity and sexual harassment are important in all organizations, and new information technology equipment and methods require continuing updates. Leadership, management, and employee development are especially important during the workforce crisis.

Job-specific training programs are required, and workers should have annual training plans for basic and advanced job skills. The plans for particular jobs should be based on the requirements of the job description and on certification requirements. By linking training to certification, the motivation of employees will rise because they see a direct incentive in their participation.

Many training methods and delivery vehicles are being developed, and these are an area of opportunity for water industry businesses, both for the actual delivery of training and for the production of training media.

Associations offer many training opportunities. Continuing education at universities or community colleges can be cost effective and help with retention. Distance education may combine digital media with degree programs. USEPA offers a great deal of free training material for the Safe Drinking Water Act and the Clean Water Act. Its Watershed Academy is accessible from its web page.

Training occurs through national conference attendance, but it is expensive due to travel, registration, and time commitments. At national conferences and association workshops, employees have access to national experts across a range of topics. Local workshops cost less than national workshops, and on-site workshops can be very cost effective. Consultants can be retained to present workshops or to train trainers. Downlink workshops from associations, in which a central office presents a program over the Internet, are becoming increasingly popular.

Among the water associations, AWWA and WEF are in lead positions as mainline associations with missions to help members with training. Each of them offers many free or at-cost resources to members and others. In addition to water associations, several others offer training programs in related areas. For example, the Urban and Regional Information Systems Association organizes conferences about GIS systems. Water utilities can also participate in training from other sectors, such as emergency response and security.

It is a common practice for lead associations to hire staff to organize continuing-education events and collect fees to offset their costs in providing the training. Associations should be in the position to offer certification training without any conflicts of interest that might arise in private firms. In some associations the fees from training programs become important parts of overall budgets. Association education staff can count on the good will and cooperation of members to suggest topics and provide free lectures and materials. Training can often be delivered through local chapters of the associations, providing a ready-made market for events and materials.

Private-sector firms such as consultants and publishers can add training to their portfolios as a source of revenue and to market their products and services.

The training business attracted my attention in the 1970s as I witnessed a surge of interest in stormwater training. I noticed that short courses and conferences could be financially profitable, whether offered through for-profit or not-for-profit venues. In the case of stormwater, no association seemed to be concentrating on this area of training, so I joined with a few others and we organized a small business to offer short courses. As in any small business, you learn quickly if you are to survive.

We learned that consultants were a better market than local governments because they could make registration choices quicker than the utilities and agencies, which were constrained by government rules and budgets. It was fun to plan our cities and programs and to deliver the instruction, which was well received. The diversity of technical topics continued to broaden as USEPA started to move into stormwater regulation-setting. We hired consultants to deliver programs on topics that we could not cover ourselves, and the business seemed promising in the beginning, especially in the growing area of computer software. We did learn that delivering short courses in hotel venues requires a lot of stamina for the travel and presentations, and you must be imaginative to hold the attention of workshop participants for several hours.

In 1982 the recession of that time, which was quite deep, put a damper on travel and training budgets of the consultants and local governments. As a result, our risk increased and profits decreased, making the business unattractive, and we closed it. This illustrates the sensitivity of the training business to recession, especially because travel and training are discretionary items, easy to cut from budgets.

Over the next two decades or so, we noticed a resurgence of the private-sector training business with many new outlets appearing. The business continues to offer many opportunities, but it will always be a niche business because so many players are in it. Also, it is attractive to some organizations to offer free or subsidized training so as to promote other lines of business, so the training business itself must be augmented by other business lines or it may be too fragile.

WATER BOOKS, JOURNALS, AND NEWSLETTERS

The business of selling media in the water industry—whether print or electronic and in various forms—has grown, just as it has with the expansion of information with the Internet. I've participated in book publishing, journals, and newsletters and remain active in these outlets, and I can testify to the rapid change that continues to occur.

In the 1960s, one of my engineering professors took an interest in the book publishing business and we witnessed his efforts to attract authors, publish the books, and sell them to a global mailing list, which was entirely through regular postal mail as there was no Internet at the time. He found that a global direct mail list of water agencies, academics, utilities, and other water-industry centers facilitated a successful niche business in water-industry publications. As competition increased, his business became less successful, and today many publishers vie for the water-industry market. Selling books is a labor-intensive and low-margin business that has become more competitive across the board. Still, the water industry continues to attract authors with many technical subjects to explain.

In our academic department, it sometimes seems that I receive more trade magazines than everyone else combined. This is probably an exaggeration because each professor follows a particular subindustry within civil engineering, but it is true that the water industry is served by a broad array of trade publications. Fields that I follow in addition to mainline civil engineering and water resources include pumps and systems, pipes and instruments, trenchless technologies, water efficiency, stormwater, plumbing engineering, and water treatment and conditioning.

An array of water-industry newsletters finds news to report daily. This service is supported by advertising or government subsidies, rather than subscriptions. Some of them provide water investment advice.

Of the thousands of libraries in the United States, a few maintain significant collections about water subjects. Also, a few databases of water titles offer bibliographic services and new forms of information archiving such as digital libraries are emerging. This NAICS category is 51912 (Libraries and archives): "This industry comprises establishments primarily engaged in providing library or archive services."

A few libraries maintain extensive water-related holdings and you can normally visit them or ask for information over the Internet. This is a short list of some libraries with interesting water-industry holdings.

AWWA Technical Library	www.awwa.org
Colorado State Library	www.cde.state.co.us
Colorado State University Water Archives	http://lib.colostate.edu
Colorado Supreme Court Library	www.state.co.us/courts/sctlib
Denver Public Library	www.denver.lib.co.us
Great Lakes Information Network	www.great-lakes.net
Hopper Law Library	http://uwadmnweb.uwyo.edu/law
Inst for Water Resources Library	www.iwr.usace.army.mil
Law Library	http://lawschool.unm.edu
Library of Congress	www.loc.gov
Montana State Library	http://msl.state.mt.us
National Science Digital Library	http://nsdl.org
Native American Water Rights	http://water.library.arizona.edu
School of Law Library	www.colorado.edu/law
Water holdings, National Agricultural Library	www.nal.usda.gov/wqic
Water Resources Center Archives	www.lib.berkeley.edu/WRCA
Wyoming State Library	www.wsl.state.wy.us

SCIENTIFIC RESEARCH AND THINK TANKS

Although the problems of water management have been around a long time, the United States has a diverse collection of water research institutes, centers, and think tanks to study the issues.

Decades ago, water research was dominated by government programs. Prior to about 1960, little research on water was conducted but during the 1960s the Office of Water Resources Research and Office of Saline Water were organized and began to publish reports about the nation's water issues. After USEPA was organized, it and other federal departments began to publish reports on many water-related subjects. The Water Resources Council, also organized during the 1960s, studied many of the nation's water systems. Policy reports from study groups such as the National Water Commission and decades of other research still contain valuable knowledge about water.

Today, the water-research activities of government agencies continue, and a number of centers have established reputations for insightful inquires. For example, the National Center for Atmospheric Research studies climate change, the USGS studies water resources, the EPA and CDC study water supply and wastewater, the USDA studies irrigation, and the DOE tracks the water-energy nexus.

Most water research in academic departments and centers is government sponsored, but the funding is administered by the schools. The academic researchers have important influence on the policies of the water industry. For example, the National Research Council issues periodic studies on topics such as drinking-water technology and policy.

The Water Resources Research Act of 1964 provided for the establishment of water-resources research institutes (WRRI) in each state, and most are still in operation but many are very small. Most of these provide limited support to small projects, usually on the basis of cost sharing among federal, state, and local interests. They are coordinated by an office in USGS and work together through the National Association of Institutes of Water Resources. These institutes are supposed to consult state and local stakeholders and to formulate research agendas. Similar to the WRRIs are the Sea Grant programs, which focus on the practical use and conservation of coastal, marine and Great Lakes resources. Sea Grant institutions are like a brain trust of coastal and oceanic science. Most major coastal states and Great Lakes universities participate. Agricultural Experiment Stations are located in the schools of agriculture of all Land Grant universities. Other academic centers include a wide variety of programs to study issues such as water quality, drinking water, limnology (study of lakes), environmental law, and transboundary water legal issues, for example.

In terms of money spent, government-sponsored research has been the largest research sector, but industry-sponsored institutes such as the Water Research Foundation and Water Environment Research Foundation have become active in the last few decades.

The Water Research Foundation (WaterRF), based in Denver and located next to the headquarters of AWWA, was originally named the AWWA Research Foundation to indicate its status as an independent spin-off from AWWA. The WaterRF was actually established in 1966, but its more active years began during the 1980s when it initiated a subscriber program of centralized research for the drinking-water community. Currently, it focuses on infrastructure, management and customer relations, water quality and water resources, and environmental sustainability. It is governed and supported by member organizations that subscribe to support research, and about 900 water utilities and 50 consulting firms and manufacturers are subscribers. Most are in the United States, and collaborating partners are around the world. The WaterRF has completed about 800 research projects valued at around $460 million. Current subscribers provide about $12 million annually, and the funding is augmented by funding from the U.S. government and collaborative partnerships. More than 700 subscriber volunteers serve on committees and add expertise in research areas.

The Water Environment Research Foundation (WERF, 2010), which came along after the WaterRF, was formed in 1989 by the Water Environmental Federation. It has produced about 300 research reports, which are valued at around $62 million. WERF is also an independent nonprofit organization with funding from subscribers and the government. Subscribers include wastewater treatment plants, stormwater utilities, and regulatory agencies, along with industries, suppliers, and consultants.

Many other think tanks and institutes engage in water research and outreach, and they often promote special goals, such as environmental sustainability and stewardship of natural resources. Examples include Resources for the Future, a Washington-based think tank that focuses on economics; the World Resources Institute, which focuses on environmental issues; and the National Water Research Institute, which was endowed by private funding.

Because water is an interdisciplinary subject, a number of university departments contribute to education in water resources. Mainly, engineering and science educators focus on it, and smaller numbers of economists, lawyers, and other social scientists participate as well. The Universities Council on Water Resources is an association for water educators. Civil engineering departments are mostly active in water education, but some schools of natural resources, law, and public health will also focus on water education.

Environmental educators may be parts of universities or of public interest programs, including advocacy groups and government agencies, such as USEPA. For example, California's Water Education Foundation has been active for years, and in Colorado the Colorado Foundation for Water Education is becoming more active.

FUTURE WORKFORCE ISSUES

Although it is currently masked by the financial crisis, the problem of maintaining an effective water industry workforce will continue into the future. The problems are loss of critical knowledge, skills, and abilities in water utilities caused by key employees leaving at the same time that systems and infrastructure are aging, regulatory requirements are increasing, and budgets are under stress.

To face their challenges, utilities require specialized skills that are ratcheting upward to use the new technologies and meet tighter regulations. While other organizations face the same issues, utilities have unique knowledge-intensive requirements, particularly at the level of technical supervisors, and this is exacerbated for small utilities.

Fortunately, solutions are available and they can be good for water-industry businesses. One solution is for utilities to become employers of choice. This is easier to say than to do, but it requires that the work of utilities rise in public esteem and for utilities to be managed effectively. Another solution is in education and training. Utility jobs should be good jobs and taken seriously by management for training and preparation of all levels of employees.

Faced with similar workforce problems, private-sector firms might adapt by merging, introducing new products, or outsourcing work, but water utilities require a stable technical workforce and cannot be as nimble as many private companies. They need integrated strategies of organizational development with leadership, training, and human resources elements, along with emerging information and knowledge-management systems.

It would help if consolidation could occur to mitigate the small-utility problem. Workforce issues that apply mainly to large utilities (such as use of computer-based knowledge-management systems) could then be handled on a broader basis. In any event, all utilities need positive incentives and work environments so employees can create value and use technology. Human resources staffs will continue to be important in capacity-building and can facilitate knowledge capture.

Most large utilities are becoming data-centered and use software packages to manage their information systems, which are used more and more to guide structured work and to retrieve data and information. This creates a large new market for IT companies that offer packages for utility management.

Associations have opportunities as well because, in developing knowledge-management systems, utilities need organizing vehicles for their communities of practice. The work of associations in a public-private industry like water can go a long way to bridge misunderstandings and provide coordination across a range of business and policy issues.

CHAPTER 16

Private-Sector Operations in the Water Industry

Although government operations dominate water handling, the private sector also has a big hand in it. Private water companies provide a significant percentage of all utility water supply and many industries and farms manage large quantities of water in their own utility-like operations. Investor-owned utilities are the largest players in electric power, which uses more raw water than any other economic sector, mainly to cool thermoelectric power plants. Privatization of government-owned systems by sale or lease to private companies remains a viable option in many places, and private sector operating contracts are in place for many water facilities.

The common thread among these topics is private-sector operations as an alternative to government operations in the water industry. Each of the topics deserves a special chapter itself, such as private water utilities and their business environment, industrial water management, farm water organizations, privatization, and contract operations. Most of these topics were introduced in previous chapters, such as the discussion in Chapter 4 about private water-supply utilities and in Chapter 7 about industrial use of water. The contribution of this chapter is to synthesize the material about private-sector water handling and to explain the range of public-private partnership activities in the water sector.

PRIVATE WATER COMPANIES

While privatization of publicly owned water systems receives a lot of attention whenever it is attempted, interest in it waxes and wanes. Privatization became popular in the United States and elsewhere during the Reagan-Thatcher era because of a number of interacting economic, social, and political factors, including the breakup of the Soviet Union. Most of the United

Kingdom's water systems were privatized in that period, and a number of experiments were launched in different countries. However, many subsequent failures and controversial deals seem to have put the brakes on new experiments with privatization of public systems.

Actually, private water companies have a long and important history in the United States, and they date back to the first organized U.S. water utilities, around 1800. Best known among these might be the New York City water supply, which was started by Aaron Burr, a former vice president who is best remembered for killing Alexander Hamilton in a duel. Burr started the New York City water system as a side activity of a bank scheme that eventually led to the predecessor of the Chase Manhattan Bank.

As secretary of the Treasury, Hamilton had promoted the first National Bank, which was approved in 1791. Burr's idea for the Manhattan Company was to create a competing bank with a stealth deal based on developing a water-supply system. A loophole in the charter of the company authorized it to use its capital to start a bank, and this was the beginning of the Chase Manhattan Bank company.

Around 1800, the perceived need for clean urban water was great because people believed that poor water quality caused yellow fever. They would leave the city during the fever season and drink "tea water" if they could afford it, rather than the commonly available supplies from local wells. While the water system was just a sideline to Burr, the New York City system has evolved to one of the world's largest (and is now publicly owned), but its beginning as a private water company marks the beginning of a strong presence by private water companies in the United States (Koeppel, 2000).

There are many other stories of U.S. private water companies operating in growing cities as the country emerged from its status as a rural colony to become an urbanized and independent nation. For example, Denver's water system was in private ownership until nearly 1920. Prior to 1872, when Denver was a small settlement to support the gold rush, Denver residents relied on private wells or stream diversions for their water. The Auraria and Cherry Creek Water Company was formed in 1859, but it never functioned effectively. From 1872 to 1878, the Denver City Water Company provided service from South Platte River supplies, and the Denver City Irrigation and Water Company was formed in 1878 to build a lake on the South Platte, with the two companies merging to form the Denver Water Company. After it merged later with several smaller companies, the Denver City Water Works Company was formed. It went into receivership in 1892 and was purchased in 1984 by the Citizen's Water Company, which had been formed by two former directors of the Denver Water Company, D. H. Moffat and W. S. Cheesman.

Also in 1894, the Denver Union Water Company was incorporated, and it took over the assets of the competing water companies and obtained a monopoly to serve domestic water in Denver with a 20-year franchise. The company built Cheesman Dam in 1905, which is an important part of the Denver system today. Several disputes followed, with Denver seeking to buy the Denver Union Water Company and trying to build a competing system, and the disputes went to the U.S. Supreme Court. Denver finally got an option in 1916 to buy Denver Union's assets, and in 1918 a bond issue was passed to buy the assets. In the same election, a charter amendment established the Denver Board of Water Commissioners, the governing board of the Denver Water Department. Thus, by 1920 the Denver system had been converted from private to public ownership, almost the reverse of today's attempts to privatize systems (Milliken, 1989).

While many if not most of these early private water companies went public as cities grew and local politics became more sophisticated, the formation of private water companies continued, thus creating opportunities for new generations of entrepreneurs. One such story is how the country's largest private water and wastewater company—American Water—got started.

The company evolved by acquisitions from its beginnings about 1886 (Cross, 1991). The main force in creating today's company was entrepreneur John Ware, who led it through its period of greatest growth. Ware had begun in the 1930s to acquire small water utilities and had become wealthy. He took note of the New Deal's Public Utility Holding Act of 1935, which was aimed at breaking up large utilities into smaller companies. He was following the American Water Works & Electric Company, which was founded in 1886 as the American Water Works and Guarantee Company and renamed in 1917 to reflect its operations in eastern, southern, and midwestern states.

The American Water Works & Electric Company filed a suit that reached the Supreme Court and resulted in a 1946 decision that that the Public Utility Holding Act Law was constitutional. American Water Works was compelled to issue a revised reorganization plan that had it sell its water works business. Ware submitted the only bid for the company and invested $13 million to gain control of a company with assets of $183 million but with deteriorated infrastructure. Ware divested the company of its electric power business and began to buy and sell small water companies. Sometimes he would divest, when cities chose to operate their own systems. However, when municipal operations favored privatization, he acquired their systems. These actions led to the formation of today's American Water, which offers water and wastewater services to 15.6 million people in more than 1,600 communities in the United States and Canada.

American Water is listed on the NYSE, its listing having been restored after an acquisition by a German company, RWE AG, and later divesture and initial public offering. RWE sold 39.5 percent of its holdings in 2007 and planned to divest its remaining share to focus on power and gas markets. It still owned about 60 percent of American Water in early 2009 (Wall Street Journal Business, 2009).

American Water's development has been mimicked by other private water companies. By collecting small to medium-sized utilities in its portfolio, a private water company can grow and take advantage of economies of scale. Although American Water is quite large, most private water companies are not as large as the biggest municipal utilities. For example, the California Water Service Company is the largest investor-owned water company in the West and the third largest in the nation. It is a subsidiary of the California Water Service Group, which serves two million people in about 100 communities. Many publicly owned utilities are much larger than this.

On the international front, some private water companies have grown to giant scales. For example, the Saur Group serves 6,700 French communities. A subsidiary named Saur International has 2,400 employees. Another French water company is GDF Suez (2010), which was formed in 1997 by a merger between Compagnie de Suez and Lyonnaise des Eaux. It is a megacorporation and employs 198,200 people globally and had revenues of €74.3 billion in 2007. This includes its activities in energy, energy services, and environment, from which it offers its drinking water, wastewater treatment, and waste management services.

In Germany, RWE AG, which bought and then divested American Water, offers electricity, gas, water and wastewater, and waste disposal and recycling services with a focus on the European market. United Utilities (2010), the largest water and wastewater company in the United Kingdom, was created by a merger of Northwest Water plc and Norweb plc. Water and wastewater are its biggest business, but other services include electricity distribution and telecommunications.

While there is an ongoing debate over the relative merits of public versus private ownership of water systems, it seems clear that privately owned water companies can deliver safe water competitively and operate as responsibly as publicly owned water companies. Whether they can be more efficient and hold costs down would depend on a case-by-case basis. The operation of private water companies focuses on the utility nature of water and wastewater services, and it is hard to see how these for-profit organizations could go very far toward responding to environmental or social needs and still serve their investors well. They might be compelled by their regulators to take certain actions, such as maintain a program for rate relief of low income residents, but these would not be very consistent.

Private water companies are represented in the National Association of Water Companies (NAWC) (2010), which is their trade association. It reports statistics from USEPA that 73 million Americans get their drinking water from privately owned companies or a municipal utility operating under a public-private partnership. These partnerships would normally involve operating contracts, such as those explained in Chapter 18. The number served by utilities that are entirely investor owned or in other private ownership would be fewer. NAWC reported further that private water companies have about 100,000 miles of distribution main, which is between 5 percent and 10 percent of all mileage in the United States. If it is 10 percent, this suggests that private water companies serve around 30 million customers, based on a total U.S. piping of one million miles. The quantity of piping is discussed in more detail in Chapter 5. Further, the private water business is reported to be a $4.3 billion per year business, which suggests, based on U.S. averages, that it supplies 30 million to 35 million people.

Other statistics quoted by NAWC are that there are about 4,200 privately owned wastewater facilities in the United States and that 20 percent of all wastewater utilities in the country are in private ownership. This results in about 3 percent of the U.S. population being served by private wastewater utilities. I cannot corroborate these statistics (see Chapter 5) because the wastewater industry has a greater percentage of public ownership than the potable water industry. The references given by NAWC stem back to surveys taken by USEPA, which are reported in the periodic Community Water Systems Survey, which is discussed in more detail in Chapters 5 and 6.

NAWC reported that more than 2,000 drinking water and wastewater facilities are operated by public-private partnerships at $1.5 billion per year, and that these are renewed more than 93 percent of the time. These statistics are explained in more detail in Chapter 18.

NAWC identified 12 private water companies as being publicly traded. This list provides a starting point for assembling a bundle of water company stocks:

- American Water
- American States Water Co.
- Aqua America
- Artesian Resources Corp.
- BIW Ltd.
- California Water Service Group
- Connecticut Water Service, Inc.
- Middlesex Water Co.
- Pennichuck Corp.

- SJW Corp.
- Southwest Water Co.
- York Water Co.

Among water-handling organizations, the private water companies are unique in being the only ones to be regulated by state public utility commissions (PUCs). PUC regulation of water companies is similar to that imposed on electric power and natural gas utilities, along with other monopoly privately owned public services. While PUC regulation is imposed on private water companies, publicly owned water utilities are regulated by local governments based on political choice, although they are regulated by the USEPA for health and environmental goals. For rates, local elected leaders take public interest into account when making rate decisions and try to balance the views of businesses, individuals, and nongovernmental organizations, as well as the needs to balance health and the environment and to sustain the economy.

PRIVATE-SECTOR INDUSTRIAL AND ELECTRIC POWER WATER USERS

The operations of private-sector self-supplied industrial and energy water users are not unlike those of water utilities. These organizations obtain permits, build and manage infrastructure, and maintain complex water systems and, if it were attractive, would have the capability to enter the water and wastewater utility businesses themselves. Once an industry has solved its problems of source of supply and treatment, it would be positioned to also provide public supply if the situation required it to do so. In fact, some of them do offer water and wastewater services as auxiliary enterprises, sometimes not even charging for the services. Chapter 2 explained how self-supplied industrial water users account for a large share of all water withdrawals, and they also hold a large fraction of the 500,000 NPDES permits in the United States. The self-supplied industries that provide public water systems as an adjunct service are surveyed by the CWSS of USEPA. Their skills, products, and services are similar to those required in water and wastewater utilities.

Electric power generation is a special class of industrial water user, and thermoelectric cooling accounts for the largest raw-water withdrawals among all water uses. They would normally not be positioned to enter the water and wastewater utility business as readily, purely on the basis of their cooling-water operations. However, electric power utilities have other infrastructure that lends itself to water utility operations, such as skilled maintenance workers, billing services, and related capabilities.

The future of industrial water and wastewater management is a global issue. The North Atlantic Treaty Organization (NATO) held a 2010 research workshop about it, focusing on problems with siting industries such as semiconductor processing and nanotechnology where water use is significant and high-quality water is needed (U.S. Environmental Protection Agency, 2010d). It noted that some industry sectors, such as paper, coffee, and sugar, use large amounts of water in their production processes. Also, industry sectors with large needs for fresh water are identified as the power industry with boiler-water needs, chemical plants, and petroleum refineries with cooling-water needs, pulp and paper, chemicals, textiles, automotive, electronic, food and beverage, metal processing, and mining industries.

Water-treatment needs are a special issue for industries, and they fall on a spectrum from inexpensive raw cooling water for power plants to very expensive ultrapure water for semiconductor processing. Industrial wastewater is challenged with pollutants such as salinity, inorganics like sodium and chlorine residuals, nutrients, dissolved organics, particulates, nitrogenous chemicals, and microbial contaminants. Industrial water treatment attracts large companies such as General Electric, Siemens Water Technology, Lyonnaise, Veolia, Mekorot, and Suez. Water desalting is an attractive business, and distillation and evaporation are attractive where energy is inexpensive. Solar energy can be used for evaporative water purification where solar exposure is high. Membrane technologies are used for industrial water applications using reverse osmosis and membrane distillation, microfiltration, and ultrafiltration.

Chemical plant operations are a special concern and are implicated in some past pollution episodes, such as the Superfund project at the Stauffer Chemical Company's Tarpon Springs site in Pinellas County, Florida. Information about the cleanup is posted on USEPA's (2010) web site and is public information. Elemental phosphorous was mined there from 1947 until the facility was closed in 1981. The mining operations contaminated soils, groundwater, and ponds on the property with contaminants such as arsenic, antimony, beryllium, and elemental phosphorous. A cleanup plan has been developed, and a Record of Decision for source control was issued in 1998. The elements of the cleanup will include some excavation of contaminated material and soil, consolidation of contaminated material in the main areas, institutional controls to include land-use restrictions, physical barriers and water-well permitting prohibitions, and on-site stabilization of material and contaminated soil. The soil cleanup began in 2010 and is scheduled for completion in 2011.

PRIVATIZATION OF PUBLIC SYSTEMS BY PRIVATE COMPANIES

Returning to the Reagan-Thatcher era when the term *privatization* had a certain buzz, especially as the state-controlled economies of Eastern Europe started to come apart, and water privatization became a hot topic globally. The privatization of the British water industry under Prime Minister Margaret Thatcher's Conservative government was the poster child of that era. The British move was in part the swing of a pendulum from socialism and government direction of the economy toward the private sector. After World War II, Labor had strong control of the British economy, and by the 1980s a great deal of state enterprise was in place.

Actually, the United Kingdom had made strong moves to make its water industry more efficient under government control. Efforts to regionalize it during the 1970s were explained by Okun (1977), and during a couple of visits to UK utilities and research centers during that era, I was impressed by their efforts and strides. Okun invited speakers to the United States and promoted the general concept of regionalization as a way to make services safer and more efficient.

These efforts toward greater efficiency through regionalization were blown away, however, by the forces of privatization. During that period, many other public services and companies were also privatized, as I explained in more detail in a book about infrastructure finance (Grigg, 2010).

The interest in the United States was led to some extent by President Reagan's philosophy that small government is better and by the philosophies that he shared with Thatcher. At the same time, the Soviet Union was coming undone and state socialism was discredited, at least partially. Economic growth in China and India and in smaller Asian countries such as South Korea, Thailand, and Taiwan began to favor the private sector over public enterprise. While this interest in private sector control unraveled a little during the global recession in 2008, the interest in government cost control and efficiency has not abated.

As a result of the experiences of the past 30 years, privatization has attracted a lot of attention and we have an accumulated experience base on it that enables us to answer the question: "Which is best for water systems, privatization or public ownership?" The answer is, of course, "it depends." What it depends on is the set of specific and local circumstances that govern the pros and cons of a particular deal.

From the standpoint of ideology, the arguments in favor of privatization are that infrastructure is an economic good and ought to be managed by the private sector and that smaller government is better. On the opposite side, the argument is that infrastructure is a public good and ought to be managed by government to resist the excesses of the private sector. The pro-privatization forces argue that the private sector is more competent than the public sector and can deliver cost savings in construction, procurement and management, hiring and training, and tax benefits. The anti-privatization argument is that the public sector is efficient and that cost savings in privatization are fictional. They consider that tax benefits are a shell game, that long-term contracts have many hidden pitfalls, and there is the potential for large rate increases.

Other arguments are that government is not reliable and people do not always trust it. The other side thinks business is not to be trusted and it is risky to lose political control, which leads to loss of jobs and loss of public benefits of water. Some think the private firms will guarantee performance, but others think that effective management by government minimizes risk. The private sector may provide access to capital in private markets and escape government debt limits, but others think the public sector should generate the capital for infrastructure.

One aspect of privatization that has prospered is private-sector operating contracts of public facilities, which are discussed in Chapter 18 as a form of outsourcing of services. Obviously, private-sector firms that operate water systems are in a good position to also offer operating services, as are engineering and construction companies with the expertise.

Another form of partial privatization is outsourcing that might be driven by managed competition between the public and private sectors. This occurs when a government entity decides it wants to unbundle some of its services and have private operators compete against public workforces for the jobs. I wrote about this in more detail in my infrastructure book as well, and the strategy has attractive features and possible pitfalls as well.

Today, most privatization efforts in the United States today are led by experienced operators, such as American Water and other large private water companies that would like to expand their holdings. It is a way to regionalize on a de facto basis by using private-sector incentives to offer alternative management arrangements to water utilities that might gain from them.

Water-Industry Businesses, Careers, and Investments

CHAPTER 17

Constructing Water-Industry Infrastructure

The water industry requires an active construction program to create and renew the infrastructure for its capital-intensive systems. It engages heavy-construction contractors to clear land and build dams and access roads, building contractors to construct facilities, and utility contractors to lay pipelines and install equipment. Many water-industry infrastructure components, such as buried pipelines, last a long time but require maintenance and rehabilitation, which creates a market for construction-related renewal products and services after installation. Water utilities and districts may perform their own renewal of facilities, but they are likely to use construction contractors who specialize in utility construction. Utility contractors also handle a large part of private-sector water-related construction. Well-drilling contractors are a special category of utility constructors engaged in groundwater-related work. The number of water wells in the nation is not known exactly, but there are millions of smaller wells and many larger ones as well.

The purpose of this chapter is to explain the extent and nature of the construction activities that are required to support the water industry. The chapter begins with an inventory of the types of contractors that perform the construction and proceeds to construction spending statistics. The last part of the chapter draws from other parts of the book to provide a look into the future of water-industry construction.

CLASSIFICATION OF WATER-INDUSTRY CONTRACTORS

The world of construction is gigantic, with around seven million employed to construct $1 trillion of facilities each year in the United States. This is cited from 2006 data in my book on infrastructure finance, and after the financial crisis the numbers declined, but the overall size of the industry is not much different (Grigg, 2010). The 2006 data show the distribution among types of construction establishments; most construction is for residential and non-residential buildings with less for heavy and civil engineering construction, which is the category that includes utility contractors and site preparation contractors, who would be involved in stormwater. Employment for utility system construction was 5.5 percent of the total, or 426,000 jobs. Another large group of water-industry workers are in the group labeled specialty trade contractors, who will install water systems related to buildings. The specialty trade contractors were 63.7 percent of the total.

The contractors are classified in the NAICS system as:

- Heavy and Civil Engineering Construction (NAICS 237)
- Utility System Construction (NAICS 2371)
- Plumbing, Heating, and Air-Conditioning Contractors (NAICS 238220)
- Site Preparation Contractors (NAICS 23891)

Within these categories, you find water and sewer line and related structures construction (NAICS 237110), with 10,506 establishments, 191,539 employees, and a payroll of $9.2 billion from the data in the 2007 Economic Census. The 2007 Economic Census did not show the breakdown among the establishments, but from the 2002 Economic Census we see that of 12,357 establishments, 7,708 were water, sewer, and pipeline construction and 4,028 were water-well contractors, with the others being all other construction. The employee count was 156,061 for water, sewer, and pipeline construction and 23,910 for water-well construction. These data give us a good idea of the overall size of the utility construction and well-drilling sectors.

A good bit of water-industry construction is contained in NAICS 37, the Heavy and Civil Engineering Construction subsector. For example, it is the group that would construct dams and their access roads. Construction projects involving water resources such as dredging and land drainage are included in this subsector. Also, land development and related road and stormwater building and utility line installation) and are included.

The utility contractor category (NAICS 2371) includes establishments engaged in construction of distribution lines and related buildings and structures for utilities (i.e., water, sewer, petroleum, gas, power, and communication). This includes structures (including buildings) that are integral parts of utility systems (e.g., storage tanks, pumping stations, power plants, and refineries) and are included in this industry group.

Most categories of construction have their own trade associations, and utility contractors have the National Utility Contractors Association (NUCA) and the American Pipeline Contractors Association, among others.

The landscaping services group (NAICS 561730) includes establishments engaged in maintenance services and/or installing landscape components, including walkways, retaining walls, decks, fences, ponds, and similar structures.

Within NAICS 238220 (Plumbing, Heating, and Air-Conditioning Contractors), we find the establishments engaged in installing and servicing plumbing, heating, and air-conditioning equipment. The percentage of plumbing work was given previously.

CONSTRUCTION SPENDING IN THE WATER INDUSTRY

While it is difficult to get detailed figures on construction spending in the water industry due to the scattered organization of statistics, we can garner a fair estimate from government accounts, which divide into public and private construction spending. During the recent economic turmoil construction spending was down significantly, but we will use the 2010 numbers for analysis. As spending ramps up, some of the construction volumes and percentages are likely to change.

Annual construction spending as of May 2010 was $842 billion, or $536 billion in private spending and $306 billion in public spending (U.S. Census Bureau, 2010). Water utility expenditures are mainly on the public side and industrial water expenditures are mainly on the private side.

Public water-related construction volumes appear in Table 17.1.

The totals were about $47 billion or 16 percent of public construction and 6 percent of all construction. However, other water-related spending is hidden behind categories such as the large category of roads and streets, which includes a great deal of drainage and flood control work. Years ago, we used the notion that 10 percent of road spending was on drainage, so

TABLE 17.1 Water-Industry Construction Volumes

Spending Category	Construction Spending, billions
Sewage and waste disposal	$25.4
Water supply	15.4
Conservation and development	6.4
Total public water spending (total is higher due to rounding)	47.3

Data source: U.S. Census Bureau, 2010

based on average figures, today's $80 billion per year in highway and street construction might include around $8 billion in drainage-related work, but road budgets are difficult to analyze to get such estimates.

Another masked set of water-related construction on the public side is in public facilities of all kinds, especially education facility spending, which is $80 billion to $90 billion per year. This includes large-site development, drainage, swimming pools, showers, and many rest room and kitchen areas. These expenditures resemble those in the industrial and commercial categories.

Total private construction includes spending on highways and streets, sewage and waste disposal, water supply, and conservation and development, which are not shown separately in government accounts. Therefore, there is no way to estimate the water-related construction spending that is contained within the private sector.

However, by probing the statistics of private construction spending, we can gain some idea of water-related activity. Residential construction declined greatly but was still at $260 billion in May 2010. Significant parts of this spending go to plumbing, site drainage and water-related expenditures such as kitchen and bath amenities. Nonresidential construction was at $271 billion, and it included similar expenditures for commercial, institutional, and industrial facilities. Electric power construction was at $53 billion, and some of this goes to cooling and hydropower expenditures. Private construction statistics include sewage and waste disposal, water supply (such as for private water companies), conservation and development, and highway and street work, but the data are not shown separately.

Any attempt to estimate total water-related construction spending in the three categories we are tracking (utility-scale, commercial/industrial, and residential) would be only a guess. The starting point would be the total of public spending, or $47 billion. If you add to that the masked public spending on drainage and public facilities, the total would rise considerably. Given the lack of detailed statistics, the private side is especially hard to estimate but it seems reasonable to estimate that 10 percent of total private construction spending is water related, or about $50 billion as of May 2010. Combining the public water expenditures at $47 billion plus and the private spending at some $50 billion would yield a grand total of some $100 to $120 billion, or in the range of 12 to 14 percent of all construction spending. Given the difficulty of classifying water-related expenditures and the lack of detailed statistics, this seems reasonable and about as far as we can go to compile an estimate of total water-related construction spending.

This spending would be distributed among sizes and types of construction. At the utility scale, water-supply construction would focus on pipes, pumps, and treatment plants, with source of supply being significant but less than the other categories. Wastewater construction would also focus on pipes, pumps, and treatment plants, with less spending on biosolids management. Both categories would include spending on controls and instrumentation, as well as appurtenances such as valves, meters and hydrants.

The flood control and stormwater sector would require construction of stormwater conveyance, storage and treatment facilities, pumps, energy dissipators, and channels, levees, and stream controls. Instream construction for hydropower, navigation, and the environment would include spending for locks and dams and reservoirs, penstocks, turbines, surge tanks, gates, river controls, and natural systems, such as wetlands. Much of this construction would be rehabilitation and renewal because new dams and major river facilities are not being constructed in the United States, although in developing countries many remain to be built.

At the medium and smaller scales, water-related construction as aligned with new and renovated facilities will focus on building systems. These include service lines, interior piping, building sewers, and drains; water tanks, hot-water tanks, and cisterns for storage; point-of-use treatment systems; water heating systems; and end-user access facilities such as toilets, sinks, tubs, and showers. Meters and valves are also needed for measurement and control in the systems. For water supply and wastewater removal, construction is required for wells, small package plants, and septic tanks.

While dam building is very limited today, a great deal of utility and landscape construction occurs. I made an analysis of the revenues of *ENR* magazine's top 400 contractors in 2004, and found that of $210 billion in revenues, the top categories were building ($113 billion), transportation ($29 billion), and petroleum ($14 billion). Water and sewer/waste system construction were reported at $3.0 billion and $4.1 billion, respectively. Together they comprise 3.4 percent of revenues of the top 400 contractors for that year (*ENR*, 2005).

FUTURE OF WATER-INDUSTRY CONSTRUCTION

As we think about the future of water-industry construction, it is difficult to escape the reality that much of it will depend on construction in the various building sectors of residential, commercial, industrial, and public facilities. You might say, as construction goes, so goes water-industry construction. The part of water-industry construction that is directly tied to such building construction would probably account for somewhere around half of the $100 billion to $120 billion in total water construction.

The other part of water-industry construction is also tied to the overall economy and its growth, which calls for more water, more energy, and more water-related services. The part that is somewhat outside this picture is the rehabilitation market, which responds to the aging infrastructure problem shared by public utilities. In Chapter 2, the assets of the water sectors were estimated at a total of $1.2 trillion, and if these depreciated at 1 percent per year (reflecting a 100-year life expectancy), the indicated renewal need would be $12 billion per year. However, many years of backlog are waiting in the wings for renewal, and some of the facilities have lifetimes shorter than 100 years.

Total public-sector water construction must respond to growth, renewal, and upgrading needs. Growth promises to be moderate, upgrading should be a slow process, and renewal is a wild card in many places, so projections for future construction seem uncertain but perhaps in the same order of magnitude as the $50 billion to $60 billion per year estimated to be the current level.

Looking across the sectors, growth, upgrading, and aging infrastructure will be drivers of water supply and wastewater construction. The assets of these two categories were estimated at $400 billion each, or a total of $800 billion or two-thirds of all water assets. Just in one category—renewal of buried pipes—utilities would like to renew them at around 1 percent per year. This would require spending of $8 billion on pipe renewal alone, which is in the ballpark of current spending levels for this purpose, according to my estimates. New trenchless construction methods may increase the appeal and possibilities for rehabilitation spending.

In the stormwater and flood control sector, spending will be less. The estimate of assets was $100 billion, but upgrades and asset replacement are easier to defer than in water and wastewater, which are much more tightly regulated. The national response to Hurricane Katrina will require large expenditures, which are being made in the New Orleans area. The expenditures like this for disaster prevention could eventually dwarf other categories of flood-related construction spending.

Another category of spending where the asset value suggests low annual spending is dams, reservoirs, and levees. In its report card, ASCE listed $12.5 billion needed over five years, or about $2.4 billion per year. That would be about 2 percent of the estimated asset value of $100 billion and certainly reasonable given the risk posed by the aging dams. Levee costs were much higher, at $50 billion needed over five years, which reflects the neglect they have suffered over many years. Closely related to dams and levees is construction for river improvements, ports, and harbors. ASCE estimated a five-year need of $50 billion to deepen and widen ship channels for larger ships, to continue maintenance dredging of ship channels, and to limit erosion and sedimentation in ports, harbors, and waterways.

Irrigation system construction is difficult to assess, both because statistics are lacking and because irrigation water use is flat or declining (see Chapter 8). The asset value that was presented in Chapter 2 includes a range of large and small systems, partly in the public and partly in the private sector. If you look closely at the nature of these systems, you can see that they start with the largest (such as Imperial Irrigation District [IID] in California) and extend to the smallest, such as an individual farm's center-pivot system. If the assets included only physical systems, they might add up to the $100 billion estimate, but these would not be likely to expand or even be renewed very aggressively. If the asset value included the value of water rights, too, the total would no doubt be higher, but this value would not point to construction projects in the future, unless they were for reallocation of irrigation rights to urban uses, such as the IID–to–San Diego water transfer (see Chapter 8).

In the industrial and energy water-use area, indications are that water use will be flat or decline, except in the case of cooling water for the expanding electric power industry. Greater efficiencies will be sought, of course, but these will require new facilities and infrastructure, and this is likely to be a bright spot in water-related construction. Also, indications are that increases in hydroelectricity will stimulate construction, although there are no indications that dramatic increases will occur.

Groundwater development and water-well construction should be a stable construction sector that is tended by specialist niche firms. With climate change and worries over future water supply, turning to a groundwater source for security makes sense, but we see no rapid increases in attention to these sources.

At the smaller scale, residential and commercial construction seems sure to pick up in the years ahead, but it is difficult to forecast when this will occur due to the deep trough it went into in 2008 and beyond. Aging service lines and premise plumbing systems will require continuing attention, but there is no indication that this will depart from the past trends in construction volumes.

If the torrid pace of development in China continues, construction there and in other fast-developing parts of Asia will overshadow U.S., European, and Japanese construction markets. Parts of Eastern Europe have a long way to go to catch up to U.S. standards in water systems, and construction pace will depend on funding and willingness to invest. Latin America also has much upgrade work to do, as does Central Asia. The dry countries of the Middle East and North Africa will require many new water facilities for urban and rural development, and the rest of Africa also displays vast needs.

Adding it all up, the needs for new water-related construction certainly justify optimistic forecasts for the future, but whether it will happen depends on complex political, social, and economic variables.

CHAPTER 18

Services to Support
the Water Industry

While water handlers such as utilities and thermoelectric energy plants are the most visible parts of the water industry, the magnitude and diversity of services they require from small to large systems dominates the industry's business activity. Water-industry support services range from the high-level professional consulting services to utilities to the routine maintenance services required by residential homeowners. As examples of service providers, think of the support required to keep a complex water supervisory control and data acquisition (SCADA) system in operation or the plumbing contractor who is called at midnight to repair a pipe break.

While it might seem like mixing apples and oranges to discuss such a wide range of services in one chapter, it aligns with the way the Bureau of Census and Bureau of Economic Affairs classify services in the economy and it provides a coherent framework to show the common elements among types of supporting service work.

This chapter explains the diverse categories of support services, with emphasis on engineering and other professional consulting services, on outsourcing of operations and maintenance services and, to a lesser extent, on outsourcing of business services. Construction is a service as well, and it was discussed in Chapter 17. Products that are supplied to the water industry are explained in Chapter 19 and, when you add them to services, you have the full range of products and services that are provided to the water handlers, who in turn provide water services to customers (Figure 18.1).

CLASSIFYING WATER-INDUSTRY SERVICES

Although water-industry services cover a wide range, for the purpose of classification they can be fit into three types of services and three levels of water-handling, as shown in Table 18.1.

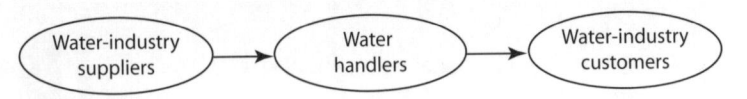

FIGURE 18.1 Product and service suppliers to the water industry

Take professional services, for example, in which consulting engineers work to support utilities and industries. This occupies a large industry, which is described in more detail later in the chapter. These services are seldom used by homeowners, but they could be. Over the years I've had a number of inquiries from homeowners who wanted professional advice about water-related issues, from flood problems to water supply.

Operations and maintenance (O&M) services are easier to envision as you can think of contract operations for treatment plants, industrial facility maintenance services being outsourced, and your plumber coming to maintain your water-heating system. Business and administrative services are perhaps the least common, but examples are shown in Table 18.1 for some that might be outsourced.

OUTSOURCING GOVERNMENT AND CORPORATE SERVICES

For the most part, the support services discussed in the chapter can be either done in-house or outsourced. For example, the engineering services for a utility can be performed by an in-house staff or let out to consulting firms. Even many of the maintenance services for a household plumbing system can be performed by the homeowner or by a contractor. Outsourcing seems to be increasing, with one driving force being strong public support to make the public sector more efficient and the other being innovation in management tools and methods that is offered by the private sector.

TABLE 18.1 Types and Levels of Water-Industry Support Services

	Examples of Types of Services		
Levels of Application	Professional	Operations and Maintenance	Business and Administrative
Utility	Engineering	Treatment plant	Meter reading
Industrial	Engineering	Maintenance	Regulatory reports
Residential	Seldom used	Plumbing repair	Seldom used

To see why outsourcing of professional, business, and operations services can be attractive in water utilities, compare in your mind's eye a bloated, inefficient government agency to a lean just-in-time business operation. If you could reach into the inefficient organization to identify its core essential processes to outsource them you could get rid of most of the bloat right away. That creates the driving force for today's interest in unbundling and outsourcing.

While government continually seeks to become more efficient, without intervention its operations tend to become more inefficient with time due to human behavior, lack of competition, and other institutional factors. While total privatization might be an answer sometimes, it may not work in most cases. Thus, outsourcing of some services is natural answer to the dilemma of inefficiency.

The problem of inefficiency afflicts organizations of all types, and there is today a move toward going leaner in all levels of management. In the private sector it is natural to use outsourced services when they can be done better and at lower cost than by in-house forces.

Some think that this focus on outsourcing is part of a fundamental shift in organizational theory, both for corporations and government agencies. The thinking is that the forces of "creative destruction" are intensifying in the private economy but also the idea of the large corporation may also be giving way to a new paradigm. The explanation is that the reason for the large corporation (or organization) was to lower transaction costs among buyers and sellers of goods and services needed for the work of the organization because it was simply too expensive and cumbersome for managers to find everything they need from the marketplace. The corporation itself serves as an allocation mechanism for the resources it uses. British economist Ronald Coase won the 1991 Nobel Prize in economics for his theories about these transaction costs. Now, the idea is that the large organization is simply too inefficient in allocating resources internally and future organizations must be smaller and nimbler (Murray, 2010)

The public sector response to these trends is seen in tax revolts, downsizing, unbundling and outsourcing. These moves are explained by Osborne and Gaebler (1992), who wrote *Reinvention of Government* and by Osborne and Hutchinson (2004), who wrote *The Price of Government.* These books focus on unbundling services and programs to uncover the ones to open to competition *(Reinvention of Government)* and to make financial decisions more effective through "budgeting for outcomes" *(The Price of Government)*. Together, these expand opportunities for managed competition and outsourcing between the public and private sectors.

Whether you believe that a fundamental change is occurring or not, the dual pressures to become more efficient and to use innovative tools and methods are certain to continue, and these lead to markets for outsourced services.

PROFESSIONAL SERVICES FOR THE WATER INDUSTRY

The heart of the professional services used by the water industry is consulting engineering, which is the business of planning, design, and related services that applies engineering principles to solve diverse problems of infrastructure and facility operations. The consulting business provided me with my first engineering job with the Ken R. White Company in Denver, and my first assignment was to work on recovery projects from the 1965 Colorado flooding. I also worked on water supply, stormwater, highway drainage, and various other municipal projects. I joined with Dave Sellards in 1968 to start a firm called Sellards & Grigg, Inc., and it operated for nearly 40 years until it was acquired by Short Elliott Hendrickson Inc. in 2006. I was active in the company for only a few years, but the experiences taught me many things about this fascinating business.

The lessons I learned about the professional services industry were useful to teach to our civil engineering students as they worked toward graduation and jobs that included consulting engineering. As I explained this business to them, I noticed many changes in it, and today's professional services industry is a lot different than it was back in the 1960s. Business organization has evolved, and the dominant players in consulting are the large multidisciplinary firms that have acquired many other firms and created conglomerates.

Today, professional service firms provide a shadow workforce for water utilities and agencies in the sense that they do work that could be done in-house. Water-related projects comprise a big portion of the professional services industry, which provides the outsourcing agents for much of the utility's professional work. You can see many examples of the tradeoff between in-house and outsourced services in the water industry, just as you can in other infrastructure-heavy sectors, such as public works.

Professional services required by water utilities go beyond engineering to include management consulting, environmental support, legal, financial, and other services. Small utilities may require across-the-board support, just as other small businesses do.

Professional service firms are classified by the NAICS as Professional, Scientific, and Technical Services (Categories 54 and 541), which comprise "establishments that specialize in performing professional, scientific, and technical activities for others."

Within this group, we have "architectural, engineering, and related services," where consultants are found. Other groups include lawyers, scientific research, financial services, and computer systems. These categories seem cumbersome, but AWWA's classification of consultant categories is more specific and shows three main groups: engineering and architecture; environmental, health and safety; and management, planning, business, and finance.

Engineering services are part of a larger category in NAICS 5413 that includes architectural, engineering, geophysical, surveying and mapping, and testing laboratories.

In the 2002 Economic Census, engineering services across all types of work showed revenues of $116 billion and payroll of $50 billion. Total employees were 861,000 (U.S. Bureau of Census, 2004). Preliminary data from the 2007 Economic Census shows these figures up to $189 billion, $73 billion, and 991,000 employees, increases that track substantial growth in engineering services (U.S. Bureau of Census, 2010). The number of establishments grew between 2002 and 2007, but revenue growth far outstripped these increases. As Table 18.2 shows, the numbers of establishments grew in all categories of professional services.

The portion of the engineering services devoted to the water sector mirror roughly the percentage of construction work in that sector, with the exception that water utilities require a good bit of environmental work that may or may not be connected to construction projects.

The business association for engineering consultants (American Council of Engineering Companies, or ACEC, formerly the American Consulting Engineers Council) reports more than 5,000 member firms are organized into 51 state and regional councils, with more than 500,000 employees

TABLE 18.2 Engineering and Related Establishments

	Establishments 2002	Establishments 2007
Engineering services	55,229	57,895
Architectural	23,269	25,144
Surveying and mapping (except geophysical)	9,118	9,690
Landscape architectural	6,225	6,394
Testing laboratories	5,048	6,449
Building inspection	4,074	5,762
Drafting services	2,674	3,198
Geophysical and mapping	738	960

Data source: U.S. Bureau of Census, 2004

responsible for more than $200 billion of work per year (ACEC, 2010). Given the number of consulting engineering establishments in the Bureau of Census data, ACEC firms are around 10 percent of the total number but they are the larger firms and account for most of the revenue and workforce.

The firms are multifaceted and have specialty groups to focus on markets within the water industry. Firms working in the water industry cut across the sectors of working for water suppliers, wastewater providers, local governments, irrigation districts, self-supplied industries, regulators, and so forth. The greatest revenues are in construction-related work, including services from design through facility operation.

Discipline groups within engineering include chemical engineering, civil engineering, construction engineering, electrical engineering, environmental engineering, erosion control, geological engineering, geophysical engineering, and mechanical engineering. All will be used in the water industry, but civil and environmental engineering will normally be the major services required.

The firms serving the water industry primarily provide planning, design, and advisory services. Some of them also perform construction services, equipment supply, and financing for public and private infrastructure projects. While the focus of each firm differs, a common business model is one in which the firm positions itself, works in broad market sectors, and finds technical niches among the business subsectors. The largest companies often grow through acquisitions of firms in niche or geographic areas.

Each year, *ENR* magazine names the "Top 500 Design Firms" and the "Top 200 Environmental Firms," as well as lists of contractors. The large multidisciplinary firms that top *ENR*'s lists may bundle water-industry services with other markets to form part of larger portfolios of engineering services. Using ENR's list of top firms and our experience, I identified a few firms to illustrate the range of professional water-related services. They mostly include the large, multidisciplinary firms serving several market sectors and in many cases, they were built around an original firm that focused on the water sector and expanded by mergers and acquisitions. A list of the top 10 would include (the list would vary from year-to-year, of course):

- CH2M Hill, Denver, CO.
- Tetra Tech Inc., Pasadena, CA.
- Black & Veatch, Overland Park, KS.
- MWH, Broomfield, CO.
- HDR, Omaha, NE.
- CDM, Cambridge, MA.
- PBS&J, Miami, FL.

- Michael Baker Corp., Moon Township, PA.
- Malcolm Pirnie Inc., White Plains, NY.
- Gannett Fleming, Harrisburg, PA.

Analysis of any of these firms would show an amazing variety of water-related work. CH2M Hill (2010) is a good example, as its headquarters are located close to our university and they interact with us frequently. The company that would become CH2M Hill was initiated by three Oregon State College students who studied under a professor named Fred Merryfield, who mentored his students and discussed an engineering partnership, which started in 1946. This was a good time to plan and build the postwar economy, and they built a successful firm. By 1969, they were ranked 102nd on *ENR*'s Top 500 Engineering Design Firm list. In 1971 they merged with Clair A. Hill & Associates of Redding, California, to create today's firm. A 1970s project to design wastewater facilities for the Upper Occoquan Sewerage Authority near Washington, D.C., and another project to be program manager for Milwaukee's Water Pollution Abatement Program created a focus for the firm. During the 1980s they formed Operations Management International (OMI) to meet demand for operation of water-treatment plants. By 1987, they were No. 3 on the *ENR* list. After a long and successful tenure by Ralph Peterson as CEO, Lee McIntire was selected in 2009 to serve as CEO. Today, CH2M Hill has more than 23,500 employees and earned $6.3 billion in 2009 revenue.

Another group of professional service firms are management consultants, which is a broad and umbrella term with many shades of meaning. In government statistics, it falls into the categories of management and technical and environmental consulting services (NAICS 541618 and 541690). This category "comprises establishments primarily engaged in providing management consulting services (except administrative and general management consulting; human resources consulting; marketing consulting; or process, physical distribution, and logistics consulting)." The work of environmental consultants is explained this way: "This industry (environmental consultants other than environmental engineering companies) comprises establishments primarily engaged in providing advice and assistance to businesses and other organizations on environmental issues, such as the control of environmental contamination from pollutants, toxic substances, and hazardous materials" (NAICS 541620).

Services that water utilities might use are listed in the *Directory of Management Consultants* (Consultant's News, 2003). Some of the water-industry studies done by these firms are: general management; financial consulting and economic studies; operations improvement, including information technology; strategic planning; legal studies; environmental impact studies; and scientific or technical studies such as agricultural, biological, chemical, economic, energy, geochemical, hydrology, safety, and security.

In general, management and environmental firms serving the water industry tend to be niches within larger groups or individual or small-scale efforts, so it is difficult to categorize them. Management consulting firms serving the water industry include firms such as EMA, Inc. of Minneapolis and Raftelis Financial Consultants Inc. of Charlotte, which give advice on topics such as human resources and financial management. Larger management consultants, such as Booz Allen Hamilton of McLean, Virginia, also work in the water industry. Big consulting engineering firms often have subsidiaries that offer management consulting. An example is Black & Veatch's Enterprise Management Solutions. Firms also work in niche areas such as Frost & Sullivan, which surveys water-industry markets, the TechKNOWLEDGEy Strategic Group, which also studies water markets and investments, and Water Systems Optimization Inc., which works on water-efficiency programs.

Environmental consulting firms include specialists that might not be represented in engineering firms. U.S. Bureau of Census (2010s) data show for 2002 that there were 93,000 management consulting establishments and 8,528 environmental establishments. Those working in the water industry are only a small set of these totals.

Lawyers (NAICS 541110) are also involved extensively in the water industry to resolve water conflicts and regulatory issues. They can help determine strategy and actions for water managers, such as to transfer ownership of water rights. State attorneys general and local government staff attorneys are normally involved in water cases, and corporate attorneys work on water and environmental issues. Law firms tend to specialize, and although NAICS does not list legal specialties, the American Bar Association has sections that suggest areas where lawyers provide support to the water industry. These include administrative law and regulatory practice; environment, energy and resources; government and public sector; health; public utilities; and science and technology.

OPERATIONS AND MAINTENANCE SERVICES

If you walk the floor of large water-industry trade shows such as the American Water Works Association's Annual Conference and Exposition (ACE) or the Water Environment Federation's WEFTEC, it is surprising to see how many operations service firms are mingled in with the equipment vendors. The Annual Convention and Exposition of AWWA, for example, draws more than 10,000 participants and features more than 500 exhibitors in major convention centers that offer 5 to 10 acres of display space for the meeting. WEFTEC is even larger, with more than 900 exhibitors and an attendance of around 17,000 (Wateronline, 2010). The services that can be outsourced tend to align with the boxes on a utility's organization chart, and this gives us a system with which to classify the categories of services.

The trends toward outsourcing and introduction of new technologies and methods are seen most clearly in operations and maintenance services. In water organizations, the units that perform operations are often grouped together under a consolidated operations section, which normally will include both forces that perform the facility operations and the maintenance. This operations section will have responsibility to operate and maintain all physical infrastructure and operating systems. As an example, in a water-supply utility it might be responsible for a dam and reservoir, a transmission pipeline, treatment plants, and a distribution system. In some cases, the dam and reservoir might be separated into a different management unit, and there might be separate subsections for treatment and distribution systems.

This is big business. In a medium-to-large utility serving a population of 500,000, the replacement value of this infrastructure might be on the order of $5,000 to $10,000 per capita, making a total that could range as high as about $5 billion. Annual revenues and expenditures might be on the order of $50 million, a number that is certain to rise (see Chapter 22 for an explanation of water rates and the forces tending to increase them).

Several categories of operations are attractive for outsourcing: treatment plant operations, pipeline operations (including leak detection, infiltration and inflow monitoring, and corrosion control), metering, and management of operations data systems.

During the 1980s there was a great deal of talk about privatizing water utility operations, including outright purchase of entire utilities. The outcomes of this heightened interest are explained in Chapter 20, and specific instances when contracts were let for treatment plant operations are explained there.

Consulting firms are attracted to contract operations because they can use their planning and design expertise to run plants and systems. Most contracts are short term and for operation of water or wastewater treatment plants. There have been few contracts to operate collection or distribution systems and pumping plants, and there have been none to operate laboratories or billing and collection systems.

Short-term contract requirements are such that most risk rests with the municipality and there is little incentive for the contractor to perform beyond minimum expectations. Funding for any major item must be approved by the municipality, and there are very limited funds for nonroutine maintenance or capital improvements.

Long-term contracts became more prevalent after 1997, when an Internal Revenue Service (IRS) rule change authorized 20-year contracts with one 5-year extension. In long-term contracts, risk is transferred to the contractor, who makes investments and performance guarantees. The contractor is responsible for management of assets and has tight maintenance requirements.

A 1986 tax law change removed tax benefits for private ownership of public assets, and operations activity converted to mostly short-term contract operations. These were successful, and most companies experienced a renewal rate greater than 90 percent.

To improve performance, there was a need to provide incentives for long-term contracts, and IRS Revenue Procedure 97-13 was issued as government water-grant programs geared down and USEPA tightened regulations under the Clean Water Act and Safe Drinking Water Act.

The 1997 IRS rules allow longer contracts but impose constraints to prevent the abuse of tax-exempt financing. Contractors cannot share in profits from system operations, but they can share in cost savings or revenue enhancements, a provision that led to gain-sharing provisions of long-term contracts.

The new regulation stimulated much activity, and within two years more than 80 cities began the competitive process for long-term contracts and 45 completed them (Johnson et al., 2002)

In one of the largest deals under consideration as this is written, Indianapolis received expressions of interest from more than 20 firms to restructure and merge the water and sewer utilities. The two utilities are currently under long-term operating contracts, and consolidation would generate long-term cost savings and hold water and sewer rates down. Some of the interested firms are Citizens Energy Group, Veolia Water, United Water, Macquarie Capital, CH2M Hill, and Black & Veatch (Jarosz, 2010).

The Indianapolis City-County Council approved moving the utilities ownership to a local nonprofit trust headed by Citizens Energy Group, which would assume the operations and capital projects and $1.5 billion in debt of both utilities. The city would receive $435 million to $460 million for infrastructure projects from the deal. Citizens would issue debt to be serviced by revenue from sewer ratepayers. Its board of directors would decide policies such as rate increases, and the company's leaders claimed they can save $43 million a year in operations costs. The review is now before the Indiana Utility Regulatory Commission.

Citizens Energy Group is actually a not-for-profit Public Charitable Trust that dates to 1887, when Indianapolis leaders organized it to operate a natural gas company for its customers and the community. It now operates its natural gas business, a district steam and chilled-water cooling system, and a utility services business. It has signed a memorandum of understanding to take on the city's water and wastewater utilities and keep them under local public ownership as a not-for-profit, rather than go through privatization.

Pipeline operations are not as easy to outsource as treatment plants, but services might include leak detection, infiltration and inflow monitoring, and corrosion control. Another possibility for outsourcing might be all metering and operations data systems, which are monitored in a data-intensive control headquarters with a SCADA system. Overall services might include GIS, databases and data conversion. Turning this over for a complete contract is unlikely because of security concerns and the need of the utility to maintain control of its own data. However, it might outsource part of this business area.

For example, the utility could outsource flow monitoring and data acquisition, reporting of operating and maintenance data, water-quality monitoring and reporting, and preparation of reports. It could also outsource preparation of consumer confidence reports, capital and operating budget forecasting and management, and regulatory agency compliance liaison.

Maintenance outsourcing provides opportunities for any category of physical assets, including buildings, fleets and any water-handling infrastructure and equipment. Water organizations are capital intensive with massive quantities of physical infrastructure and equipment. To deal with their many issues they are moving toward software-based enterprise asset management and maintenance management systems. Two categories deserve special attention: condition assessment and pipeline and ditch maintenance and renewal.

Condition assessment for wastewater is part of a cadre of services that are offered to help utilities respond to USEPA regulatory requirements. Services they might include are closed-circuit TV inspections, manhole structural inspection, smoke testing, sanitary sewer evaluation survey, flow meter rentals, and training and education. Equipment and facilities maintenance can include inspection of equipment and systems, instrument calibration and troubleshooting, chemical replenishment, filter maintenance and servicing, and emergency generator exercising and service.

Outsourcing of O&M services is a global phenomenon. The large water utilities described in Chapter 16 are engaged in it, as well as large consulting engineering firms. We can expect additional players in the future, including management companies from rising economic powers such as China, South Korea, and India.

PLUMBING—MAINTENANCE SERVICES FOR BUILDING SYSTEMS

Of course, the most familiar water-related maintenance service is plumbing, which as a craft evolved with the earliest pipes and fittings. The word *plumbing* actually derives from the Latin word for lead, and early plumbers would use lead to fabricate their own plumbing solutions. Today, the plumbing field has branches dealing with buildings and industrial systems, and the skills and tools used are similar to those required in larger urban water transmission and distribution systems.

The history of plumbing is fascinating to those who have an interest. The earliest flush toilet has been identified from the palace of King Minos on the island of Crete, dating back to about 1700 B.C. Rome had advanced systems, but after it fell, western civilization declined during the Dark Ages. While royalty enjoyed more comfortable lives than peasants, even kings and queens died from typhoid and dysentery. New plumbing devices were invented as civilization advanced. The earliest known flush toilet of modern times was by Sir John Harington, who put it into a castle of Queen Elizabeth I about 1595. The earliest patent for a flush toilet was in 1775 to Alexander Cumming.

Modern plumbing and public health emerged about the same time, during the latter part of the 19th century. George Waring's 1876 book, *The Sanitary Drainage of Houses and Towns,* was published in this period. Also, the development of venting and drainage procedures helped make indoor plumbing more acceptable.

Plumbers and gas fitters were placed into a single category by the Census Bureau until the 1880s. The Plumbing-Heating-Cooling Contractors Association began as the National Association of Master Plumbers in 1883. The Mechanical Contractors Association of America and the United Association plumbers union began in 1889, and the American Society of Sanitary Engineering began about 1900 (*History of Plumbing in America,* 1987). Plumbing has continued to develop as a trade and a business. While today's tools and methods have improved from the past, plumbing still requires a lot of hard work in dark, cramped spaces.

The 2002 and 2007 Economic Census data show trends in the number of plumbers and volume of their work (Table 18.3).

The value of business done in 2002 for plumbing, heating, and AC contracts was $100 billion, and of this, $18 billion was for plumbing, with $49 billion for heating, ventilation, and air conditioning (HVAC). The number of establishments for plumbing was 37,615 and apparently there are about the same number of plumbing and HVAC as specialist firms, but the HVAC firms do more dollar-volume work.

TABLE 18.3 Trends in Plumbing Employment and Volume

	2002 Economic Consensus	2007 Economic Consensus
Establishments (includes plumbing, heating, and HVAC)	87,501	91,693
Employees	974,368	975,796
Payroll, $ billions	35.9	45.4

Data source: U.S. Bureau of Census, 2004

The administrative or business services might be outsourced by small water utilities, but large ones would tend to handle functions such as financial accounting, human resources, public relations, and meter reading in-house. These categories offer opportunities for consulting support, but they are not major markets for outsourcing. Due to its workforce issues, the water industry requires outside help for training, especially operator training, and it will be discussed later.

Another category of services is for training and operator certification, which might be provided by community colleges or by local and regional associations working together to identify needs and meet them through cooperative programs.

CHAPTER 19

Equipment for
the Water Industry

The water industry requires a massive inventory of equipment, from the smallest pipes and valves to the largest pumps and turbines. While there are many types of equipment, they can be classified into a few categories, with each one containing a wide group of types and sizes. Chapter 2 explained the water-industry's suppliers, which are the groups that supply infrastructure, equipment, materials, and services to the water handlers, who supply water and water-related services to its customers.

The equipment required by the water industry ranges across small to large systems, and need for it is driven by a number of factors, as shown in Figure 19.1 for large systems. These drivers were explained in Chapter 10.

This chapter provides an overview of the markets for equipment and supplies for the range of organizations in the water industry, from the large-scale systems of utilities to the individual residential plumbing system. The chapter presents an overview of the equipment markets and does not try to present detail on specific products or markets, but it provides links to sources of information with greater detail.

EQUIPMENT CATEGORIES

It is impossible to derive an accurate estimate of the size of the water-industry equipment market, but portions of it (such as annual purchases of large pipe) run in the $5 billion range, and for that reason it might be reasonable to estimate the total size of the market in the $20 billion range. As part of the market is tied to homebuilding and other construction, the market will be subject to wide fluctuations.

It is also difficult to estimate employment in the water industry supplier sector. The Bureau of Labor Statistics (BLS) lists "manufacturing of iron,

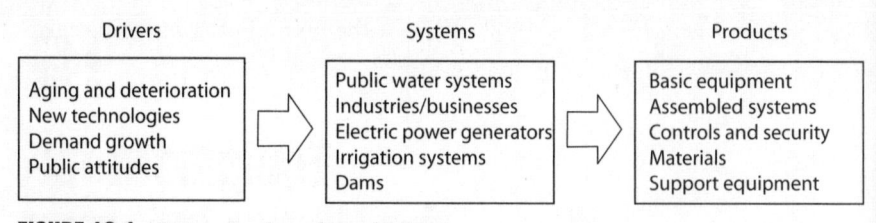

Drivers	Systems	Products
Aging and deterioration New technologies Demand growth Public attitudes	Public water systems Industries/businesses Electric power generators Irrigation systems Dams	Basic equipment Assembled systems Controls and security Materials Support equipment

FIGURE 19.1   Drivers and products for large water systems

steel pipe, and tube from purchased steel" at 26,000 jobs; manufacture of plumbing fixtures at 15,000 jobs; manufacture of pumps and pumping equipment, including measuring and dispensing, at 28,000 jobs; and whole-sale trade of plumbing equipment at 89,000 jobs. Retail trade of these categories might be in similar ranges. Construction employment in these categories is higher. Plumbing and HVAC contractors are 934,000 jobs; within this category, other BLS publications report about 550,000 total plumbing contractor employees. Employment in water and sewer system construction is 198,000 jobs.

Water-industry suppliers normally work across industries. The main equipment suppliers of components, such as pipe, pumps, valves, meters, and tanks, also serve oil and gas and other industries that use fluids for processing. Instruments and controls used in water can be used for electric power as well as other industrial applications. Therefore, it is difficult to assess how changes in the water industry will affect these businesses, which also serve other industries.

Equipment for the categories of water handlers—utilities, industries, irrigators, commercial-scale buildings, and residences—is not normally classified in any unified systems. However, it makes sense to look at the equipment in categories such as pipes, pumps, and meters, even if there is a wide gap between scales of equipment, such as between small copper pipe used in a residence and the giant ductile iron pipe used by a utility.

While government economic statistics classify manufacturers and vendors of equipment, it is difficult to glean information about water equipment from them. A more detailed view can be created from the AWWA (2010b) guide to suppliers, which provides a starting point for a classification system, and from similar lists from other associations, such as the Water Environment Federation and the Water and Wastewater Equipment Manufacturers Association (WWEMA, 2010). WEF's WEFTEC is the largest overall trade show and covers most categories of equipment (see Chapter 23). WWEMA covers all categories, but membership seems most focused on manufacturers of treatment systems and equipment.

Using the lists of these associations, the following short list was created to lump categories into coherent market and product groups. It is still a long list, but it provides a way to make sense of the myriad offerings you see at water trade shows. It omits equipment that applies to other industries as well, such as vehicles, safety and security equipment, and ordinary tools and construction equipment.

■ Analytical laboratory and field test equipment, including leak detection.
■ Chemicals.
■ Computing, communications, and information technology control equipment.
■ Construction and maintenance equipment.
■ Corrosion control equipment.
■ Meters and related automatic meter reading (AMR) equipment.
■ Pipe, fittings, appurtenances, seals, and gaskets.
■ Pumps.
■ Tanks.
■ Valves and hydrants.
■ Treatment systems.
■ Well equipment.

These categories of equipment are tracked by NAICS categories. As the following short list of NAICS example categories illustrates, the problem in using them is to separate the water-related markets from other markets:

327332: Iron and Steel Pipe and Tube Manufacturing from Purchased Steel (also there are categories for Concrete Pipe Manufacturing and Plastics Pipe and Pipe Fitting Manufacturing).

33391: Pump and Compressor Manufacturing (these apply across many industries, and the same is true for 33291: Metal Valve Manufacturing).

33399: All Other General Purpose Machinery Manufacturing (treatment systems are classified here).

334514: Totalizing Fluid Meter and Counting Device Manufacturing (meters are in this category).

334516: Analytical Laboratory Instrument Manufacturing (includes analytical laboratory and field test equipment, including leak detection).

Some categories of equipment do not fit within one category. Examples are corrosion control, wells, and safety and security equipment.

You can use the same classification system for smaller systems as for the larger categories, with the addition of a category for access point equipment such as faucets, sinks, toilets, and related equipment. The listings include plumber tools, supplies and equipment such as cleanout equipment, seals, and other special tools and equipment.

LARGE-SCALE WATER SYSTEMS

If we now consider the equipment needed for water handling by large-scale systems, we can focus on this list of infrastructure systems that were introduced in Chapters 3–9:

- Dams and reservoirs.
- Large groundwater pumping plants.
- Transmission water pipes.
- Water-treatment plants.
- Water-distribution systems.
- Collection and outfall sewerage systems.
- Wastewater treatment plants.
- Sludge processing equipment and facilities.
- Large-scale stormwater facilities.
- Flood control pumping plants.

This wide range of types of facilities will be operated by the types of organizations discussed in Chapters 2–9, which include water and wastewater utilities, districts and other organizations; stormwater and flood control authorities; thermoelectric power producers; irrigation districts; large self-supplied industries; and other dam owners, such as federal agencies.

The equipment categories given previously provide us with a way to study the purchasing needs of these organizations. There are too many types of equipment to discuss in detail, but a few examples give us a good picture. For example, water and wastewater utilities have inventories of anywhere from two million to four million miles of mostly buried pipe. While the pipe is long lasting, the market for new installations and renewal is still large.

In the case of water supply, equipment needed for sources includes well equipment, diversion gates, and storage and pumping equipment, for example. Treatment includes a range of water conditioning equipment, whether for utilities, industries, residences, or swimming pools, for example. Distribution includes all pipe, meters, pumps, valves, fittings, and any in-line equipment. Access points include sinks, toilets, faucets, urinals, sprinklers, hoses, or other points of public access. The needs for new and replacement valves and hydrants are large, and extend into the industrial and commercial arenas as well. Meters and related AMR equipment will be required mostly for public water-supply utilities, but requirements for analytical laboratory and field-test equipment applies across the board because of regulatory reporting and other quality-control requirements.

Another category of large-scale equipment is for water and wastewater treatment. In addition to public water and wastewater systems, industrial water treatment is a large and diverse market for this equipment (see Chapter 7).

Perhaps the category of equipment that is used across most large-scale industries is pumps, as they are required anywhere that water is moved, whether for irrigation, flood control, public systems, industry, or even recreational venues such as water parks.

The future might include smart pipes and valves. This was studied in a Water Research Foundation (2010) project that included a smart-pipe demonstration unit with water pipe and sensors with a transmittal unit along its length. The project may be extended into a new phase to study the underground environment and parameters such as temperature, vibration, conductivity, and powering of the sensors.

COMMERCIAL-SCALE EQUIPMENT

Moving down the size ranges from large- to commercial-scale systems, we begin to see the emphasis shift to equipment of end users, rather than the larger water handlers. In commercial-scale systems, and in residential-scale applications as well, the numbers of devices increases greatly, and in the case of commercial (and industrial systems), the variety of water-use scenarios also increases greatly.

In Chapter 2, the following categories of commercial water users were highlighted:

- Lodging.
- Office buildings.
- Commercial retail and wholesale (for example, automotive, food/beverage, shopping centers, other commercial such as drugstores).
- Warehouses.
- Health care (hospitals and medical buildings, and special care).
- Educational (including preschool, primary/secondary, higher education, and other educational, such as gallery/museum).
- Religious.
- Amusement and recreation (such as theme/amusement parks, sports, performance/meeting center, social center and movie theater/studio).

This category also includes government uses to meet public needs, such as firefighting, and institutional uses are included in the list above, such as religious, health-care, and educational institutions. Small manufacturing establishments would have the same types of water systems, mainly to serve their employees, customers, and other local needs.

As you envision the water systems required for these facilities, think of large-scale plumbing systems that meet multiple and often usual needs. For example, under lodging, a hotel or motel will require a large water tap, internal water-handling facilities to ensure continuous and high-quality service to its guests, water for swimming pools, and kitchen water. Its needs on the wastewater side will mirror these, and it will produce substantial peak-hour demands, both on the water supply and wastewater side.

A school would feature similar demands, and its requirements will vary with size and type of school. Peak demand will be a major consideration during recess and sporting events, and fire protection will also be critical. Schools can include large expanses of open space and sport fields, which require a lot of irrigation water.

Hospitals and health-care facilities have even more critical water needs, and they cannot tolerate being down due to power failures. They may be especially sensitive to water-quality fluctuations. These and other commercial systems may have to meet performance standards such as high-quality, 24/7 production, warnings and alerts with instrumentation for reliability, and operators to check on operation. They may require special point-of-use (POU) equipment (see Chapter 21).

RESIDENTIAL EQUIPMENT

As you can see from its statistics, residential housing is far and away the largest sector of the construction market and the largest end user of water services. The United States has 130 million housing units, and each one requires water services. Most are owner-occupied, but many are also rental units. Each residential unit requires water supply and wastewater systems, and most also have stormwater facilities.

The water systems of commercial and residential units can be thought of as supply and end-user systems. The service-line pipe and the meter that come from the water main, together with the building piping system, comprise the supply system. The access units of sinks, faucets, toilets, and other appliances, such as hot tubs and swimming pools, are end-user devices.

Plumbing equipment for buildings comprises pipe and pumps and NAICS category 332913 (Plumbing Fixture Fitting and Trim Manufacturing). The explanation of this category is: "This U.S. industry comprises establishments primarily engaged in manufacturing metal and plastics plumbing fixture fittings and trim, such as faucets, flush valves, and shower heads." Another category is NAICS 32711 (Pottery, Ceramics, and Plumbing Fixture Manufacturing): "This industry comprises establishments primarily engaged in shaping, molding, glazing, and firing pottery, ceramics, and plumbing fixtures made entirely or partly of clay or other ceramic materials."

The firms that operate in this sector make practically a who's who of the homeowner plumbing equipment industry and include names such as American Standard Companies; Crane Plumbing LLC; Fluidmaster, Inc.; Kohler; Masco Corp of Indiana (Delta Faucets); Moen, Inc.; Mueller Industries, Inc.; Oatey, Inc.; and Zurn Plumbing Products Group. Their products are on display at home-improvement stores and kitchen and bath trade shows as well as at plumbing expositions.

The grouping of point-of-use, point-of-entry, treatment systems, package plants, septic tanks, and related components includes several NAICS categories, such as those for plumbing components, those for larger treatment systems, and NAICS 327390 (Other Concrete Product Manufacturing).

The landscape industry, including sod farms, is also a significant user of water and water-management products. The NAICS code that applies is 444220 (Nursery, Garden Center, and Farm Supply Stores): "This industry comprises establishments primarily engaged in retailing nursery and garden products, such as trees, shrubs, plants, seeds, bulbs, and sod, that are predominantly grown elsewhere." Some of the company names associated with these products are Orbit Irrigation Products Inc., Rain Bird, and Toro Company, Irrigation Division.

Swimming pools represent a special class of water users. Vendors for pool equipment fall into the same categories for pumps, filters, pipes, and so forth. Manufacturers of pool equipment include Hayward Pool Products (Hayward Industries) and Pentair Pool Products, among others.

MARKET STUDIES

Market studies help reveal both the approximate sizes and the trends of purchases in the categories of equipment. Given the diversity of the water industry's markets, you would expect that the studies would be in the niches where firms operate, rather than the entire industry.

Frost & Sullivan (2005), a management consulting firm, offers its Global Water & Wastewater Market Subscription Program, which tracks trends, market size and shares, and other business information. In 2005 it forecast that the municipal water-equipment market would be $5.22 billion by 2011, growing slowly from $4.09 billion in 2004 (not including pipe and fittings). This forecast is in the same range as the capital expenditures for equipment that we note in Chapter 12. The firm tracks diverse topics and niches, such as desalination, instrumentation, package wastewater treatment plants, meters and pumps, and regional markets.

Drivers of the pipe market include residential construction, obsolescence of systems, and improvements in public water systems. A business press forecast was that U.S. demand for water and wastewater pipe is expected to increase 6 percent annually to $19 billion in 2014, equivalent to approximately five billion feet. Plastic pipe was expected to grow at the fastest pace due to construction and new applications in drain, sewer, and water supply. New plastic materials and joining methods may help this growth. For example, resins and molecularly oriented PVC are new applications. Also, polyethylene pipe may exhibit growth. Concrete pipe demand is driven by drain and storm sewer applications and some large diameter water applications. The report includes a review of demand-drivers, such as macroeconomics, demographics, construction, utility and transportation spending, farming, and regulatory factors. Markets analyzed include municipal and all other construction. Types of pipe include sewer and drain, potable water, transmission and distribution, and irrigation (PR Newswire, 2009).

The valve market breaks into several subgroups: water treatment, distribution (for utilities, industries, commercial and residential and fire protection), and wastewater. Most valves are sold off-the-shelf. Prices range from a few dollars for a house valve to large sums for engineered valves for large applications. Types of valves include mostly old designs for gate valves, butterfly valves, check valves, ball valves, needle valves, and more. Materials include cast iron, composite plastic and metal, and fabricated steel.

Usually, the markets are dominated by a few large players. For example, North America's $1.5 billion market is dominated by Pratt and Dezurik, which do about 60 percent of the business. The European market is dominated by Tyco Water, AVK, Viking, and Saint-Gobain. Tyco Water is a division of Tyco Flow Control, which is a subsidiary of Tyco International Ltd. The Henry Pratt Company was a subsidiary of Tyco but was sold to Mueller Water Products in 1999. Saint-Gobain, in Nancy, France, manufactures ductile iron pipe and associated fittings and valves.

There seems to be about 5 percent growth in the valve market (at least before the recession), mostly in rehabilitation. Growth markets follow migratory patterns. Market characteristics are dominated by standards and organization. In the United Kingdom, for example, the market is dominated by a few water companies and their purchase managers. Maintenance is a big part of the market as the utilities want service along with the valves. In the future, automation of the water sector could drive new valve business to develop economical and smart valves that measure variables such as water quality and infrastructure condition (Global Water Intelligence, 2006).

The Hydraulic Institute (2010) issues a market report on pumps. Its *World Pump Market Report* provides analysis and forecasts by end-use industry and pump applications for a number of countries, by pump type. The report is available to institute members and includes detail on macroeconomic developments such as GDP growth by world region. Then it considers the pump market size by world region and special topics such as China and other competitors in world pump markets. It considers types of pumps by world region and looks at industries that include mining, oil and gas, chemicals, power, food and drink, pharmaceuticals, pulp and paper, manufacturing, marine, construction and, finally, water and sewerage.

Suppliers to the categories of water systems coordinate their expositions through professional and trade organizations, such as AWWA and WEF, which serve multiple professional and policy purposes, as well as business interests. Otherwise, no trade association represents all water-industry suppliers, but the Water and Wastewater Equipment Manufacturers Association (WWEMA) represents a range of them and is an identifiable voice of the supplier industry.

The trade associations with a focus on a single product category, rather than the full industry, deal mostly with business issues, including international trade in water equipment. They usually serve niches of the water industry such as for a particular type of pipe or water treatment chemicals.

While a number of trade and professional organizations hold expositions where equipment is displayed, only a few comprehensive water trade shows are held. Vendors want to allocate their scarce marketing funds to the expositions where the customer interest will be the highest, and this tends to focus their energy on a few shows. The expositions where you can see the most equipment at one time are AWWA's Annual Conference and Exposition and WEF's WEFTEC. Smaller trade shows include Stormcon, an exposition organized by *Stormwater* magazine and the annual meeting of the Association of State Flood Plain Managers. There are also trade shows that feature hydroelectric equipment (electric power trade shows), irrigation equipment (agricultural exhibits), and dam safety and instrumentation equipment (Association of State Dam Safety Officials). For smaller-scale equipment, Aquatech 2009 in Chicago drew about 2,300 attendees, mostly from the Midwest. The previous year, when it was in Las Vegas, the show drew close to 3,000 (Water Quality Association, 2009). In 2005, in Las Vegas, the event drew 4,200 and had 331 exhibiting companies. The business has been following the ups and downs of real estate and the economy.

REGULATION OF QUALITY OF WATER-INDUSTRY EQUIPMENT

Water-industry equipment is quality-assured by similar procedures as other manufactured products and must follow legislated rules and regulations. For example, the no-lead rule for plumbing solder was authorized through the 1996 Amendments to the Safe Drinking Water Act. Some equipment, such as pipes and valves, must comply with standards issued by authorities such as the American National Standards Institute, the American Water Works Association (AWWA), and NSF International.

AWWA's volunteer members of standards committees oversee around 150 standards for 24 categories of products and processes in water supply. These are sold through AWWA to raise revenue to maintain the association's efforts. The American National Standards Institute (ANSI, 2010) is the centerpiece of the U.S. voluntary standards system. It was created after a 1916 meeting between several professional associations, coordinated by the American Institute of Electrical Engineers, which is now called IEEE. The associations invited several federal agencies to join, including the Departments of War, Navy, and Commerce. ANSI adopted its current name in 1969 and has been increasing its activity with new requirements and involvement, and has led in coordination with other national and international standards organizations. NSF International (2010) was started in 1944 and at one time was named the National Sanitation Foundation. Now, it labels itself the "The Public Health and Safety Company" and strives to be a world leader in standards development, product certification, education, and risk management for public health and safety, including food, water, indoor air, and the environment. NSF has the Water Treatment and Distribution Systems Program to certify drinking-water treatment chemicals and system components. Two standards are of particular note: NSF/ANSI Standard 60: Drinking Water Treatment Chemicals and NSF/ANSI Standard 61: Drinking Water System Components. The latter standard deals with health effects of all devices, components, and materials that contact drinking water.

EXAMPLES OF WATER-INDUSTRY SUPPLIER COMPANIES

Water-industry trade shows are a great place to learn about the business and its new products. You can attend them to view the "big" pumps and systems or you can see new small-scale equipment at home and garden shows. I like to talk to the representatives at the trade shows or even salespeople at home-improvement stores to track the trends, but while this has been interesting, I have yet to learn of a game-changing new technology or system. The water industry is too regulated and slow changing for that.

At the trade shows, the equipment seems to fall into the categories outlined by AWWA or even by NAICS categories. The trade show I attend most often is AWWA, and the following are some of the companies that you will find displaying there or at similar shows.

As the water industry does a lot of monitoring and reporting, analyzers and test equipment are in widespread use, both for the laboratory and field. One of the leading instrument companies is Hach, which produces a range of water-quality instrumentation. Honeywell is a Fortune 100 company that produces a range of controls used in the water industry, and it is a good example of a large company for which water is just one of many markets. Intuitech markets models of full-scale water-treatment processes to enable consulting engineers and utilities to evaluate their processes. Armfield Limited produces water-laboratory equipment for technical education and has expanded to the general field of industrial research and development. You might see their experimental setups in the labs of engineering colleges.

Perhaps the fastest-growing category of equipment is computing, communications, and information technology. At the trade shows, you will find ESRI, the GIS company with many utility applications for planning and asset management. Another computer graphics company to track is Autodesk, which produces computer-aided design equipment for engineers and planners. GBA Master Series Inc. is one of a group of companies that produce enterprise software systems for maintenance and asset management. Haestad Methods, which has been acquired by Bentley Systems (a competitor of Autodesk), distributes computer-based models for water systems.

Millions of meters are used in water systems, and you find a number of companies vying for contracts to supply utilities and other water users. A list of these companies would include Neptune, Econet Systems, Badger Meter, Datamatic, Dynasonics, and Itron. In addition to the meters themselves, the companies are also producing automatic meter reading (AMR) systems and services. Closely connected to meters are the leak detection equipment and services, with Gutermann Leak Detection and Hughes Supply Company being commonly seen at trade shows. One category of remedial equipment is for corrosion control, and you will see, for the example, the CorrPro Companies on display.

Perhaps the largest number of companies will be displaying pipes and valves. Pipe companies will include Charlotte Pipe and Foundry, American Ductile Iron Pipe Co., Griffin Pipe Products Inc., and Dresser Piping

Specialties, among others. In addition, you will see the trade associations of the pipe companies, such as DIPRA, the Ductile Iron Pipe Research Association. Valve producers will include ISCO Industries, Clow Valve Co., and DeZurik.

Ameron International Corporation is a good example of a broad-based pipe supplier. It sells fiberglass pipes, fittings, and well screens for various industrial uses. Its water transmission group provides concrete pipe systems for water supply, wastewater, and stormwater systems. Ameron's Infrastructure Products group provides ready-mix concrete, aggregates, concrete pipe, and box culverts. Mueller Water Products, Inc. has water equipment in three divisions: Mueller Company, U.S. Pipe, and Anvil. Mueller Company manufactures fire hydrants, valves, meters, and tools and fittings. U.S. Pipe manufactures and sells ductile iron pipe and related products. Anvil also manufactures pipe fittings and related products for mechanical, fire protection, and other piping systems.

Full-treatment systems are offered by some companies, such as GE Infrastructure Water and Process Technologies. Another company with similar products is Severn Trent Services, a division of Severn Trent plc, which also owns the UK water utility with the same name.

In addition to these categories of equipment, you will find companies displaying pumps, chemical products, construction and maintenance equipment, safety equipment, tanks, and security equipment. Calgon Carbon Corporation, an example of a longstanding chemical supplier, also serves the industrial process, environmental, and food markets. Its activated carbon and service segment sells activated carbon to remove organic compounds from water, air, and other liquids and gases, and leases and maintains carbon-adsorption equipment.

The household end of the water business is closer to the home and bath improvements than to the utility industry. American Standard is a well-known company that produces valves and toilets, and its roots date to before 1900. It was named the American Radiator & Standard Sanitary Corporation in 1929 and became the world leader in toilets and radiators. It was taken private in 1988 by an investment banker (Kelso & Co.), which formed ASI Holding Corporation to acquire and merge with American Standard. Its name was changed to American Standard Companies, Inc. in 1994. It has acquired the Trane Company to enter air conditioning, and now it also has divisions for plumbing products, automotive products, and medical diagnostic technologies. The company has divested the water products and been renamed Trane, but the American Standard name has been sold to Bain Capital Partners, LLC, for use in water-related products.

CHAPTER 20

Commodity Water: Transfers, Exchanges, and Water Banks

Water scarcity would seem to create an attractive business opportunity to sell it like a commodity, similar to oil and gas. The idea in selling water as a commodity is to obtain supplies (usually raw water but perhaps also treated water) from a source and sell it to a willing buyer. The water might be sold as permanent rights, as a lease, or in terms of some volume delivery. Permanent rights are explained in Chapter 14, which is about water law. A lease of water might involve the right to divert or pump a supply for a limited time. A volumetric delivery, for example, would require an agreement to deliver a certain number of gallons or acre-feet.

As there are many ways to sell commodity water, the goals of this chapter are to outline the theory, give examples of ways it can be sold, and provide a framework to conceptualize this area of the water business. In some ways, commodity water is a sound business concept, but water is different from other resources and, given its social and political aspects, this is an area to tread carefully in, especially for speculative ventures. The chapter will conclude by outlining the channels where commodity water seems to work and those that have not worked out very well, at least so far.

SALE OR LEASE OF COMMODITY WATER: THE THEORY

The starting point for the commodity water business is the idea that there is a growing demand for water and if one can nail down a supply, it becomes a valuable commodity to sell. This opens up many questions, such as what kind of water, at what price, on what delivery terms, and other contractual questions. The supplies of water could come from tapping a stream or lake, pumping groundwater, or buying it from third parties.

Demands for water would normally come from the big users, which are mainly cities, utilities, industries, and farms. Chapter 2 explained the quantities required by the categories of users. These demands could be stimulated by growth, loss of supplies, or the attraction of lower-cost, higher-reliability supplies.

Packaging the water and organizing exchange and delivery mechanisms are where the rubber hits the road because of legal, political, and financial constraints. As examples will show, these constraints have proved to be fatal flaws for a number of proposals.

A buyer of commodity water might prefer to get the water through an agent than develop it himself. The agent might have a competitive advantage or economy of scale, have unique access to water supplies or have superior technical and financial capacities to develop and deliver the water. For example, here in Colorado we have agents who specialize in finding and marketing water rights for sale. They might be the same agents who specialize in farms and ranches because the water sold is often from irrigation rights. Another example would be a water entrepreneur who developed a project that yielded water supplies, which would be marketed to local utilities and industries.

The legal issues involve state doctrines of water rights, which differ around the country, or any number of other roadblocks, such as federal permits to sell or exchange water. In Colorado, for example, buying water rights through the appropriation doctrine procedures is well established and seems to provide the requisites for a market for commodity water. However, the law works against speculation. Financial arrangements can also be tricky, but they might not be as difficult as legal and political obstacles.

MECHANICS OF WATER TRANSFERS

Developing commodity water involves transferring it, which can lead to big legal, political, and financial problems. The types of transfers might involve location, timing, ownership, or type of use. If transfers involve moving the right to use water from one place to another, it can be like wheeling electricity across a grid. Sometimes water wheeling can involve paper transactions rather than movement of actual water, which is heavy and expensive to move.

Lund and Israel (1995) classified transfers as permanent; contingent transfers/dry-year options; spot-market transfers; water banks; transfer of reclaimed, conserved, and surplus water; and water wheeling or exchanges.

Location of a transfer might involve interbasin transfer, which almost always involves conflict, or change in location within a watershed. Storage in a reservoir or a water bank changes the timing of water movement and availability. Ownership transfers change the right to divert or use water from one party to another. Change in type of use moves the water from, say, a farm field to a municipal application. Compacts represent transfer of water rights between sovereign governments and are a way to negotiate between political stakeholders in an interstate river basin.

EXAMPLES OF VENTURES TO SELL WATER AS A COMMODITY

One way to explain how commodity water ventures might work is to give examples. Some of these are generic and familiar scenarios and others may seem like wild schemes.

Megascale transfers can involve schemes such as China's ongoing south-to-north transfer scheme, the California Water Project, and proposals to divert Alaska water, Columbia River water, or Mississippi River water to western states. Examples of large regional transfers include the Colorado Big Thomson (CBT) project and the ongoing project to transfer Imperial Irrigation District water to San Diego. Smaller regional transfers might be the Virginia Beach water transfer or Atlanta's attempts to transfer water from the adjacent river basins. Inter–local transfers based on contracts are practiced by the Tampa Bay Water utility and Colorado's CBT project transfers. Smaller transfers occur by diverting water from one local watershed to another via a wastewater treatment plant. Finally, you can have change from type of use as in changing irrigation to industrial water.

Federal, state, and local water projects usually yield extra water that must be marketed. The government agencies that develop the projects must find customers to pay for some of the project benefits to offset the need for full taxpayer funding of the infrastructure. For example, when the Corps of Engineers developed Buford Dam above Atlanta on the Chattahoochee River, it offered cities the opportunity to purchase water entitlements. The fact that Mayor Hartsfield declined the chance to buy water led to some of the headaches Atlanta currently faces in its water-supply situation (see Chapter 3).

Another version of water development is the "produced water" that sometimes occurs from oil and gas development. The drilling taps aquifers as well as seams of oil and gas, bringing sometimes large quantities of water to the surface. If this water can be captured and packaged, it might prove valuable as a commodity to sell. Another version of this might be the groundwater that must be pumped out in dewatering operations from construction excavations, but this would not usually be a long-term supply.

Once a utility or industry has developed its water supply, it might have extra water to sell wholesale to other utilities or industries. This is actually a common practice among water utilities, and many of the nation's 52,000 public water supplies operate on the basis of wholesale water. For example, Chicago, which gets its water from Lake Michigan, serves a number of adjacent cities with wholesale supplies. These can either be raw or treated water, depending on the situation.

Utilities in growing areas must look ahead to buy or develop water in advance of their future needs. The story of Los Angeles' development of water in the Owens Valley is well known in the water industry and is the basis of the movie *Chinatown*. A more recent effort to bring new water over long distances was the Virginia Beach project to develop water from Lake Gaston, along Virginia's border with North Carolina (see Chapter 4).

During the 1980s, the small Denver suburb of Thornton perceived a need to develop a new water supply, and it undertook a secret campaign to purchase farms and water supplies in northern Colorado. This effort followed a failed regional water-development plan called the Two Forks project (see Chapter 3).

One of the largest-scale recent efforts to develop and sell commodity water is the agreement between San Diego and the Imperial Irrigation District of California to salvage irrigation water and transfer it to the city (see Chapter 8).

The organization of water companies to develop and market supplies has seemed like a good opportunity. In one version, this can be like a real estate company that simply deals in water rather than in property.

An example of another version was the Enron spinoff of a water company known as Azurix. This move into public utilities launched a business model to buy water as a commodity and use the Internet as a marketing exchange for trading water. At the time, Enron vice chair Rebecca Mark said the company would purchase water assets in Europe and South America. They also agreed to buy Wessex Water plc, a UK-based water and wastewater utility, but the venture proved unsuccessful.

Entrepreneurs may see in water the opportunity to develop megadeals. You can see the attractiveness if you think about capturing a small spring. . . .

For example, an investment group named American Water Development Inc. (AWDI) attempted to export groundwater to Denver during the 1990s, but it was unsuccessful after legal challenges. Currently, a Colorado entrepreneur (Aaron Million) is planning a project to divert water from the Green River and transport it across Wyoming to supply cities and districts along Colorado's Front Range. Figure 20.1 shows the approximate route of the pipeline, which would divert water from Flaming Gorge Reservoir.

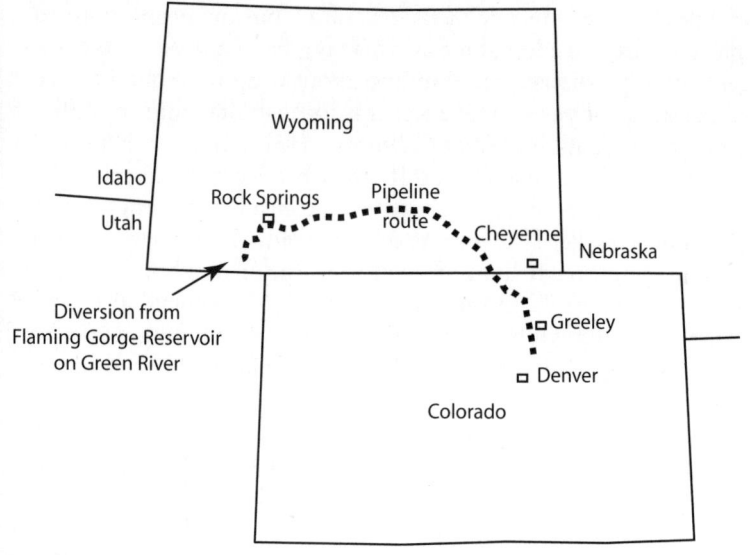

FIGURE 20.1   Approximate route for Flaming Gorge Project

A similar idea has been cooked up in Texas, where T. Boone Pickens started a company known as Mesa Water (2010). The idea is to use the Ogallala Aquifer to transfer water to communities that need it. The company's opportunity is based on pumping groundwater from a four-county area in the northeastern corner of the Texas Panhandle, where they estimate 81 million acre-feet of available water with an annual recharge rate of 80,000 acre-feet. Given the low irrigation potential of this area, they assert that the best use of the water is to export it to other places in Texas. The success of this venture is unknown at this time.

One version of water development that has attracted much interest is the concept of the city–farm cooperative program. In this arrangement, a city and farm partner such that the city has the right to use water supplies during dry years and the farm can use them in normal years when there is a water surplus.

This city–farm scheme is a version of the ongoing process to transfer water from farms to cities across the western United States. I witnessed this the first time during the early 1970s when, as a consulting engineer, I was advising a utility on its future water supply and local agents came by with irrigation water shares in hand to market to the utility. That was a matter of willing buyer and willing seller, but newer versions of city–farm deals seem to offer additional win–win possibilities.

This is more in the category of far-out ideas, but the proposal to tow icebergs has been around a long time and may not be totally out of the question. Weeks (1980) reviewed the thinking about it up to about 1980. He concluded that it might work to take icebergs to Australia, but very difficult to get them as far as Saudi Arabia or California. He traced the origins of the concept of towing icebergs back to the 1850s, when ice was transported for use as a refrigerant and small icebergs were transported from southern Chile as far north as Peru for use as a refrigerant. Fast forward to the 1950s, and the semipopular literature began to speculate about taking ice to water-thirsty Southern California. Later, Prince Mohammed al Faisal al Saud became interested while he was charged with developing water supplies for Saudi Arabia. Water delivered to Saudi Arabia would be for human consumption and might command higher prices than some of the irrigation and industrial schemes. Weeks' conclusion about this possibility was that it would depend on the economics and, of course, it has not happened in the last 30 years. Nevertheless, the idea continues to be debated.

There have been recent schemes to export iceberg water to dry areas. For example, the Iceberg Corporation of America announced a venture to export freshwater from Greenland. Its partner is the shipping company Allan Idd Jensen, of Greenland, and the joint venture would be named Aquapolaris. Iceberg has been harvesting ice from icebergs and producing and selling spring water, as well as water to produce vodka and beer. The source would be a waterfall that discharges into a fjord and would facilitate loading onto ships. There is no indication in the report of the quantities of water that might be involved, but the company appears focused on the beverage market.

WATER BANKS

To increase the security of raw water supply, the concept of the water bank may be used for storing water for dry years. You might say, "Isn't a reservoir a water bank?" It is, but the concept of the water bank goes beyond the physical storage of water to include the accounting for water so that it can be allocated to its rightful users when they call for it. For example, a water bank might be operated by an irrigation company, which earmarks shares of water that are stored in a reservoir owned by another entity, and the irrigation might even pay rent for the use of the storage space. The irrigation water could then be allocated when needed at a time when its value in use is highest.

In 2009, the California Department of Water Resources (2010) established the Drought Water Bank by purchasing water upstream of the

Sacramento–San Joaquin Delta and this water was transferred to at-risk water users using State Water Project or Central Valley Project facilities. This was an example of a state agency taking action to secure additional water during times of need to add to security of water users who needed it.

Texas' Water Bank enables the voluntary transfer of water rights between buyers and sellers, either on a temporary or permanent basis. It is managed by the Texas Water Development Board (2010) and transfers require permits from the Texas Commission on Environmental Quality.

So, a water bank acts to facilitate transfers, but there are many versions, and some can store water as well as facilitate arrangements.

CONSTRAINTS ON WATER-SUPPLY DEVELOPMENT

The many obstacles to developing commodity water are similar to constraints on water-supply development by any party. These have been studied and summarized by Graham et al. (1999), who cited examples to provide a classification system for them.

- Conditions imposed by states to regulate interstate transfers.
- Limitations on interbasin transfers within states.
- Endangered species and other environmental legislation.
- Bureau of Reclamation constraints on agricultural water uses.
- Tribal rights.
- Obstacles to cooperation among local utilities and interlocal transfers.
- State limitations on water rights.

Commodity water is a tough sell, not because the economics of it won't work but because of human, political, and legal problems. Still, it remains a viable consideration for utilities and public agency players, and private developers someday may find new opportunities that pay off.

CHAPTER 21

Bottled Water and Point-of-Use Treatment

While the most common way in the United States to get drinking water is directly from utilities through our taps, point-of-use (POU) and bottled-water companies also supply drinking water. The bottled-water business is large and has been growing, but the POU business is smaller and more stagnant. However, both are important parts of the overall water business and can serve as barometers to changes in the industry.

In many ways, POU and bottled water are different businesses, but they have interfaces and relationships with utilities. Bottled-water vendors are closer to the food and beverage industry than to the water-utility industry, and their product lines may include soda drinks and other beverages. Point-of-use companies may provide and service water-treatment systems, but they may also provide drinking fountains or even bulk bottled-water services.

As we present later, statistics on bottled water sales are good. However, the POU business is not well defined and is hard to measure. The sales and service of treatment devices is probably on the order of a $1 billion per year industry and, if you add in all end-user devices found in residential, commercial, and industrial facilities, it will be much larger. The bottled-water business is many times this size, and if you expand its definition to include products such as flavored water, it becomes even larger.

An understanding of the point-of-use and bottled water businesses helps us to understand consumer preferences and trends in the overall drinking water business. Referring back to Chapter 10, it is possible that the future of water utilities might include services that mimic or coordinate with point-of-use systems that are offered by the private sector. If that happened, both POU and bottled water could take on much greater roles in drinking water.

This chapter presents an overview of the point-of-use and bottled-water businesses. It provides a conceptual description of the businesses and, although it does not include exhaustive statistics, it offers links to information for those who seek it.

CONVENTIONAL AND NONCONVENTIONAL WATER SERVICES

The mainline water-supply utility business has had a watchful eye on the POU and bottled-water businesses for a long time. In some ways, it seems an affront to utilities that people would pay high prices for bottled water when they can get high-quality tap water for such a low price. In the same way, they wonder why a customer would need a POU device when they supply high-quality water in the first place.

Of course, there is a lot of psychology in people's choices about their drinking water, and bottled water has a certain cachet to it, as well as being convenient. The ever-present bottle of water around the corporate conference table is evidence of the convenience and, when you check into a motel, your room may offer you a bottle of exotic-sounding water, for a fee.

Although both POU and bottled water are substantial businesses, neither is large enough to catch the attention of government statisticians. The sales of bottled water are recorded by the Bottled Water Association and will be explained later. POU sales are very hard to track because so many different devices and services are involved. In spite of this lack of statistics, the water industry understands that it is important to study why people are attracted to bottled water and POU devices and what the future will hold.

To look into the future of POU and bottled water, the Water Research Foundation sponsored a study on trends of supplying water in conventional and unconventional ways, to include POU systems (Raucher et al., 2004). This study was part of the foundation's ongoing program of research that responds to needs identified by the utilities, who have a natural interest in promoting innovation in urban water services

The study began by explaining how water utilities must bundle two distinct products: a small volume of high-quality water for drinking and bulk water for many uses, including fire protection. This is an expensive way to do business because to deliver the small quantity of high-quality water, the utilities must treat and distribute massive quantities and be ready for the ultimate test—fire—at any moment.

Because customers will continue to insist on high-quality water for drinking, the utility industry is thinking about new approaches that include POU treatment, point-of-entry (POE) treatment, neighborhood-scale treatment, water reuse and dual water systems, and bottled water. Perhaps it can bundle its products and services in different ways and perform better across the board.

The study concluded that there is no magic bullet for the future. It found that POU and package devices can perform well and unconventional approaches such as POE can be very cost effective. However, risks include greater microbial threats in water, and new technologies and stronger controls may be needed. This might occur, for example, because the more reliance is placed on POU/POE systems, the greater the number of control points needed and the more difficult the regulation will be. Also, regulatory and statutory barriers may promote and inhibit POU and POE approaches at the same time, and the industry will look to federal guidance and state regulatory agency actions to assess the future of unconventional approaches.

POINT-OF-USE WATER BUSINESS

The services and equipment provided through POU suppliers were introduced in Chapters 18 and 19 and their operations can be viewed as an integrated business. However, this is a challenge because, like other niches of the water business, POU services are not well defined. Basically, they comprise all of the water-treatment and water-vending devices that are offered at the end-user level.

While there is no centralized database, magazine publishers seek to define the market, and *Water Conditioning & Purification (WC&P)* magazine has been a central player in POU services and products for a long time. Its editorial calendar displays the major categories of water-treatment products and system applications that include any place where water is dispensed or processed by customers.

WC&P started publishing in 1959 as a family-owned company serving the water-treatment industry, and it strives to be the voice of the POU and POE business community. Another information resource is the Water Quality Association (WQA), which was established in 1973 by the merger of the Water Conditioning Association International and Water Conditioning Foundation. Its laboratory had already begun testing and certifying products in 1960.

In spite of these media outlets, we do not know the size or characterization of the POU/POE industry niche. Maxwell (2003) writes frequently about the size of the water business, and in an article in *WC&P* he addressed the POU/POE market by referring to studies by firms such as Frost & Sullivan, which estimate the business at $800 million to $1 billion of revenue per year, but with a caveat that we lack good assumptions and industry definitions to bolster these estimates. The categories he included are water conditioners, POU/POE residential and commercial treatment devices, chemicals, and materials to keep them running.

I consulted the North American Industrial Classification System (NAICS) to see how this industry is classified and found, as in other parts of the water business, that statistics are mixed with many other services and products. For example, water softener installation is classified under Plumbing, Heating, and Air-Conditioning Contractors (NAICS 238220). Bottled Water Manufacturing has its own code (NAICS 312112), but water-purification equipment manufacturing is mixed in with Other Commercial and Service Industry Machinery Manufacturing (NAICS 333319) and wholesaling of water-softening systems is with Plumbing and Heating Equipment and Supplies (Hydronics) Merchant Wholesalers (NAICS 423720). Wholesaling of water coolers is with Refrigeration Equipment and Supplies Merchant Wholesalers (NAICS 423740). The water-conditioning service provider companies that serve customers directly are in NAICS 54390, which is for Other Direct Selling Establishments and also includes miscellaneous categories like flea markets, fruit stands, and home-delivery newspaper routes. As a result of this inquiry into NAICS I concluded that it would be practically impossible to consult government statistics to study the size of the POU market.

Koslow (2004) provided some detail about the market and wrote that the market is small and highly fragmented. The usual estimate for consumer water treatment systems is about $1 billion, but he thought it is closer to $1.25 billion when you include refrigerator filtration systems. The North American markets have grown, but the ones in Europe are stagnant. However, markets in Asia are more promising.

It seems that both new technology and more effective marketing are needed if this industry is to grow. Stimulation can occur through threats such as terrorism and the periodic news about contaminants such as MTBE, perchlorate, radium/radon, arsenic, endocrine disrupters, and pharmaceuticals. Publicity about these comes from NSF International and the WQA, which are vested in the industry's future.

Technologies are advancing, both to detect and remove contaminants. Advances in manufacturing make high-performance products more affordable, and tighter regulations may follow advances in more sensitive analytical methods. However, high levels of contaminant removal will also depend on quality control of manufacturing and consumer maintenance of devices.

General merchandise retail devices such as gravity-flow carafe and faucet-mounted filter systems should be low in cost and simple to install and maintain. These are sold by companies such as Brita (Clorox) and Procter & Gamble (PUR Division). The do-it-yourself market includes devices sold by Sears, Home Depot, Lowes, Ace Hardware, and others. The systems might include reverse osmosis, softeners, and water-filtration systems with more capability than carafe and faucet-mounted systems. Suppliers include Sta-Rite Industries, General Electric—Smartwater Division, Ecowater, Watts Water Technologies, and Culligan. Refrigerator filtration has grown in recent years, and 30 percent of refrigerators sold in North America now have water-filtration systems.

The market has changed, and dealers and service firms have had to respond to actions of big-box retailers. In the 1980s, the consumer water industry was dominated by local dealers, who performed installation and maintenance of systems for water softening and treatment. Now, dealer networks such as Culligan, Rainsoft, Kinetico, and Ecowater must respond to the new business environment and engage in direct retail operations. For example, Ecowater supports Sears Kenmore, and Culligan/USFilter sells directly to consumers. Recently, our family received an offer from 3M for a free in-home water screening that would presumably lead to a purchase from 3M Clean Water Solutions. All of this activity means that the traditional water-treatment dealer remains under pressure.

The market for consumer devices might respond to a dramatic event, such as terrorist threats or a breakdown in water quality. Water filtration companies may add health claims to existing products to get attention, even if the chemicals mentioned are unlikely to occur in household water. Meanwhile, the steady stream of news about water-related contaminants such as MTBE, perchlorate, radium and radon, arsenic, endocrine disruptors, and pharmaceuticals raises public awareness more gradually. An example is the recent USEPA action on arsenic to reduce the maximum contaminant level from 50 parts per billion (ppb) to 10 ppb. This is hard to deal with in municipal systems, and POU devices can be expensive and difficult to maintain.

The future of the industry will require products that achieve reduced cost while addressing new health claims. For example, responding to microbiological threats could be a market opportunity if viruses, bacteria, and oocysts are seen to be serious threats.

Markets in developing countries are also quite large, but revenues might not be attractive and local manufacturers may be able to market low-cost devices.

BOTTLED WATER SALES

Although bottled water is a large segment of the beverage business, the quantity of it consumed in the United States is minuscule compared to the public water supply. According to the Beverage Marketing Association (2010), the annual rate of consumption in 2009 was only about 8,400 MG (of nonsparkling water). On a daily basis, this would be 23 MGD, and it compares to 44,200 MG per day of public supply (see Chapter 2). In other words, the daily supply of bottled water is only about 1/2,000th of the supply of municipal water.

To keep this in perspective, the public supply amounts to about 150 gpcd, and if each person drinks his or her recommended eight glasses or so, less than one gallon per day is actually consumed by drinking.

Although the quantity of water consumed is small compared to public supply, revenues are substantial. In 2009 wholesale sales of bottled water were about $11.2 billion. If you provide only a modest markup, this comes to on the order of $20 billion at the retail level. If you assume that a 16-ounce bottle sells for $0.50, the revenue is even higher, at about $33 billion per year. Total revenues of all water-supply utilities were on the order of $40 billion, so the financials of the bottled water business are actually competitive with theirs, even if the quantities are much lower. That shows that even if bottled water consumption is way below tap water consumption, people's willingness to pay for it is much more.

While consumption of bottled water declined during the financial crisis, it rose dramatically over the previous two decades. This data from the Beverage Marketing Corporation (2010) shows recent experience (Table 21.1).

Bottled water is the second largest commercial beverage category in the United States (Weber, 2008). Its sources can be either ground or surface water or treated municipal water systems. Groundwater can be artesian or

TABLE 21.1 Bottled-Water Consumption

	Gal/cap
1999	16.2
2000	16.7
2001	18.2
2002	20.1
2003	21.6
2004	23.2
2005	25.4
2006	27.6
2007	29
2008	28.5
2009	27.6

Data source: Beverage Marketing Corporation, 2010

shallow-well water and can have different mineral contents. The water can be delivered in different containers, including regular bottles or larger ones, either plastic of glass.

In the United States, most bottled water is sold in the same state where it is bottled. About 5 percent is imported, and about 25 percent is from municipal sources. Some brands use reverse osmosis and filtration and add minerals and may label the water as from public sources. Some bottlers produce sparkling, flavored, and vitamin-enhanced water.

People seem to like bottled water as a convenient choice. People think that it is consistently safe, healthy, and of good taste. A phone survey of Washington residents in 2007 showed that 55 percent prefer tap water over bottled water and that men, people over 35, and households without children are more likely to prefer tap water, while women, people under 35, and households with children are more likely to prefer bottled water. This is, of course, just one survey and the data may be dated.

People in the United States seem to be gravitating toward lower-cost bottled water, and the main industry trend is toward flavored water. The leading suppliers globally are Nestlé, Danone, Coca-Cola (Dasani), and PepsiCo (Aquafina). Marketing slogans and strategies look for ways to promote remote locations, artesian aquifers, lack of contact with man, healthy minerals and far from any pollution. Imported brands that sell well in the United States include Fiji Water (a Paramount Citrus product), Poland Springs (from Nestlé), and Evian (a Danone product).

In developing countries, people often have few choices for drinking water, and if they can afford it at all, they may drink bottled water. Studies have shown, to the surprise of the researchers, that people are willing to devote high percentages of household income to have safe water. This flies in the face of conventional wisdom that people are unwilling to pay higher rates for water.

Bottled water is regulated as a food product by the Food and Drug Administration (FDA) and by some states. FDA rules are similar to those of the Safe Drinking Water Act (SDWA) but more stringent on lead. There is no mechanism for international inspections. The International Bottled Water Association has voluntary standards, but no enforcement mechanism. Several nongovernmental studies showed some violations of standards. A 1999 study by the National Resources Defense Council (NRDC) tested 103 brands and found that 22 percent violated California standards, mostly for arsenic and synthetic organic compounds. Case Western Reserve University compared 57 bottles to Cleveland tap water and found some violations, but all were safe to drink.

Environmental issues of bottled water center on the plastic that is used and the use of energy to bottle and transport the water. Plastic packaging has also attracted attention for health issues. About 30 percent of the global production of polyethylene terephthalate (PET) is used for bottled water, and most end up in landfills or as litter. Several chemicals in plastics are suspected of leaching and being carcinogenic or endocrine disruptors. These are phthalates, which include the organic chemical DEHP, which is used to make PVC, and bisphenol A, which might leach from polycarbonate containers such as water coolers, bottles, and baby bottles or food containers. In addition to concerns about plastic, health advisories say not to reuse bottles because of the risk of bacterial growth in open bottles with irregular surfaces.

WHAT IS NEXT FOR BOTTLED WATER AND POU?

While bottled-water sales have enjoyed a long period of rapid growth, the increase seems to have leveled off, at least during the recent recession. It may be that the public has internalized its concerns about the health of tap water and now has made its choices. Time will tell. In any event, utilities are aware of public concern and are taking steps to raise public confidence to the extent they can. The Consumer Confidence Report required by the 1996 SDWA Amendments was aimed at that goal. Meanwhile, bottled water continues to be one of a number of consumer choices and there is a lot of competition among distributors of it. If this data is any indication of young persons' preferences, the future will not see large increases. Many students I see at my university have a slot on their backpack for a stainless steel water bottle that is refilled with tap water.

POU suppliers must not see a lot of growth ahead, although equipment firms continue to develop and distribute new products. There seems to be a certain resignation among dealers in the POU industry that competition from online and big-box retailers has dimmed the prospects for the local water-services firm that provides office drinking-water systems, water softeners, and household water filters. This industry is looking for a stimulus for its business. For example, in 2010, the Water Quality Association was looking to a study by Batelle Institute to raise awareness of the green benefits of water softeners, while at the same time some states were looking at tighter regulation of water softeners because of the discharges of brine, especially into septic tank systems.

If you think about an ideal water-supply system for the future, it might be an optimized one that distributes safe bulk water to zones of cities, which have their own storage and POE treatment systems. The regional storage systems for bulk water could be supplemented by regional source-of-supply systems that could serve as reserves for emergencies. Then, drinking water of high quality and reliability could be distributed locally in smaller pipes that run alongside the larger bulk pipes, which could also be used for fire-fighting and sale of lower-cost water for purposes such as landscape irrigation. The POE systems could be supplemented by POU treatment for additional protection and processing that meet special needs. This sort of idealized system would have to be evaluated in the light of economic and political realities and might never come to pass. In any event, the future of drinking water, including bottled water and POU systems, will continue to evolve in response to social and financial pressures that cannot be predicted.

CHAPTER 22

Safe Water for All:
The Ultimate Water Business

f Adam Smith was 100 percent correct and an "invisible hand" will meet our needs through the market place, then this should include safe drinking water. If Karl Marx was 100 percent correct that the capitalist system is corrupt and we need a utopian system "From each according to his ability, to each according to his needs," then a cooperative or government solution is required. However, something must be broken, because somewhere around a billion people in the world lack access to safe water and sanitation.

In fact, this problem is due not only to the failure of capitalism and socialism but also to poverty, corruption, civil war, and a host of related ills. The bottom line is that many people remain at risk for disease and suffering unless safe water and sanitation can be provided for all.

The problem is being addressed through a business approach, but it requires public-private cooperation and, in many cases, the private part is not-for-profit business. This is a short chapter to summarize this part of the water business and how it relates to the rest of the water activity described in the book.

HOW THE PROBLEM DEVELOPED

The problem is lack of access to safe water and sanitation. The safe-water part means to have enough affordable drinking and household water for families, especially the vulnerable and children. The sanitation part means to have safe and convenient toilet facilities where human waste does not threaten health.

Estimates vary, but current ones peg the number of people around the world who lack access to safe water at around 1 billion. One estimate, published by the United Nations (2010) is that 894 million people lack the

20–50 liters per day of fresh water they need for drinking, cooking, and cleaning. The same source reported that 2.5 billion people lack access to basic sanitation, and this includes almost 1 billion children.

This appalling situation did not occur overnight but is a legacy of centuries of deprivation and conflicts, and the question now is, what can be done? There is no shortage of international meetings about it and, thankfully, donor assistance has been significant. However, the 2010 UN-Water Global Annual Assessment of Sanitation and Drinking-Water (GLAAS) report showed a drop in donor assistance to solve the problem (World Health Organization, 2010). This was in spite of evidence that improved water and sanitation would lower health-care costs, increase school attendance and boost productivity. WHO estimated that improved access to sanitation and water produces impressive economic benefits and increases a country's gross domestic product significantly. One estimate was that poor water, sanitation and hygiene services claim the lives of 1.5 million children under the age of 5 every year from diarrhea alone, a greater toll than the combined impact of HIV and AIDS, malaria, and tuberculosis.

WHAT IT WILL TAKE

Safe water and sanitation are problems of poverty, which has multiple and complex causes. Many people have a heart to help others escape from poverty, which is such a visible and oppressive curse. At my university, we have had any number of programs meant to assist people in overcoming poverty, whether for safe water, jobs, education, or other needs. One of my heroes at the university, Maurice Albertson, devoted his life to it. He saw the solution in people being equipped and enabled to solve their own problems at the village level and organized an International Conference on Sustainable Village-Based Development, which led to an organization named Village Earth. According to Bill Morgan, a long-term university president, Albertson had the "land grant virus," which meant he devoted his life to outreach and service. Albertson himself explained that the Sermon on the Mount was the centerpiece of the Bible, with its focus on helping others.

It might be an oversimplification, but what it will take to provide safe water and sanitation is to overcome poverty. However, safe water and sanitation will help people escape poverty. This is illustrated by Figure 22.1, which shows how public health leads to economic development, which creates jobs and business opportunities, which lead to higher incomes and greater capacity to afford safe water and sanitation. The

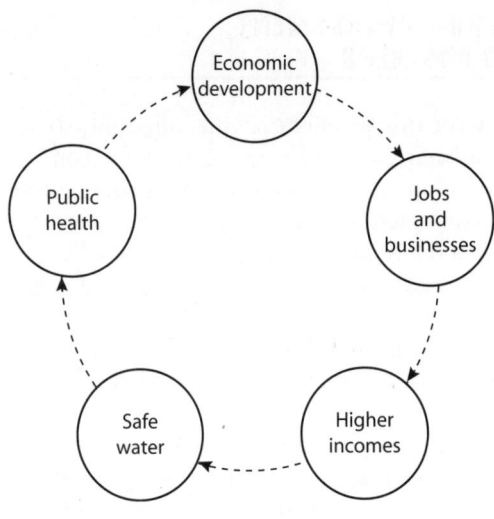

FIGURE 22.1   Safe water and poverty

figure is a simplified "causal loop" diagram, which is a tool of systems thinking that originated after the best-selling business book *The Fifth Discipline* (Senge, 1990). My students use this diagram as a tool to explain complex problems, leading to research into their causes. The problem is that life is not as simple as the diagram shows; for example, in the case of the variables shown on Figure 22.1, there are many, many other influences on poverty at work and it is simply impossible to show them coherently in one diagram.

In spite of this complexity, the job that must be done is to confront the massive problems facing us. This is the lesson given by former congressman Tony Hall, who has devoted great effort to alleviation of hunger. He gave talks at our university and in the community in 2010 and, in explaining his frustration at some of the complexities and roadblocks, he summarized with advice from Mother Teresa: to do what is in front of us. So, by providing safe water and sanitation we do something to help, even if it is not the complete solution.

How to approach the problem has been the subject of many policy discussions and most people agree that it is not a matter of giving someone a fish, but of teaching them to fish. This advice has been improved by pointing out that they also need fishing gear and their fishing holes need to have fish; in other words, holistic solutions are needed.

RESPONSES FROM GOVERNMENT, DONORS, AND BUSINESS

My experience with this problem has included mostly government solutions, but I have been involved with others who approached it through donors and business solutions. Government and donor solutions take more or less the same approaches of finding productive projects or programs to invest in. The main difference might be in the level of commitment. Donors might be more personally invested and more careful with funds than government employees. This will not always be the case, of course, but it rings true for the general situation.

The government solution is one of international, national, or community development, where the government invests in projects or programs that are meant to help. For example, a government might allocate funds to build a small rural water tank and distribution system. A donor might do the same thing and might bring people there to actually help in the construction. If the project were large, it might require a government approach.

Perhaps the ultimate government program is through the United Nations, which is an association of governments and involves global programs of assistance through agencies such as the United Nations Children's Fund (UNICEF), the Food and Agriculture Organization (FAO), and the UN Development Programme (UNDP). Agencies such as the World Health Organization (WHO) might not build projects but would have community education programs. The World Bank is a quasi-government organization that would provide funds to build projects that are managed by governments. The U.S. Agency for International Development (USAID) is an example of a national-level government agency with a clear mission of international development.

My experience with government foreign-aid programs includes a number of the agencies mentioned, and it has impressed me with the complexity of the development process and how closely it is linked to the overall political and cultural situation in a country or locality. For example, I participated in an FAO mission to Somalia in 1982 that was to assist in the development of a national water-planning program. The breakdown of law and order in that country shows how futile such development efforts will be in the absence of necessary conditions being fulfilled. Still, the motivation was good and my personal opinion, after many years of participating in such programs, is that although there will be failures the overall result will be positive and the important thing is to keep trying and improving.

Donors comprise a more diverse field of players than governments. Perhaps a way to explain them is in categories. The UN system, national government donors, and development banks were already mentioned.

The other two categories that come to mind are business and private philanthropy.

Business philanthropy includes organizations such as Water for People, which is run by the AWWA. Its executive director, Ned Breslin (2010), explained his philosophy about the best ways to attack the problem. Breslin has a lot of experience on the water and sanitation front, and he applauded the current good will that the sector enjoys and the efforts to push legislation, increase finance, and get celebrities, musicians, schoolchildren, and volunteers involved. However, he deplores the focus on short-term results, sending people overseas for quick fixes, and the lack of attention to the real, long-term, and sustainable results. The actual situation, according to Breslin, is that emerging data show that about 50,000 rural water points are broken in Africa, that $215 million to $360 million has been wasted because of poor implementation, and that the number would be far higher if all donors were counted. However, this data is not getting publicity because perceptions of failure could threaten the "cause."

He thinks we have to get away from welfare and charity to focus on development, with water and sanitation interventions that truly assess the financial details that will influence long-term success. He has observed that the current practice of NGOs is to dodge the hard work by thinking incorrectly that communities suffer from cashlessness, not just water poverty. He thinks that charitable approaches lead to poor project implementation because paying 100 percent of the costs establishes dependency. Better philanthropy would draw from business principles and ask hard questions about how sustainability will occur.

Rotary International is another business-related association with an outreach program. It currently has a focus on water, and I was a member of a committee that funded several water projects in Latin America and Asia. We would typically work with a local Rotary Club in the receiving country, which would be responsible for accountability on the local scene.

Private philanthropy involves organization such as the Bill and Melinda Gates Foundation, the Ford Foundation, and a number of smaller NGOs such as Lifewater International, a Christian organization founded by William A. Ashe in the 1970s. The Ashe family used outings into Mexico to help orphanages, camps, and churches install new water systems, and its water-pump business enabled them to expand their work. The NGO was established in 1977, and its work has grown.

The complexity of safe water as a business was demonstrated by a project undertaken by graduate business students at Colorado State University who organized a project titled Running Water International for the university's Global, Social, and Sustainable Enterprise Program. They were addressing the problem of poor drinking-water quality in developing countries and introduced a household water filter that was appropriate for conditions in Kenya. On the surface it appeared that the market was right. There was an urgent need, a local workforce, and materials were available, and they had a good business plan. They did well and launched a promising enterprise. But as explained to me by their leader, Becky Fedak, their experience showed the mixed social-business aspects of water. They had to deal with the fact that competitors included nonprofits who gave the products away and other sociopolitical issues such as relationships with a state-owned water-supply company. These challenges required that their business plan be crafted to avoid traps created by social and political conditions.

TOWARD THE FUTURE

Given its close connection with poverty, the safe-water and sanitation issue is about conditions for people living on the bottom rungs of the economic ladder. While many people in developing countries live in what is defined as poverty, their conditions are not nearly as dire as those of the nearly 1 billion people in Asia, Africa, and Latin America who lack access to safe drinking water or the 2.5 billion who lack access to safe sanitation.

Safe water and sanitation is the ultimate water business because it challenges our economic and social system to use private (and public) business to meet these compelling human needs. For the most part, the combination of public and private sector efforts are meeting needs in the United States and other developed countries, but with the dire global statistics it is easy to see that much more is needed.

Perhaps the same phenomenon that is occurring with telecommunications will emerge for water and sanitation. People in developing countries had no hope that they could eventually be given secure housing and landline telephones. In most cases, the land lines could not be built. But with cell phones they have bypassed the land-line technology, and now billions of people are in touch with this portable technology.

POU water systems have some of the same possibilities, where even if people lack secure housing with premise plumbing systems they may have access to a safe community source, or even their own well protected by a POU treatment system. These do not have to be expensive, but they must be operated and maintained well. By the same token, sanitation can be portable, but the systems must be designed well, as well as operated and maintained. So, at the end of the day it is not all about cost but much of it is about management and accountability, which have, after all, business implications as much as products and services do.

CHAPTER 23

Water Investments, Careers, and Business Opportunities

The preceding chapters have explored the corners and mainstream of the water industry. They presented a model of it, explained details of its sectors, and covered its business aspects ranging from finance to purchases of products and services to its workforce. This final chapter is a capstone that explains water industry investments, business opportunities, and careers. It addresses three realities of water as a business. First, although the need for water will only become more compelling, you have to look hard for investment opportunities in its industry because the business is so diverse. However, this very diversity offers opportunities to create many kinds of businesses. Finally, it may be that the most attractive part of the water business is in the career opportunities that it offers. When students ask about careers, I often say that the water business is a place where you can "do well by doing good." By this, I mean that you can have a satisfying career while doing work that meets human needs at the same time that it protects the environment. If we need any example, you can look at William Ashe, who built off of a successful pump business to start Lifewater International (see Chapter 22).

WATER-INDUSTRY INVESTMENTS

Although it is a $200 billion-plus industry, the full water business has only a few focused high-profile stocks to buy. These tend to be the handful of large, listed private water companies. Also, suppliers to the water industry tend to work in multiple industries and it is hard to find those to invest in where you can be sure that rising demand for water will lead to investment growth. Bonds are another matter and can be attractive investments. Many tax-exempt bonds are secured with reliable revenues from public water enterprises, although these are not without some risks.

Water Companies

The core business model of water-supply utilities is to provide water supply (and sometimes also wastewater) services as regulated monopolies. Most large water-supply utilities are government owned, such as the Chicago Department of Water Management, the Los Angeles Department of Water & Power, and the Massachusetts Water Resources Authority. The investment opportunities offered by the publicly owned organizations are restricted to municipal bonds, but they also purchase large quantities of products and services.

Privately owned water companies range from public companies listed on stock exchanges (investor-owned water utilities) to small businesses serving only a few water taps. Only the privately owned utilities are regulated in the United States by state public utility commissions. Publicly owned utilities are mostly self-regulated for business performance, subjected only to the political systems in which they operate. Of course, all utilities are regulated for health, safety, and environment by federal and state regulations.

Private water companies mostly operate the same way as publicly owned utilities, but they offer ownership possibilities as well, either through direct ownership or the purchase of shares, as in the case of the larger listed utilities. Another difference is that the officers of some private water companies are apt to be paid much more in compensation than those of publicly owned utilities.

The proportion of U.S. water services provided by private water companies has remained close to 15 percent for over 50 years (measured by customers served or volume of water handled). Investor-owned water-supply utilities accounted for about 14 percent of water revenues and about 11 percent of water-system assets in 1995. Investor ownership of wastewater utilities is less than water-supply utilities because of several reasons, including federal subsidies of wastewater treatment plants.

In the United States, the privately owned water companies are represented by the National Association of Water Companies, founded in 1895, with about 340 members. Their press releases offer a good way to keep up with trends affecting the private water companies.

Examples of major U.S. privately owned water companies that are listed on stock exchanges were given in Chapter 16.

Municipal Water Bonds

The tax-exempt municipal bond market is $2.7 trillion of the $33 trillion total bond market, as of 2009 (Grigg, 2010). Of this, a significant percentage is for water and wastewater issues. Water-supply and wastewater utilities are especially capital intensive and require most of their funding for long-lived assets such as buried pipelines. Therefore, municipal bonds are a good avenue to raise capital for utilities that qualify for them. A typical issue would be to build water-supply, treatment, or distribution facilities or the same on the wastewater side.

Revenue bonds are the most common type of bond issued by water and sewer agencies, but general obligation bonds are also used on occasion. Revenue bonds are repaid from revenues of an enterprise, so the relatively stable user fees for water and wastewater are an ideal revenue source.

Although municipal bonds would seem like safe investments, risk of default is present. For example, the sewer bonds of Jefferson County, Alabama, were given "junk" status in 2008 and the county faced bankruptcy in 2009. Some analysts think that water bond credit ratings do not reflect the full and growing risks of water shortages and legal battles over water supplies. No regulatory agency has full oversight over all of the municipal bond industry. Disclosure requirements of corporate bonds do not apply to municipal bonds, and the Government Accounting Standards Board's guidelines lack enforcement power (Levitt, 2009).

Municipal bond issues can reflect water-scarcity risk. The risk is that bonds may drop in value when threats to water supplies become apparent and it might be more expensive to raise money. Allegations are that rating agencies are not considering differences between secure sources and insecure water sources with cities such as Los Angeles and Atlanta cited as facing the greatest risks. A report by Ceres and Water Asset Management relied on a measure of risk by a unit of PricewaterhouseCoopers. The major bond rating agencies disputed the conclusion. They insisted that cost and availability of water was an important element in their analysis. The Los Angeles Department of Water and Power called the study's conclusions "uninformed and miscalculated" (Barringer and Henriques, 2010).

Water Funds

It is a challenge to assemble a broad-based water fund because, for the same reason that not many water stocks are available, water-investment indices and funds are difficult to organize. The industry's activity is widely dispersed among the subsectors and water is mostly a local business. So, the difficulty in creating baskets of stocks that focus only on the water industry lead to water portfolios in funds that are relatively small because companies they might hold, such as General Electric Co. or ITT Corporation, are engaged in many other businesses and water is a minor part of their business activity. Still, some water funds are available.

For example, PowerShares Global Water Portfolio (PIO) and First Trust ISE Water Index Fund (FIW) had major holdings in Nalco Holding Company, Kemira Oyj, Kurita Water Industries Ltd., and Hyflux Ltd. (water treatment, chemicals, processes); Millipore Corporation (bioscience and pharmaceutical); Flowserve Corporation (flow control equipment); Roper Industries, Inc. (energy systems and controls); Aqua America, Inc. (water utility); Pentair, Inc., ITT Corporation, Crane Company, and Idex Corporation (manufacturing); Veolia Environnement ADR and Suez Environnement Company (environmental services); Arcadis NV (consulting services); and Valmont Industries, Inc. (irrigation and other equipment) (Grigg, 2010). This mixture illustrates the diversity of utility-supplier components of the water industry.

Water-Industry Indices

Several indexing companies track the water industry. For example, Dow Jones Brookfield (2009) offers a family of infrastructure indices organized by sector, and water is one of the sectors. Also, water infrastructure is a subset of the Global Infrastructure index, but it includes only utilities: United Utilities Group plc; Severn Trent plc; Aqua America, Inc.; Pennon Group, plc; Northumbrian Water, plc; Companhia de Saneamento Basico do Estado de Sao Paulo; American Water Works Co.; California Water Services Co.; and American States Water Company. The Macquarie Global Infrastructure Index Series (MGII), managed by FTSE (2009), also includes a sector for gas and water utilities.

Private Equity

Private equity can invest in the water industry, just as it can in other businesses. For example, American Standard was purchased by an investment banker in 1998 (see Chapter 19). In the utility arena, the Saur Group, which began as one of France's three main water companies, is now held in private equity ownership (see Chapter 16). The AXA private equity (2009) group purchased a share of Saur in 2007 when the PAI investment fund resold it to them, the Séché Environnement industrial group, and the Caisse des dépôts et consignations. The three partners created a holding group to manage this investment, and AXA Private Equity has a 20 percent equity stake in the partnership.

WATER-INDUSTRY BUSINESS OPPORTUNITIES

Business opportunities in the water industry will generally track the services and products explained in Chapters 18 and 19. The flow of funds in the water industry that was explained in Chapter 2 showed a conceptual diagram to explain the operation of the industry, and anywhere the funds flow might offer a business opportunity, other than the internal flows to pay salaries and internal expenses within utilities. The source of funds was from households and businesses in the form of fees, purchases, or tax payments. Most of these flow through the water supply, wastewater, and stormwater utilities, which are the primary utility-based water services. Industrial and energy utility water systems also account for large parts of the fund flows. The government sector is also significant and it includes environmental protection, regulatory controls, large-scale flood control, and security, some of which can be outsourced.

BUSINESS DRIVERS

As Chapter 10 explained, water looks like a business sector with continual growth and profit opportunities ahead. Population growth, economic growth, and environmentalism will place pressures on water systems and these factors can be positive for water businesses. However, other attributes of the water business, such as heavy politics and regulation, can dampen our enthusiasm. While it is capital intensive, the water industry requires infrastructure that is mostly long-lasting, and annual capital investments for renewal can be small and even zero during times of funding cutbacks.

For example, several million miles of buried water supply and wastewater pipes in the United States have a replacement value in excess of $500 billion, but the replacement rate is very slow due to the long service lives. In the case of water-supply mains, the replacement rate averages about once in 200 years, so an asset inventory that might be on the order of $400 billion generates construction activity of only a few billion dollars each year for renewal. As a result of this slow renewal rate for buried pipes, the country experiences many failures of buried pipes each year.

This is one example of a general situation explained by Cui and Davis (2008), who wrote, "Water may be the world's most critical commodity. But it has been a tough market for many investors to tap profitably lately." They traced a wave of water investment vehicles that sought to capitalize on rising need for clean water, but showed how water-oriented stocks are exposed to economic problems such as the housing decline. They explained how water is different from other commodities because it can be traded only in regional markets. Although the sector is large, they explained that investors were forced into a small set of opportunities.

TYPES OF BUSINESSES

The main business opportunities of the water industry are derived from the requirement that water handlers purchase goods and services from the support sector. This leads to the diverse group of product and service suppliers, which are explained in Chapters 18 and 19.

Many of the water-industry equipment suppliers have gained their market share through decades of customer engagement and service. Think of pipe, meters, valves, and other expensive capital equipment and you can find examples such as were cited in Chapter 19. New entrants to the equipment-supply business would normally either purchase an existing line or enter through a niche formed by a new technology. That is why we see more new entrants in the software and other technology sectors, as opposed to the older lineups of basic infrastructure components.

Water-industry service businesses can be formed by spinning off knowledgeable staff from utilities or by consultants who see an opportunity to get started with a contract in a field such as leak location, asset management, or corrosion control. These amount to unbundling and outsourcing of work that could be done internally by utilities.

Perhaps the easiest type of firm to start is to offer professional services, although staying in business can be a challenge. A professional services firm can be started with very little capital, but it would be very sensitive to cash flow to stay in business.

Finally, buying a water utility might sound attractive, but it can be a slippery slope for players other than the highly experienced private water utilities that already have a portfolio of acquisitions. In the case of private equity, it could obtain the expertise and advice needed to acquire utilities, of course.

CAREERS IN THE WATER BUSINESS

For most people interested in the water industry, finding a job is probably the place to start. While it is not easy to track jobs in such a diverse industry, several hundred thousand jobs are available in more than 100,000 water-management organizations. Also, many good jobs are available in the supplier and regulator sides of the business.

The water industry employs around 1 million workers drawn from most of the occupations tracked by the U.S. Bureau of Labor Statistics (2010). The full employment base of the United States is 130 million jobs (as of 2009, down from a peak of 137 million in 2007), which are distributed among numerous industries and occupations. Of these jobs,

108 million are in the private sector, of which only 19 million are goods-producing (mostly manufacturing and construction). Most water-industry jobs are among the 112 million service-producing jobs, such as those in professional service firms and government, for example.

Water-industry jobs can be found in water and wastewater utilities, stormwater and flood control organizations, irrigation agencies, hydropower producers, navigation, recreation, and environmental management. The water industry's large support sector can be considered as a shadow workforce and account for many water-industry jobs working hand-in-hand with service providers in tasks such as consulting, construction, and contract services. Regulatory jobs are mostly with the federal and state governments. Planning offers fewer jobs, but they are interesting and important because many people share water resources.

Work in the water industry offers many challenging and rewarding opportunities. Many engineers, operators, technicians, scientists, and administrative workers work to build, operate, and renew water systems. Managers in the industry make decisions about water control and the business processes to operate their programs. Many of these jobs pay well and offer considerable satisfaction and growth potential.

Mobility is good in the water industry, both for promotion and lateral moves. A person training in one part of it can find opportunities in other parts. Managing a city water system would qualify you to manage a larger, integrated water and wastewater system. Your training as a construction supervisor for a federal water project might qualify you to be a project manager in a city water utility.

During a downturn, it might seem difficult to see the promise of careers in any industry, but the water industry has been wringing its hands over a workforce crisis. The problem was explained in Chapter 15 and, although there is a financial crunch currently, the workforce issue looks like a long-term one.

Perhaps the best way to explain jobs in the water industry is by examples:

Managers of water agencies and utilities. Managers in the water industry have responsibility for all operations of their organizations. Many utility managers started as engineers, but other career routes to management are available. These managers interact extensively with the public and elected officials.

Civil and environmental engineers. Civil engineers build and manage water-management facilities and processes. The BLS (2010) estimated in 2008 that the nation had 278,000 civil engineers, and around half work on water issues in one way or another. In addition, another 54,000 environmental engineers do similar work, with a focus on designing and evaluating treatment processes and issues relating to water quality. For 2011, *U.S. News & World Report* (2010) identified civil engineering as one of the best careers with strong growth forecast for the next decade. This was based on Labor Department predictions of 68,000 new jobs in 10 years due to infrastructure repair and expansion of communities and development of new ones. Their current median earnings are $76,590 (as of 2009), and the top 10 percent earned more than $118,000.

Water-resource scientists and managers. For the person who likes to work outside, being a water resource scientist or manager might be the ticket. Many water organizations obtain and manage their own water resources, a task that involves watershed management, groundwater systems, water conservation programs, or cooperative work with others in sharing river or reservoir water. Backgrounds in engineering, science, or hydrology can be helpful for these jobs.

Managers of technical systems and water-system operators. The water industry has many technical systems to manage. One manager might oversee the operation of treatment plants. Another might operate pipeline systems, and another might be responsible for operation of dams on a river system. Operators require training in plant systems and can enter the field from different backgrounds. These jobs range in responsibility from that of the manager of technical systems in a metropolitan area to the operator of a small system serving only a few hundred people.

Construction managers. Managing the infrastructure of the water industry requires a well-trained workforce of construction specialists and administrators. Not only must new systems be built, systems are aging and require renewal, which can be more complex than building new systems.

Consultants. Many professional jobs supported by the water industry are in consulting firms. These firms require workers with similar skills as utility personnel. Consultants work on planning, design, and management studies. A consultant can work for engineering firms or for management consulting firms.

Scientists. Scientists from the natural and life sciences work for the water industry in research, field studies, and laboratory analysis. Ecologists are needed to study water habitat.

Electrical, mechanical, and chemical engineers. Electrical and mechanical engineers work on control processes, instrumentation, and process engineering. Their work would be similar to the same tasks in manufacturing plants or in other utility sectors. Chemical engineers would focus on treatment operations, much the same as environmental engineers.

Information technology specialists. The complexity of databases and control systems requires specialists in information technology. Today's SCADA systems and control systems for all water facilities, as well as the computing networks for water agencies, create many needs for IT workers.

Landscape and water conservation specialists. Water conservation requires specialists in landscape, irrigation, and water-use studies. With rising demand for water set to collide with environmental awareness, water conservation will be an important field for the future.

Public information and education specialists. The water industry involves the public in many of its operations and requires the organization of public meetings, brochures and news releases, and work to educate the public about water. Backgrounds in journalism, education, communications, and related fields are helpful for these positions.

Managers of financial, administrative, and legal affairs. Water organizations face complex issues of public finance, labor and personnel rules, and compliance with regulatory requirements. The large investments in infrastructure require specialists in contracts, and the workforce requires personnel officers. These tasks involve business administration, human resources fields, or law.

The water industry's workforce of engineers, financial managers, administrators, lawyers, and support workers is similar to the workforces in related utility fields such as electric power, energy, and telecommunications. Also, the water industry involves strong components of health and environment. As in these other fields, the right academic background or training is an important choice to work in the water industry.

You can prepare for work in the water industry through academic fields or vocational paths. When advising students on career options, I often explain that upward mobility in an industry depends on getting your foot in the door in a lower-level job and then proving yourself by good work and learning. Following that advice, good academic fields to prepare for water-industry work are those where most jobs are, such as civil, environmental, and other engineering fields. Another field with many jobs is environmental or public health, which is normally offered in a different academic department than engineering. While they lead to fewer jobs, technical fields such as agriculture and agricultural engineering, biology and fisheries, and chemistry offer good possibilities. Administrative fields such as law, natural resource management, and policy sciences can also lead to management roles in the water industry. Vocational paths to good water-industry jobs might become available for people with military or industry training, operator licenses, and construction management.

Information about jobs in the water industry is widely available. In addition to universities and community colleges, sources include associations such as the American Consulting Engineers Council, American Public Works Association, American Society of Civil Engineers, American Water Resources Association, American Water Works Association and Water Environment Federation. Federal agencies offering career advice (and jobs) include the Army Corps of Engineers, Bureau of Reclamation, Environmental Protection Agency, Natural Resources Conservation Service, Fish and Wildlife Service, and Geological Survey. Water and wastewater agencies at the local level also offer jobs and career advice.

WATER BUSINESS CLUSTERS

A number of water business clusters are emerging around the world. A business cluster is a network of businesses, suppliers, and institutions that work in a related field and can benefit by cooperating with each other. The concept is that innovation occurs in networks, and by cooperating with others who have similar interests new possibilities emerge for all. The business cluster concept comes in varied forms. One form is the "innovation cluster," which is promoted by the Obama administration. Secretary of Labor Gary Locke stated, "encouraging the growth of innovative clusters is a national priority . . . creating ecosystems where universities, venture capital, entrepreneurs, and skilled workers are all amplifying each others' talents" (American Society for Engineering Education, 2010).

One version of the innovation cluster is the research park, such as Research Triangle Park in North Carolina, which was founded in 1959. Its success has led to imitations and there are about 150 university-based research parks around the country now. These types of business clusters cut across many fields and are focused on the innovations themselves. A business cluster for water focuses on one industry, similar to the business cluster we have in northern Colorado that focuses on creating clean energy jobs in the region. Our region is working to organize a similar cluster focused on innovations in water management. A number of other clusters around the world also focus on water.

Reports from promoters of water clusters cite a global water-infrastructure business at $425 billion per year and climbing. This figure is related to the U.S. estimate I presented in Chapter 12 of around $240 billion per year and to reflect all revenues, not just expenditures on equipment and services. Since most people consider the water industry to be only the utilities, the relevant number from Chapter 12 would be $80 billion for U.S. water and wastewater expenditures. As the U.S. population is 5 percent of the world's population but more like one-quarter of the population of highly developed areas, it suggests a world water industry in the same range as the global estimate of $425 billion. The billions who live in poverty require water services, but the expenditures would be low. The citations of such a large world water industry would seem to exaggerate the market for services and equipment because a large share of those funds is spent on labor.

Some water-business clusters are built around the awarding of a water prize and the hosting of a water conference. This is the case of the Singapore water promotional activities, which include the Lee Kuan Yew Water Prize. It tends to focus attention on the organizers as people with a future in the water business, whether on the basis of public or private activities. Singapore had 14,000 attendees at its International Water Week trade show in 2010. Singapore has $50 million a year in government subsidies and a reputation for innovation and competitiveness. Its government expects the water sector to contribute $1.2 billion to its economy by 2015 and create 11,000 jobs. It is home to more than 50 water-engineering companies, including General Electric Co., Siemens AG, and Black & Veatch Corp. of the United States; Delft Hydraulics of the Netherlands; and Nitto Denko of Japan. It has national companies, such as Hyflux Ltd. and Keppel Corporation. Singapore also has two research universities and 12 research institutes dedicated to water engineering. Its strategic location is in Asia, which has almost three billion people.

Israel has a focus on water-business development with an emphasis on export of water technologies. The name is Novel Efficient Water Technologies (Israel NEWTech), which is part of the National Water Technology Program at the Ministry of Industry. The focus is on treatment of wastewater for reuse, advanced desalination, water security, and water management (Ritch, 2010).

In Holland, the Wetsus cluster focuses on water-treatment technology. It is located in Leeuwarden in the province of Friesland, where there are a number of water companies. It includes technology companies, water boards, water companies, end users, consulting engineers, financial institutes, and universities. This "water-hub" initiative is supported by the Ministry of Economic Affairs, which designated Leeuwarden as the national water technology focal point (Wetsus, 2010).

The province of Ontario has announced a "clean-water technology capital" to focus on water-sector growth projections based on energy and chemical use in water systems, extracting energy or materials value from wastewater, water reuse, and water infrastructure renewal (Lorinc, 2010). One of its visible participants is XPV Capital of Toronto, a venture-capital firm that invests exclusively in the water sector.

Milwaukee has a legacy of a machine-shop economy and can manufacture stainless steel water-treatment systems for water technology companies, such as General Electric Co. and Siemens AG. Milwaukee formed the Water Council and lined up civic and political support and even added funding for water research to match National Science Foundation grants for water research projects at the University of Wisconsin-Milwaukee and Marquette University. In 2010, Milwaukee hosted its fourth annual Water Summit, which had a theme of "Blue Footprint," which the Water Council has trademarked. Milwaukee seeks to attract the engineering and manufacturing operations of water-related companies and to encourage universities to develop technologies to clean, conserve, and re-use water. UWM has a harbor campus, which is home to the Great Lakes WATER Institute. The university has plans for a new campus for its School of Freshwater Sciences and a business incubation park. Marquette has launched a water-law curriculum.

The United Nations designated Milwaukee as one of 14 Global Compact cities and the only one devoted to water research. Milwaukee has also made an application to the state public service commission to allow reduced water rates for new industries so they can use their high water capacity from Lake Michigan as an economic development tool (Barrett, 2010b).

Another water prize is the Stockholm Water Prize, which is conferred during a week of activities annually and is well known among the water academic community. Dubai also is seeking to organize a water cluster. Our local community has organized one, called the Colorado Water Innovation Cluster, and we had our inaugural reception in November 2010. Northern Colorado is home to a large group of innovative water businesses, and the idea of a business cluster seems to be catching on.

ASSOCIATIONS

Water-industry associations have been mentioned throughout the book, and they are a great way to network and learn about the water business. In fact, given the public-private and scattered nature of the water industry, it seems to me that associations take on more important roles there than in other parts of the economy. Figure 23.1 illustrates their pivotal role in coordinating among the support sector, which supports the water providers, who are regulated and governed to control their activities.

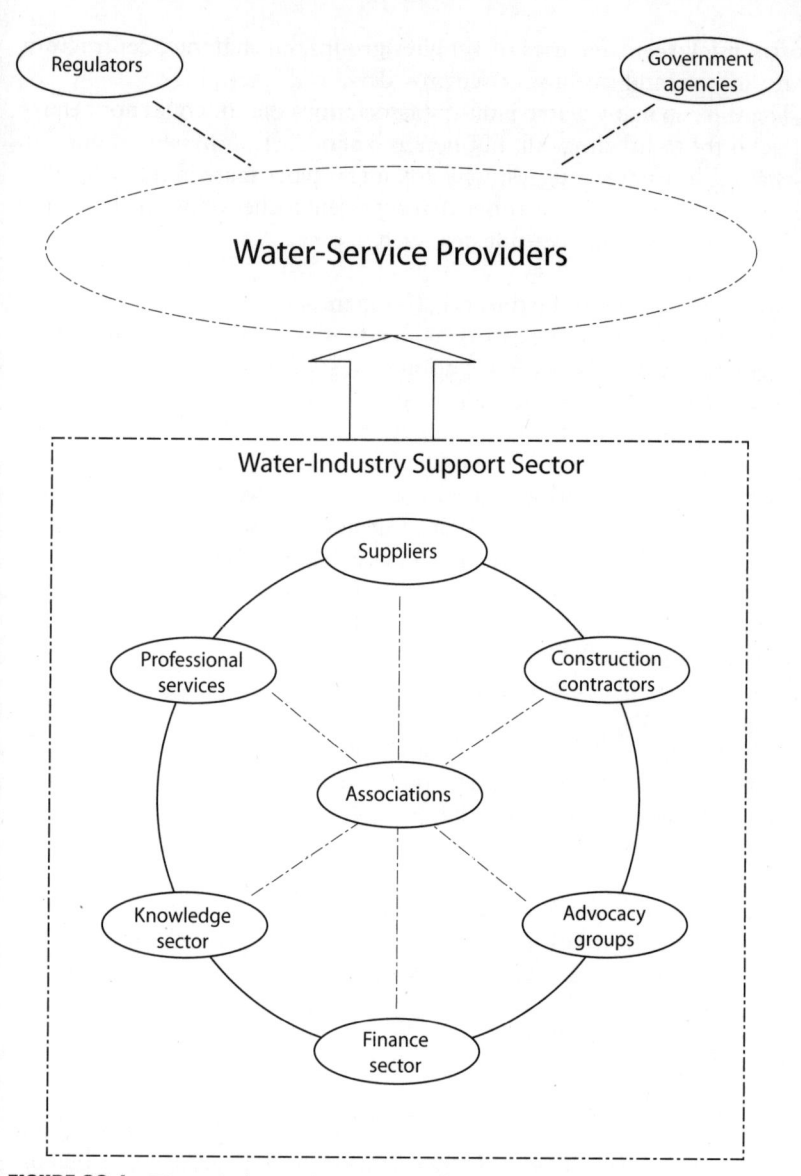

FIGURE 23.1 Water-industry association roles

Much of the business activity of the water industry is done through the larger professional associations, such as AWWA and WEF. These serve also as umbrella groups for small niches of manufacturers and distributors who need a place to plug in. Other business associations of interest to the water industry track the categories of supplier groups, consultants, contractors, private utilities, and various service providers.

There are so many water-industry associations that it would not be productive to try to list them all, but here is a short list of influential ones. In most cases, their names suggest why you might participate in them. The list does not include trade associations that represent niches of products, even if a niche represents a massive industry, such as pipe:

- American Council of Engineering Companies.
- American Pipeline Contractors Association.
- American Public Works Association.
- American Society of Civil Engineers.
- American Society of Plumbing Engineers.
- American Water Resources Association.
- American Water Works Association.
- Association of Metropolitan Water Agencies.
- Association of State and Interstate Water Pollution Control Administrators.
- Association of State Dam Safety Officials.
- Association of State Drinking Water Officials.
- Association of State Flood Plain Managers.
- International Water Association.
- Irrigation Association.
- National Association of Clean Water Agencies.
- National Association of Water Companies.
- National Groundwater Association.
- National Institutes for Water Resources.
- National Rural Water Association.
- National Utility Contractors Association.
- United States Society on Dams.
- U.S. Committee on Irrigation and Drainage.
- Water and Wastewater Equipment Manufacturer's Association.
- Water Environment Federation.
- Water Quality Association.

Some international organizations are professional associations, and some are quasi-governmental. United Nations organizations can be considered as "government," but in a different sense than U.S. agencies. A number of international organizations provide substantial information and networking opportunities, but they focus more on science and political coordination than they do on business.

Acronyms

7Q10	Seven-day ten-year low flow
AAAS	American Association for the Advancement of Science
AACLP	All-American Canal Lining Project
AAEE	American Academy of Environmental Engineers
AASC	American Association of State Climatologists
AAWRE	American Academy of Water Resources Engineers
ABA	American Bar Association
ABC	Association of Boards of Certification
ACC	American Chemistry Council
ACE	Annual Conference and Exposition
ACEC	American Council of Engineering Companies
ACF	Apalachicola-Chattahoochee-Flint
ACPA	American Concrete Pipe Association
ACPPA	American Concrete Pressure Pipe Association
ACWD	Association of California Water Districts
ADB	Asian Development Bank
AEHS	Association for Environmental Health and Sciences
AEM	Association of Equipment Manufacturers
AF	Acre-feet
AFS	American Fisheries Society
AGC	Associated General Contractors of America
AGWA	Association of Ground Water Agencies
AICHE	American Institute of Chemical Engineers
AIDIS	U.S.A. Chapter of the Inter-American Assn of Sanitary & Environmental Engineering
AIH	American Institute of Hydrology
AIMMPE	American Institute of Mining, Metallurgical, and Petroleum Engineering
AIPG	American Institute of Professional Geologists
AISI	American Iron and Steel Institute
AMCF	Association of Management Consulting Firms

AMI   Advanced metering infrastructure
AMWA   Association of Metropolitan Water Agencies
APA   Administrative Procedures Act
APA   American Planning Association
APCA   American Pipeline Contractors Association
APHA   American Public Health Association
APWA   American Public Works Association
ASCE   American Society of Civil Engineers
ASDSO   Association of State Dam Safety Officials
ASDWA   Association of State Drinking Water Administrators
ASDWO   Association of State Drinking Water Officials
ASFPM   Association of State Flood Plain Managers
ASIWPCA   Association of State and Interstate Water Pollution
             Control Administrators
ASLA   American Society of Landscape Architects
ASME   American Society of Mechanical Engineers
ASPA   American Society for Public Administration
ASPE   American Society of Plumbing Engineers
ASTM   American Society for Testing and Materials
AWBD   Association of Water Board Directors—Texas
AWRA   American Water Resources Association
AWT   Association of Water Technologies
AWT   Association of California Water Agencies
AWWA   American Water Works Association
AWWARF   AWWA Research Foundation (now WaterRF)
BCA   Benefit-cost analysis
BGD   Billion gallons per day
BLS   U.S. Bureau of Labor Statistics
BTWF   Big Thompson Water Forum
CAFOs   Concentrated animal feeding operations
CAFR   Comprehensive annual financial report
CBA   Colorado Bar Association, Water Law Section
CBO   Congressional Budget Office
CBT   Colorado Big Thomson project
CCR   Consumer Confidence Report
CDC   Centers for Disease Control and Prevention
CEQ   Council on Environmental Quality
CFR   Code of Federal Regulations
CMAA   Construction Management Association of America
COG   Councils of government
CRWUA   Colorado River Water Users Association
CSO   Combined sewer overflow

CSQA	California Stormwater Quality Association
CWA	California Water Association
CWA	Clean Water Act
CWC	Colorado Water Congress
CWNS	Clean Watersheds Needs Survey
CWS	Community water system
CWSRF	Clean Water State Revolving Fund
CWSS	Community Water Systems Study
CWWA	Colorado White Water Association
DBP	Disinfection byproduct
DEP	New York City Department of Environmental Protection
DIPRA	Ductile Iron Pipe Research Association
DNR	Departments of natural resources
DOE	Department of Environment
DWM	Chicago Department of Water Management
DWR	California Department of Water Resources
DWSRF	Drinking Water State Revolving Fund
DWU	Dallas Water Utilities
EDF	Électricité de France
EIS	Environmental Impact Statement
EPA	Environmental Protection Agency
EPRI	Electric Power Research Institute
EQ	Environmental quality
ESA	Endangered Species Act
EU	European Union
EWRI	Environment and Water Resources Institute
FAO	Food and Agriculture Organization
FDA	Food and Drug Administration
FEMA	Federal Emergency Management Agency
FERC	Federal Energy Regulatory Commission
FIRM	Flood insurance rate maps
FPA	Federal Power Act
FWS	Fish and Wildlife Service
GAO	Government Accountability Office
GASB	Government Accounting Standards Board
GDP	Gross domestic product
GLAAS	Global Annual Assessment of Sanitation and Drinking-Water
GO	General obligation
gpcd	Gallons per capita per day
HAZUS	Flood loss estimation software
IA	Irrigation Association
IBT	Interbasin transfer

ICMA	International City and County Management Association
ICR	Industrial cost recovery
IFIM	Instream Flow Incremental Methodology
IHS	Indian Health Service
IID	Imperial Irrigation District
IRP	Integrated resource planning
ISF	Instream flows
IWRM	Integrated Water Resources Management
LACSD	Los Angeles County Sanitary District
LADWP	Los Angeles Department of Water & Power
LCR	Lead and Copper Rule
LID	Low-impact development
MCDA	Multicriteria decision analysis
MCL	Maximum contaminant level
MCM	Million cubic meters
MGD	Million gallons per day
MS4	Municipal separate storm sewer systems
MWD	Metropolitan Water District of Southern California
MWRA	Massachusetts Water Resources Authority
MWRD	Metropolitan Water Reclamation District of Greater Chicago
NACO	National Association of Counties
NACWA	National Association of Clean Water Agencies
NAFSMA	National Association of Flood & Stormwater Management Agencies
NAICS	North American Industrial Classification System
NARUC	National Association for Regulatory Utility Commissioners
NATO	North Atlantic Treaty Organization
NAWC	National Association of Water Companies
NCWS	Noncommunity Water Systems
NED	National Economic Development
NEPA	National Environmental Policy Act
NFIP	National Flood Insurance Program
NGO	Nongovernmental organization
NLUD	National Land Use Database
NMFS	National Marine Fisheries Service
NOAA	National Oceanic and Atmospheric Administration
NPDES	National Pollutant Discharge Elimination System
NPDWR	National Primary Drinking Water Regulations
NPS	Nonpoint sources
NRRI	National Regulatory Research Institute
O&M	Operation and maintenance
OCSD	Orange County Sanitary District

Ofwat	Office of Water
OMB	Office of Management and Budget
P&G	Principles and Guidelines
P&S	Principles and Standards
PCB	Polychlorinated biphenol
PHABSIM	Physical Habitat Simulation
PIF	Plant investment fees
PILOT	Payment-in-lieu-of-taxes
POE	Point-of-entry
POTW	Publicly owned treatment works
POU	Point of use
PUC	Public utility commission
PVO	Private volunteer organization
PW&E	Houston Public Works and Engineering Department
RBC	River basin commission
RD	Regional development
SCADA	Supervisory control and data acquisition
SDCWA	San Diego County Water Authority
SDWA	Safe Drinking Water Act
SEMAPA	Bolivian State Water Agency
SFPUC	San Francisco Public Utilities Commission
SFWMD	South Florida Water Management District
SIA	Social impact assessment
SIFMA	Securities Industry and Financial Markets Association
SWB	Social well-being
TBL	Triple bottom line
THM	Trihalomethanes
TMDL	Total maximum daily load
TVA	Tennessee Valley Authority
TWM	Total Water Management
UCOWR	Universities Council on Water Resources
UDFCD	Urban drainage and flood control district
UIC	Underground injection control
UN	United Nations
UNDP	UN Development Programme
UNESCO	United Nations Education, Science, and Cultural Organization
USAID	U.S. Agency for International Development
USBEA	U.S. Bureau of Economic Affairs
USCID	U.S. Committee on Irrigation and Drainage
USDA	U.S. Department of Agriculture
USDI	U.S. Department of the Interior
USDOE	U.S. Department of Energy

USEIA	U.S. Energy Information Agency
WASH	Water and Sanitation for Health
WaterRF	Water Research Foundation
WC&P	*Water Conditioning & Purification* magazine
WEF	Water Environment Federation
WERF	Water Environment Research Foundation
WFD	Water Framework Directive
WHO	World Health Organization
WQ 2000	Water Quality 2000
WQA	Water Quality Association
WRDA	Water Resources Development Act
WRPA	Water Resources Planning Act
WRRI	Water resources research institutes
WSD	Miami-Dade Water & Sewer Department
WWAP	World Water Assessment Programme
WWEMA	Water and Wastewater Equipment Manufacturers Association
WWTP	Wastewater treatment plant

References

American Council of Engineering Companies. 2010. About ACEC. www.acec.org. November 16, 2010.

American National Standards Institute. 2010. ANSI: Historical overview. www .ansi.org/about_ansi/introduction/history.aspx?menuid=1. December 14, 2010.

American Society for Engineering Education. 2010. Catalyst. www.prism-magazine .org/sept10/feature_01.cfm. December 11, 2010.

American Society for Training and Development. 2010. About ASTD. www.astd .org. December 15, 2010.

American Society of Civil Engineers. 2010. 2009 Report Card for America's Infrastructure. Dams. www.infrastructurereportcard.org/fact-sheet/dams. March 20, 2010.

American Water Works Association. 1996. Water://Stats: The Water Utility Database. Denver.

American Water Works Association. 2000. Principles of Water Rates, Fees, and Charges, Manual M1, EDN Fifth Ed. Denver.

American Water Works Association. 2000. "Walkerton Coroner's Office Investigating Deaths." *Mainstream*. 44(7) 1,3.

American Water Works Association. 2010. IWA/AWWA Water Audit Method. www.awwa.org/Resources/WaterLossControl.cfm?ItemNumber=48055. March 7, 2010.

American Water Works Association. 2010. QualServe. www.awwa.org/Science/ qualserve/. December 15, 2010.

American Water Works Association. 2010b. Sourcebook Online. http://sourcebook .awwa.org. December 15, 2010.

American Water. 2009. February 26. http://online.wsj.com. March 8, 2009.

American Water. 2009. Investor Relations: Financial Statements. www.amwater .com. July 13, 2009.

AMSA. 2002. AMSA 2002 Financial Survey: A National Survey of Municipal Wastewater Management Financing and Trends. Washington, DC.

Anglian Water. 2010. About Us. www.anglianwater.co.uk/about-us/who-we-are/. October 17, 2010.

Asian Development Bank. 2006. ADB's Dams and Development E-paper: A Reservoir of Knowledge on Dams. www.adb.org/water/articles/dams.asp. August. September 6, 2010.

Association of California Water Agencies. Coping with Future Water Shortages: Lessons from California's Drought, Sacramento.

Association of State Dam Safety Officials. 2009. Investment in Infrastructure: Focus on Dams. ASDSO Press Release January 29, 2009. www.damsafety.org. March 21, 2010.

Association of State Dam Safety Officials. 2010. Dam Safety 101. www.damsafety .org. November 25, 2010.

Association of State Dam Safety Officials. 2010a About ASDSO. www.damsafety .org. August 12, 2010.

AXA Private Equity. 2009. Infrastructure Investment: SAUR. www.axaprivateequity .com. June 4, 2009.

Barnard, Jeff. 2009. Klamath River Dam-Removal Project Will Be World's Biggest. *Christian Science Monitor*. September 30. www.csmonitor.com/USA/Politics/ 2009/0930/klamath-river-dam-removal-project-will-be-worlds-biggest. December 5, 2010.

Barrett, Joe. 2010a. Levees Fall Off Face of Map. *Wall Street Journal*. November 29, 2010. A4.

Barrett, Joe. 2010b. Water Plan Aims to Help Jobs Flow. *Wall Street Journal*. November 30. A6.

Barringer, Felicity, and Henriques, Diana. 2010. Water Scarcity a Bond Risk, Study Warns. *New York Times*. Business Day.October 20, 2010. www.nytimes.com/ 2010/10/21/business/21water.html?_r=2&ref=energy-environment. November 4, 2010.

Barzilay, JoshuaI., Weinberg, Winkler G., and Eley, J. William. 1999. *The Water We Drink: Water Quality and Its Effects on Health*. Rutgers University Press. New Brunswick.

Baumann, Duane D., Boland, John J., and Hanemann, W. M. 1998. *Urban Water Demand Management and Planning*. McGraw-Hill. New York.

Bernstein, Peter L. 2005. *Wedding of the Waters: The Erie Canal and the Making of a Great Nation*. W. W. Norton and Co. New York.

Beverage Marketing Corporation. 2010. Bottled Water Perseveres in a Difficult Year. www.beveragemarketing.com/?section=pressreleases. March 5, 2010.

Breslin, Edward D. 2010. Rethinking Hydro-Philanthropy: Smart Money for Transformative Impact. *Journal of Contemporary Water Research and Education*. *Universities Council on Water Resources*. August. 145: 65–73.

Burns, N., Cooper, C., Dobbins, D., Edwards, J. and Lampe, L. 2001. Security Analysis and Response for Water Utilities. American Water Works Association. Denver.

Buyalski, C., Ehler, D., Falvey, H., Rogers, D., and Serfozo, E. 1991. *Canal Systems Automation Manual. Volume 1*. U.S. Bureau of Reclamation Water Resources Technical Publication. Denver.

California Department of Water Resources, 2010. 2009 Water Bank. www.water .ca.gov/drought/bank/. December 2, 2010.

California Water Service Group. 2009. Investor relations. www.calwatergroup.com. July 13, 2009.

Carbon Disclosure Project. 2010. CDP Water Disclosure 2010 Global Report. https://www.cdproject.net/en-US/Programmes/Pages/cdp-water-disclosure .aspx. March 16, 2011.

Carlton, Jim. 2005. Can a Water Bottler Invigorate One Town? *Wall Street Journal.* Page B1. June 9, 2005.

Casselman, Ben. 2009. Planning the "Ike Dike" Defense. *Wall Street Journal.* June 4. A3.

Center for Public Integrity. 2008. The Water Barons. http://projects.publicintegrity .org. November 14, 2008.

CH2M HILL. 2010. Company History. www.ch2m.com/corporate/about_us/ history.asp. December 10, 2010.

Chaker, Anne Marie. 2010. Gardening Without a Sprinkler. *Wall Street Journal.* D1, 2. Wednesday, August 18, 2010.

Chávez, Franz. 2006. Cochabamba's 'Water War,' Six Years On. IPS News. http:// ipsnews.net/news.asp?idnews=35418. October 17, 2010.

Citizens Energy Group. About the Trust. 2010. www.citizensenergygroup.com/ AWater.aspx. August 22, 2010.

City of Fort Collins. 2009. Comprehensive Annual Financial Report. December 31.

City of Fort Collins. 2010. Departments: Utilities. www.fcgov.com/utilities/. October 8, 2010.

City of Fort Collins. 2010b. 2011-2012 Budget Process. www.fcgov.com/city manager/budget.php. October 8, 2010.

Colorado Department of Public Health and Environment. 2010. Water Quality Control Commission Regulations. www.cdphe.state.co.us/wq/index.html. September 20, 2010.

Colorado Water Resources and Power Development Authority. 2010. State Revolving Funds Program Update. www.cwrpda.com/Programs.htm. November 24, 2010.

Consultant's News. 2003. *Directory of Management Consultants.* Kennedy Publications. Peterborough, NH.

Council for Agricultural Science and Technology. 1988. Effective Use of Water in Irrigated Agriculture. Report 113. Ames, Iowa.

Craun, Gunther F., Hubbs, Stephen A., Frost, Floyd, Calderon, Rebecca L., and Via, Steve H. 1998. Waterborne Outbreaks of Cryptosporidiosis. *Journal AWWA.* 90(9) 81–91. September.

Crichton, David. 2002. UK and Global Responses to Flood Hazard. *Water International.* 27(1): 119–131.

Cross, Gilbert. 1991. A Dynasty of Water: The Story of American Water Works Company. American Water Works Company. Vorhees, NJ.

Cui, Carolyn, and Davis, Ann. 2008. Water's Slippery Seduction: Investors Flood Sector amid Economic Falloff, Limited Opportunities. *Wall Street Journal.* March 29. B1.

Cyre, Hector J. 1982. Stormwater Management Financing. APWA Congress, Houston, September 1982.

DeNileon, Gay Porter, and Stubbert, John. 2005. Employment Outlook Good for Operators, Grim for Utilities. *AWWA Opflow.* 31(5): 1, 4.

Edwards, Kathleen, and Braun, Martin Z. 2010. Jefferson County Sewer to Get Receiver, Judge Says. *Bloomberg Businessweek.* September 07, 2010.

www.businessweek.com/news/2010-09-07/jefferson-county-sewer-to-get-receiver-judge-says.html. November 24, 2010.

Edwards, Marc. 2010. Hidden Dangers of Residential Plumbing. Technical Keynote: WQA Aquatech USA. March 10, 2010. http://s36.a2zinc.net/clients/wqa/wqa10/public/enter.aspx. August 4, 2010.

Egypt Ministry of Water Resources and Irrigation. 2009. Minister's Message. www.mwri.gov.eg. December 26, 2009.

Engemoen, Marc, and Roger E. Krempel. 1985. Utility Approach to Comprehensive Stormwater Management. *Public Works Magazine.* April.

Environmental Business Journal. 1999. US Water Industry. XII(7/8). San Diego.

Environmental Protection Agency Region 4. 2010s. Superfund. Stauffer Chemical Company (Tarpon Springs). www.epa.gov/region4/waste/npl/nplfln/stautsfl.htm. October 10, 2010.

European Public Health Alliance. 2010. From: How Will Water Shape the 21st Century? Update 67. www.epha.org/a/694. September 15, 2010.

Evans, Ben. 2010. Court Ruling Cutting Off Atlanta from Federal Reservoir Could Have National Implications. http://abcnews.go.com/Politics/wireStory?id=10023051. November 6, 2010.

FAO. 2007. *Egypt's Experience in Irrigation and Drainage Research Uptake.* International Programme for Technology and Research in Irrigation and Drainage.

Finley, Bruce. 2010. "Denver Water Raising Rates for 20th Straight Year." *Denver Post.* November 18. 2B.

Food and Agriculture Organization. 2010. Hunger. www.fao.org/hunger/en/. November 30, 2010.

Frost & Sullivan. 2010. About Our Water & Wastewater Service. www.frost.com/prod/servlet/vp-about.pag?vpid=2843824. August 29, 2010.

FTSE. 2009. Macquarie Global Infrastructure Index Series.

Funding Universe. 2010. Suez Lyonnaise des Eaux. www.fundinguniverse.com. October 17, 2010.

GDFSuez. 2010. Activities. www.gdfsuez.com. December 14, 2010.

GE Power and Water: Water and Power Technologies. *Handbook of Industrial Water Treatment.*www.gewater.com/handbook/index.jsp. July 30, 2010.

Georgia River Network. 2010. About GRN. www.garivers.org. December 7, 2010.

Getches, David H. 1990. *Water Law in a Nutshell.* West Publishing Co. St. Paul.

Glennon, Robert. 2009. *Unquenchable: America's Water Crisis and What to Do about It.* Island Press. Washington, DC.

Global Water Intelligence. 2006. Ebb and Flow of Valve Market. Vol 7, Issue 9 (September 2006). www.globalwaterintel.com/archive/7/9/market-insight/ebb-and-flow-of-valve-market.html. August 30, 2010.

Grigg, N. 2006. Workforce Development and Knowledge Management in Water Utilities. *Journal AWWA.* September.

Grigg, N. and Zenzen, M. 2009. *The Water Workforce: Recruiting and Retaining High Performance Employees.* AWWA Press. Denver.

Grigg, Neil S. 2003. *Colorado's Water: Science and Management, History and Politics.* Aquamedia Publications. Denver.

Grigg, Neil S. 2007. Water Sector Structure, Size and Demographics. *Journal, Water Resources Planning and Managemenet*, ASCE. 133(1): 60–66 (January/February).

Grigg, Neil S. 2008. *Total Water Management: Leadership Practices for a Sustainable Future*. AWWA Press.

Grigg, Neil S. 2011. *Water Governance and Management: Integrated Policy, Regulation, and Capacity-Building*. IWA Press. London.

Grigg, Neil S. 1985. *Water Resources Planning*. McGraw-Hill. New York.

Grigg, Neil S. 1996. *Water Resources Management: Principles, Regulations and Cases*. McGraw-Hill. New York.

Grigg, Neil S. 2005. *Water Manager's Handbook. A Guide to the Water Industry*. Aquamedia Publications. Denver.

Grigg, Neil S. 2010. *Infrastructure Finance: The business of infrastructure for a sustainable future*. John Wiley & Sons. New York.

Grimond, John. 2010. For Want of a Drink: A Special Report on Water. *Economist*. 395(8693) (May 22): 1–20.

Hardin, Garrett. 1968. "The Tragedy of the Commons," *Science* 162(3859) (December 13, 1968): 1243–1248.

Herman, R., Olivo, T., and Gioia, J. 2003. *Impending Crisis: Too Many Jobs, Too Few People*. Oakhill Press. Winchester, VA.

History of Plumbing in America. 1987. *P&M Magazine*.www.plumbingsupply.com/pmamerica.html. November 16, 2010.

Hoffman, Steve. 2009. *Planet Water: Investing in the World's Most Valuable Resource*. John Wiley & Sons. Hoboken, NJ.

Houtsma, John, deMonsabert, Sharon, and Gutner, Sandy. 2003. U.S. Wastewater Contract Operations: Contract Details and Views of Contracting. European Regional Science Association. 2003. Congress. Jyväskylä, Finland.

Howe, Charles W. 1993. Water Pricing: An Overview. Water Resources Update. Issue 92. Summer. Universities Council on Water Resources, Carbondale, Illinois.

Hydraulic Institute. 2010. World Pump Market Report. www.pumps.org/content_detail.aspx?id=1548. August 29, 2010.

Iceberg Corporation of America Forms Joint Venture to Export Greenland Water. 2000. Business Wire. August 24, 2000. www.allbusiness.com/company-activities-management/product-management-branding/6495093-1.html. August 17, 2010.

Imperial Irrigation District. 2010. Budget Plan 2010–2011. www.iid.com/index.aspx?page=72. December 3, 2010.

Imperial Irrigation District. 2010a. IID Water History. www.iid.com/index.aspx?page=125. December 3, 2010.

Instream Flow Council. 2010. About Us. www.instreamflowcouncil.org/index.htm. June 19, 2010.

Interagency Floodplain Management Review Committee. 1994. Sharing the Challenge: Floodplain Management into the 21st Century. Washington, DC, June.

Interagency Task Force Report (USDI, USDA, EPA). 1979. Irrigation Water Use and Management. Superintendent of Documents, Washington, DC.

Jarosz, Francesca. 2010. Indianapolis Water, Sewer Utilities Sale Survives Political Battle. IndyStar.com. Posted July 27, 2010. August 22, 2010.

Johnson, Robin A., McCormally, John, and Moore, Adrian T. 2002. *Long-Term Contracting for Water and Wastewater Services*. Reason Foundation. Los Angeles.

Kelda Group. 2010. Kelda Group. www.keldagroup.com. October 17, 2010.

Kenny, Joan, Barber, Nancy, Hutson, Susan, Linsey, Kristin, Lovelace, John, and Maupin, Molly. 2009. Estimated Use of Water in the United States in 2005. U.S. Geological Survey Circular 1344. Reston VA.

Koeppel, Gerard T. 2000. *Water for Gotham: A History*. Princeton University Press. Princeton, NJ.

Koslow, Evan. 2004. Consumer Water Filtration: Emerging Trends and Developments. *Water Conditioning and Purification*. April. 46(4): 10–12.

Lea, Dallas M. 1985. Irrigation in the United States. USDA-ERS. AG ES840815. Washington, DC.

Levitt, ArthurJr. 2009. Muni Bonds Need Better Oversight. *Wall Street Journal*. May 9–10.A15. CCLIII(108).

Life Water. 2010. Fighting Poverty through Safe Water. www.lifewater.org. December 12, 2010.

Lorinc, John. 2010. Ontario's Clean Water Tech Cluster. Green: A Blog about Energy and the Environment. http://green.blogs.nytimes.com. August 25, 2010.

Lund, J., and Israel, M. 1995. Optimization of Transfers in Urban Water Supply Planning. *Journal of Water Resources Planning and Management*, ASCE. 121 (1): 41–48.

Mann, John, and Runge, Jon. 2009. State of the Industry Report 2009. *Journal AWWA*. 101(10): 36–46.

Mannion, J. ed. 1998. The Changing Water Utility: Creative Approaches to Effectiveness and Efficiency. AWWA. Denver.

Maxwell, Steve. 2003. How Big Is the Water Industry Anyway? *Water Conditioning & Purification*. September: 45(9): 12–13.

Maxwell, Steve. 2010. The New Water Frontier: Looking Forward through Lessons Learned from the Recent Past. *Journal AWWA*. 102(9): 98–99.

Maxwell, Steve. 2010. A Look at the Challenges–and Opportunities–in the World Water Market. *Journal AWWA*. 102(5): 104–116.

McWhirter, Cameron. 2010. Crucial Trade Waterway under Threat. *Wall Street Journal*. December 14. A8.

Means, E., Ospina, L., West, N., and Patrick, R. 2006. *A Strategic Assessment of the Future of Water Utilities (2030). Top Trends Seen by Utility Leaders*. AWWARF: Denver.

Means, Ed. 2001. Future Trends in the Water Supply Industry. Speech at AwwaRF breakfast, AWWA convention., Washington DC.

Means, Edward G., III, Ospina, Lorena, and Patrick, Roger. (2005). Ten Top Trends and Their Implications for Water Utilities. *Journal AWWA*. 97(7): 64–75.

Mehan, G. Tracy, III 2007. God Gave Us the Water, but Who Pays for the Pipes? *Water & Wastes Digest*. 47(5), May.

Melosi, Martin. 2008. *The Sanitary City: Environmental Services in Urban America from Colonial Times to the Present*. University of Pittsburgh Press. Pittsburgh, PA.

Mesa Water. 2010. The Mesa Water Project. www.mesawater.com/project/default .asp. December 11, 2010.

Michaud, C. F. 2009. Industrial Water Treatment: Size Doesn't Matter. Water Conditioning and Purification, February. Online. www.wcponline.com/pdf/ 0902Michaud.pdf. December 1, 2010.

Mintzberg, H., and Van der Heyden, L. 1999. Organigraphs: Drawing How Companies Really Work. *Harvard Business Review* (September–October): 87–94.

Molden, David, ed. 2007. *Water for Food, Water for Life: A Comprehensive Assessment of Water Management in Agriculture*. International Water Management Institute. Sri Lanka. Earthscan Publications. London.

Moss, M., Smigiel, D., and Sulewski, J. 2005. Knowledge Management Approach to the Water Industry. AwwaRF Report.

Murray, Alan. 2010. The End of Management: Corporate Bureaucracy Is Becoming Obsolete: Why Managers Should Act Like Venture Capitalists. *Wall Street Journal*. August 21-22, 2010. W3.

Naisbitt, John. 2010. Megatrends. www.naisbitt.com/bibliography/megatrends .html. September 10, 2010.

National Association of Water Companies. 2010. Private Water Service Providers Quick Facts. www.nawc.org. August 23, 2010.

National Human Resources Association. 2010. About NHRA. www.humanre sources.org/about_main.cfm. December 15, 2010.

National Hydropower Association. 2010a. About Us. http://hydro.org/. March 16, 2011.

National Hydropower Association. 2010b. Hydrofacts. www.hydro.org. September 19, 2010.

National Land Use Database Partnership. 2010. NLUD: Land Use and Land Cover Classification. www.nlud.org.uk. March 13, 2010.

National Research Council. 2002. Privatization of Water Services in the United States: An assessment of issues and experiences. National Research Council. Washington, DC.

National Research Council. Water Science and Technology Board. 2006. Drinking Water Distribution Systems: Assessing and Reducing Risks. Washington, DC.

National Water Resources Association. 2010. A Brief History of the National Water Resources Association. www.nwra.org/history.php. August 12, 2010.

Natural Resources Defense Council. 2010. Stormwater Strategies: Community Responses to Runoff Pollution. www.nrdc.org/water/pollution/storm/chap2.asp. October 24, 2010.

Noji, Eric K. 1997. *The Public Health Consequences of Disasters*. Oxord University Press. New York.

North Poudre Irrigation Company. 2004. *Feasibility of Rehabilitation of North Poudre Reservoir No. 1*. http://cwcb.state.co.us. December 24, 2009.

Northern Colorado Water Conservancy District. 2010. About Horsetooth.com. Frequently Asked Questions. http://abouthorsetooth.com/html/faq.asp. December 5, 2010.

Northumbrian Water Group plc. 2010. About us. www.nwg.co.uk. October 18, 2010.

NSF International. 2010. About NSF. www.nsf.org. December 14, 2010.

Okun D. 1977. *Regionalisation of Water Management: A Revolution in England and Wales.* Applied Science Publishers. London. 1977.

Olstein, M., Marden, D., Voeller, J., Jennings, J., Hannan, P., and Brinkman, D. 2005. Succession Planning for a Vital Workforce in the Information Age. AwwaRF report.

Osborne, D., and Hutchinson, P. 2004. *The Price of Government: Getting the Results We Need in an Age of Permanent Fiscal Crisis.* Basic Books. New York.

Osborne, David, and Gaebler, Ted. 1992. *Reinventing Government: How the Entrepreneurial Spirit Is Transforming the Public Sector.* Reading, MA. Addison-Wesley.

Oscilloscope. 2010. Flow. www.flowthefilm.com. December 7, 2010.

Pennon Group plc. About Us. www.pennon-group.co.uk. October 17, 2010.

Plastino, Michael. 2008. Clean Watersheds Needs Survey (CWNS 101) 2008. A Webinar Presentation. www.epa.gov/owm/mtb/cwns/cwns101.pdf. November 28, 2010.

PR Newswire. 2009. Reportlinker Adds Water & Wastewater Pipe Market. June 24 www.prnewswire.com/news-releases/reportlinker-adds-water--wastewater-pipe-market-97118884.html. August 30, 2010.

President's Water Resources Policy Commission. 1950. A Water Policy for the American People. December 17. U.S. Government Printing Office. Washington, DC.

Raucher, R., Hagenstad, M., Cotruvo, J., Narasimhan, R., Martin, K, Arora, H. Regunathan, R., Drago, J., and Pontius, F. 2004. Conventional and Unconventional Approaches to Water Service Provision. AwwaRF Report. Denver.

Rice, Leonard, and White, Michael D. 1987. *Engineering Aspects of Water Law.* John Wiley & Sons. New York.

Rijsberman, Frank R. (1987). *Development of Strategies for Planning for Improvement of Irrigation SystemPperformance.* Ph.D. Dissertation. Colorado State University.

Ritch, Emma. 2010. Israel to Export $2.5B in Water Technologies by 2011. Clean-Tech Group News. http://cleantech.com/news/4319/israel-export-25b-water-technologies. August 24, 2010.

Rogers, Peter. 1993. *America's Water: Federal Roles and Responsibilities.* MIT Press. Cambridge, MA.

Rosen, J.Frey, M., Stevens, K., Miller, D., Sobrinho, J., Ergul, A., and Pinkstaff, L. 2003. Application of Knowledge Management to Utilities. AwwaRF Report.

Rouse, Michael. 2007. *Institutional Governance and Regulation of Water Services: The Essential Elements.* IWA Publishing. London.

Runge, J., & Mann, J. 2005. State of the Industry Report, 2005. *Journal AWWA*. 97 (10): 58–67.

RWE. 2009. Investor Relations. www.rwe.com. July 13, 2009.

Sagardoy, J.A. 1986. Organization, Operation and Maintenance of Irrigation Schemes. *FAO Irrigation and Drainage Paper* 40. www.fao.org/docrep/x5647e/x5647e06.htm. December 26, 2009.

Sandia National Laboratories. 2010. The Energy-Water Nexus. www.sandia.gov/energy-water/. November 30, 2010.

SAUR Group. 2010. History. www.saur.com/en/index.html. October 17, 2010.

Schilling, Kyle, Copeland, Claudia, Dixon, Joseph, Smythe, James, Vincent, Mary, and Peterson, Jan. 1987. The Nation's Public Works: Report on Water Resources, National Council on Public Works Improvement, Washington, DC.

Schmid, Joe. 2010. In Singapore, Milwaukee Water Industry Has a Role Model. JS Online. www.jsonline.com/business/98719254.html. December 12, 2010.

Senge, Peter M. 1990. *The Fifth Discipline: The Art & Practice of the Learning Organization*. Doubleday, New York.

Severn Trent Water. 2010. About Us. www.stwater.co.uk. October 16, 2010.

Siedler, Moses. 1982. Obtaining an Analytical Grasp of Water Distribution Systems. *Journal AWWA*. December.

Simon, Stephanie. 2010. Water Surge: Hydropower, Once Shunned Because of Environmental Concerns, Is Making a Comeback. *Wall Street Journal*. R3.

Sjarief, Roestam. 1995. Holistic Monitoring & Evaluation of Irrigation Development: A Model for Management Control. Ph.D. Dissertation. Colorado State University.

Southern Water. 2010. About Us. www.southernwater.co.uk. October 18, 2010.

Stedman, Lis. 2010a. GLOBAL: World Bank Report Highlights Urban Cost of Climate Change Adaptation (07/12/10). www.iwapublishing.com/template.cfm?name=news565. December 13, 2010.

Stedman. Lis. 2010b. ASIA: ADB Announces First Water Infrastructure Private Equity Fund. Water 21 IWA Publishing. www.iwapublishing.com/template.cfm?name=news558. November 23, 2010.

Task Force on the Natural and Beneficial Functions of the Floodplain. 2002. The Natural & Beneficial Functions of Floodplains. U.S. Government Printing Office. June.

Tennessee Valley Authority. 2010. Environment Report: 4.23 Power. www.tva.gov/environment/reports/ros_eis/4-23_power.pdf. October 13, 2010.

Texas Water Development Board. 2010. Finance Assistance Programs Index. www.twdb.state.tx.us/assistance/financial/financial_main.asp. December 7, 2010.

Texas Water Development Board. 2010. Texas Water Bank and Water Trust. www.twdb.state.tx.us/assistance/waterbank/waterbankMain.asp. December 2, 2010.

Thames Water. 2010. Our Investors. www.thameswater.co.uk/cps/rde/xchg/corp/hs.xsl/7565.htm. October 17, 2010.

The Nessie Curve. 2010. What It Is. http://nessiecurve.com/home. October 18, 2010.

Toro. 2010. History of Toro Micro Irrigation. www.toromicroirrigation.com/history.aspx. September 28, 2010.

Tucker, L. S., Millan, Jaime, and Burt, Will. 1972. Metropolitan Industrial Water Use. American Society of Civil Engineers Urban Water Resources Research Program. New York. Available from NTIS PB212 578.

U.S. Army Corps of Engineers and Federal Emergency Management Agency. 1997. National Inventory of Dams. (Electronic resource).

U.S. Army Corps of Engineers Institute for Water Resources. 2009. The U.S. Waterway System. Transportation Facts. www.iwr.usace.army.mil. December. September 19, 2010.

U.S. Army Corps of Engineers. 2005. Our Mission. www.usace.army.mil/who .html#Mission. January 24, 2005.

U.S. Bureau of Labor Statistics. 2010. Establishment Data. Historical Employment. B-1. Employees on Nonfarm Payrolls by Major Industry Sector, 1960 to Date. ftp://ftp.bls.gov/pub/suppl/empsit.ceseeb1.txt. September 26, 2010.

U.S. Bureau of Labor Statistics. 2010. Occupational Outlook Handbook, 2010–11 Edition. www.bls.gov/oco/oco2003.htm. August 19, 2010.

U.S. Bureau of Labor Statistics. 2010a Occupational Outlook Handbook, 2010–11 Edition. Engineers: Employment. www.bls.gov/oco/ocos027.htm#emply. September 27, 2010.

U.S. Bureau of Reclamation. 2005. Bureau of Reclamation: About Us. www.usbr .gov/main/about. December 15, 2010.

U.S. Census Bureau. 2004. Architectural, Engineering, and Related Services: 2002. EC02-541-03

U.S. Census Bureau. 2010. Construction Spending. www.census.gov/const/www/ c30index.html. August 1, 2010.

U.S. Census Bureau. 2010. Industry Statistics Sampler. NAICS 54133 Engineering Services. www.census.gov/econ/industry/ec07/a54133.htm. November 16, 2010.

U.S. Census Bureau. 2010a Economic Census. Management, Scientific, and Technical Consulting Services: 2002. www.census.gov/prod/ec02/ec0254i06.pdf. December 10, 2010.

U.S. Centers for Disease Control. 2010. Surveillance for Waterborne Disease and Outbreaks Associated with Recreational Water Use and Other Aquatic Facility-Associated Health Events—United States, 2005–2006, and Surveillance for Waterborne Disease and Outbreaks Associated with Drinking Water and Water Not Intended for Drinking—United States, 2005–2006. www.cdc.gov/mmwr/ pdf/ss/ss5709.pdf. August 4, 2010.

U.S. Centers for Disease Control. 2010. Water-Related Diseases, Contaminants and Injuries. www.cdc.gov/healthywater/disease/. August 4, 2010.

U.S. Department of Commerce. 2002. Water and Wastewater Technologies Export Plan. Washington, DC.

U.S. Department of Energy. 2006. Energy Demands on Water Resources: Report to Congress on the Interdependency of Energy and Water. Washington, DC. www.sandia.gov/energy-water/docs/121-RptToCongress-EWwEIAcomments-FINAL.pdf. November 30, 2010.

U.S. Department of Energy. 2010. History of Hydropower. www.1.eere.energy.gov/ windandhydro/hydro_history.html. March 21, 2010.

U.S. Energy Information Agency. 2006 Energy Consumption by Manufacturers—Data Tables. www.eia.doe.gov/emeu/mecs/mecs2006/2006tables.html. August 19, 2010.

U.S. Energy Information Agency. 2010. Annual Energy Review 2009: Energy Perspectives Overview. www.eia.gov/aer/pdf/perspectives_2009.pdf. December 1, 2010.

U.S. Environmental Protection Agency and U.S. Agency for International Development. 2004. Guidelines for Water Reuse. EPA/625/R-04/108. September.

U.S. Environmental Protection Agency. 2002. Clean Water and Drinking Water Gap Analysis. www.epa.gov/ogwdw/gapreport.pdf. March 16, 2011.

U.S. Environmental Protection Agency. 1978. Report to Congress: Industrial Cost Recovery. Volume I. Executive Summary (MCD-52). December. Washington, DC.

U.S. Environmental Protection Agency. 1996. Wastewater Needs Survey. Washington, DC.

U.S. Environmental Protection Agency. 1999. Understanding the Safe Drinking Water Act. EPA 810-F- 99-008. December.

U.S. Environmental Protection Agency. 2002. The Clean Water and Drinking Water Infrastructure Gap Analysis. EPA-816-R- 02-020.

U.S. Environmental Protection Agency. 2003b Factoids: Drinking Water and Ground Water Statistics for 2002. Washington, DC.

U.S. Environmental Protection Agency. 2009. Office of Water. www.epa.gov/OW/ June 30, 2009.

U.S. Environmental Protection Agency. 2010. Drinking Water Contaminants. www.epa.gov/safewater/contaminants/index.html. August 4, 2010.

U.S. Environmental Protection Agency. 2010. Safe Drinking Water Information System. www.epa.gov/enviro/html/sdwis/sdwis_query.html. December 14, 2010.

U.S. Environmental Protection Agency. 2010. Stormwater Program. http://cfpub.epa.gov/npdes/home.cfm?program_id=6. September 14, 2010.

U.S. Environmental Protection Agency. 2010a. Community Water Systems Survey. http://water.epa.gov/aboutow/ogwdw/cwssvr.cfm. November 21, 2010.

U.S. Environmental Protection Agency. 2010b. Clean Watersheds Needs Survey: 2008 Report to Congress. www.epa.gov/cwns. August 15, 2010.

U.S. Environmental Protection Agency. 2010c. What are water quality standards? http://water.epa.gov/scitech/swguidance/waterquality/standards/. September 19, 2010.

U.S. Environmental Protection Agency. 2010d. NATO Advanced Research Workshop on Security of Industrial Water Supply and Management. www.epa.gov/nrmrl/events/program_schedule09152010.pdf. December 9, 2010.

U.S. Environmental Protection Agency. 2010e. Stauffer Chemical Company (Tarpon Springs). www.epa.gov/region4/waste/npl/nplfln/stautsfl.htm. December 15, 2010.

U.S. Environmental Protection Agency. 2010f. Clean Water and Drinking Water State Revolving Funds. http://water.epa.gov/aboutow/eparecovery/index.cfm. November 23, 2010.

U.S. Environmental Protection Agency. 2010g. Community Water Systems Survey. http://water.epa.gov/aboutow/ogwdw/cwssvr.cfm. November 21, 2010.

U.S. Federal Emergency Management Agency. 2002. The National Flood Insurance Program Program Description. www.fema.gov/business/nfip/. September 16, 2010.

U.S. Federal Emergency Management Agency. Chronology of Flood Laws. Unpublished document. Washington, DC.

U.S. Federal Highway Administration. 2010. Hoover Dam Bypass Project. www.hooverdambypass.org/project_funding.htm. November 24, 2010.

U.S. General Accounting Office. Federal Efforts to Monitor and Coordinate Responses to Drought, GAO/RCED-93-117, June 1993.

U.S. General Accounting Office. 1994. Water Pollution: EPA Needs to Set Priorities for Water Quality Criteria Issues, GAO/RCED-94-117, June.

U.S. Geological Survey. 2009. Water Use in the United States. http://water.usgs.gov/watuse/. December 16, 2009.

U.S. Geological Survey. 2010a. Industrial Water Use. http://ga.water.usgs.gov/edu/wuin.html. August 19, 2010.

U.S. Government Accountability Office. 2005. Management Issues Requiring Attention in Utility Privatization. Washington, DC.

U.S. Natural Resources Conservation Service. 2010. Watershed Rehabilitation Information. www.nrcs.usda.gov/programs/wsrehab/. November 25, 2010.

U.S. News & World Report. 2010. Best Careers 2011: Civil Engineer. http://money.usnews.com/money/careers/articles/2010/12/06/best-careers-2011-civil-engineer.html. December 15, 2010.

United Nations. 2010. Graphs and Statistics: Drinking Water and Sanitation. www.unwater.org/statistics_san.html. December 12, 2010.

United States Society on Dams. 2010. About USSD. www.ussdams.org. August 12, 2010.

United Utilities. 2010. About United Utilities. www.unitedutilities.com. December 14, 2010.

Urban Drainage and Flood Control District. 2010. Urban Storm Drainage Criteria Manual. Denver. www.udfcd.org/downloads/down_critmanual.htm. December 6, 2010.

van Shilfgaarde, Jan. 1992. Irrigation: A Blessing or a Curse. *The Abel Wolman Distinguished Lecture.* Speech to the National Research Council. Washington, DC.

Vaughan, Roger J. 1983. *Rebuilding America. Vol. 2. Financing Public Works in the 1980's.* Council of State Planning Agencies. Washington, DC.

Veolia. 2010. History. www.veolia.com/en/. October 17, 2010.

Viessman, Warren, Jr., and Welty, Claire. 1985. Water Management: Technology and Institutions. Harper & Row. New York.

Vista Consulting Group. 1997. Guidelines for Implementing an Effective Integrated Resource Planning Process. AWWA Research Foundation. Denver.

Wall Street Journal Business. 2009. RWE CFO Repeats Co. Still Aims to Fully Divest.

Wall Street Journal. 1991. Lox Horizons. Editorial. May 29, 1991.

Water 21. IWA Publishing. www.iwapublishing.com/template.cfm?name=news 558. November 23, 2010.

Water and Wastewater Equipment Manufacturers Association. 2010. Membership. www.wwema.org. August 2, 2010.

Water Environment Research Foundation. 2010. About WERF. www.werf.org//AM/Template.cfm?Section=Home. December 15, 2010.

Water Environment Research Foundation. 2010. About WERF. www.werf.org. October 10, 2010.

Water Quality Association. 2010. WQA Overview. http://www.wqa.org/sitelogic .cfm?id=2. March 16, 2011.

Water Quality Association. 2009. WQA Aquatech USA 2009 Numbers Show a Chicago Success. www.wqa.org/pdf/pressreleases/wqaa09_attendance.pdf. March 8, 2010.

Water Research Foundation. 2010. About Us. www.waterresearchfoundation.org. October 10, 2010.

Water Research Foundation. 2010. Smart Sensors for Buried Utility Location and Performance Monitoring—3129. www.waterrf.org/search/detail.aspx?Type=2&PID=3129&OID=3129. December 10, 2010.

Water Resources Power and Development Authority. 2010. The Authority. www .wapda.gov.pk. August 12, 2010.

Water Smart Innovations Conference. 2010. WSI 2010 Thanks You. www.water smartinnovations.com/index.php. October 19, 2010.

Wateronline. 2010. WEFTEC Continues to Climb Tradeshow Week's Top 200. www.wateronline.com August 20, 2010.

Wateronline.com. 2009. Resolution by Canadian Municipalities Targets U.S. Water and Wastewater Equipment Industry. June 10, 2009. http://www.wateronline .com/article.mvc/Resolution-By-Canadian-Municipalities-Targets-0001. March 16, 2011.

Weber, Patrick. 2008. Bottled Water: Tapping the Trends. PNWS-AWWA 2008 Annual Conference. Vancouver, WA. February 28.

Weeks, W. F. 1980. Iceberg Water: An Assessment. *Annals of Glaciology* 1. International Glaciological Society.

Welsh Water. 2010. Company Information. www.dwrcymru.co.uk/English/Company/index.asp. October 17, 2010.

Wessex Water. 2010. About Us. www.wessexwater.co.uk. October 18, 2010.

Wetsus. 2010. Centre of Excellence for Sustainable Water Technology. www .wetsus.nl. November 8, 2010.

White, Gilbert F. 1969. Strategies of American Water Management. University of Michigan Press. Ann Arbor.

Wirthman, Lisa. 2010. A hero for smartest students. Denver Post. October 23, 2010. http://www.denverpost.com/recommended/ci_16409822. March 16, 2011.

World Bank. 2010. World Bank Lending for Large Dams: A Preliminary Review of Impacts. http://lnweb90.worldbank.org. September 6, 2010.

World Business Council for Sustainable Development. 2005. Facts and Trends: Water. Geneva. www.wbcsd.org. July 28, 2010.

World Commission on Dams. 2001. Dams and Development: A New Framework for Decision-Making. www.dams.org.

World Health Organization. 2010. UN-Water Global Annual Assessment of Sanitation and Drinking-Water (GLAAS). www.who.int/water_sanitation_health/publications/9789241599351/en/index.html. December 12, 2010.

World Water Assessment Programme. 2006. *Water: A Shared Responsibility*. The United Nations World Water Development Report 2. UNESCO, Paris, and Berghahn Books, New York.

Yahoo Finance. 2010. Fitch Rates Los Angeles Dept of Water & Power Water Revs "AA+" & Affirms Outstanding; Outlook Stable. http://finance.yahoo.com/news/Fitch-Rates-Los-Angeles-Dept-bw-3598773118.html?x=0. November 23, 2010.

Yorkshire Water. 2010. About Us. www.yorkshirewater.com/ December 15, 2010.

Milly, P., Betancourt, J., Falkenmark, M., Hirsch, R., Kundzewicz, Zbigniew, Lettenmaier, D., and Stouffer, R. 2008. Stationarity Is Dead: Whither Water Management? *Science* 1, 319(5863) (February 2008): 573–574.

Zuckerman, Gregory, and Kranhold, Kathryn. 2005. Water Sector Rides a Wave of Strong Demand. *Wall Street Journal*. April 15, 2005. C1, 4.

About the Author

Neil S. Grigg is a professor in the department of civil and environmental engineering at Colorado State University. He has worked for over 40 years as a professor, consulting engineer, and public official in the water industry. He graduated from the U.S. Military Academy and has graduate degrees in water resources engineering from Auburn and Colorado State. As a state government official in North Carolina, he had responsibility for natural resources agencies, air- and water-quality regulation, and oversight for wastewater construction grants. He has served for over 20 years in a U.S. Supreme Court appointment as the river master of the Pecos River. He is an experienced municipal consultant and was cofounder of a Denver-area consulting firm that focused on water industry projects. He served for 12 years as a member and 3 years as president of the Fort Collins Water Board. His international experiences include work on water policy and finance issues in several countries. Since 2000, he had worked closely with the water-utility industry on studies of emergency management, infrastructure condition assessment, risk modeling, workforce development, and integrated management strategies. He currently serves on several editorial advisory boards, including the *Journal of the American Water Works Association*. In 2010 he became co–principal investigator of a National Science Foundation project to train Ph.D. scientists in integrated studies of water issues.

Index